The Composition of the Narrative Books of the Old Testament

The Composition
of the Narrative Books
of the Old Testament

Reinhard G. Kratz

Translated by John Bowden

t&t clark

Published by T&T Clark International
A Continuum imprint
The Tower Building, 11 York Road, London SE1 7NX
15 East 26th Street, Suite 1703, New York, NY 10010

www.tandtclark.com

Translated from the German *Die Komposition der erzählenden Bücher des Alten Testaments*, published 2000 by Vandenhoeck & Ruprecht, Göttingen.

© 2000 Vandenhoeck & Ruprecht
English translation © 2005 John Bowden

British Library Cataloguing-in-Publication Data
A catalogue record for this book is available from the British Library

ISBN 0567089207 (hardback)
      0567089215 (paperback)

Typeset by BookEns Ltd, Royston, Herts.
Printed on acid-free paper in Great Britain by CPI Bath

Contents

Preface

This book offers an introduction to the narrative works of the Old Testament, as far as possible without presupposing any hypotheses, simply on the basis of some undisputed fundamental assumptions like a distinction between the Priestly and the non-Priestly text in the Pentateuch, the special position of Deuteronomy, a Deuteronomistic revision in the books from Joshua to Kings, or the literary dependence of Chronicles on the books of Samuel and Kings. Moreover further distinctions in literary criticism and redaction criticism are not based on preconceived views, but on observations on the text made a long time ago. However, today these often figure under another name. Still, whether one speaks of literary criticism or canonical criticism and sometimes sees the same interfaces as literary joins, narrative strategies, rhetorical figures, or compositional structures makes no fundamental difference. The crucial thing is how precisely one takes the text. It is a great mistake to think that anyone who is for the final canonical shape must be against literary criticism, and anyone who is for criticism must have something against the final shape. 'Synchronicity' and 'diachronicity' are not mutually exclusive, but are dependent on each other.

However, this book does require one thing of its readers: to look at the texts of the Old Testament. I have made an effort to present the material in such a way that not only are biblical passages cited, but their content is always described in a few words. But the reader's own precise reading of the biblical text cannot and should not be a substitute for this. So that the argument can also be followed by those using a modern translation, I have dispensed with quotations from the Hebrew; some terms are given in transliteration. Only the sometimes unavoidable differentiation of verses into a, aα, aα[1], etc. follows the Massoretic accents. They denote in order individual sentences or clauses in a verse, and the observant reader can also find them in a translation. In cases of doubt indications for identifying the wording are given.

The book is arranged in such a way that it can be read either from beginning to end or in individual complexes. Surveys, summaries and tables, some of which go into more and some into less detail, may make it easier to use. The conclusion once again sums up the results and sketches out the picture of the history of religion and theology that arises from the analysis.

I am grateful to Eva Jain, Martin Hallaschka and Thomas Thiem for their help; Stefanie Stubbendiek did the index [index for this English translation compiled by Sarah Armstrong].

Reinhard G. Kratz
Göttingen, March 2000

Preface to the English Edition

The text has been reviewed and at some points revised for the English edition, but I saw no need to make far-reaching changes. Apart from some marginal polemic, the notices and reviews that have been brought to my attention have been predominantly friendly. They are as follows: *Frankfurter Allgemeine Zeitung*, 10 May 2000, 56; *Revista Biblica Brasileira* 17, 2000, 634f.; *International Review of Biblical Studies/ Internationale Zeitschriftenschau für Bibelwissenschaft und Grenzgebiete* 47, 2000/1 (no page numbers); *Old Testament Abstracts* 24, 2001, 571f.; *Journal for the Study of the Old Testament* 94, 2001, 67f.; *Interpretatie*, April 2001, 31; *Zeitschrift für Altorientalische und Biblische Rechts-geschichte* 7, 2001, 415-67; *Theologische Rundschau* 67, 2002, 152-5; *Theologische Literaturzeitung* 127, 2002, 623-5; *Zeitschrift für Alttesta-mentliche Wissenschaft* 114, 2002, 312f.; *Deutsches Pfarrerblatt* 9, 2002, 481-3. The bibliographies have been supplemented above all by titles in English. I should emphasize once again that I have made no effort at completeness; I have quite deliberately made only a selection of titles through which, if necessary, readers may move on to the secondary literature. My choice has been above all of works which treat the subject as a whole and not just parts of it.

This book is based on the historical-critical analysis of the biblical sources, of the kind customarily also made of the secular writers of antiquity; however, for a number of reasons the tradition in the Old Testament is much more complicated. The book is arranged in such a way that it can also be useful to those who are sceptical about biblical criticism: I would ask them not to jib at the method but to pay attention to the content. We do not need to share specific findings of literary criticism and redaction criticism to recognize that the narrative books are composed of different parts. This book is an introduction to proposals discussed for more than 250 years as to where these parts are to be located and to illuminate the way in which they have been brought together in the narrative works of the Old Testament.

I am particularly grateful to the translator, Dr John Bowden; he has done his work with a deep understanding of the subject-matter and with great care, and in addition has adjusted the bibliography for English readers at a number of points. I hope that the translation will help to revive the exchange between German- and English-language biblical study, which for a number of reasons has unfortunately ground to a halt.

Reinhard G. Kratz
Wissenschaftskolleg/Institute for Advanced Study
Berlin, February 2003

Introduction

The history of the people of Israel is told twice in the Old Testament, once at the beginning in the series of books from Genesis to Kings, and once again at the end of the Hebrew Bible in the books of Ezra, Nehemiah and Chronicles.[1] The dominant view is that the two literary complexes are made up of three originally independent composite works: the Tetrateuch or Pentateuch[2] (Genesis–Numbers + Deut. 34); the Deuteronomistic history, abbreviated as DtrG (Deuteronomy–Kings); and the Chronistic history, abbreviated as ChrG (1–2 Chronicles, Ezra–Nehemiah). The connection in ChrG arises out of the overlap in the text in 2 Chron. 36.22f. and Ezra 1.1-3 and thus is evident, despite the anachronistic sequence of the books in the Massoretic canon, in which according to most manuscripts Ezra–Nehemiah stand before Chronicles. The only dispute is over whether it is original. By contrast, the division of the series of books from Genesis to Kings into the Tetrateuch and DtrG is less obvious; it does not agree either with the canonical division into Torah (Pentateuch) and Former Prophets (Joshua–Kings) or with the course of the narrative.

The division hypothesis is not particularly old. It derives from Martin Noth,[3] and replaced the view previously customary, for which Julius Wellhausen[4] produced the classical argument, that the whole was composed of a Hexateuch extending from Genesis to Joshua and the books of Judges, Samuel and Kings, which had undergone a Deuteronomistic revision, thus extending the Hexateuch into an Enneateuch. Here Deuteronomy took on a key role. Since Wilhelm Martin Leberecht de Wette[5] it has been regarded as an entity *sui generis*, displaying relations in both directions. On the one hand it recapitulates the narrative of the Tetrateuch and concludes the Pentateuch (the part of the canon which is the Torah) with the death of Moses in Deut. 34; on the other hand it provides a narrative and theological transition to the books of Joshua–Kings which follow. What happens to Deuteronomy is decisive for whatever literary division is made. If it is taken out, the connection in the Hexateuch between Genesis–Numbers and Joshua follows quite automatically: after the patriarchs and the exodus from Egypt, the people of Israel go through the wilderness to the gates of the land promised to them by their God. There Moses dies, and the people occupy the promised land under the leadership of Joshua. Without the continuation, the Tetrateuch lacks a tail, without the prehistory the books of Joshua–Kings lack a head. Thus in Wellhausen,[6] Joshua, Judges, Samuel and Kings appear more as an appendix than as the continuation of the Pentateuch or Hexateuch presupposed in them, and so are left hanging in the air. Conversely, Noth[7] felt compelled to postulate an earlier narrative of the settlement as the original conclusion of the Tetrateuch in Genesis–Numbers. This conclusion was suppressed by the books of Deuteronomy and Joshua added to DtrG and got lost in the formation of the Pentateuch (up to and including Deut. 34, but without the Deuteronomic law) and the link with DtrG (with Deuteronomy as the conclusion of the Pentateuch and Joshua–Kings as an appendix). Moreover in both cases the death of Moses in Deut. 34 to some degree serves as a substitute for Deuteronomy, which was inserted only subsequently, whether for the necessary transition from Genesis–Numbers to Joshua in the framework of the Hexateuch, or for the necessary conclusion of the Tetrateuch or Pentateuch, which was still independent before being connected with DtrG.

In short, with or without Deuteronomy, one cannot fail to notice the narrative connection between the exodus, the wandering in the wilderness and the settlement in Exodus, Numbers and Joshua. Deuteronomy does not offer a real alternative to this, but merely represents a digression in the action, which, while marking a caesura, does not remove the connection. So we have reason to ask whether the division into Tetrateuch/Pentateuch and DtrG is justified. It already seems very strange that two works like Genesis–Numbers and Deuteronomy–Kings, which are dependent on each other, initially came into being independently, were subsequently connected, and then divided up again. Either the break between the two literary works has been wrongly chosen, or the model does not fit and must be given up in favour of the older accumulation hypothesis. But it is also possible that both possibilities are right and that the number of breaks between Genesis and Exodus, Numbers and Deuteronomy, Joshua and Judges, Judges and Samuel allow both the assumption of formerly independent literary entities and the accumulation hypothesis.

As for the literary composition of the individual books, again things are simplest in the case of ChrG. Chronicles is based on the books of Samuel and Kings, and, if one includes the genealogies in 1 Chron. 1–9, on the narrative connection from Adam to Zedekiah in Genesis–Kings. This existing source material, which in some stretches is more or less identical with the transmitted Massoretic text, has been written out word for word, though here and there it has been changed and expanded with special material. Likewise, Ezra and Nehemiah are composed of different bits of sources, though these have not been preserved separately; this source material has been arranged for a specific purpose, commented on or supplemented. The only remaining question is that of literary integrity, that is, whether the books of Chronicles, Ezra and Nehemiah were composed all at once or display traces of growth, whether in the use of sources or in the special material.

In an analogous way, earlier sources of varying provenance are posited for the books of the Deuteronomistic work, that is, for Deuteronomy and Joshua–Kings – a law book in Deuteronomy, individual narratives and annals in Joshua–Kings. These were collected together in successive stages, put in a historical context, and given a literary revision, according to Noth by one author in a single process, and according to most more recent scholars by several redactors. Here too the dispute is only over the precise division between tradition and Deuteronomistic redaction, and also the literary differentiation of the redaction itself within the individual books and in the relationship of the books to one another.[8]

The greatest problem is posed by the Pentateuch or Tetrateuch, for which a completely different pattern of explanation has become established. Instead of tradition and redaction, here sources are divided; in other words, the text is dissected into two, three or more parallel narrative threads: the Yahwist (J), the Elohist (E), the Jehovist (JE) who brings together J and E, and the Priestly Writing (P).[9] Wellhausen[10] already saw Joshua as an appendix to the Pentateuch, only remote in terms of sources; Noth[11] no longer found the threads of any sources here, as in the second half of Numbers. This and the other kind of Deuteronomistic redaction in Joshua–Kings, which is hardly compatible with the character of the written sources, above all in Genesis, were also responsible for the division of Genesis–Kings into two independent composite works. But the difficulties only begin here: the E source has been preserved only in fragments, if at all. J and P prove increasingly (once again) to be literary entities with many strata, now that it has been demonstrated that their literary make-up cannot be simplified by transferring all the differences to the history of the tradition, that is, to the (oral) prehistory of the individual 'themes' of the Pentateuch. For some scholars even P does not exist as an independent source but as redaction. The pre-Priestly connection between the patriarchal history and exodus, which always suffered from the fact that the division of sources had begun in Genesis and was extrapolated from there, is increasingly disputed. The unravelling of sources fails at the latest from Exod. 25, where we can really identify only P or the strata closest to it. Where the sources end is quite uncertain.

In short, the usual division of sources in the Tetrateuch has an uncertain basis and at present is disintegrating. Only one thing is certain: the demarcation of the Priestly Writing (which in turn has many strata), whether as a source or as redaction. This has remained more or less unchanged since Theodor Nöldeke's 1869 *Untersuchungen zur Kritik des Alten Testament*. Everything else, that is, the whole of the non-Priestly text, is an open question. Still, a new consensus is forming, to the effect that here too, in the (non-Priestly) Tetrateuch, as in the Deuteronomistic and Chronistic works, we have to look not for parallel narrative threads but for individual traditions, which are brought together in a basic writing and expansions. The relationship between the two versions, the non-Priestly (JE) and the Priestly Tetrateuch (P), is not dissimilar to that between DtrG and ChrG or the incorporation of Dtr into the Chronistic history.[12]

The journey through the narrative books of the Old Testament which follows investigates both the extent and nature of the composite works and, inseparably from this, the literary composition of the individual books. To keep the account as simple as possible and to make it easier for both experts and beginners to make decisions on the text, I shall begin from the literary blueprint of the final shape as it has been handed down to us. This automatically leads to questions about the history of its origin. These are treated with different degrees of intensity, depending on how far the consensus among scholars extends and where dissent begins. I shall dispense with long methodological prefaces or accounts of the history of research, simply for reasons of space, but also because in the clarification of open questions no novelties should be reported; all that is needed is for some elementary, long-known textual findings to be brought together as clearly as possible and evaluated in well-tried but sometimes new ways. For the same reason bibliographical references have been restricted to essentials. A selection of works is given – in chronological order – before each section; in addition to this, where necessary there is a reference to further titles on the topic. I also draw attention here once and for all to the current Introductions to the Old Testament and the relevant articles in the lexica (*TRE, AncBD*, etc). Of course Wellhausen[13] and Noth,[14] who have analysed the questionable areas of text more or less completely and who each summed up the state of research in their time, have been constant companions. As yet there is no such synthesis for the present situation. But that synthesis is the indispensable presupposition for any account of the history of Israel, its religion and theology. Most such accounts today tend to be written on the basis of hypotheses which have either long been disproved or at least have become questionable. I begin with the Chronistic history, where the state of affairs is clearest. From this we can gain criteria for assessing the far more difficult situation in Genesis–Kings.

Notes

1. No account is taken of Ruth and Esther or the so-called apocryphal history books (Tobit, Judith, 1 and 2 Maccabees).
2. The terms Tetrateuch (Genesis–Numbers), Pentateuch (Genesis–Deuteronomy), Hexateuch (Genesis–Joshua) and Enneateuch (Genesis–Kings, 1–2 Samuel and 1–2

Kings each count as one book) denote the extent of a literary complex and not always the precise number of books.

3. M. Noth, *Überlieferungsgeschichtliche Studien* (1943), reprinted 1957, esp.180ff. (partial ET of pp. 3-110, *The Deuteronomistic History*, [2]1991), abbreviated as *ÜSt*; *Überlieferungsgeschichte des Pentateuch*, 1948 (ET *A History of Pentateuchal Traditions*, 1972, abbreviated as *Pentateuch*).

4. J. Wellhausen, *Die Composition des Hexateuchs und der historischen Bücher des Alten Testaments* (1876–78), [3]1899 = [4]1963 (abbreviated as *Comp.*); id., *Prolegomena zur Geschichte Israels* (1878 as *Geschichte Israels* I), [6]1905 (ET *Prolegomena to the History of Ancient Israel*, reissued Cleveland 1957, abbreviated as *Proleg.*).

5. W.M.L. de Wette, *Dissertatio critico-exegetica qua Deuteronomium a prioribus Pentateuchi libris diversum, alius cuiusdam recentioris auctoris opus esse monstratur*, 1805; id., *Beiträge zur Einleitung in das Alte Testament* I–II, 1806–1807 (reprinted 1971), I, 265ff.; II, 385ff.; id., *Lehrbuch der historisch kritischen Einleitung in die Bibel Alten und Neuen Testaments, Erster Teil*, [3]1829, 237-40, 242f.

6. *Comp.*, 116f., 207, 301.

7. Noth, *ÜSt*, 210f., 211-16; Noth, *Pentateuch*, 33 n. 127.

8. I use the term 'redaction' for all the literary procedures which in any way relate to pre-existing material, the 'tradition', regardless of whether these go to make up a literary complex, presuppose it and develop it in writing, supplement or gloss it. The term is not important; what is meant will be clear from the context.

9. Wellhausen, *Comp.* and *Proleg.* are basic; Noth, *Pentateuch*, 5-41, esp. the listings of the state of the text on pp.17-19 (P), 28-32 (J) and 35-6 (E), takes things further.

10. Wellhausen, *Comp.*, 116f.

11. Noth, *ÜSt*, 180ff.; Noth, *Das Buch Josua*, HAT I/7, [3]1971, 7-9.

12. R.G. Kratz, 'Redaktionsgeschichte/Redaktionskritik', *TRE* 28, 1997, 367-78: 372-5, gives a short survey; K. Schmid, *Erzväter und Exodus*, WMANT 81, 1999, provides far more extensive information.

13. See above n. 4 (*Comp.* and *Proleg.*), the historical synthesis in id., *Geschichte Israels* (1880) and *Israelitisch-jüdische Religion* (1905), reprinted in id., *Grundrisse zum Alten Testament* (ed. R. Smend), TB 27, 1965; id., *Abriss der Geschichte Israels und Judas, Skizzen und Vorarbeiten* 1, 1884, 3-102; id., *Israelitische und jüdische Geschichte* (1894), [7]1914.

14. Thus n. 3 (*Pentateuch* and *ÜSt*), the historical synthesis in id., *Geschichte Israels* (1950, [2]1954, [3]1956), [10]1986 (ET *History of Israel* [2]1959).

A. The Chronistic Writings

I. Chronicles

1. Survey

W.M.L. de Wette, *Beiträge zur Einleitung in das Alte Testament I: Kritischer Versuch über die Glaubwürdigkeit der Bücher der Chronik mit Hinsicht auf die Geschichte der Mosaischen Bücher und Gesetzgebung*, 1806 (reprinted 1971); L. Zunz, *Die gottesdienstlichen Vorträge der Juden, historisch entwickelt*, 1832; Wellhausen, *Prolegomena*, 171ff.; A.C. Welch, *The Work of the Chronicler: Its Purpose and Its Date*, SchL 1938, London 1939 (reprinted Munich 1980); Noth, *Überlieferungsgeschichtliche Studien*, 110-80; T. Willi, *Die Chronik als Auslegung*, FRLANT 106, 1972; P.R. Ackroyd, *The Chronicler and His Age*, JSOT 107, 1991; G. Steins, *Die Chronik als kanonisches Abschlussphänomen*, BBB 93, 1995; M.P. Graham and S.L. McKenzie (eds), *The Chronicler as Historian*, JSOT.S 238, 1997.

Aids

P. Vannutelli, *Libri Synoptici Veteris Testamenti*, 1931; A. Bendavid, *Parallels in the Bible*, 1965–69 (1972); J.D. Newsome, *A Synoptic Harmony of Samuel, Kings and Chronicles*, 1986; I. Kalimi, *The Books of Chronicles – A Classified Bibliography*, 1990.

Commentaries

K. Galling, ATD 12, 1954; W. Rudolph, HAT I/21, 1955; J.M. Myers, AB, 1965; H.G.M. Williamson, NCB, 1982 (reprinted 1987); T. Willi, BK 24, 1991f.; S. Japheth, OTL 1993; G. Knoppers, AB, 2002.

Research

T. Willi, 'Zwei Jahrzehnte Forschung an Chronik und Esra–Nehemia', *ThR* 67, 2002, 61-104.

1.1   The two books of Chronicles, in Hebrew *dibrē hayyāmīm*, 'occurrences of the days', Greek Παραλειπόμενα, 'passed over', Latin *verba dierum*, since Jerome Χρονικόν *totius divinae historiae*, were originally one book. The sub-division into two books, which makes good sense, goes back to the Greek translation of the Old Testament, the Septuagint, from where it reached the Latin version, the Vulgate, and finally the Hebrew textual tradition. In the Greek and Latin canon and therefore in many modern translations Chronicles belongs among the historical books; in the Hebrew canon it is counted among the hagiographa and stands either right at the beginning or right at the end of the third part of the canon.

The narrative spans an arch from the first human being, Adam, to the Babylonian exile and the edict of Cyrus, king of Persia, which reverses the exile. Three stages are distinguished within this arch: 1. From Adam to Saul (1 Chron. 1–10). 2. The foundation of the Davidic kingdom which unites Judah and Israel and the building of the temple in Jerusalem under David (1 Chron. 11–29) and Solomon (2 Chron. 1–9). 3. The Davidic kingdom from the division of the kingdom under Rehoboam to the end of the Jewish state (2 Chron. 10–36).

1.2   The structure is based on other biblical material, from which extracts are made and worked on, and enlarged with sometimes a considerable amount of special material. For the history of humankind in 1 Chron. 1.1–2.2, what Wilhelm Rothstein has called the 'genealogical vestibule', 1 Chron. 1–9, draws almost exclusively on the genealogies in Gen. 5; 10 and 11.10ff.; 25; 35; 36; Exod. 1.1-5; for the tribes of Israel in 1 Chron. 2–9 essentially on Gen. 46 and Num. 26, before the prehistory is concluded with the death of Saul in 1 Chron. 10/1 Sam. 31, and in 1 Chron. 11/2 Sam. 5 the main narrative, the history of the Davidic kingship over Israel, begins. Alongside this, in 1 Chron. 2–9 there is a wealth of additional genealogical, geographical and historical material, some of which has been combined from scattered information in biblical texts like Josh. 13–22, but the majority of which has no basis in the Bible.

The excerpt and special material in 1 Chron. 1–10 reduce the whole narrative course of Genesis–1 Samuel, with the exception of a few narrative insertions, the so-called historical glosses, and the Saul narrative in ch. 10, to a bare skeleton of names, places and numbers. This is not meant to replace the historical narrative but to compress it to essentials. Just as the Israel of Genesis, the people of twelve tribes, has emerged from the history of humankind in Gen. 1–11 and is part of humankind, so too the Davidic kinship of Chronicles has emerged from the history of humankind and is part, indeed even the representative, of the people of twelve tribes. The genealogies say who Israel is and show it its place on earth, which the Davidic kingship occupies vicariously for the tribes of Israel after the death of Saul until the exile. Who represents Israel after the end of the state of Judah is indicated by the genealogy of the sons of David in 1 Chron. 3, which is extended into the post-exilic period; the list of the inhabitants of Jerusalem in 1 Chron. 9, which is partly identical with Neh. 11; and the conclusion in 2 Chron. 36.22f., which points forward to the continuation in Ezra–Nehemiah.

1.3   The biblical basis for the second part, the founding phase of the Davidic monarchy in 1 Chron. 11–2 Chron. 9, is 2 Sam. 5–1 Kgs 11. After the death of Saul in 1 Sam. 31/1 Chron. 10, the Chronicler jumps directly to David's accession to rule over all Israel in 2 Sam. 5/1 Chron. 11–14. Here various lists of persons following 2 Sam. 23/1 Chron. 11.10ff. and taken from the special material (1 Chron. 12), along with the first action of moving the ark from 2 Sam. 6.1–11/1 Chron. 13, are put between the accession to the throne (2 Sam. 5.1-10/1 Chron. 11.1-9) and the first building enterprises, descendants and successes in war (2 Sam. 5.11-25/ 1 Chron. 14). Following the basic biblical material in 2 Sam. 6.12ff., in 1 Chron. 15–16 there occurs the moving of the ark to Jerusalem. In 1 Chron. 15.1-24 this has been given a new introduction and transition with a list of those bearing the ark and relevant instructions. Over and above the original source material in 2 Sam. 6.12ff./1 Chron. 15.25–16.3, perhaps inspired by 2 Sam. 6.21, it ends in 1 Chron. 16.4ff. with a solemn act of worship composed of passages from Pss. 105; 96 and 106.

After that, large stretches of the biblical source material are reproduced without interruption: 2 Sam. 7 = 1 Chron. 17; 2 Sam. 8 = 1 Chron. 18; 2 Sam. 10.1–11.1 + 12.26-31 = 1 Chron. 19.1–20.3; 2 Sam. 21.18-22 (not vv. 15-17) = 1 Chron. 20.4-8; 2 Sam. 24 = 2 Chron. 21. The principle of selection is obvious. After Nathan's promise in 2 Sam. 7/1 Chron. 17, all the accounts of wars and lists of officials which have not been used elsewhere (2 Sam. 20.23-26 = 8.16-18/1 Chron. 18.15-17 or 2 Sam. 23/1 Chron. 11) are taken up from the original. The chapters on David and Mephibosheth (Meribaal) in 2 Sam. 9, which evidently no more fitted the notions of the Chronicler than the stories about David and Saul in 1 Samuel, the chapters about David and Bathsheba in 2 Samuel 11–12, and the domestic fights in 2 Sam. 13–21 are omitted. The song of David and the last words of David in 2 Sam. 22.1–23.7 were either not in the material the Chronicler had, or have been passed over because the story of his punishment and cryptic aetiology of Zion in 2 Sam. 24 was to become the legend about the site of the temple and the altar of burnt offering in 1 Chron. 21.18–22.1 (cf. 2 Chron. 3.1) on which the extensive special material in 1 Chron. 22–29 depends.

Like 2 Sam. 13–20, the machinations over the throne at the transition from David to Solomon in 1 Kgs 1–2 are also passed over. The farewell discourses of David in 1 Chron. (22 and) 28f. (cf. 1 Kgs 2.1ff.) lead directly to the accession of Solomon in 1 Chron. 29.20-25, orientated on 1 Kgs 1.28-40 but formulated freely, to which all the sons of David submit (v. 24), and to David's end in 1 Kgs 2.10-12/1 Chron. 29.26-30. The account of the reign of Solomon essentially coincides with the material the Chronicler has before him. In some places two shells are put around the kernel of the history of Solomon, the building of the temple in 1 Kgs 6–9 (without the palace, 7.1-12)/2 Chron. 3–8: various measures for building the temple, especially the relations with Huram/Hiram of Tyre in 1 Kgs 5.15-32/2 Chron. 2 and 1 Kgs 9.10-28/2 Chron. 8, and Solomon's wisdom and splendour in 1 Kgs (2.46;) 3.4-15; 10.26-29 (instead of 3.16–5.14, esp.5.6)/2.Chron. 1 and 1 Kgs 10/2 Chron. 9. There are no deeper reasons for the omission of 1 Kgs 3.16–5.14 in 2 Chron.; it must be solely to tighten the story up and concentrate on the core of the history of Solomon. When it is repeated in its original place in 2 Chron. 9.25-28, the passage preferred for this, namely, 1 Kgs 10.26-29/2 Chron. 1.14-17, is to some degree assembled crosswise from 1 Kgs 5.6, 1; 10.27, 28. The omission of Solomon's idolatry and the rebellions against him in 1 Kgs 11 is also self-evident. The text goes immediately from 1 Kgs 10 to the concluding comment in 11.41-43/2 Chron. 9.29-31.

The composition is dominated by the notion that both David and Solomon did their bit towards building the temple and with the foundation of the kingship of Judah over all Israel became involved in the foundation of the temple cult in Jerusalem. The special material in particular gives this impression. Alongside this, in the excerpt we see the beginning of a tendency for David to be specially concerned with the military defence of the kingdom against outsiders and Solomon with the building of the temple. The former laid the foundation for the foreign policy of the Davidic monarchy over all Israel and the latter the foundation for its cult.

1.4   In the third stage, too, the period from the division of the kingdom to the exile in 2 Chron. 10–36, for long stretches Chronicles follows the material on which it is based in 1 Kgs 12–2 Kgs 25, though with one qualification: exclusively those passages are selected and used which refer to the (Davidic) kingdom of Judah, but these are used more or less in full. This determines the course of the text of Chronicles, as seen in Table A.I.1.

This survey first of all gives the parallels as a whole and then in brackets especially those passages in the text of Chronicles which represent the material used. Omissions from it are rare and often cannot be distinguished from interpretative reformulations. Moreover as well as the passages about the northern kingdom, with the exception of 1 Kgs 15.1/2 Chron. 13.1 the usual synchronism of the kings of Judah and Israel is consistently deleted; the kings of the north are mentioned only where this is unavoidable, above all at the beginning of the history of the divided kingdoms and as a negative background to the claim of the kings of Judah to represent all Israel: 1 Kgs

Table A.I.1

1 Kgs 12.1-24; 14.21-31	= 2 Chron. 10–12	Rehoboam (10.1–11.4; 12)
1 Kgs 15.1-8	= 2 Chron. 13	Abijah (13.1-2, 22f.)
1 Kgs 15.9-24	= 2 Chron. 14–16	Asa (14.1-4; 15.16–16.6; 16.11–17.1)
1 Kgs 22.1-35, 41-51	= 2 Chron. 17–20	Jehoshaphat (18; 20.31–21.1)
2 Kgs 8.16-24	= 2 Chron. 21	Jehoram (21.5-11, 20; 22.1)
2 Kgs 8.25-29 (9f.)	= 2 Chron. 22.1-9	Ahaziah
2 Kgs 11.1-20	= 2 Chron. 22.10–23.21	Athaliah
2 Kgs 12.1-22	= 2 Chron. 24	Joash (24.1-14, 23-27)
2 Kgs 14.1-22	= 2 Chron. 25	Amaziah (25.1-4, 11f., 17-28; 26.1f.)
2 Kgs 15.1-7	= 2 Chron. 26	Uzziah/Azariah (26.3-4, 21-23)
2 Kgs 15.32-38	= 2 Chron. 27.1-9	Jotham (vv. 1-3, 7-9)
2 Kgs 16.1-20	= 2 Chron. 28	Ahaz (28.1-4, 5, 16-27)
2 Kgs 18–20	= 2 Chron. 29–32	Hezekiah (29.1-2; 31.1, 20f.; 32)
2 Kgs 21.1-18	= 2 Chron. 33.1-20	Manasseh (33.1-10, 18-20)
2 Kgs 21.19-26	= 2 Chron. 33.21-25	Amon
2 Kgs 22.1–23.30	= 2 Chron. 34–35	Josiah (34; 35.1, 18-27; 36.1)
2 Kgs 23.31-35	= 2 Chron. 36.2-4	Jehoahaz
2 Kgs 23.36–24.7	= 2 Chron. 36.5-8	Jehoiakim
2 Kgs 24.8-17	= 2 Chron. 36.9-10	Jehoiachin
2 Kgs 24.18–25.21	= 2 Chron. 36.11-21	Zedekiah and the end
2 Kgs 25.22-30/2 Chron. 36.20f., 22f.		Exile and change to salvation

12/2 Chron. 10.1–11.4; 1 Kgs 15.1, 7/2 Chron. 13.1ff.; 1 Kgs 22/2 Chron. 18, etc.

The excerpt from the biblical source is the framework of the composition. The gaps in the text cited in brackets which are evident from the survey are filled in with Chronistic special material. For the most part the following passages (all in 2 Chronicles) are involved: 11.5-23 in chs 10–12 (Rehoboam); 13.3-21 in ch. 13 (Abijah); 14.5-14; 15.1-15; 16.7-10 in chs 14–16 (Asa); 17.1-19; 19.1–20.30 in chs 17–20 (Jehoshaphat); 21.2-4, 12-19 in ch. 21 (Jehoram); 24.15-22 in ch. 24 (Joash); 25.5-16 in ch. 25 (Amaziah); 26.5, 6-20 in ch. 26 (Uzziah/Azariah); 27.3-6 in 27.1-9 (Jotham); 28.(6-8,) 9-15 in ch. 28 (Ahaz); 29–31 in chs 29–32 (Hezekiah); 33.11-17 in ch. 33.1-20 (Manasseh); 35.2-17 in chs 34–35 (Josiah).

After the constitution of Israel within the framework of humankind in the first part (1 Chron. 1–10) and the political and cultic foundation of the Davidic monarchy over Israel in the second part (1 Chron. 11– 2 Chron. 9), the third part (2 Chron. 10–36) focuses exclusively on the continuation of the history of the Davidic kingship over Judah as the one and only kingship over all Israel legitimated by Yhwh. The history of Judah stands for the history of Israel.

2.   The genealogies

M. Oeming, *Das wahre Israel*, BWANT 128, 1990; Willi, BK 24, 1991ff.; id., *Juda – Jehud – Israel*, FAT 12, 1995, 119ff.

2.1   The genealogies in 1 Chron. 1–9 stand out from the narrative which follows, both in the way in which they use sources and in their special material. The reduction of the material in Genesis–1 Samuel on which it is based to the genealogical lists and corresponding additional material is unique in Chronicles with the exception of 1 Chron. 12; 15f. and 23–27, but has points of contact with the lists in Ezra–Nehemiah (Ezra 2/Nehemiah 7, etc.). But the genealogies cannot be cut out altogether, as is sometimes done, since without them there is no beginning. Neither 1 Chron. 10 nor 1 Chron. 11 are possible beginnings. The start would be much too direct, and one would have to reckon either with the text being broken off in the course of the secondary prefixing of chs 1–9 or with a deliberately fragmentary extract for whatever purpose. Certainly this cannot be ruled out completely, as is shown by the example of 3 Ezra,[1] a compilation from 2 Chron. 35–36, Ezra 1–10 and Neh. 8, but of course here as elsewhere in the fragmentary hypothesis this is always a solution of desperation and should be adopted only when nothing better is on offer. In the case of Chronicles the genealogies offer themselves as a natural beginning that is required by the narratives, in the present version with a plausible transition from 1 Chron. 8–9, the genealogy of Benjamin and Saul, through the death of Saul in 1 Chron. 10, to David's accession to rule over Israel in 1 Chron. 11. The question remains whether the present version is also original.

2.2   A first section enumerates the names from Adam to the twelve tribes of Israel: 1 Chron. 1.1–2.2. In succession there are excerpts from Gen. 5; 10; 11.10-26; 25; 36 and 35.22-26 or Exod. 1.1-5. The only addition here is the renaming of Abraham in 1 Chron. 1.27 after Gen. 17.5 in the formulation of Gen. 36.1, 8. But the genealogies have been heavily revised. Here two forms can be distinguished:

1.   Only the bare names have been taken over from Gen. 5 and 11.10-26, without keeping the recurrent scheme of the (Priestly) material on which it is based; they are simply put one after the other in 1 Chron. 1.1-4 and 1.24-27. They represent a sequence of generations up to the three sons of Noah, Shem, Ham and Japheth, in one case and up to Abraham in the other.
2.   Under the heading 'the sons of X' the genealogical branching of each last generation into children and grandchildren follows, in such a way that the main line – which before this has always been

mentioned in first place – comes at the end, following the law of final emphasis: in 1 Chron. 1.5-23, after Gen. 10, the sons of Japheth (vv. 5-7), Ham (vv. 8-16) and Shem (vv. 17-23) and their descendants; in 1 Chron. 1.28–2.2, after Gen. 25; 36 and 35.22-26; or Exod. 1.1-5, the sons of Abraham and their descendants: v. 28 (cf. Gen. 25.9) the sons of Abraham, vv. 29-31 the sons of Ishmael, vv. 32-33 the sons of Keturah, v. 34 (referring back to v. 28) the sons of Isaac, vv. 35-54 the sons, kings and princes of Esau/Seir, 1 Chron. 2.1-2 the twelve sons of Israel. The basic scheme of the second form comes from Gen. 10, where already the two formulae 'the sons of X' and 'X was the father of Y', etc. are used indiscriminately. These are taken over unchanged in 1 Chron. 1.5-23 and the material is also introduced into them in 1 Chron. 1.28ff., partly with, partly against, the original. The other formulae in the basic material, headings, historical notes, etc, are usually deleted, but not in every case. I cannot recognize any regularity here or in the distribution of the two genealogical formulae.

On the basis of its dependence throughout on the genealogies of Genesis and the more or less equal disposition of the material in 1 Chron. 1.1–2.2, the section gives the impression of being a unity. The omission of vv. 17-23 in manuscript B (Vaticanus) of the Greek translation has no significance; it arises from a mistake by the copyist. Verses 11-16/Gen. 10.13-18 in the same manuscript have possibly been passed over because of the omission of Gen. 10.10-12; in fact they are not necessary. The sons of Keturah in 1.32-33/Gen. 25.1-4 drop out of the framework, v. 28 being taken up in v. 34a, as do the sons of Seir and the list of the kings and rulers of Edom in 1.38ff., 43ff. which most scholars regard as additions. A series of plausible reasons have been advanced for the irregularities,[2] but the considerations necessary for them could also have occurred to those who supplemented the material. On the whole it makes no difference.

Of more importance is the beginning of the Israelite genealogy in 1 Chron. 2.1-2: 'And these are the sons of Israel'. If we use as a basis the formula 'sons of X' taken over by the Chronicler in 1.5ff. from Gen. 10 and imitated in 1.28, 34b, 35ff. contrary to the material he had before him, leaving aside the doubtful exceptions in 1.33, 43a, 54, it is the first and only transition which on the model of Exod. 1.1 (cf. also Gen. 35.26b) begins the introduction of the series of tribes with the demonstrative. 1 Chronicles 2.1-2 is not only the completion and climax of ch. 1 but at the same time the introduction to the genealogies of the tribes of Israel which follow; these are not dependent on the derivation from Adam. So here we could have an original beginning to Chronicles, only later expanded by ch. 1 and the genealogies of Genesis. I shall be returning to this.

2.3   The simplest form in 7.13, 'The sons of Naphtali: Jahziel, Guni, Jezer and Shallum, sons of Bilhah', leads to the framework of the relations between the generations in chs 2–9. The scheme consists of the introductory formula 'sons of X', with which we are already familiar, and a list of names; in substance it is based on Gen. 46 and Num. 26, where one or two generations are given for each tribe: 1 Chron. 2.3-4 (taken up again in 4.1) the sons of Judah; 4.24 the sons of Simeon; 5.(1f.), 3 the sons of Reuben; 5.27 (6.1) the sons of Levi; 7.1 'the' sons of Issachar; 7.6 Benjamin;[3] 7.13 the sons of Naphtali; 7.14 the sons of Manasseh; 7.20 the sons of Ephraim; 7.30 the sons of Asher; 8.1f. 'and Benjamin was the father of'. The beginnings in 5.11 'and the sons of Gad, they dwelt', and 5.23 'The sons of the half tribe of Manasseh, they dwelt' diverge from the scheme in so far as they only continue the history of the settlement of Reuben in 5.8-10.

With the exception of Naphtali in 7.13 and originally perhaps also of Dan in 7.12, where only one generation is listed, everywhere the genealogical branching into the next generations follows the headings. Here, however, we have not only descendants but also other themes like kinship relationships, dwelling-places and pasturages, numerical strengths and specific historical facts. The information is offered in a variety of forms. Alongside the basic scheme 'the sons of X', for each first and further generations we also have 'X, son of Y', or 'X, his son Y', or the birth formula with yld, 'bear' or 'beget', and the object, in the case of women in the qal, of men in the niphal or hiphil. Where we have a history of settlement the root $y\check{s}b$, 'dwell', regularly appears; the founding fathers of cities are often called $'\bar{a}b$, 'father', in the formula 'X, the father of place Y'. Generations, chiefs and warriors are counted, and as a rule here are also lists in which all this is entered ($yh\acute{s}$ hithpael). As in the doubtful cases of chs 1 and 2.1, there are different headings or endings to individual sections ('these are', 'and these are', 'all these are', etc.).

The best way of getting an overview is to begin where only a little material is provided. That is the case with the tribes of the northern kingdom in ch. 7. In the case of Issachar (vv. 1-5), in the first section on Benjamin (vv. 6-12), and in the case of Asher (vv. 30-40), the headings (vv. 1, 6, 30) are followed only by the next generations, in 7.31 once with a reference to the father of a city, and at the end the sums of the chiefs and warriors according to the lists. The genealogies of Manasseh (vv. 14-19) and Ephraim (vv. 20-29) are already rather more complicated and have historical glosses: in the case of Manasseh the title 'father of Gilead' suggests the area of settlement; in the case of Ephraim in vv. 28-29 the descendants are also followed by a short list of dwelling places. In the case of Simeon in 4.24-43 the descendants (vv. 24-27) and the dwelling places (vv. 28-33) are followed by a written list of rulers (vv. 34-38, 41) and various actions taken in extending their dwelling places (vv. 39-43). In the case of

Reuben in 5.1ff. both the subsequent generations (vv. 1-3, 4-8) and the dwelling-places (vv. 8-10, 11-26) are expanded with alien members that are attached directly; however, the joint campaign in vv. 18ff. and the common end under Tilgath-pileser in vv. 6, 25f. make these a unity. Here we already find almost the degree of complexity there is finally in the genealogies of Judah (chs 2–4), Levi (ch. 6) and Benjamin (chs 8–9).

Some of the padding can also be derived from biblical sources, but the bulk of it belongs to the special material of Chronicles. We can clarify the procedure by which the framework has been filled out by means of the Judah genealogy, which has been discussed a good deal since Wellhausen's 1870 dissertation. The head is formed of the list of the first three sons of Judah in 2.3 according to Gen. 46.12a; Num. 26.19, from which the information about the mother and the birth of the next two sons following Gen. 38 in 1 Chron. 2.3-4 is inseparable. With the words from Gen. 46.12bα the formula 'the sons of Perez' goes over to the next generation in v. 5; vv. 6-8 construct the pendant 'and the sons of Zerah' from 1 Kgs 5.11 and Josh. 7.1,18. The transition to the generation after that, the third generation, is then made by the important v. 9, which draws all that follows after it, with the mixed formula 'and the sons of Hezron, what was born to him, Jerahmeel and Ram and Chelubai'. Here the genealogy of Perez is picked up again from v. 5 in order to take the genealogy in vv. 10-15 in the scheme 'X fathered (*hōlīd*) Y' from Ram to David, and in vv. 16-17 to lead to the sisters of the sons of Jesse and their children by yet another scheme. This is based on scattered reports (1 Sam. 16.6ff.; 17.13f.; 2 Sam. 17.25) which have been read together and combined with Bethlehem through Obed and Boaz (Ruth 4.17) in the same way as in Ruth 4.18-22; through Bethlehem with Salma (1 Chron. 2.51, 54); through Salma and the two Jewish rulers of the time of the exodus and the wilderness, Nahshon and Amminadab, both taken from Num. 2.3, with the name Ram, known only from 1 Chron. 2.25, 27 and Job 32.2 among the southern Palestinian clans with whom David is said once to have had dealings (1 Sam. 25; 30.14 and 27.10; 30.29); through them with Hezron, who 'dwelt in farms' (cf. Josh. 15.3); and through Hezron with the genealogy of Judah. It continues in 1 Chron. 2, lacking a biblical basis, with the sons of Chelubai/Caleb (vv. 18-24 and again vv. 42-50aα, 50aβ-55) and Jerahmeel (vv. 25-33, 34-41), the two other sons of Hezron from v. 9 and brothers of Ram, the ancestor of David. Like Zerah in vv. 6-8, they complete the genealogy of the main line with very far-reaching and complicated ramifications in terms of family descent and the history of their settlement. 1 Chronicles 3–4 are a kind of appendix, which takes the material in ch. 2 further and supplements it. 1 Chronicles 3 brings the continuation of the David genealogy. In the first part this pays special attention to the geography, which combines ch. 3 with the Calebite lists of ch. 2: the 'sons' of David from Hebron and Jerusalem in 3.1-4, 5-9 according to 2 Sam. 3.2-5; 5.5, 14-16.[4] The opportunity is then taken also to attach the names of the kings of Judah from Solomon to Zedekiah in 1 Chron. 3.10-16, which are dealt with by the basic biblical material of Chronicles and of course by Chronicles itself, and the descendants of Jehoiachin, who survives the exile, in vv. 17-24, for which there is no biblical tradition except for the fact of his survival (2 Kgs 25.27ff.). 1 Chronicles 4.1-23 begins again with 'the sons of Judah'; however, by this it does not mean the actual children, as in 2.1, but the descending line of generations, and adds genealogical, geographical and historical material on some clans from ch. 2. The conclusion is formed by Shelah, the only survivor of the three 'Canaanite' sons of Judah from 1 Chron. 2.3/Gen. 38; 46.12; Num. 26.20, who has been forgotten up till then. It continues like this or in a similar way until the narrative begins in ch. 10.

As things are, no order can be recognized in the disposition of the material of chs 2–9 – in contrast to ch. 1. The basic principle of the genealogical branching, in which not all but always one or several 'sons' of a generation are taken into the next generation or the generation after that, is clear; everything else seems to be interspersed here and there, depending on the author's knowledge. It is clear that the filling out of the framework increases at the beginning with Judah and David (chs 2–4), in the middle with Levi (ch. 6), and at the end with Benjamin and Saul (chs 8–10); this beyond doubt represents a focusing of the content and points to a certain congruence between the main pieces on the one hand and the subsidiary pieces that have been inserted into them in chs 4–5 and 7 on the other. But even that does not explain everything, above all the haphazard way in which, now in this form and now in that, in the one case there is more and in another less, and in yet another case nothing at all. The same goes for the inner ordering of the individual passages. Today scholars tend to discover this in the description of internal relations or to force the accumulated material into chiastic, concentric or other kinds of arrangement. Here a good deal of material has to be passed over to arrive at the desired result. But none of this can disguise the fact that the filling-in of the framework of 1 Chron. 2–10 seems impossible to sort out in detail, and even if it was not done without an aim, it was certainly done without a plan.

2.4   Earlier research concluded from this that the genealogies did not come into being all at once, but successively. We can ask whether that does not simply shift the problem to another literary level, rather than resolving it. Now of course what matters is in fact not so much whether one puts the responsibility for the confusion, one could even say for the literary complexity and the complexity of the content, on one author or several authors, anonymous tradents from the same milieu who for always the same or similar purposes added one thing or another. However, the second possibility is more plausible, because it corresponds to the nature of Jewish tradition developed in Qumran and in the rabbinic literature, which can be grasped more clearly in Chronicles than in any of the other Old Testament writings, and because with a fairly short explanation, the simple differentiation of hands, it comes closest to the differentiated state of the text. If we want to see it that way, here the elements of the text which lie on top of one another and perhaps expand, make more precise or develop one another by modification or even by correction, are merely divided between different literary strata.

Thus Noth,[5] who was followed by many others, saw the framework demonstrated above after Num. 26 and Gen. 46 as the original text, and the extensive filling in of this framework as expansions by a later hand. The hypothesis would be illuminating were it not burdened by too many text-critical uncertainties, especially in 7.12f., where Noth begins, and assumptions of abbreviations and transpositions of the text. As the framework presents itself in the present text, it is not original, at any rate not as a whole.

We must start from what is there. This includes the fact that the list of the twelve tribes of Israel shows considerable irregularities both in order and substance. The order does not correspond completely either with 1 Chron. 2.1-2 (Gen. 35.22-26; Exod. 1.1-5) or with the original material on which it is based, Gen. 46 and Num. 26. We can understand that Judah is given the preferential place in first position instead of Reuben, even without the later explanation in 1 Chron. 5.1f., which anticipates the older beginning in 5.3. However, the question is why the exchange did not also take place in 2.1-2. The present position of Reuben (with Gad and half-Manasseh) before Levi and the transpositions in the sphere of the northern tribes in ch. 7 are more difficult to explain. We get the impression that this is a consequence of 2.1-2, where Dan, perhaps on the basis of the division of Joseph governed by the context in Exod. 1.1-5, is put before Joseph and Benjamin, whereupon in ch. 7 Naphtali (with or without Dan) is put before Joseph = Ephraim and Manasseh. It will probably never be possible to elucidate how in this way the position of Benjamin, first between Issachar (and Dan) and Naphtali, Manasseh and Ephraim, and secondly after Asher, is connected with this. As for the content: Zebulon and, in the text as it has been transmitted, Dan are completely absent; Gad together with half-Manasseh is only an appendage of Reuben; Judah (chs 2 and 4), Benjamin (7.6-12 and chs 8–10) and Manasseh (5.23-26; 7.14-19) occur twice, Manasseh always in connection with another tribe, once with Gad in the trio of east Jordanian tribes after Num. 32 and parallels, the other time with Ephraim as a representative of Joseph. We are forced to conjecture that 1 Chron. 2–9 originally did not set out to depict the system of the twelve tribes at all, but was only subsequently assimilated to the system out of necessity. That by no means excludes the possibility that the assimilation which Noth assumes took place gradually; on the contrary, it supports it – it is shown by the inconsistencies in the overall layout and also by the haphazard way in which the framework is filled out.

Another point to note is that the transition from the lists of tribes in 1 Chron. 2–9 to the narrative in chs 10 or 11ff. is not completely smooth. The incomplete repetition of the Saul genealogy of 8.29-40 in 9.35-44 bridges the list of the citizens of Jerusalem in ch. 9 (Neh. 11.3-19). The list can be seen as a development of the information about places of abode in 8.28, 32 (cf. 9.34, 38), which, like the genealogy of David in 3.17ff. anticipating the end of the history of the Davidic kingdom in 2 Chron. 36, provides the continuity with post-exilic Jerusalem and stands between the two genealogies of the Benjaminite Saul as ch. 3 stands between the genealogies of Judah. In both cases we have a kind of annexe to the preceding lists in ch. 2 on the one hand and ch. 8 on the other, that is, secondary insertions. They can be clearly recognized from the way in which they are taken up again: 4.1 takes up 2.3, and 9.35-44 restores the early link between ch. 10 and 8.29-40 (9.1a?). If we take that together with the first, it follows that what comes at the beginning is not the genealogy of the tribes but the genealogy of the royal houses, Judah/David in ch. 2 and Benjamin/Saul in ch. 8, at all events with Levi in the centre (ch. 6).

If we further note that the two genealogies are in turn full of material about family descent and the history of settlements, of the kind that is typical of the system of tribes in chs 2–9, and that this material is largely secondary, it seems likely that we should also differentiate here. Here we can be guided by Noth, who distinguished the framework from the filling-in by means of the compositional seams. For ch. 2 this produces basic material in 2.3-15, which always pursues only one of the 'sons' of a generation genealogically and in this way leads purposefully from Judah to David: vv. 3-4 (without v. 3b), 5, 6, 9,[6] with a supplement in vv. 16f. Granted, this is a secondary filiation, which combines different reports, including some that have been handed down to us only in 1 Chron. 2 (vv. 25, 51), but that does not mean that the genealogy presupposes the lists in 1 Chron. 2. Even without 1 Chron. 2 we could know of the relationships between Judah (Gen. 38), Bethlehem, the son of Salma and the home of the clan of Jesse (1 Sam. 16.1; 17.12) together with the family of Ruth (Ruth 1.1f.) on the one hand and the tribes of southern Palestine, among them Ram, on the other. Accordingly, the lines through Perez (cf. Ruth 4.12) and his son Hezron, who lives in the wilderness (Josh. 15.3), as the father of the clans from which the Judahite leaders of the time of the exodus and wilderness in Num. 2.3 emerge, can be drawn from general knowledge, inferred in some way or devised ad hoc, like the names of the three brothers of David which are not mentioned in 1 Sam. 16.6ff.; 17.13, or the sibling relationship of the women named from 2 Sam. 17.25 in 1 Chron. 2.16f. (cf. 2 Sam. 19.14).

In analogy to this one might conjecture that the original stratum of 1 Chron. 8 lies in the tribal genealogy of vv. 1-5, 29, 31, corresponding to 2.3–5.9, and in the genealogy of the house of Saul in vv. 33-40, corresponding to 2.10-15 (both times we have the striking *yld* in the hiphil). But the unity of form and content is not preserved even in these two texts, which are very close to each other. The narrative which follows may still explain why the beginnings in 2.3 and 8.1 and the sequence of generations is not formulated in the same way and why the genealogy ends here with David, and there goes beyond Saul and embraces the whole clan of the sons of Saul. But it is also the case that in ch. 8 neither v. 29 nor v. 33 attach smoothly to vv. 1-5, any more than they do to vv. 6-28, and that the opening in vv. 29-31 (32), which is needed for v. 33, is already part of the notes about the history of settlements in the tribal lists. That means that chs 2 and 8, too, are not on the same level. This leads us to conclude that the core of 1 Chron. 2–9 is in 2.3-5, 9-15. As ch. 10 ends the Benjaminite genealogy in chs 8–9, the elevation of David to be king over Israel in ch. 11 might have been the original continuation of the Judah/David genealogy of 2.3-15. In connection with this, the Judah/David genealogy in ch. 2 may initially have been supplemented by Benjamin/Saul in chs 8 and 10 and in a further stage by Levi in ch. 6; here was the framework around which finally the system of the twelve tribes of Israel, sporadically supplemented from Gen. 46 and Num. 26 and other sources, finally clung.

The Judah/David genealogy in 2.3-5, 9-15 is a passable start for the history of the kingship of David and Judah, which begins in ch. 11. However, in 11.1 we have 'Then all Israel gathered together to David at Hebron.' Now it would be very remarkable if this Israel had not been introduced previously in some way, especially as the notion of all Israel also plays an important role in the continuation of the Chronistic narrative. The kingship of David over Judah is and remains kingship over Israel, even after the division of the kingdom. Therefore I think it probable that not only the Judah/David genealogy in 2.3-15 but also the list of the twelve tribes of Israel in 2.1-2 is part of the original stratum. The work could also have begun with this, as we saw above and as we see with Exod. 1.1. Initially there was as yet no inconsistency with the system of the tribes in chs 2–9, and the list fits well into the governing principles in 2.1-15 (without vv. 6-8), according to which only one of the sons of the same generation is ever taken into the next. In the case of the twelve sons of Israel in 2.1-2, this son is Judah in 2.3. Of course this could also have been preceded by the derivation of Israel from humankind in ch. 1, but I would like to see it more as a later phase in growth, quite different from the lists of tribes in chs 2–9 by virtue of the way in which the basic biblical source material has been treated.

Perhaps it is the first step towards completing the tribes in 1 Chron. 2–9 in accordance with Gen. 46 and Num. 26.

2.5   A last question about the genealogies concerns the origin of the secondary material, especially the texts which have no biblical basis. There is an air of desperation about attempts to isolate old source material. We gain nothing by assigning the whole of the special material to a single source: that simply pushes the question further on. And the fact that later and earlier traditions or situations can be distinguished within the material does not mean that we have an old source. So the lists in 2.25-33 and 2.42-50aα must have first found their way into the text, in order, starting from 2.9 and the ancestors of David from the wilderness period, to repristinate the old (pre-exilic) conditions with Caleb in the south (around Hebron), before later hands in 2.50aβ-55 expanded their own relations with Caleb in the north, sought a balance in 2.18-24, and thus interrupted the series of sons from 2.9. As not all this can go back to a source, only fragments remain. These also came to the editors in quite different ways from the 'bits of sources' or could have been invented by them, derived from their own time, or reconstructed – perhaps even accurately in some cases. With this kind of material the question of sources is fruitless. It is more fruitful as far as possible to explain the information from the Old Testament tradition, which alongside the clear excerpts from basic material offered more or less appropriate points of contact for all kinds of independent combinations and scriptural exegeses. In addition to this we must of course also reckon with knowledge from (oral) tradition, in whatever way it was handed down, which gradually found its way into the tradition. However, we cannot decide what is tradition and what spontaneous invention in every case.

3.   The special material

P. Welten, *Geschichte und Geschichtsdarstellung in den Chronikbüchern*, WMANT 42, 1973; J. Weinberg, *Der Chronist in seiner Mitwelt*, BZAW 239, 1996, 130-47.

3.1   In a way, the distinction between excerpt and special material in the narrative part of Chronicles is artificial. Even where Chronicles follows the material on which it is based, it goes its own way in matters small and great. The special material is only a special case of the excerpt in which the basic biblical material is supplemented with additional details or larger pieces, that is, is rewritten. Here we can check by the original what we also have to reckon with elsewhere in the growth of the writings of the Old

Testament: the elaboration of a text by additions ranging from the individual addition to the larger insertion and, as this is a rewritten Bible, also the abbreviation and reformulation of the original. Nevertheless, for practical reasons a separate treatment of the textual material which is manifestly not part of the parallel is called for if we are to construct a picture of the literary composition of Chronicles.

In the second part of Chronicles, 1 Chron. 11–2 Chron. 9, there are three major insertions into 1 Chronicles: ch. 12; chs 15–16; and chs 22–29. These enrich the narrative material of the original with lists and a festival liturgy.

The special material of the third part, 2 Chron. 10–36, has been listed above under 1. It fills in the gaps which the basic biblical material shows in the history of the kings of Judah. In 1–2 Kings the account as far as 2 Kgs 17 as a rule limits itself to the pure (Deuteronomistic) framework scheme, which gives only external information and offers hardly any narrative material. Both are collected in short blocks or interspersed individually (1 Kgs 14.21–15.24; 22.41-51; 2 Kgs 8.16-29; 11–12; 14.1-22; 15.1-7, 32-38; 16), and only from 2 Kgs 18 on is the narrative broader. This is in complete contrast to the history of the Israelite monarchy, which is developed substantially in 1 Kgs 12–13; 1 Kgs 16–2 Kgs 10; 13; 15.8-31; 17. Chronicles keeps to the framework provided, but reverses the proportions: in place of the history of the Israelite monarchy which has been omitted, the special material fills out the framework scheme of the kings of Judah and supplements the existing narrative material.

Here the following principles prevail: as a rule the point of contact is a brief comment within the framework scheme of the kings of Judah, which was the occasion for a broader narrative.[7] But often a statement which in the original biblical material refers to the northern kingdom serves as a point of contact and is transferred to Judah.[8] In addition, the narrative material which was in the original is commented on in the special material in Chronicles and linked with the historical information in the framework scheme.[9]

3.2   One consequence of the principle of filling out by means of what is in the original biblical material is that the special material is not distributed equally through the excerpt, and that there is no fixed order. When that has been taken into account, there is nevertheless a striking degree of regularity in both distribution and content.

First the distribution. The bulk of the special material comes with the kings on whom a positive verdict is passed in the original, above all David (1 Chron. 12; 15–16; 22–29), then from Rehoboam to Jehoshaphat (2 Chron. 10–20), and from Joash to Josiah (2 Chron. 24–35). Here the positive verdict is usually, but not consistently, transformed into two phases, one positive and one negative. The exceptions are Abijah (2 Chron.

13), who is judged positively by comparison with the basic material, Jotham (2 Chron. 27), Hezekiah (2 Chron. 29–32) and Josiah (2 Chron. 34–35), in whose case there are no qualifications – a quite remarkable series. The special material appears quite massively in the case of David and the first four kings after the division of the kingdom, Rehoboam, Abijah, Asa and Jehoshaphat, in 2 Chron. 10–20, presumably as a counter-balance to the broad narrative of the original from 2 Kgs 18, which in the case of Hezekiah is broadened even further. The insertions are sparser in the case of Solomon in 2 Chron. 1–9 and in the stretch from Joash to Jotham in 2 Chron. 24–27, where the original in 1 Kgs 3–11 and 2 Kgs 12 and 14 already offers some narrative material. By contrast, the special material stops suddenly in 2 Chron. 21–23, that is, with the kings Joram and Ahaziah, who are related to the house of Ahab and are therefore judged negatively both in the original and in Chronicles, and the queen mother Athaliah, through whom the relationship runs. It is the same with Amon and the last kings before the end in 2 Chron. 33.21ff.; 36, for whom there is sometimes even a very abbreviated excerpt from the original. But here too there are exceptions to the rule: Jehoram in 2 Chron. 21, Ahaz in 2 Chron. 28 and Manasseh in 2 Chron. 33.

In content, on closer inspection some constantly recurring themes and stereotyped formulations which Peter Welten has aptly called 'topoi'[10] crystallize. There is the building activity and, usually coupled with it, the constitution of the army and a successful foreign policy (victories and tributes) in the case of David (1 Chron. 12; 27), Rehoboam (2 Chron. 11.5ff.), Asa (2 Chron. 14.5f., 7, 8ff.), Jehoshaphat (2 Chron. 17.1ff.), Amaziah (2 Chron. 25.5ff), Uzziah/Azariah (2 Chron. 26.5ff.), Jotham (2 Chron. 27.3-6), Hezekiah (2 Chron. 32.2-8, 22f., 27-29, 30) and Manasseh (2 Chron. 33.14). Then there is the holy war with Abijah (2 Chron. 13.3ff.), Asa (2 Chron. 14.8ff.) and Jehoshaphat (2 Chron. 20) – there are also corresponding successes with Uzziah/Azariah and Jotham (see above). There is the organization and reform of the cult with David (1 Chron. 15–16; 22–29) and Rehoboam (2 Chron. 11.13ff.), Asa (2 Chron. 14.4; 15.1ff.), Jehoshaphat (2 Chron. 17.6, 7-9; legal reform 19.4ff.), Hezekiah (2 Chron. 29–31), Manasseh (2 Chron. 33.15-17) and of course Josiah (2 Chron. 35). There are also prophetic addresses or similar passages which comment on defeats in war, cultic wickedness and other sins in the phases of the history of the monarchy which are judged to be negative, in the cases of Rehoboam (2 Chron. 12.1ff.), Asa (2 Chron. 16.7-10, 12), Jehoshaphat (2 Chron. 19.1-3; 20.35-37), Jehoram (2 Chron. 21.12ff.), Joash (2 Chron. 24.15f., 17ff.), Amaziah (2 Chron. 25.7ff., 14ff.), Uzziah/Azariah (2 Chron. 26.16ff.), Ahaz (2 Chron. 28.9ff., 16f.), Manasseh (2 Chron. 33.10, 11ff.) and Josiah (2 Chron. 34.22-28; 35.20ff.).

To some degree the topics of the special material coincide with the perspectives in accordance with which the texts of the original have been selected in 1 Chron. 11–2 Chron. 9, and each time they have some basis in the biblical material written out in 2 Chron. 10ff. The topics serve to emphasize the focal points in the content of the Chronicler's work, the development of the power of the kingdom of Judah granted by Yhwh, the concern of the kings of Judah for the temple in Jerusalem, and the responsibility of the kings for their sins against God and his law. From this perspective the special material gives the impression of being coherent, more or less unitary, and distributed according to a plan over the whole work. In contrast, here, as with the dispersal of the material, there are also inconsistencies: first in the placing, in which it does not become clear why there is this topos here and that there, and in some places this or that combination and accumulation of topoi; secondly in the topics themselves, which look very different. This is evident, say, from a comparison of the cultic institutions under David and the kings that follow.

3.3   The problem lies in the deviations from the rule. The differences in the distribution of the material and in the formulation and the placing of the topics, which sometimes seems quite fortuitous, cannot be explained by dependence on the context alone. Rather, the differences lead one to suppose that the special material did not come into being all at once, but was gradually written into the excerpt made by the Chronicler from the original.

However, literary-critical reconstruction is not easy: consequently it has so far been attempted only by a few, mostly half-heartedly, if it has been attempted at all.[11] The main difficulty is to find a suitable criterion for distinguishing between original and secondary special material. For the special material as a whole is 'secondary' by comparison with the excerpt from the original, and in some cases is completely absent. However, we cannot therefore simply delete it completely and reckon that a pure copy of Samuel–Kings formed the starting point. In quite a few places the excerpt presupposes the special material.[12] For the same reason, the other possibility, of beginning from the lowest common denominator of the topics in 2 Chron. 27.3-6, is also to be ruled out. The framework scheme in 2 Chron. 27.2 has other things in view than just the notices about building which are supplemented here and the successful wars crowned with tribute. So the only way left is to proceed through the excerpt to the original. The literary-critical reconstruction will depend on how firmly the special material is rooted in the context of the extract in accordance with the principles explained above. In passages not required by the excerpt, the relationship to the rest of the special material is decisive. In addition, the integrity of each passage must be examined independently.

According to these principles and the general consensus, at least the lists in 1 Chron. (11.41ff.); 12 and 23–27 and the festal liturgy in 1 Chron. 15–16 are to be regarded as secondary. Their subsequent insertion has also left traces at other points, for example, 2 Chron. 5.11-13; 7.6; 8.14f.; 23.13, 18f., and of course above all in 2 Chron. 29–31 and 34–35 (esp. 34.12f.; 35.4,15).[13] In 1 Chron. 11f., 11.41ff. and 12.24ff. pick up the text of the biblical original and are further filled out in 12.1-23. Perhaps even the list from 2 Sam. 23 has been added later; 1 Chron. 13.1 or 13.5 attaches well both to 1 Chron. 11.10ff. and to 11.9. In chs 15f. the original narrative thread runs from 15.1, 3 through 15.25–16.3 to 16.43 (cf. 2 Sam. 6.12-20). The appointment of the levites in 15.2 and 16.4 and the commissioning of priests and levites by name in 15.11-15 (explicitly referring back to 13.1-4) and 16.39f. – this latter passage cannot be separated from 16.37f.; did it originally attach to 16.4? – give the impression of being an addition which attracted further names of levites, singers and gatekeepers and the composition of psalms. The festal liturgy replaces the painful scene of 2 Sam. 6.20-23. The point for the insertion of the lists in chs 23–26 and 27 lies in 23.2/28.1;[14] the original transition to chs 28f. in connection with 23.1 is either 23.2aα, less the priests and levites, or 28.1, less the assimilations to ch. 27. However, the great closing scene at the end of David's reign in 1 Chron. 22 and 28f. is hardly a unity. Apart from the references back for example, in 28.11-21[15] caused by the insertion of chs 23–27, in chs 28–29 David's gifts and prayer must be secondary. Both interrupt the enthronement of Solomon in 23.1; 28.1-10; 29.20-30 after 1 Kgs 1f. and are full of repetitions. As for the 'second' enthronement in 28.1, 2-10; 29.20-25, which uses motifs from 1 Kgs 1.19, 25, 28-40 and 2.1ff and is inserted between the first transference of the kingship in 23.1 (after 1 Kgs 1.1, 30) and the concluding note in 29.26-30 (after 1 Kgs 2.10-12), we may leave aside what is original here and what has been added. At all events the second instruction of Solomon and the leading men in Israel by the aging David (cf. 22.2-5; 23.1 after 1 Kgs 1.1) in 22.6-19 and 28.1-10 is dubious. The anticipation of 1 Kgs 5 (and 1 Chron. 29.1ff.) in 22.2-19 (cf. 2 Chron. 2.1,16f.) is the first step from the founder of the empire to the founder of the temple and its worship. He makes bread for his successor 'so far that nothing remained but to put it in the oven'.[16]

Further on, the relationship between excerpt and special material becomes rather more complicated. The scholarly consensus therefore clearly diminishes. On the basis of the criterion discovered above, however, here too we should reckon with supplementations. The following passages are relevant:

2 Chronicles 11.5-23

The notice about building in 11.5-12 is not required by the excerpt, but is best suited as a background to the defeat in 12.1ff. Taking up 11.1-4, Judah and Benjamin are regarded as the domain which Rehoboam first fortifies and then loses again: 11.13-17 (cf. 13.9-11) is a first addition to this, and vv. 18-23[17]a second. Verse 23 directs attention back to vv. 5-12.

2 Chronicles 13.3-21

The account of the war expands 1 Kgs 15.7b/2 Chron. 13.2b and does away with the negative theological judgment and the contradiction with 2 Chron. 11.1-4/1 Kgs 12.21-24 in 1 Kgs 15.3-6.[18] In vv. 3-18 there is a contrast between people of Judah and people of Israel, in vv. 19-21 – as in 1 Kgs 15.7/2 Chron. 13.2 – between kings Abijah and Jeroboam. One of the two versions could have been added, most likely the first. The speech of Abijah in vv. 4-12 which interrupts the account of the war in vv. 3, 13-18 gives a different reason in v. 7 from that mentioned in 11.1-4 for Rehoboam's restraint in the quarrel with the north and is also not completely consistent, especially in vv. 9-11. It is by no means certain that the summary in 13.22 refers to the speech, as the questionable formulation presumably means only 'his ways and his affairs' (cf. 28.26). However, as it can also mean 'his ways and his words' it was perhaps the catalyst for the insertion of an address by Abijah.

2 Chronicles 14.5-14; 15.1-15; 16.7-10

The excerpt in 2 Chron. 16.11f./1 Kgs 15.23 requires the note about building in 14.5f. and the sermon about punishment in 16.7-10 and only through that the Cushite war in 14.8ff. This in turn depends on the note about the army in 14.7. But the textual complex contains a series of additions: 14.4 is a resumption of 14.2, connects the cultic well-being with the 'rest' of 13.23b and 14.5bα ($\check{s}q\underline{t}$), and does not fit well with 15.17/1 Kgs 15.14;[19] 14.5bα anticipates v. 5bβ and is connected with 13.23b and 14.4; 14.6 duplicates v. 5, presupposes the clumsy dating of the rest in 13.23b,[20] and ends with a recapitulation of v. 5bβ. 16.8f. and the Cushite war in 14.7, 8ff., which disturbs the peace until the thirty-fifth year of Asa in 15.19, are also suspect. As in 2 Chron. 17.10 and 20.29f. the 'fear of Yhwh' is evidently meant to guarantee rest from enemies. 15.16-18 attach as well to 14.14 as to 14.5(f.). The second reform of the cult in 15.1-15, competing with 14.1-4, is quite certainly an addition. It is a variation on motifs from 14.2-4, 6, 8ff., confuses the dating system of chs 14–16 with 15.10f., and ends with a resumption of the motif of rest from 14.5, 6 in 15.15.

2 Chronicles 17.1-19; 19.1-20.30

A comparison between the excerpt (2 Chron. 20.31ff.) and the special material shows 17.1-5[21]/18.1b to be the closest parallel. 17.10-19 can be recognized as an insertion by the resumption of v. 5 in 18.1a. As in 14.5f., 7, notes about building and the army follow one another in 17.12-13, 14-19, which develop 17.1f.; as in 14.7, in 17.14-19 the army is divided into Judah and Benjamin, and as in 14.8ff., in 17.10-11 the 'fear of Yhwh' falls on the peoples round about. Here, however, they are not plundered, but like the people of Judah in 17.5 voluntarily offer their 'gifts'. 2 Chronicles 17.6, 7-9, which break the connection between 17.1-5 and 18.1 or 17.10ff., are quite separate, as are 19.4(b)ff. and 20.1ff. (with a recapitulation of 17.10 and 14.4-6; 15.15 in 20.29f.); they insert themselves between the prophetic interpretation in 19.2f. (4a) and the continuation of the excerpt in 20.31ff. The introductory formula 20.31-33 stands at the end because precisely the same thing happens in 1 Kgs 22.

2 Chronicles 21.2-4, 12-19

We can doubt the episode 2 Chron. 21.2-4, which is no better and no worse placed than 2 Chron. 13.23b or 22.1, but like 11.18ff. represents an alien body by comparison with the rest of the special material and duplicates the reason for the bitter end of Jehoram and his family. If we regard the text as secondary,[22] we have to delete the reason given in 21.13b, which is syntactically lame. Everything else is presupposed in the excerpt of the framework scheme.

2 Chronicles 24.15-22

The two-fold reasons given for the end of Joash in 2 Chron. 24.17-22 are indispensable. Verses 17-19 are focused on vv. 23-24, vv. 20-22 on v. 25. The precise correspondence between action and outcome in vv. 20-22, 25 and the reference back in 26.5 (like 24.2) argue for originality.

2 Chronicles 25.5-16

The main notion is the reason given for the defeat of Israel, taken from the victory over Edom in 2 Kgs 14.7/2 Chron. 25.11f., with the worship of the Edomite gods in vv. 14-16, censured by an anonymous prophet, cf. vv. 19f. The remarks about the composition of the army in 2 Chron. 25.5-10,13,

which distinguish Judah and Benjamin from the other Israelites (Ephraimites) and in v. 13 anticipate the punitive judgment of vv. 22-24, follow
another subsidiary idea.

2 Chronicles 26.5-20

As previously in the case of Asa (14.5ff.) and Jehoshaphat (17.1ff.), the
remarks in vv. 6-15 about the success of v. 5 presupposed in 26.16ff. seem at
least in part to be an addition. It can be recognized by the two concluding
notes in vv. 8, 15b, the first of which refers to the victories and tributes in
vv. 6-8 (cf. 17.10f.; 27.5f.), the second to the building of fortresses and the
constitution of the army in vv. 9-10, 11-15a (cf. 11.5-12; 14.5f.,7; 17.12f., 14-
19; 27.3f.).

2 Chronicles 28.(6-8), 9-15

A special interest in the events in the north is shown by the carrying away of
the captives in 2 Chron. 28.8, 9-15. This interrupts the connection between
2 Kgs 16.5,[23] 6ff. in 2 Chron. 28.5(-8), 16ff. and seeks to harmonize the
contradiction between the original (2 Kgs 16.5) and the excerpt (2 Chron.
28.5-8). 2 Chronicles 28.17-19 again takes the line of v. 5, which in turn has
been supplemented in vv. 6, 7 and 8.

2 Chronicles 29–31

We find the skeleton of the purification of the cult spun out of 2 Kgs 18.4, 5-
7 in 2 Chron. 29.3, (4f.,) 16-17, 36 and 2 Chron. 31.1,[24] 20f. All the rest have
been inserted: the burnt-offering ordained by Hezekiah in 29.20, 27a, 29; the
(Passover) Mazzoth feast in 30.1, 6a, 13f., 21a, 26 and everything else,
namely the cleansing of the temple with speeches, sacrifices and music in 2
Chron. 29; the invitation to the tribes of the north for Passover in 2 Chron.
30; and the ordinances for service and offerings in 2 Chron. 31.2ff. As in the
case of David and Solomon, the founder and builder of the temple, here
Hezekiah and Josiah, the forerunner and the completer of the restoration of
the temple and the cult, are put in parallel with one another. The
exclusiveness of Josiah's Passover in 2 Chron. 35.18 already tells against the
Passover under Hezekiah; moreover it disrupts the original connection
between the opening of the temple and the purification of the cult.

2 Chronicles 33.11-17

Both 33.18-20 and 33.23 speak only of the conversion of Manasseh in vv. 11-13. The high places and idols installed beforehand and mentioned once again in 33.19 are still presupposed in 33.22 ('all the idols!') and also in Josiah's reform in 34.3ff. The reform of the cult in 33.15-17 therefore introduces the difference between 'alien gods' and the worship of Yhwh on the high places, but this only covers over the inconsistency in a makeshift way. It is therefore presumably secondary by comparison with the fortification of the cities in 33.14, which demonstrates the rule over them that has been regained.

2 Chronicles 35.2-17

The excerpt from the note about the Passover in 2 Kgs 23.21, 22f. forms the framework in 2 Chron. 35.1, 18-19; the preparations necessary for it embrace vv. 2, 7, 16-17. The services of the priests and levites, singers and gatekeepers and further gifts in 2 Chron. 35.3ff., 8ff., 15 (cf. also 34.12f.) interrupt the connection and from v. 10 anticipate the institution. Moreover they spoil the proportions, if we set the Passover against the expansion of the note about Necho from 2 Kgs 23.29f. in 2 Chron. 35.20-25.

3.4   The bulk of what is certainly original in the special material, which the excerpt from the basic biblical material necessarily requires, is made up of passages which with scanty means elaborate and explain individual pieces of the excerpted basic biblical material used in 1 Kgs 12–2 Kgs 25/2 Chron. 11–36. These pieces of the basic material are the ones in which after the broad description of the foundation of the kingdom under David and Solomon, in 2 Sam. 5–1 Kgs 10/1 Chron. 11–2 Chron. 9 the narrative thread becomes perceptibly thinner and with few exceptions the history of the kings of Judah is limited to the framework scheme and some annalistic notes. So it is not at all surprising that the special material originally begins only here. The difference from the use of the basic biblical material in Chronicles proves to be quite small. If the concentration on the history of the kings of Judah in 1 Chron. 11–2 Chron. 9 is achieved by the selection of narrative material which presents David as a hero in war and the founder of the kingdom; Solomon as a powerful ruler and founder of the temple; and both as examples of piety, in 2 Chron. 10–36 it is achieved by extracts from the framework scheme of Judah which measures successors by the two founder figures and in this sense is simply extended somewhat here and there.

The main purpose of the expansion is didactic: 'In the kingdom of Yahweh, what is at work is not a natural and human pragmatism but the divine pragmatism ... Sin is always punished and guilt never fails to incur misfortune.'[25] Therefore military defeats, illnesses leading to death and other unpleasant events which disturb the picture of the kings of Judah on whom a positive judgment is passed, are interpreted as divine punishment for sins committed: 2 Chron. 12.1ff.; 16.7-10, 12; 19.1-4a; 20.35-37; 24.15f., 17-22; 25.14-16, 19f.; 26.5, 16-20; 32.24-26, 31; 35.20ff. Conversely, the evil may not escape just punishment: 13.(3-18,) 19-21; 21.12-19; 22.7; 28.16ff. continuing 28.5, 6-8; 33.11-13, where a conversion is inferred from a long reign.

The divine pragmatism is expressed at many points by prophets, for whom in the basic material 1 Kgs 22/2 Chron. 18; 2 Kgs 18–20/2 Chron. 32; 2 Kgs 22.14ff./2 Chron. 34.22ff. and of course the many prophets of the northern kingdom provided the model. The prophets proclaim the law in the sense that the fate of the kings always depends on whether or not they obey Yhwh. According to this criterion, in anticipation or in retrospect they bring the actions of the kings and the events of history into the connection between action and outcome that is guided by Yhwh. Punishment is directed against individual kings, not against the kingdom or the people as a whole, with the exception of the reaction to the finding of the law under Josiah (2 Chron. 34.21, 23-25, 28), which for the period of Josiah is already relativized in the basic material. Yhwh, too, observes his law, which the Chronicler quotes from his basic material in 2 Chron. 25.4. Thus in Chronicles the Davidic-Judahite kingship over Israel ceases not because from the beginning it contained within itself a tendency towards evil and downfall, but because each of the last kings failed as individuals (2 Chron. 36). That opens up the way for the continuation of the history of Judah indicated by the Chronicler 2 Chron. 36.20f. The role of the prophets best fits into the source notes of the framework scheme taken over from the basic biblical material, in which Chronicles often refers to prophetic designations. The prophets are both preachers of the law and sacred authors at the same time. The extract from the sources about the history of the kingship of Judah made under the aegis of divine pragmatism is derived from them.

The divine pragmatism also includes the fact that the kings of Judah in Yhwh's realm are endowed with power and glory. Where nothing of this kind appeared in the basic biblical material, it has been reconstructed from the information in the framework scheme or in some other way from the basic material (which is why initially not the same thing is said of everyone). It has then successively been expanded and assimilated. This leads to the cluster-like collections of 'topoi', varying slightly in order, which certify that the kings of Judah engaged in lively building activity, usually of fortresses, once even in a renovation of the temple. There was a numerically strong army in Judah and Benjamin, and there were triumphs over Philistines, Ammonites, Moabites, Edomites, Cushites and Meunites and of course Israelite aggressors: 2 Chron. 11.5-12; 13. (3-18,) 19-21; 14.5 and vv. 6, 7, 8ff. (16.8f.); 17.1-5 and vv. 10-11, 12-13,14-19 + 18.1a; 26.(2,) 5 and vv. 6-8, 9-10, 11-15; 27.3-4, 5-6; 29.3, (4f.,) 16f., 36; 32.2-8, 22f., 27-29; 33.14. In addition to the points of contact in the closer context the topoi[26] have as a model the buildings, wars and tributes under David and Solomon; evidently the collection of themes at the beginning of the reign of David in 1 Chron. 11 and 14.1ff. (cf. v. 17) after 2 Sam. 5 was particularly influential. For Joash (2 Chron. 24.4ff.), Amaziah (2 Chron. 25.11f.), Hezekiah (2 Chron. 32) and Josiah (2 Chron. 34f.), there were already corresponding elements in the basic material. However, the outward splendour and the strength of the Judahite kingship apply only to the kings on whom a positive judgment is passed. In their case this sharpens the contrast with the apostasy which usually takes place at the culmination of power and the punishment that follows. The difference from the rulers on whom a negative judgment is passed, who have none of this, and from the phases in which the kings on whom there is a positive judgment but who for a time lose the divine blessings, clarifies the true issue. 'Merit is always the obverse of success ... Power is the index of piety, with which accordingly it rises and falls.'[27]

This picture does not alter fundamentally, but it does change notably with the addition of further secondary pieces of the special material. These first introduce a feature that is usually regarded as typical of the Chronicler and in part also recurs in Ezra–Nehemiah,[28] namely, the temple and the cult as the centre of the monarchy of Judah. This is sometimes accompanied by detailed lists of cultic personnel, sacrifices, gifts, etc.: 1 Chron. 15–16; 23–26 and the secondary additions in 1 Chron. 22; 28–29; 2 Chron. 11.13-17; 13.3-18 (vv. 4-12); 14.4; 15.1-15; 17.6, 7-9; 19.4ff. (legal reform); 29-31; 33.15-17; 35.3ff., 8ff.[29] Of course the original excerpt reported the building of the temple, the wickedness of the cult and reforms, partly with, partly without support in the basic material. At a few places the priests and levites already appear in the basic material where the theme is appropriate and to the degree that these are clearly not additions[30] (1 Chron. 15.26 for 2 Sam. 6.13[31] and 2 Chron. 5.4f. for 1 Kgs 8.3f.; 2 Chron. 23.1ff.; 24.5-7; 29.4f., 16; 34.9, 30). But it is the secondary parts and the additions in the excerpt to which these gave rise that make the secondary element the main element and idealize the Davidic Judahite kingdom in the way that we find in the present composition. They make David, the founder of the empire, the founder of the temple and the cult; thus Solomon is indirectly degraded to his assistant. Wherever possible, the priests, levites, singers and gatekeepers installed by David are involved over and above what is indicated in the basic biblical material; offerings and gifts are made, all kinds of sacrifices are offered and worship, and feasts are celebrated.

A further change is evident from the way in which sporadically the relationship with the brothers and fellow-tribesmen in the north – listed in 1 Chron. 2–9 and dominant in the basic material – becomes a theme.[32] That, too, is not a completely new perspective. Already in the original stratum the royal house of Judah claims to represent all Israel (cf. for example, 2 Chron. 12.1, 6) and may not get mixed up with the Israelite royal house in either political or family matters (cf. 2 Chron. 18.1; 20.35ff.). The claim to represent all Israel is fulfilled, say, with the bringing in of the ark in 2 Chron. 5.2f./1 Kgs 8.1f. and of course with Josiah's reform in 2 Chron. 34.6f., 9, 32f. (and afterwards also in 31.1) on the basis of 2 Kgs 23.3-20 or with the occupation of the cities of Ephraim in 2 Chron. 17.1f. (after 16.1-6). The geographical and genealogical fixing of the sphere of rule on 'Judah and Benjamin' taken over from 1 Kgs 12.21-24/2 Chron. 11.1-4 in the notes about the army (cf. 2 Chron. 11.10, 12; 14.7; 17.17-19) serves to provide the demarcation. But in time the latter in particular necessarily provoked the question of the members of the northern tribes. The genealogies in 1 Chron. 2–9 are an answer to this. Further answers are given by 1 Chron. 12; 13.1-4, 27; 2 Chron. 11.13ff.; 13.4ff.; 15.1ff. (v. 8 written out from 17.1f. with no reference in the preceding text); 23.2-3a; 25.5-10, 13; 28.(7-8,) 9ff.; 30.1ff.; 35.18b.

As in the excerpt and in the original special material, so too in the secondary special material the law of Moses or the law of Yhwh is the criterion. It is simply quoted very much more often here; it is taken very literally and implemented specifically in the temple cult initiated by David and realized by Solomon. Whereas the excerpt from the basic biblical material initially had to cope with the shadow sides of the kings of Judah, and held together the positive and negative aspects of the period of the monarchy in Judah, the later writers could concentrate exclusively on the bright side and elaborate that powerfully. Accordingly, seen as a whole, the Chronistic paraenesis in good and bad, the divine pragmatism or, as it is also called, the doctrine of retribution is the primary element, and the episodes and lists relating to the cult and tribal history, also including paraenetic episodes – converging with 1 Chron. 2–9 and Ezra–Nehemiah – are secondary. For the sake of simplicity we can follow Kurt Galling in distinguishing between a first Chronicler for the original stratum of Chronicles and a second Chronicler for the cultic expansions and all further expansions. This division is practical and therefore makes sense. However, not all the additions in the special material can have been made at once; they found their way into the text gradually. The sequence can only be explained case by case.

3.5   As in 1 Chron. 2–9, here too we must ask where the special material discussed here comes from. It should be said straight away that the answer to the question here is no more certain than it is in the case of 1 Chron. 2–9. We can only weigh probabilities. The assumption of a version of the history of the kings which contained everything that distinguished Chronicles from Samuel–Kings is improbable. The source postulated would be identical with Chronicles, so it makes more sense to keep with that. By contrast, it is conceivable that Chronicles has a special source especially for the deviations from the original, and in particular for the special material on which it drew. However, this possibility does not arise for everything, but only for those phenomena which neither have some support, which is often very hidden, in the basic material, nor correspond to the tendency of the Chronistic excerpt and those who supplemented it. In so far as the deviations, abbreviations or surpluses can be derived from the basic source material or from the theme and the purposes of Chronicles, the assumption of a special source is superfluous. Information to which that does not apply consists of personal names, places and numbers. Therefore the quest for a special source usually concentrates mostly on the notices about building, the constitution of the army and the wars, which it is thought cannot have been invented.[33] Strangely, it does not concentrate so much on the detailed ordinances of the cult, which are attributed to the Chronicler. Over against that stands the older view which sees all this information as no more than the invention of the Chronicler.[34] This latter view can appeal, first, to the fact that the themes all also occur in the basic material and can be extrapolated, regardless of whether the material fits the context well or not – because it has perhaps been added later. Secondly, it can indicate that the mere names, places and numbers could have been available to anyone at any time, regardless of whether they are correct or not – as must be assumed in the case of the fantastic numbers.

That means that it is impossible to decide whether the information which cannot be derivative comes from a special source or has been freely invented. So the third possibility, which seems most likely, represents a kind of compromise. It is that the information which cannot be explained either from the original material or from the theology of the Chronicler is a mixture of knowledge and invention – one might also say oral tradition. Whether the Chronicler got the information from elsewhere or whether he made it up for himself makes no fundamental difference.

The reason why this solution does not satisfy many scholars is that the historicity of the information depends on it. If we may reckon with a special source or with authentic oral tradition, the way is free to infer reliable reports about the pre-exilic history of Israel from Chronicles as well. A popular move is, say, to reconstruct a pre-exilic supreme court in Jerusalem from 2 Chron. 19.6ff. in combination with Deut. 16.18-20; 17.8ff. One can only warn against such historical combinations. The organization of the cult and the administration in the time of David and Solomon can with equal justification be got from 1 Chron. 23–27. But the difference between the Chronistic texts and the literary parallels or the actual circumstances in the time of the Chronicler do not guarantee the authenticity and great age of the information. One or other detail may be quite correctly remembered or known, but since the Chronicler is trying to reconstruct the pre-exilic period historically on the basis of the material he has before him and his own views, the bulk of the material must reflect the circumstances or the programme of his own period – the Persian-Hellenistic period.

4.   Basic material and excerpt

T. Willi, *Die Chronik als Auslegung*; S.L. McKenzie, *The Chronicler's Use of the Deuteronomistic History*, HSM 33, 1985; I. Kalimi, *Zur Geschichtsschreibung des Chronisten*, BZAW 226, 1995; J. Weinberg, *Der Chronist in seiner Mitwelt*, BZAW 239, 1996, 121-30.

4.1   The relationship between the basic biblical material and the excerpt is stamped by the greatest possible fidelity to the text of the original. That does not exclude changes in the way in that this is rendered by the Chronicler. The excerpt is a rewriting and exposition of the basic biblical material all in one.

The most important change concerns the state of the text. Chronicles does not write out the whole text of Genesis–Kings, but makes a selection. From Adam it goes through the genealogies of Genesis in rapid strides to Israel (indeed the description may have originally begun with the list of the twelve sons of Israel in 1 Chron. 2.1-2). From them it runs through Judah to David in 1 Chron. 2; from David, if we leave out of account the secondary filling out of the tribal genealogies, to the beginning of the Davidic-Judahite kingship over Israel in 1 Chron. 11 following 2 Sam. 5. From there on Chronicles recapitulates the history of the Davidic-Judahite monarchy: the beginning is formed by a selection from 2 Sam. 5–24, which apart from the history of the ark in 1 Chron. 13–16^{35}/2 Sam. 6 (dovetailed with the accession in 2 Sam. 5) and the purchase of the temple site in 1 Chron. 21/2 Sam. 24, is really interested only in the wars of David (1 Chron. 14 after 2 Sam. 5.17ff.; 1 Chron. 18–20 after 2 Sam. 8; 10–12; 21), which are meant to explain why he was not allowed to build the temple (1 Chron. 22.8; 28.3), but only his successor Solomon (1 Chron. 22.8; 28.3). After a freely formulated transition in 1 Chron. (22 and) 28f. in place of 1 Kgs 1f.,[36] there follows the account of the time of Solomon, after 1 Kgs 3–11, in 2 Chron. 1–9. The excerpt from the framework scheme and those narratives of Kings which deal with the kings of Judah (1 Kgs 12–15; 22; 2 Kgs 8; 11–12; 14–16; 18–25) is attached to Solomon in 2 Chron. 10–36.

The omissions are the obverse of the selection. In Gen. 1–2 Sam. 4/1 Chron. 1–10 they pass over everything except the constitution of Israel, which is initially simply presupposed and developed in the form of a list in the secondary material. In 2 Sam. 5–1 Kgs 11/1 Chron. 11–2 Chron. 9 – as is already the case with the omission of 1 Sam. 1–2 Sam. 4 (cf. 1 Chron. 11.3) – they avoid any superfluous or inappropriate contact between David and the descendants of Saul (2 Sam. 9; 21; 22.1f.), any wrangling or unpleasantness over the succession to David (2 Sam. 11.2–12.25; 13–20; 1 Kgs 1f.) and any deviation from Solomon's main task (1 Kgs 3.16–5.14). As is understandable from the very nature of the tradition, there is no omission in the excerpt from the Judahite history extending from 1 Kgs 12 to 2 Kgs 25 in 2 Chron. 10–36, but every passage is worked on, for example, by the consistent omission of the synchronism except in 2 Chron. 13.1. Where the basic biblical material is itself broad, it is markedly condensed and in the process the content is also rewritten.[37] The reduction of the material, particularly at passages like 2 Kgs 18–20 or 23.4ff., which must have come in very handy for the present form of Chronicles, confirms indirectly that the original form must have been very much slimmer, and that the present proportions produced by the fillings-out from the special material are secondary. Conversely, the changes, say, in 2 Chron. 33.10,11f. or 2 Chron. 36[38] show how sparse are the means with which the Chronicler originally undertook the rewriting. At a number of places the text excerpted presupposes knowledge of the omissions.[39] Chronicles is not meant to replace the original but to interpret it.

Transposition is another means of reception, between selection and omission. Three cases stand out: the dovetailing of 2 Sam. 5 and 6 in 1 Chron. 11–16 and the incorporation of 2 Sam. 23 into 1 Chron. 11/2 Sam. 5; the placing of 1 Kgs 10.26ff. in 2 Chron. 1.14ff., despite the repeated reproduction of it in 2 Chron. 9.25ff.; and the placing of the reform of Josiah from 2 Kgs 23.4-20, 24 in 2 Chron. 34.4ff. In the first case, scholars are fond of making the Chronicler's predilection for everything cultic responsible; he is said to have made his David embark on the task of bringing in the ark as quickly as possible. But presumably there was another decisive factor. Just as the failure of the first attempt is explained by Uzzah's false move, so too the success of the undertaking attached to 2 Sam. 6.12ff., with no motivation whatsoever and prepared for only by the blessing of the house of Obed-Edom, will have a basis in David himself. The Chronicler found it in 2 Sam. 6.17: when building his houses in Jerusalem David also thought of a place for the ark (1 Chron. 15.1; 17.1ff.). Therefore the first approach in 2 Sam. 6.1ff./1 Chron. 13.1ff. is put immediately after the occupation of Jerusalem and the first building up of the city in 2 Sam. 5.1-10/1 Chron. 11.1-9, but before the note about building in 2 Sam. 5.11f./ 1 Chron. 14.1f.; the second approach is put after it. The insertion of the list

2 Sam. 23 in 1 Chron. 11.10ff. (with expansions in 11.41ff.; 12.1ff.) seems to have been caused by the beginning of 2 Sam. 6.1, which reflects 1 Chron. 13.1-4 and later 13.5. The second case is connected with the ring-shaped composition of the Solomon tradition in the basic biblical material and the existing doublet in 1 Kgs 5.6; 10.26. In the third case the weight is simply distributed differently. Other transpositions such as the isolation of the sins of Rehoboam and the Shishak episode from 1 Kgs 14.22-28 in 2 Chron. 12.1ff. before 1 Kgs 14.21, 29-31/2 Chron. 12.13-16, or duplications (cf. 2 Chron. 21.5, 20; 27.1-8) are caused by the filling-out of the framework scheme and are less striking.

Finally, changes in the wording of the text excerpted should be mentioned. As a rule they are not serious, but often they are very significant. Three sorts of change occur: reformulations, deletions and additions. I have already touched on some of these in discussing special material, especially abbreviations or replacements in the framework scheme of the kings of Judah,[40] and also additions to and reformulations of the framework scheme in respect of the special material. However, that is only a fraction of the deviations, larger and smaller, which occur in the reproduction of the text of the basic biblical material. The details are a matter for special investigations which survey the phenomena and catalogue them. To get at least an impression, here is a sample from a consecutive passage. I have selected the reproduction of 2 Sam. 7 in 1 Chron. 17, which clearly indicates different types and at the same time the scope of such deviations; here I have limited myself to the prophecy of Nathan in 1 Chron. 17.1-15.

Most deviations are of an orthographic, grammatical or lexical kind: plene writing replaces defective writing (vv. 8, 9, 11, 13); the normal form replaces a consecutive imperfect of the first person singular with a cohortative ending (v. 8); the infinite construct replaces the finite verb (v. 11); the transitive form replaces the intransitive (vv. 13, 14 with a change of subject); the long form replaces the contracted personal suffix (v. 9); the simple 'see' replaces the imperative 'look' + independent particle –*na* (v. 1), but by way of exception the long form of the first-person-singular personal pronoun is preserved (v. 1, but cf. v. 16); conjunctions (vv. 1, 11),[41] prefixed or double prepositions (vv. 4-7, 9, 10, cf. also v. 14) and the rhetorical question (v. 4) are simplified; stylistic improvements are made with slight omissions (vv. 2, 6, 8, 12), additions (article, v. 4) and alterations of the position of words or syntax (vv. 4, 10, 12); replacement words sometimes serve to clarify (David for 'the king', vv. 1f.; 'treat harshly', v. 9; 'build', v. 10 assimilating to v. 12; the usual word for 'vision' in v. 15): sometimes they reflect the terminology and conceptual horizon of the Chronicler ('the ark of the covenant of Yhwh' for 'the ark of God', v. 1; God for Yhwh, vv. 2f.; 'Israel' for 'the sons of Israel' in vv. 5f.;[42] simple 'lead out' for 'lead out of

Egypt', v. 5; 'humble', v. 10; 'go with the fathers', v. 11; the abstract 'kingdom', vv. 11, 14; the periphrasis for David's predecessor, avoiding the name Saul, v. 13).

Alterations based on content, which interpret the text, work with the same means: it is no accident that the omission of 'rest' from 2 Sam. 7.1b in 1 Chron. 17.1, with which the substitution of the word in 17.10 converges, already points forward at this place to the reason that the Chronicler gives in 1 Chron. 22.8; 28.3 as to why it was not David but Solomon who might build the temple: David was a man of war. In order to obviate the misunderstanding that the ark was still in the tent of meeting, in v. 1 it is under tent-cloths, namely under the cloths of the tent set up by David (15.1; 16.1), and according to v. 5 went from tent to tent and from dwelling (to dwelling).[43] The substitution of a word in v. 11 ('one of your sons' instead of 'one from your loins') introduces the shift of the promise of a dynasty addressed to David to the promise of the builder of the temple; this is already announced with the addition of the article in v. 4 ('the house') and perhaps also with the substitution of a word in v. 10 ('build' a house instead of 'make' a house). The threat of punishment from 2 Sam. 7.14b is omitted for the same reason in 1 Chron. 17.13: it is not to strike David's successor. Finally there is a subtle reformulation of 2 Sam. 7.16 in 1 Chron. 17.14:

And your house and your kingdom shall be made sure for ever before me; your throne shall be established for ever. (2 Sam. 7.16)
And I will confirm him in my house and in my kingdom for ever and his throne shall be established for ever. (1 Chron. 17.13)

The promise originally addressed to David passes over to Solomon; the house and kingdom pass over to Yhwh himself.[44] So after and alongside all the linguistic and stylistic deviations, including those of expression and general convictions, here there is a clear and incisive change of historiographical and theological conception.

4.2   Like the special material, this differentiated finding in the excerpt also raises the question whether the basic material of Chronicles was not the version of (Genesis and) Samuel–Kings that we now have but some other version. Scholars like to postulate a separate source at least for the surpluses, or they make a reference to oral tradition. But what applies to the special material applies even more to the relationship between basic material and excerpt. The basic material postulated would not look very different from Chronicles, and in turn we would have to investigate its relationship to the present version of Samuel–Kings. And that Genesis and Samuel–Kings were not yet available to the Chronicler in the version that has been handed down to us can be decisively refuted by the fact that those parts which have been omitted, and indeed particularly those parts, are often presupposed in Chronicles, though this does not exclude post-Chronistic additions in Genesis–Kings. It is quite different if knowledge from other traditions or writings, for example, other biblical books, has also found its way into the excerpt.

The only points of contact for the use of other or at least additional sources offered in Chronicles are its references to sources.[45] The following titles are mentioned: Book of the Kings of Israel and Judah (1 Chron. 9.1); 'Words' (things) of Samuel the Seer, Words of Nathan the Prophet, Words of Gad the Seer (1 Chron. 29.29); Words of Nathan the Prophet, Prophecy of Ahijah the Shilonite, Vision of Iddo the Seer (2 Chron. 9.29); Midrash of Shemaiah the Prophet and Iddo the Seer (2 Chron. 12.15); Midrash of Iddo the Prophet (2 Chron. 13.22); Book of the Kings of Judah and Israel (2 Chron. 16.11); Words of Jehu, the son of Hanani, which are recorded in the Book of the Kings of Israel (2 Chron. 20.34); Midrash on the Book of Kings (2 Chron. 24.27); Book of the Kings of Judah and Israel (2 Chron. 25.26); 'the rest was written by the prophet Isaiah, son of Amoz' (2 Chron. 26.22); Book of the Kings of Israel and Judah (2 Chron. 27.7); Book of the Kings of Judah and Israel (2 Chron. 28.26); Vision of the Prophet Isaiah, son of Amoz, in the Book of the Kings of Judah and Israel (2 Chron. 32.32); 'Words' of the kings of Israel, Words of 'his' seers (2 Chron. 33.18,19); Book of the Kings of Israel and Judah (2 Chron. 36.8).

For a long time scholars have been clear that the different titles always denote one and the same book, the Book of the Kings of Israel and Judah, which is cited either by this, its main title, or by sections contained in it, the prophetic writings: 'The peculiar mode of naming the individual sections – at a time when chapters and verses were unknown – has its origin in the idea that each period of the sacred history has its leading prophet ... but also at the same time involves the notion that each prophet has himself written the history of his own period.'[46] And that this Book of the Kings of Israel and Judah is none other than that which Chronicles knows simply and solely from the books of Samuel and Kings handed down to us is demonstrated by the fact that the Chronistic citations of sources (with the exception of 1 Chron. 9.1; 29.29f.) stand, or (with the exception of Jehoram and Amon in the case of Ahaziah, Athaliah, Amon, Jehoahaz, Jehoiachin and Zedekiah) are lacking, where they also stand, or are lacking, in Samuel–Kings, though in Chronicles they are unified and redefined. Moreover, generally speaking the majority of the prophetic writers and the prophets are figures whom the Chronicler has brought together from the basic biblical material in Samuel–Kings; only in individual cases has he combined them freely.[47] The intention is evidently that Chronicles should rest on the same sources, or more correctly on the one prophetically inspired source, as the books of Samuel and Kings, which for their part are regarded as an extract from this source. Accordingly, in an alteration of the references to sources which have been adopted, they are derived from the one source. In fact Chronicles knows of this source only from Samuel–Kings themselves. The source quotations, too, thus specifically confirm the assumption that the present version of Samuel–Kings served as the basic material.

4.3   The only qualification that needs to be made here is a text-critical one.[48] In some cases the simplest explanation of the deviations is that Chronicles does not presuppose the present Massoretic text of Samuel–Kings but another recension. The possibilities are: (1) Chronicles is original and Samuel–Kings were subsequently corrupted;[49] (2) Samuel–Kings are original and Chronicles was subsequently corrupted;[50] (3) Samuel–Kings have preserved the original text; Chronicles is based on a version which differs from M (see below); (4) Both versions are damaged.[51] The third possibility has received new support from the discovery of fragments of Samuel in Qumran (4QSam), particularly in those cases in which Chronicles and 4QSam agree against M^{Sam}, sometimes with and sometimes without G^{Sam}. An especially vivid example is the relationship between 1 Sam. 6.13 and 1 Chron. 15.26. By comparison with the Massoretic versions, the help for the levites and the number of the sacrifices which are also listed elsewhere seem to be additions by the Chronicler. G^{Sam} has a rather different text from M^{Sam} in the first half of the verse and speaks of 'seven choirs' which were with them instead of 'six steps', but it is by no means a witness for the variants in Chronicles. In the first half, 4QSam^a confirms the reading of 2 Sam. 6.13a indirectly, namely, by the present position; in the second half it confirms the reading of 1 Chron. 15.26b. That allows us to conclude that in v. 26a Chronicles offers an independent formulation, but in v. 26b is based on an original which deviates from 2 Sam. 6.13 M.[52] Whether such a pre-Chronistic variant of the text of Samuel which has found its way into Chronicles – in the sense of the two possibilities (1) and (2) mentioned above – is older or younger than the Massoretic text is another question. The orthography of Chronicles in particular may represent an earlier state of the textual tradition than the Massoretic version of Samuel; otherwise the relationship has to be explained instance by instance. The mechanical distribution by means of the surpluses, which some scholars practise today, works the rule of the *lectio brevior* to death.

So in so far as we do not have scribal errors, that is, chance mistakes, or subsequent alterations to the original, we have to reckon with two things in Chronicles: the word-for-word adoption of the original, which over wide stretches is identical with M but in places is also different from it, and a deliberate alteration of the original for reasons which are not only text-critical and exegetical but also relate to content and theology. The instances of textual history that I have just discussed are evidence that the procedure of reception practised by the Chronicler in matters great and small is not an individual instance but at many places functions according to the rules of the ancient textual tradition. Therefore the boundaries between the textual tradition of the original and the redaction of the Chronicler are fluid, just as they are between the Chronistic redaction and its supplementers. If we like, we can regard the origin of Chronicles, including the successive filling-out of the excerpt by the special material, as a process of productive tradition of the text. It is productive in so far as the tradition does not just copy and safeguard the text but always also edits it, improves it and interprets it; in other words, it is exegesis. And the tradition of the text is a microcosm of the genesis of Chronicles, as it is of the Old Testament writings generally.

4.4   Finally, we turn once again to the wider picture and the whole work. We have rejected out of hand the possibility that, as in the history of the text, so too in the coming into being of Chronicles, not everything goes back to an original contained in Samuel–Kings but at least some material goes back to a different original which has now disappeared, because the hypothesis has no heuristic value. Of course that does not mean that Chronicles had no preliminary stage at all. As the analysis of the genealogies and the special material showed, the preliminary stages are contained in Chronicles itself. Thus the question arises whether perhaps the excerpt from the original also had a preliminary stage.

There are some reasons for doubting the literary unity of the excerpt. These relate to: the beginning (1 Chron. 1 or 2.1f.); the originality of the Saul chapter in 1 Chron. 10, which belongs more to the preceding genealogies than to the following narrative and interrupts the connection between the genealogy of David in 1 Chron. 2 and the beginning of the history of the Davidic kingship in 1 Chron. 11; the dovetailing of 2 Sam. 5–6 in 1 Chron. 11–13; the prefixed list 2 Sam. 23 in 1 Chron. 11.1ff.; the twofold closing scene of the history of David in 1 Chron. 21–22, 23.1 + 28f., one composed of 2 Sam. 24 and 1 Kgs 5, the other orientated on 1 Kgs 1.f.; the doublet 2 Chron. 1.14ff./9.25ff. after 1 Kgs 5.6; 10.26ff. Further inconsistencies arise from the combination of passages taken over word for word with the Chronistic revision of the original or with the special material (for example, 2 Chron. 15.16-18 after 14.4 and 15.8 or 20.31-33 after 17.6).

As far as the latter is concerned, scholars tend to content themselves with the view that the Chronicler wrote out the material before him quite mechanically, and in so doing did not notice that he was contradicting his own intentions. Given the many careful reformulations of the original, that is quite improbable. By contrast, most difficulties can be explained quite simply if we reckon both with expansions in the sphere of the special material and also with secondary filling out of the excerpt from the basic material. The development of the special material must be the rule in the case of inconsistencies between excerpt and special material, especially in 2 Chron. 10–36, where the framework scheme of the history of the kings of Judah has been written out. The secondary filling-out from the original could be responsible for the clumsy positioning of 1 Chron. 10; 11.10ff.; 21f. and the doublets in 2 Chron. 1.14ff.; 9.25f. I would not venture to resolve the dovetailing of 2 Sam. 5–6, although the disruptive part 1 Chron. 13, together with the original stratum of chs 15f., can easily be detached; the connection of 1 Chron. 14.1ff. to 11.1-9 (after 2 Sam. 5) is smooth; and 17.1 as the first mention of the ark with 2 Chron. 1.4; 5.2ff. as a retrospect and continuation, and as the occasion for a subsequent filling-out (cf. 2 Chron. 1.1ff./1 Chron. 13.1-4, 5ff.), are completely satisfactory for the beginning.

The advocates of the so-called block model who delete out of hand the whole conclusion in 2 Chron. 35–36 and replace it with the compilation of 2 Chron. 35–36 + Ezra 1–10 in 3 Ezra have few scruples. Anyone who regards 3 Ezra or the supporting Semitic basic material as original must regard the Massoretic text as secondary. That does not work, simply because 3 Ezra 1 presupposes the text of 2 Chron. 35, expanded in the light of the late additions in 1 Chron. 23ff., and for its part, apart from mistakes in reading and translation, considerably alters the Massoretic text in 3 Ezra 1,10, 21-22, 26, 30f., 32, 35f., 41. Had this been just the literary continuation of 2 Chron. 34, as suggested by the abrupt intervention in 3 Ezra 1.1, it was certainly not the original one. Moreover, the version of the book of Ezra including Neh. 8 in 2 Ezra is not the original form, but an epitome. But more on that later. The end of Chronicles is reached in 2 Chron. 36.20f. with the prospect of the end of the exile. With or without the crowning line in 36.22f. this points to the continuation of the history of the kings of Judah in the history of the Persian empire.

5. Result

Chronicles is based on biblical material, above all on Genesis and Samuel–Kings, in the version which has been handed down to us. Sometimes, however, especially in Samuel, it is based on a form of the text which deviates from the Massoretic text. It is composed of excerpts from the basic material and the special material, attached to the excerpts both through literary links and in terms of content, and fills in the gaps. We need not assume additional, extra-biblical sources either for the excerpt or for the special material, apart from insights and ideas which the Chronicler draws from other traditions or writings, known to us and unknown, and allows to flow into excerpt and special material.

However, within Chronicles itself we have to distinguish different stages of the development of the text. At the beginning stands the excerpt from the history of the kings of Judah from 2 Sam. 5 to 2 Kgs 25, which starts with the list of the twelve sons of Israel and the genealogy of Judah up to and including David in 1 Chron. 2 and extends from 1 Chron. 11 to 2 Chron. 36. Here already we have the first pieces of special material which fill out the dry framework scheme of the kings of Judah after David and Solomon with narrative material and introduce isolated notes taken from annals in the basic material into the theological context of action and outcome, that is, offer a theology of retribution, and connect these notes with a judgment on the piety of the kings in the framework scheme, for better or worse. As things developed, the excerpt from the basic material was supplemented, and the special material was markedly expanded. Gradually the introductory part came to contain the origin of Israel from the history of humankind in 1 Chron. 1, the lists of tribes in 1 Chron. 2–9, and the end of the kingdom of Saul in 1 Chron. 10. This is followed by the efforts of David to establish the cult in 1 Chron. 13; 15f.; 22 and the ordinances about estate and service in 1 Chron. 11.10ff.; 12; 15–16; 23–27, some expansion of the older notes about buildings, the army and war with the kings of Judah after David and Solomon, the extended accounts of the 'holy war'. Here too extensive Priestly notes about the cult and the law and explanations of tribal history focused on the attachment of the north. The origin of Chronicles thus proves to be a long literary process, which is always an exposition of the original biblical material and at the same time an exegesis of Chronicles itself.

The proposals for dating range from the sixth to the second century BC.[53] If the identification is accurate, the *terminus ad quem* is the fragment of a manuscript of Chronicles (4Q118) found in Qumran Cave 4. If we take note of the biblical books used or quoted in Chronicles, we may not go back too far in time, and if we also take into account the literary stratification, we must make differentiations in the dating. My view is that the beginning, the extract from the Davidic Judahite kings from Samuel–Kings in accordance with the Torah, is conceivable even in the Persian period (middle of the fourth century BC). The intention is either to offer distinctive opposition to the sometimes fluid Persian empire or to give a distinctive political and theological identity to the young province of Judah in the framework of the Achaemenid empire, which was once again rising to become the sole power around 350 BC, over against the province of Samaria. The late Persian period and the Hellenistic era down to the time of the Maccabees seem to be the time of the extensive expansions related to politics and military matters, the cult and tribal history. The criteria of the basic writing to some degree become independent in the supplements: the kingship of Yhwh in the hands of the house of David, which assumes tremendous proportions, and the Torah, which becomes the universal criterion, especially for the cult and its ordinances and the constitution of Israel, the people of twelve tribes. Thus in terms of literary and theological history, Chronicles is moving towards the two books of Maccabees.

Table A.I.2

Basic document		Supplements
Excerpt	Special material	Secondary special material
1 Chronicles		
		1.1-54
2.1-2, 3a, 4-5, 9-15		2.3b, 6-8, 16-17
		2.18-9.44; 10.1-14
11.1-9(, 10ff.)		11.41–12.41
(13-)14		
(15.1, 3, 25-29; 16.1-3, 43)		15.2, 4-24; 16.4-42
17.1–22.1		
23.1		
		23.2-26, 32; 27.1-34
(28.1, 2-10; 29.20-25)		28.11–29.19
29.26-30		
2 Chronicles		
1–9		
10.1–11.4	11.5-12	11.13-17, 18-23
12		
13.1-2, 22-23	13.3-21	13.4-12
14.1-3, 4	14.5, 6, 7, 8-14	
		15.1-15
15.16–16.7, 10-14	16.8-9	
17.1-5	17.10-19	17.6, 7-9
18		
19.1-4a		19.4b-11; 20.1-30
20.31–21.1, 5-20		21.2-4, 13b
22.1–24.27		
25.1-4, 11-12, 14-23		25.5-10, 13
26.1-5, 16-23	26.6-15	
27.1-2, 7-9	27.3-6	
28.1-4, 5, 16-7	28.6-8	28.9-15
29.1-2	29.3-5, 16-17, 36	29.6-15, 18-35
31.1, 20-21		31.2-19
32	32.2-8, 22-23, 27-29	
33.1-13, 18-25	33.14	33.15-17
34		34.12f.
35.1-2, 7, 16-27		35.3-6, 8-14, 15
36.1-21		36.22-23 (with Ezra 1.1-3).

Notes

1   The text is easily accessible in the German edition by K.F. Pohlmann in JSHRZ I/5, 1980; or in the English version by R.H. Charles, *APOT* I, 1-58.

2   Willi, BK 24, 18f., 21f., and ad loc.

3   The text is disturbed at this point. Perhaps the original reading in 7.6, 12aα is 'the sons of' Benjamin, and in 7.12aβ the sons of 'Dan'. Cf. Noth, *ÜSt*, 118 and commentary ad loc.

4   2 Sam. 5.14-16 appears once again in 1 Chron. 14.3-7.

5   Noth, *ÜSt*, 118-22.

6   We may follow Noth, *ÜSt*, 119 n. 4, in altering or omitting the difficult formulation; at all events with Willi, BK 24, 78f. and ad loc. it is to be regarded as a formulation by the Chronicler which introduces 2.10ff. but does not require the continuation in 2.18ff.

7   Cf. 1 Kgs 14.25-28/2 Chron. 12.2ff.; 1 Kgs 15.7b/2 Chron. 13.2b, 3ff.; 1 Kgs 15.22, 23/2 Chron. 14.5ff.; 2 Kgs 14.7/2 Chron. 25.5ff.; 2 Kgs 14.22/2 Chron. 26.2, 5ff.; 2 Kgs 15.35(, 37)/2 Chron. 27.3ff.; 2 Kgs 16.5f., 7ff./2 Chron. 28.5ff., 16ff.; 2 Kgs 18.4(-7)/2 Chron. 29f.; 2 Kgs 21.17/2 Chron. 33.11ff.,18; 2 Kgs 23.21-23/2 Chron. 35; 2 Kgs 23.29f./2 Chron. 35.20ff.

8   Cf. for example, 1 Kgs 12.25, 26ff./2 Chron. 11.5ff., 13ff.; 1 Kgs 16.1, 7 (Jehu ben Hanani)/2 Chron 16.7ff.; 19.1-3; 1 Kgs 17–2 Kgs 2 (prophet Elijah)/2 Chron. 21.12ff.; 1 Kgs 22.39/2 Chron. 17.12f.; 1 Kgs 20 or 2 Kgs 3/2 Chron. 20; 2 Kgs 9f./2 Chron. 22.7 as an example for 2 Chron. 21.2-4, 13.

9   Cf. for example, 2 Chron. (15.19;) 16.1–17.1, after 1 Kgs 15.16-22, 23-24; 2 Chron. 26.16-20, 21-23; 27.2 after 2 Kgs 15.3, 4-7; 2 Chron 24.17ff., 23ff. after 2 Kgs 12.18ff.

10   Cf. the survey in Welten, *Geschichte*, 187f.

11   Cf. Noth, *ÜSt*, 112-17, and the commentaries by I. Benziger, KHC 20, 1901; Galling, ATD 12; W. Rudolph, HAT I/21. J.W. Rothstein and J. Hänel, KAT 18.2, 1927, is quite impossible to take in.

12   Thus for example, 2 Chron. 12.13f., 15f./1 Kgs 14.21-31, the isolation and development of the Shishak episode of 1 Kgs 14.22-28 in 2 Chron. 12.1ff.; 2 Chron. 16.11f./1 Kgs 15.23, the breach of faith in 2 Chron. 16.7ff. which leads to sickness, and indirectly the buildings and the fortifications in 2 Chron. 14.5ff.; 2 Chron. 26.21, 22f./2 Kgs 15.5, 6f. and 2 Chron. 27.2/2 Kgs 15.34f., the cultic wickedness in 2 Chron. 26.16.ff.; 2 Chron. 33.22f./2 Kgs 21.20-22, the conversion of Manasseh in 2 Chron. 33.11ff.; 2 Chron. 35.26f./2 Kgs 23.28-30, the isolation of the Necho episode of 2 Kgs 23.29f. in 2 Chron. 35.20ff.

13   Cf. Noth, *ÜSt*, 112ff.; Willi, *Auslegung*, 194ff.; Steins, *Chronik*, 417ff.

14   Cf. Num. 27.12ff./Deut 31–34 or Josh. 13.1; 21.34-45/23.11.

15   With a recapitulation of 28.10 in 28.20; cf. 22.13.

16   Wellhausen, *Proleg.*, 181.

17   The name and father's name of Maacah, mother of Abijah in 2 Chron. 11.20-22, correspond with 1 Kgs 15.2b, but not with 2 Chron. 13.2a. G contaminates both readings in 2 Chron. 13.2 (Maacah, the daughter of Uriel of Gibeon). According to Noth, *ÜSt*, 143 n. 1, 2 Chron. 13.2 still had the original text of 1 Kgs 15.2b before it, whereas 2 Chron. 11.20ff. presupposes an alteration following 1 Kgs 15.10. But perhaps the mistake was also caused by 2 Chron. 11.20ff.; 2 Chron. 14.1f. does not offer 1 Kgs 15.10; 2 Chron. 15.16 mentions only the deposition of the 'queen mother' Maacah (not 'his mother', like 1 Kgs 15.13), who could be also understood as the grandmother of Asa and mother of Abijah and identified with Micaiah of 2 Chron. 13.2; thus in 2 Chron. 11.20ff., through 1 Kgs 15.10, the daughter of Uriel became a 'daughter' (granddaughter) of Absalom.

18   The note about the persistent wars between Rehoboam and Jeroboam in 2 Chron. 12.15b/1 Kgs 14.30 which has been taken over from the original material and is not covered in either place also contradicts 2 Chron. 11.1-4/1 Kgs 12.21-24, but the mistake is already in the original material. However, perhaps we may also understand the plural 'wars' and the deletion of the prepositions in 2 Chron. 12.15b to mean that here the thought is not of wars 'between' the two but of the wars of either the one or the other.

19   In view of comparable cases it is improbable that the Chronicler was not concerned about the precise relationship between his own formulation and the material he had before him (cf. for example, Wellhausen, *Proleg.*, 193; most recently Japheth, OTL, 707). Rudolph, HAT 1/21, 241, 263, reckons with a secondary elaboration from 1 Kgs here, as in 2 Chron. 20.31-33/1 Kgs 22.42ff. But the opposite is the case: 2 Chron. 14.2 corresponds to 1 Kgs 15.12 and like the abbreviation of 1 Kgs 22.43f., 47 in 2 Chron. 20.32f. (and the deletion of 2 Kgs 23.7 in 2 Chron. 34.3ff.) takes into account the omission of 1 Kgs 14.23f. in 2 Chron. 12.1. 2 Chronicles 15.17 distinguishes the high places 'from Israel' from the alien altars, mazzeboth and asheroth abolished in 14.2. It is the alien or Judahite high places in 14.2, 4 (also added in 14.2?), the account of the reform in 15.1ff. and the addition in 17.6 (see below) which cause the confusion.

20   The limitation of the 'rest' to ten years before the Cushite war, to which in turn 2 Chron. 15.11(?); 16.8f. relate, is possibly meant to balance out the difference between the information in the original material in 1 Kgs 15.7b, 33; 16.8 (twenty-sixth year of Asa) and the deliberate alteration of it in 2 Chron. 15.19; 16.1 (the thirty-sixth year of Asa with a continuation in 16.12, 13): if ten years precede this, Asa's war with Baasha falls in the twenty-sixth year after the Cushite war.

21   2 Chron. 17.6 stands in blatant contradiction to 20.33, as does 14.4 to 15.17 (see n. 19). The addition presupposes 14.2; 15.17, but presumably not yet the corresponding measures under Asa in 14.4 (15.8ff.). The reference back in 19.3bα (*asheroth*, feminine plural) originally goes back rather to 15.16; 17.3f. and will have led to the addition of 17.6.

22   Thus Noth, *ÜSt*, 143 n. 1.

23   Here M reads 'Aram' throughout, but 2 Chron. 28.17 must at least have had before it the kethib of v. 6 ('and the Edomites came to Elat', etc.), which is also attested in the versions.

24   Perhaps without 'from all Judah and Benjamin and completely in Ephraim and Manasseh'.

25   Wellhausen, *Proleg.*, 194; cf. Noth, *ÜSt*, 172f.

26   The family histories in 2 Chron. 11.18ff. and 21.2-4 (cf. 13.21), the holy war in 2 Chron. 13.3-18; 20.1ff. (cf. 14.8ff.; 17.10f.; 26.6-8; 27.5f.), the scenes from the war of northern Israel in 2 Chron. 25.5-10, 13; 28.8, 9ff., and the lists in 1 Chron. 11.41ff.; 12; and 27 (cf. 2 Chron. 14.7; 17.14-19; 26.11-13) are close in theme but later insertions.

27   Wellhausen, *Proleg.*, 209.

28   Cf. Wellhausen, *Proleg.*, 171ff., 187ff.; Noth, *ÜSt*, 173ff., is more differentiated; more recently, for example, G. Steins in E. Zenger et al., *Einleitung in das Alte Testament*, Studienbücher Theologie I, 1, 1995, 173f.

29   As 1 Chron. 11.41ff.; 12; 27 show, the additions to the earlier 'topoi' do not belong here. Cf. above n. 26.

30   1 Chron. 13.2 (cf. 13.1-4 and 2 Chron. 1.2ff.); 2 Chron. 5.11-13; 7.6; 8.14f.; 23.2-3a, 13aβ, 18-19; 34.12-13; 35.18b.

31   Independently of this 1 Chron. 15.2, 11-15; 2 Chron. 35.3. The passages about donors are 1 Sam. 6.15; 2 Sam. 15.24; and Deut. 10.8.

32   Cf. Noth, *ÜSt*, 178f.; in detail H.G.M. Williamson, *Israel in the Book of Chronicles*, 1977; Willi, *Auslegung*, 161f., 190ff.

33   Cf. Noth, *ÜSt*, 139ff.; Welten, *Geschichte*, 191-4. Both pass very moderate judgments.

34   Cf. Wellhausen, *Proleg.*, 207-12.

35   1 Chron. 13 inserted between 11.1-9, 10ff. and 14.1ff.; 15.1, 3, 25–16.3, 43.

36   1 Chron. 22.2-19 or 23.1; 28.1-10; and 29.20-30.

37   2 Kgs 16.6ff. in 2 Chron. 28.16ff.; 2 Kgs 18–20 in 2 Chron. 32; 2 Kgs 22–23, esp. 23.4-20, 24 in 2 Chron. 34–35; 2 Kgs 21.10-16 in 2 Chron. 33.10, 11ff.; 2 Kgs 23.31–24.21 in 2 Chron. 36.

38   Omission of the negative theological censure and the tribute in the case of Jehohahaz, the son of Josiah, 2 Kgs 23.32, 35 in 2 Chron. 36.1-4; deletion of the punishment for Manasseh and the international political motive in the case of Jehoiakim, 2 Kgs 24.2-4, 7 in 2 Chron. 36.5-8; deletion of the reference back to the sin of the fathers in 2 Kgs 23.37; 24.9, 19 in 2 Chron. 36.5, 9, 12; concentration on the temple vessels and Yhwh as author of the destruction in 2 Kgs 24.5, 8f., 11 in 2 Chron. 36.17, 18f., 20.

39   1 Chron. (10 and) 11.2f., the kingship of Saul and the anointing of David by Samuel in 1 Sam. 16, which becomes a word of God proclaimed by Samuel; 1 Chron. 11, the references back from 2 Sam. 23 to the time of the battles with Philistines under Saul; 1 Chron. 13, the prehistory of the ark in 1 Sam. 4–6, esp. 6.21–7.2; 1 Chron. 14.3 (the twofold 'still'), the women and sons from Hebron in 2 Sam. 3.2-5; 1 Chron. 15.29 the Michal episode in 2 Sam. 6.20-23; 2 Chron. 1.18; 8.1, the building of the palace in 1 Kgs 7.1ff.; 2 Chron. 8.1, the marriage of Solomon to an Egyptian princess in 1 Kgs 3.1; 7.8; 2 Chron. 10–11; and 13.3ff., the Jeroboam tradition in 1 Kgs 11–14; 2 Chron. 22.7f., the revolution of Jehu in 2 Kgs 9f., etc.

40   1 Kgs 14.23f. and connected with it 1 Kgs 15.12; 22.47; 2 Kgs 23.7; also 1 Kgs 15.3-5; 22.48 (v. 45 is used in 2 Chron. 20.35-37); 2 Kgs 15.4, 37; 18.8, 14-16 and of course the synchronism with 2 Kgs 17 in 18.9-12; 23.26f.; 24.2-4 (corresponding to the alteration of 21.10ff. in 2 Chron. 33.10, 11ff.).

41   But with 'And it shall happen when' Chronicles has perhaps also preserved the original text.

42   The difference between 'judges' and 'tribes' in v. 6 lies only in the vocalization. On the basis of v. 10 here Chronicles is original; the reading in 2 Sam. 7.7 is secondary.

43   Here as in the basic material the text seems disturbed; even G ('I was in tent and habitation') is no help.

44   Because of the confusion of the suffixes in the versions – in 2 Sam. 7.16, G reads 'his house and his kingdom', in 2 Chron. 17.14 'in my house and in my kingdom' – McKenzie, *Chronicler's Use*, 64, assumes that the reasons are purely text-critical (confusion of yod and waw). But that does not explain the decisive change, from the second-person suffixes related to David into the third-person suffixes related to Solomon, which are attested by both G in Samuel and Chronicles and M in Chronicles. The third-person-singular suffix has found its way into the tradition from 1 Chron. 17.14b, 'his throne'. In Chronicles, G presupposes a text in which at least already at one point there is the first-person-singular suffix ('my house') referring to Yahweh. That could be a miswriting of the third-person suffix, but at another point (2 Chron. 9.8) a corresponding change goes back to Chronicles itself.

45   See Wellhausen, *Proleg.*, 224ff.; Noth, *ÜSt*, 133-5; Willi, *Auslegung*, 229ff.; R.G. Kratz, 'Die Suche nach Identität in der nach-exilischen Theologiegeschichte', in *Pluralismus und Identität* (ed. J. Mehlhausen), VWGTh 8, 1995, 279-303: 292ff.

46   Wellhausen, *Proleg.*, 225f.

47 Cf. Noth, *ÜSt*, 134 n. 3.
48 Cf. M. Rehm, *Textkritische Untersuchungen zu den Parallelstellen der Samuel–Königsbücher und der Chronik*, ATA 13.3, 1937; Willi, *Auslegung*, 69ff. (with further literature); McKenzie, *Chronicler's Use*.
49 Cf. (after Rudolph) for example, 1 Chron. 18.17/2 Sam. 8.18; 1 Chron. 19.9/2 Sam. 10.8; 2 Chron. 13.2/1 Kgs 15.2 (2 Chron. 11.20) or the omission through homoioteleuton of 2 Chron. 6.5b, 6a in 1 Kgs 8.16.
50 Cf. (after Rudolph) for example, 2 Sam. 5.2/1 Chron. 11.2; 2 Sam. 6.11/1 Chron. 13.14; 2 Sam. 7.21f./1 Chron. 17.19 or the omission of 2 Sam. 23.10-11 in 1 Chron. 11.13f., of 2 Sam. 12.27-29 in 1 Chron. 20.1.
51 Cf. 2 Sam. 7.6/1 Chron. 17.5.
52 This latter point can still be conjectured in a whole series of inconspicuous variants which McKenzie, *Chronicler's Use*, 41ff., has listed; but it is also a possibility for serious omissions like 2 Sam. 5.4f. in 1 Chron. 11.1-9 (but cf. 1 Chron. 3.4; 29.27) or additions like 1 Chron. 21.16, which 4QSam[a] attests against M and G, provided that in one or other place there is not a secondary omission of text.
53 I. Kalimi, 'Die Abfassungszeit der Chronik: Forschungsstand und Perspektiven', *ZAW* 105, 1993, 223-33; G. Steins, 'Zur Datierung der Chronik: Ein neuer methodischer Ansatz', *ZAW* 109, 1997, 84-92.

II.   Ezra–Nehemiah

1.   Survey

C.C. Torrey, *The Composition and Historical Value of Ezra–Nehemiah*, BZAW 2, 1896; id., *Ezra Studies*, Chicago 1910; Noth, *Überlieferungsgeschichtliche Studien*, 110-180; S. Mowinckel, *Studien zu dem Buche Ezra–Nehemia: I. Die nachchronistiche Redaktion des Buches, Die Listen*, SNVAO II.3, Oslo 1964; *II. Die Nehemiadenkschrift*, SNVAO II/5, Oslo 1964; *III. Die Ezrageschichte und das Gesetz Moses*, SNVAO II/7, Oslo 1965; A.H.J. Gunneweg, 'Zur Interpretation der Bücher Esra–Nehemia: Zugleich ein Beitrag zur Methode der Exegese' (1981), in id., *Sola Scriptura* 2 (ed. P. Höffken), 1992, 9-24; S. Japhet, 'Composition and Chronology in the Book of Ezra–Nehemiah', in *Second Temple Studies 2* (ed. T.C. Eskenazi and K.H. Richards), JSOT.S 175, 1994, 189-216; T. Willi, 'Juda – Jehud – Israel', FAT 12, 1995, 41-117.

On 3 Ezra

K.F. Pohlmann, *Studien zum dritten Esra*, FRLANT 104, 1970; D. Böhler, *Die heilige Stadt in Esdras α und Esra–Nehemia*, OBO 158, 1997; Z. Talshir, *I Esdras: From Origin to Translation*, SCS 47, 1999; Z. Tashir and D. Talshir, *I Esdras: A Text Critical Commentary*, SCS 50, 2001.

Commentaries

G. Hölscher, HSAT II, 1923, 491-62; W. Rudolph, HAT I/20, 1949; K. Galling, ATD 12, 1954; J.M. Myers, AB., 1965; H.G.M. Williamson, WBC 16, 1985; A.H.J. Gunneweg, KAT 19/1, 1985; 19/2. 1987; J. Blenkinsopp, OTL, 1989.

Research

T. Willi, *ThR* 67, 2002, 34-103.

1.1   Ezra and Nehemiah were originally one book. The division into two books goes back to the Greek and Latin textual tradition. In the Septuagint they were called Esdras β (chs 1–10 and 11–23), and from Origen onwards also Esdras β and Esdras γ, in Jerome's Vulgate *Liber Ezrae* I and II. Alongside the canonical version there is also a compilation of 2 Chron. 35–36 + Ezra 1–10 + Neh. 8, which also contains the special tradition of the competition of the three pages and in the Septuagint is called Esdras α and in the Vulgate 3 Ezra. *4 Ezra*, an apocalypse from the first century AD, which has only the name and a love for the written Torah in common with the canonical Ezra, has been handed down only in Latin and in other versions.

The present composition of Ezra–Nehemiah is tripartite: Ezra 1–6 deals with the mission of Sheshbazzar, Zerubbabel and Jeshua[1] and the building of the second temple; Ezra 7–10 with Ezra's mission, the bringing of the gifts for the temple and the implementation of the Torah; Neh. 1–13 with Nehemiah's mission, the building of the walls and the new obligation on the people to observe the law, which Ezra joins him in imposing on them. Post-exilic Israel from the Babylonian Gola to the return to the promised land is constituted in these three stages, which mark out the centre of Judaism in respect of the cult, normative law and politics.

The renewed appearance of Ezra alongside Nehemiah in Neh. 8–10 (8.9) and 12.26, 36, and the return of the question of mixed marriages from Ezra 9–10 and Neh. 10 and 13, already indicate that the three parts are dovetailed together. And these are not the only overlaps: the list of those returning home in Ezra 2 is repeated in Neh. 7; the first attempt at building the wall in Ezra 4 prepares for Neh. 1ff.; the temple of Ezra 1–6 and the gifts brought for it also remain an important theme in Ezra 7ff. and Nehemiah; the hostilities over the building of the temple and the wall in Ezra 3.3; 4.1-5, 6ff. continue in Nehemiah; festivals and sacrifice accompany the same stages in Ezra 3.4ff.; 6.16ff., 19ff.; 8.35; Neh. 8.13ff. and 12.27ff., 43; Ezra's penitential prayer in Ezra 9 has a parallel in Neh. 9; echoes of it can also be found in Neh. 1; a continuous line seems to be intended in the chronology of the Persian kings with Ezra 4.5, 6, 7ff., 24 and 6.14f.; 7.1ff.; Aramaic documents link Ezra 4–6 with Ezra 7; the first-person style and certain formulations link Ezra 7f. with Neh. 1ff.

All in all, we may see this as a well-thought-out composition. Some scholars even discover some kind of scheme, for example, 'the scheme of task, resistance and overcoming the resistance',[2] or 'two themes in an alternating series (A–B, A'–B', A" –B")', focusing on the building of the temple and the wall on the one hand and on the obligation on the people to obey the Torah on the other. Accordingly the text is divided into six 'main sections': Ezra 1–6 + 7–19; Neh. 1.1–7.4 + 7.5–10.40; 11.1–12.47 + 13.1-31.[3] The correct insight here is that the many cross-connections are meant to give an impression of the coherence and unity of the post-exilic era. However, that cannot disguise the fact that the text is not made for one of the schemes, but is composed of individual parts.

1.2   In the first part, Ezra 1–6, the Aramaic section Ezra 4.8–6.18 stands out from the Hebrew framework in 1.1–4.6 and 6.19-22. A remark in 4.7b gives the impression that petitions to the Persian authorities, a summary of which is given in 4.6f., are being cited in the original. But that is only half the truth. 4.7b refers to the letter in v. 7, but not to the two sets of correspondence in 4.8-23 and Ezra 5–6, the first of which goes over to narrative again in 4.17, 23 and the second of which has its own narrative framework in 5.1-5; 6.1-2; and 6.13-15 after a transition in 4.24. Moreover the whole narrative of Ezra 1–6, which starts from the return of the Golah (Ezra 1–2), is concluded in a very similar way in 6.16-18 and 6.19-22, once in Aramaic and again in Hebrew, with a festal act, the sacrifices at the consecration of the temple and a Passover. After that we can distinguish roughly three levels: the Hebrew-Aramaic framework narrative about those who return in Ezra 1.1–4.7 and 6.16-18, 19-22; the quotation of the Aramaic Artaxerxes correspondence in Ezra 4.8-23; and the Aramaic chronicle of the building of the temple in Ezra (4.24), 5.1–6.15. Whereas the Hebrew framework depends on the Aramaic parts, and of these Ezra 4.8ff. depends on the Hebrew introduction in 4.5, 6f., the Aramaic chronicle in Ezra 5–6 is independent in substance. So here we have a separate earlier piece of tradition forming the basis of the narrative Ezra 1–6, which is dependent on it.

In Nehemiah, too, an older core stands out from the later composition. The substance of the book of Nehemiah consists of the so-called Nehemiah memoir, composed in the first person, in Neh. 1.1–7.5 + 12.(27,) 31–13.31. This reports the building of the wall, the consecration of the wall and various other measures taken by Nehemiah. In between comes first a list of the inhabitants of Jerusalem in Neh. 7, which Ezra 2 repeats, and which is continued in Neh. 11.1ff.; and secondly the second appearance of Ezra after Ezra 7–10 in Neh. 8–10, which contains the public reading of the Torah, a great penitential prayer and the obligation imposed on the people to keep the law. Both interrupt the original connection between the completion of the building of the wall in 7.1-5 and the consecration in 12.27ff.

The Ezra tradition in Ezra 7–10 and Neh. 8–10 is distinct from the Aramaic chronicle of the building of the temple and the Nehemiah memoir, but connected with both in many ways. As in Ezra 4–6, an Aramaic document is quoted in Ezra 7.12-26, introduced by 7.11, framed by the Ezra narrative in 7.1-10 and 7.27f.; 8–10, and taken further in Neh. 8–10. The Ezra narrative begins in the third person, but after the quotation of the Aramaic document in 7.27-28 it goes over to the first person like the

Nehemiah memoir. It extends to Ezra 9.5 and also comprises the prayer in 9.6-15. After that the style again changes into the third person. The Ezra tradition is also connected with the two other parts thematically. The main theme of Ezra 7–8 is the bringing of gifts for the temple from Ezra 1–6; the main theme of Ezra 9–10 is the dissolution of the mixed marriages in accordance with Neh. 10 and 13. Nehemiah 8–10 refer back to the designation of Ezra in 7.1-10 as a priest and scribe knowledgeable in the law. In Ezra 7–10 and Neh. 8–10 the narrative presupposes the Aramaic document in Ezra 7.12ff.; this in turn is hardly viable by itself and depends on the introduction and narrative development, at least in Ezra 7–8.

2. The chronicle of the building of the temple in Ezra 5–6

E. Meyer, *Die Entstehung des Judenthums*, 1896 (reprinted 1987); A.H.J. Gunneweg, 'Die aramäische und die hebräische Erzählung über die nachexilische Restauration – ein Vergleich' (1982), in id., *Sola Scriptura*, 2, 25-8; H.G.M. Williamson, 'The Composition of Ezra I–VI', *JTS* 34, 1983, 1-30; T. Krüger, 'Esra 1–6: Struktur und Konzept', *BN* 41, 1988, 65-75; S.C. Matzal, 'The Structure of Ezra IV–VI', *VT* 50, 2000, 566-9; B. Porten, 'Theme and Structure of Ezra 106: From Literature to History', *Transeuphratene* 23, 2002, 27-44.

2.1   The beginning with waw copulative + perfect in 5.1 ('And prophets appeared') is not a good one, but it is the start of a narrative which extends up to 6.15: Haggai and Zechariah, son of Iddo, prophesied among the Jews in Judah and Jerusalem. Then Zerubbabel the son of Shealtiel and Jeshua the son of Jozadak set out to build the temple in Jerusalem (5.1f.; 6.14). At the same time, which, as we know from the introduction and present transition in 4.24 (which is perhaps original),[4] or only from Haggai and Zechariah, is the second year of Darius, Tattenai the governor of Transeuphratene and Shethar-Bozenai[5] and his colleagues came and asked the elders of Judah who had given them permission for their action. They too wrote to the Persian king, to whom they reported their conversation with the elders, and received the answer that all was in order and that they should not hinder the building. Tattenai, Shetgar-Bozenai and their colleagues followed the king's commandment precisely, and with the support of the two prophets Haggai and Zechariah the elders of the Jews continued to build. They completed the building at the command of their God and the kings of Persia on the third day of the twelfth month in the sixth year of King Darius.

The narrative is well rounded, introduces the protagonists of the action at the beginning, immediately comes to the point, and takes the span opened in (4.24;) 5.1-5 to its end in 6.13-15. The beginning does not presuppose chs 1–4; on the contrary, the persons appear and are introduced as though they were not known previously. That in part they already appear and act in 2.2 and 3.1–4.5 can only mean that the Aramaic chronicle in Ezra 5–6 did not know the preceding chs 1–4 and that these were prefixed at a secondary stage to extend the action forwards. There is more or less a consensus on this conclusion, except that most scholars count the Aramaic Artaxerxes correspondence in 4.8-23 with the earlier chronicle in Ezra 5–6, and some count the beginning of the chronicle in 4.24; 5.1-5 (and the two prophets in 6.14) as part of the redactional framework in Ezra 1–4. So we must look at the further indications of the separation of the original chronicle from the secondary framework.

Ezra 1 puts in narrative form what the elders of the Jews present to the Persian authorities in 5.13-16 in order to justify themselves, and what brings to light the discovery of the edict of Cyrus under Darius in 5.17–6.5. The main difference is that the precise measurements for the ground plan of the temple given in 6.3-5 are missing from the version of the edict in Ezra 1, and instead the homecoming of the exiles, which is not mentioned in Ezra 6, is allowed. Moreover the contributions from the state treasury promised in Ezra 6 are replaced in Ezra 1 by gifts, requested or made voluntarily. The main difference runs throughout the whole passage: whereas in Ezra 5–6 apart from Zerubbabel and Jeshua in 5.2 only the elders of the Jews, that is, the population of Judah which remained in the land and their leaders, are responsible for building the temple, in Ezra 1–4 and 6.16-18, 19-22 those who have returned from exile, that is, the Babylonian Golah, its priests and levites and singers and gatekeepers in their divisions, have the say. They stand for the totality of the twelve tribes of Israel in the territory of Judah and Benjamin, and not just in Judah and Jerusalem, as in 5.1. Moreover 5.13-16 speaks of Sheshbazzar as an unknown – to both the Persian official and the reader ('one with the name Sheshbazzar', 'that Sheshbazzar') – figure whom Cyrus has appointed governor. By contrast, Ezra 1 knows that he was a 'ruler of Judah' well known to the Persian king and the treasurer, what and how many vessels he brought, and of course that he was one of those returning who are listed in Ezra 2 (1.11). A further difference is that according to 5.16 he, and not, as is reported in 3.1ff., Zerubbabel of the house of David and the priest Jeshua, renewed the foundations of the temple building.

Other features follow the same line: the justification of the elders in Ezra 5.13-16 depends on the assertion that work on the temple has been carried on without interruption since the issuing of the edict of Cyrus, simply so as not to scorn the king's law. This is certainly contradicted by the new beginning in 5.1f. and, if it is original, even more by the note in 4.24, according to which the work stopped until the second year of Darius, but both passages leave open the question whether there had already been building before that and how long the work had been stopped. By contrast, Ezra 1–4 has very precise information about all this. It does not share the view of either 5.1f. or 5.16, but combines the two. According to 5.1f. it attributes the initiative to Zerubbabel and Jeshua (3.1ff.), but according to 5.16 it makes the work begin immediately after the edict of Cyrus and the return of the Golah in the first year of Cyrus. Shortly afterwards it is brought to a standstill, still in the time of Cyrus, as a result of hostile attacks (4.1-5) and a preliminary correspondence, about which not a word is said in Ezra 5–6 (4.6, 7, 8ff.). In short, Ezra 1–4 presupposes the contradiction between (4.24,) 5.1f. and 5.16 and smooths it out by means of information which it has taken from Ezra 5–6 and freely combined. Accordingly we can hardly assume that Ezra 1–4 and 4.24; 5.1-5 come from the same author, who would be responsible for the contradiction.

The Aramaic correspondence with Artaxerxes in 4.8-23 also belongs to the efforts at assimilation, and so it is not part of the chronicle Ezra 5–6, but part of the secondary framework. It is not about the temple, but about a first attempt at building the city and the wall, and as an example of the lively correspondence mentioned previously is dependent for content, chronology and literature on 4.5, 6-7. The charges made in it by the officials, goaded on by the enemies of Judah and Benjamin, are not directed against the elders of the Jews but against the members of the Golah who have returned home (4.12). Moreover the chronology does not agree with Ezra 5–6: like 1.11ff. and 4.5, Ezra 5–6 mention only Cyrus and Darius; here it is most likely that Cyrus II (559–530 BC) and Darius I (522–486 BC) are meant. 4.6 and vv. 7, 8ff., mention in succession Ahasuerus (Xerxes) and Artaxerxes; here only Xerxes I (486–465/464 BC) and Artaxerxes I (465/ 464–425 BC), who immediately follow Darius I and precede Darius II (424– 404 BC), can be meant. In order to sort out the inconsistency, scholars are fond of arguing that for reasons of content and composition the author or redactor accepted an anachronism.[6] However, this assumption is superfluous. After Cyrus II and Darius I in Ezra 1.1–4.5, Xerxes I and Artaxerxes I in 4.6 and 4.7, 8ff., 4.24 and 5.1ff. do not take place again under Darius I but under the next, second, Darius, who moreover is followed by a second Artaxerxes (404–359/358 BC), with whom the king of the same name (but written differently) in Ezra 7ff. and Nehemiah could be identified. The sequence of the kings in 6.14f. (Cyrus–Darius I–Artaxerxes I–Darius II) agrees with the chronology suggested by 4.6, 7ff. However, here too it is not original, but the result of the secondary addition of 'and Artaxerxes, the king of Persia' in 6.14 (the same writing of the name as in 4.7, 8ff.), which goes against the original sequence Cyrus (II)–Darius (I).

Ezra 4.8-23 shows that the distinction between Aramaic chronicle and Hebrew narrative framework is not the whole story. The secondary framework goes over into Aramaic. Finally, that is also the case at the end of Ezra 5–6. Ezra 6.16-18 are indeed in Aramaic, but have the priests and levites and the rest of the Golah who have returned as their subject. The consecration of the temple is a first conclusion, and the Hebrew Passover in 6.19-22 a second, secondary conclusion.

2.2   I have already dealt with the beginning and end of the Aramaic chronicle of the building of the temple in Ezra (4.24;) 5.1–6.15 and the uncertainties as to whether it begins in 4.24 or 5.1 – connected with the prefixing of the secondary framework. In addition, in Ezra 5–6 we must once again distinguish between the narrative framework and the documents quoted, in accordance with not only the narrative mode but also the literary composition.

The prophets Haggai and Zechariah play a role only in the framework (5.1; 6.14) and not in the core of the narrative; Zerubbabel and Jeshua appear only in the beginning in 5.2 and not again after that. The introductory verses 5.3-4 have been taken from the document quoted in 5.6ff. and are in literary dependence on it, as is shown by the quotation from 5.9 in v. 4 ('We spoke to them about it thus'), which has been displaced in the narrative. Ezra 5.5 foresees a good outcome for the matter with the 'eye of God', which has presumably been taken from Zech. 4.10. Haggai and Zechariah were also behind the formulation of 5.1f. The presuppositions are: first, the redactional pieces in Hag. 1.1b, 12-14; 2.2, 4, 20f., which bring together the two original prophetic sayings of Haggai handed down with dates in Hag. 1.1abα,[1] 4, 8 and 1.15b; 2.1, 3, (6,) 9a with Zerubbabel and Joshua (in that order); secondly, the secondary epexegeses in Zech. 1–8, which refer the original visions of Zechariah in Zech. 1–6 (which themselves have grown up successively) to the temple building introduced from Haggai and likewise associate it with Zerubbabel (in Zech. 4) and Joshua (in Zech. 3); finally, the thoroughgoing chronological framework, which brings together Haggai and Zech. 1–8 in turn to make a kind of chronicle of the building of the temple. The assimilation in Ezra 5.1f.; 6.14 introduces a first correction to the attitude of loyalty to the state in Ezra 5.6ff. and 6.3ff. by attributing the building of the temple not only to decrees of the Persian kings but also to the initiative of the Jewish prophets and their continued support of the undertaking, that is, to God himself. It follows from this that at least the beginning in Ezra (4.24,) 5.1-5 and the two prophets in 6.14 – were they added later? – are older than the narrative framework in Ezra 1.4 and 6.16-22, but later than the correspondence in 5.6ff.

There are also quite a few inconsistencies within the correspondence.[7] How they are to be explained is decided by the transition from 6.5 to 6.6, where the edict of Cyrus in 6.3-5, according to 6.1f. part of the narrative, goes over immediately into Darius' answer to Tattenai's letter in 5.1-17, which in turn makes no reference to the edict of Cyrus. This is usually reckoned to be carelessness, but recently it has also been thought to be a deliberate narrative strategy on the part of the author or a mistake by a copyist. However, it is quite improbable for the person who in 6.1f. creates a narrative transition for the quotation of the edict of Cyrus to know nothing of it two verses later, and there is no basis for the assumption of disruption in the text. 3 Ezra 6.26 is clearly a smoothing-over. The most obvious explanation is therefore the literary-critical one: either the whole Cyrus history in Ezra 5.11–6.5 or Darius' answer in 6.6-12 with the implementation in 6.13 is secondary.

In the one instance the Darius correspondence in 5.6, 7bβ, 8(, 9f.) and 6.6-12 (or only 6.6-7,[8] 12b) forms the basis for the secondary dramatization in narrative form. We would have enquiry and answer connected in the form of a protocol, and therefore only very loosely, the answer – perhaps under the heading of 6.1a – being added to the 'copy' of the letter. In the first instance the dramatization of these notes would involve the introduction in 5.1-5, the regulations for the implementation of the simple words of 6.6-7 in vv. 8-10, 11-12a, and the narrative conclusion in 6.13,15, and further – as a next stage? – the Cyrus history in 5.(9f.)[9] 11–6.5, which drew after it not only 6.14, that ties everything together, but also the second introduction of the correspondence in 5.7abα, which is dependent on 5.6; this again leads into the narrative and in its formulation corresponds to the first introduction of the edict of Cyrus in 6.2.

In the second instance the very reduced narrative of the rediscovery of the edict of Cyrus in 5.6–6.5 forms the basis, to which we can also add the dating 6.15 as a conclusion. It is in turn made up of the 'copy' in 5.6, 7bβ, 8, the edict of Cyrus in 6.3-5[10] (cf. v. 4 with 5.8) introduced with *dikrōnāh*, 'memorandum', in 6.2b and the secondary narrative features in 5.7bα, 8-17a; 6.1-2, 15. It would subsequently have been expanded – on the basis of a misunderstanding of the order given in 6.1a – by the instructions of Darius in 6.6-12 and the narrative framework in (4.24;) 5.1-5, 17b; 6.13f., which is dependent on it and on 5.9f.

Just as 5.1f.; 6.14 was occasioned by Haggai and Zech. 1–8, so the historical retrospect in 5.11ff. must have been occasioned by the prophecy about Cyrus in Isa. 44.28; 45.12f. It develops in a nutshell the picture of history which shapes the scheme of the Chronistic history indicated by the textual overlap in 2 Chron. 36.22f./Ezra 1.1ff.[11] Either the Darius history narrated after Haggai/Zechariah was supplemented by the Cyrus history, in which 4.24; 5.1f. was corrected in 5.16, or the already combined Cyrus–Darius history was assimilated to Haggai/Zechariah, with 5.16 being corrected in 4.24; 5.1f. It is hard to decide which of the two possibilities is the right one. I tend towards the former.

2.3   The question of the authenticity of the documents which have found their way into Ezra 5–6 is a much-discussed one. Here parallels from the ancient Near East play an important role, especially the papyri from Elephantine (the indigenous name is Yeb), and in particular the petition of the Jewish garrison (two copies of which have been preserved) about the rebuilding of their temple which was destroyed and plundered in the fourteenth year of Darius II. This too was approved by the Persian authorities.[12] The elders of the Jews in Ezra 5–6 argue in the same way as their brothers on Elephantine, who announce their loyalty to the Persian kings and refer to the history of the foundation of the temple and the behaviour of an earlier king, in this case Cambyses. The Jews of Elephantine spontaneously promise the prayers and sacrifices which Darius requires in Ezra 6.10 for himself and his sons. We get even nearer to the historical witnesses with the quotations in the 'copy' of the letter of Tattenai, which initially are put only in a loose sequence. The report on the approval of the rebuilding of the temple in the fortress of Yeb is a similarly brief note of a conversation headed *zkrn*, 'memorandum'. This is not an official document, but the anonymous protocol of a negotiator which quotes, or gives the gist of, the decision of the governor of Judah, Bagohi (Bagoas), and the governor of Samaria, Sanballat, represented by his son Delaiah. The petition for the rebuilding by five sponsors from Syene and Yeb mentioned by name has been preserved only in a formless copy or summary.[13] The same is true of the famous Passover letter of Darius II[14] from former, happier days, which the Jewish negotiator Hananiah writes to his brothers in Yeb, and in which he reports directly or indirectly the decision of the Persian king on matters relating to the Passover communicated through the satrap Arsham (Arsames). Not only the serious gaps in the text but also the complicated process of transmission leave open the question whether Hananiah is quoting the king or the satrap or reproducing the basic approval and making it concrete in his own words.

The parallels are striking, but mean no more than that the documents in Ezra 5–6 have been composed in the manner customary in the Persian period, perhaps in so far as similar copies were present in Jerusalem, even composed specially on the model of official procedure under Darius II. Moreover the question cannot be answered independently of the literary composition. It could even be that literary criticism first provides proof of authenticity. For it makes it possible to distinguish between earlier and later tradition in Ezra 5–6 and opens up the core of the tradition: the extracts from the protocol in 5.6, 7bβ, 8 and 6.6-7, 12b, and perhaps the memorandum in 6.3-5. The more fragmentary the information, the higher the chances that we have authentic tradition. However, we must not expect authenticity in the literal sense. As in the examples from Elephantine, at all events we can reckon with the free reproduction of relevant formulations, reduced to essentials, and in the case of the mention of Sheshbazzar in 5.14-16 even with just the remote recollection of a detail.

2.4   The prolongation forwards of the chronicle of the building of the temple in Ezra 5–6 begins with the rendering of the recollection of the edict of Cyrus quoted in 6.3-5 and the mission of Sheshbazzar of 5.13-16 in narrative form, with the decisive changes that I have already mentioned: Yhwh, the God of heaven and of the people of Israel, gains a direct influence on events; the people of God, which is divided into heads of families, priests and levites from Judah and Benjamin, comes into the foreground; the return of the exiles is added; the financing is organized through gifts; and the temple vessels brought by Sheshbazzar 'the ruler of Judah' are listed in detail (Ezra 1.1-4, 5-6, 7-11). After the list of those returning home in Ezra 2, which mentions Zerubbabel and Jeshua at their head, the narrative thread of Ezra 1 continues in 3.8ff.: in the second year after the arrival, in the second month, Zerubbabel the son of Shealtiel and Jeshua, the son of Jozadak, their brothers and all those who had come to Jerusalem from the exile, set to work (v. 8) and laid the foundation for the rebuilding of the temple (v. 10a). Many of the old people who knew the temple from former times wept, and many broke out in shouts of joy (vv. 12f.). As though attracted by the noise of the crowd, the enemies of Judah and Benjamin, namely the population settled by the Assyrians who had not gone into exile, came and wanted to share in the building. But Zerubbabel, Jeshua and the other heads of families from the Golah refused, and insisted that they alone should carry out Cyrus' command. The enemies goaded on the officials and thus prevented the building from the days of Cyrus until the reign of Darius (4.1-5).

This is the main strand of the narrative. Various subsidiary strands branch off it, the majority of which must be secondary.

We can already ask whether the list in Ezra 2 originally belongs there or is a later attempt to fill the gap between the departure in Ezra 1 and the arrival in Ezra 3, and moreover adds the names that according to 5.10, Tattenai wants to have written down. According to Ezra 1–4 the 'elders of the Jews' who act in Ezra 5–6 are of course no longer the Israelites who remained in the land but those who returned from the Golah (cf. 6.16ff.). The list is identical with that in Neh. 7, but fits the context better in Ezra 2, especially as the external framework is secondary and evidently made for the context. The framework in 2.1-2, 70 identifies the persons listed under the heading in v. 2b explicitly as those who are returning and who settle in the cities of Judah (cf. also 2.59-63), and – in an appendix (v. 2) – lists eleven leaders who together with Sheshbazzar in 1.11 embody the number of the twelve tribes of Israel. With a view to Ezra 3ff., first Zerubbabel and Jeshua are mentioned, and after them one Nehemiah. In 2.68f. the theme of giving from Ezra 1 is taken up again. Both appear in Neh. 7.6f., 69-71, 72 with a few but significant adaptations: instead of eleven there are twelve names; the syntax of the appendix in Ezra 2.2 is assimilated in Neh. 7.7a to 7.6/Ezra 2.1; instead of giving for the rebuilding of the temple (Ezra 2.68), we have giving for 'the work' (cf. Ezra 3.8f.; 6.22, the building of the temple, here in Neh. 2.16, etc. the building of the wall) and for the 'treasury (of the work)' (thus with Ezra 2.69); among the givers the Hattirshata ('governor') from Ezra 2.63/Neh. 7.65 is also mentioned, whom Neh. 8.9; 10.2 identify with Nehemiah. Accordingly, it seems to me most likely that Neh. 7 is dependent on Ezra 2 and not vice versa. In any case no argument can be made out of the even and uneven numbers. As the versions show, the numbers and names especially are a happy hunting ground for mistakes or personal contributions by the copyists.

However, its priority over Neh. 7 does not mean that the list in Ezra 2 is original. That Zerubbabel and Jeshua are initially not mentioned at all, are mentioned in Ezra 2.2 simply by name – in an appendix – and together with others, but in 3.2, 8, as in 5.1f., are mentioned with patronymics could indicate that the list was inserted later to fill in the gap and document the homecoming. Ezra 3.1 presupposes the conclusion of the list in 2.70; by contrast, 3.8 attaches better to 1.11. It is impossible to make out the origin of the lists of persons divided into laity, priests, levites, singers, gatekeepers and temple slaves. As in 1 Chron. 2–9; 15f. and 23–27, here and in the list of temple vessels in Ezra 1.9-11 some register or concrete conditions of the post-exilic period may lie in the background;[15] in both instances the framework has been assimilated to the context.

The building of the altar and the feast of tabernacles in 3.1-7 also form a digression from the main narrative. In many respects the scene anticipates the foundation of the temple in 3.8ff., but in 3.6f. is explicitly separated from it in order to refer back by means of a measure subsequently attributed to Cyrus as a preparation for the foundation of the temple, of which there is no mention in Ezra 1, to the old connection between Ezra 1 and 3.8ff. In language and content the deviations in 3.8bβγ, 9, 10b-11 go together; here priests and levites are appointed to guard the building works and strike up their song. The divergences can be recognized as additions in 3.8f. (cf. 2.40) by the harsh syntactical construction ('they began and they ordered') and inconsistency in content (at all events the subject is 'all those returning home'), and in 3.10f. by the resumption of v. 10a in v. 11bβ. Instead of the cry of joy (vv. 12f.), the noise of the trumpets can now be heard.

The double conclusion in 6.16-18 and 6.19-22 is the counterpart to the prefixing of 1.1–4.5 and its supplementations. Like Ezra 1–4, both passages understand by the 'elders of the Jews' in Ezra 5–6 or the 'people in Judah and Jerusalem' in 5.1 those who are returning from the Golah; 6.19-22 in addition, and in contrast to 4.1-5, admits to the Passover those Israelites who remained in the land and have dissociated themselves from the uncleanness of the peoples of the land. The first of the two versions, given in Aramaic following Ezra 5–6 and completely attuned to the building of the temple, must have been written by the author of the original stratum in 1.1-11; 3.8abα, 10a, 12f.; 4.1-5; the second, written in Hebrew and like 3.1ff. interested in the proper celebration of the main festivals, here the Passover, comes from the person who produced the supplements. Both strata, the supplements even more than the basic document, are evident from their close contacts with 1–2 Chronicles, the conclusion in Ezra 6.19-22 especially with 2 Chron. 30 and 34, the additions in Ezra 3 with the secondary special material in 1 Chron. 23ff.

Finally, the letters in Ezra 4.6, 7, 8-23, which interrupt the theological and thematic connection of 4.5 and 4.24; 5.1ff., lead us astray. At first glance 4.5 and 4.24 look like doublets and a recapitulation caused by the insertion of 4.6-23. But that is not the whole story. Verse 5 says that from the days of Cyrus to the reign of Darius the enemies paralysed the building by bribing the minister; v. 24 says that ('thereupon')[16] the works on the temple stopped until the second year of Darius. So the statements are not saying the same thing twice but supplementing each other. That they are nevertheless similar is because the author of Ezra 1.1–4.5, who was writing in Hebrew, had to find an appropriate transition to the Aramaic narrative in Ezra 5–6. He solved the problem by making the Hebrew text go over into Aramaic by a kind of pick-up line; here he may either have found 4.24 in some form and revised it, or formulated it himself. In this way he was able on the one hand to compensate for the contradiction between 5.16 and (4.24;) 5.1f., and on the other to cope with the change in language by means of a reasonably tolerable connection. The other possibility, that the transition already presupposes the insertion in 4.6-23, would mean that 4.24; 5.1-5 and the two prophets – possibly added later – in 6.14 were not older but younger than Ezra 1–4. However, the early dating of Zerubbabel and Jeshua in 2.1–4.5, which presupposes 5.1f., tells against that.

At all events, the linguistic and literary seam became the occasion for further supplements. Ezra 4.6, 7 combines the bribery of the officials in vv. 4f. with the correspondence in Ezra 5f. and derives from that protest letters (from the enemies themselves or the bribed officials) to the king. With the indication that the correspondence was of course carried on in Aramaic, the official language of the Persian empire in the west (4.7b), the additions sought to smooth over the transition in language. Moreover they introduce a new chronology, and date Ezra 4.24; 5.1ff. to the time of Darius II (cf. 6.14f.), perhaps in recognition or even denial of his services to the Jewish temple at Elephantine. As the petition of the Egyptian Jews shows, these were not looked on kindly in Jerusalem. So they claimed the support of the king. On the model of the correspondence and narrative framework in Ezra 5–6, and anticipating the building of the walls under Nehemiah, at a next stage both the enquiry and the answer and the corresponding report of the completion in 4.8-23 were added, and were in turn glossed in vv. 9f. Presumably this is a pure literary fiction which seeks to integrate the building of the temple into the overall complex of the rebuilding of the city and at the same time demonstrate the heightened hostility and its refutation by the unconditional loyalty of the Jews shown in the building of the temple. It moves within the chronology introduced by 4.6, 7 and assimilated in 6.14f.

That the insertions in 4.6, 7, 8-23 are late and disrupt the earlier connection between 4.24; 5.1ff.; and 4.5 is also confirmed indirectly by the sequence of texts in 3 Ezra. This offers the following chronology: Cyrus (3 Ezra 2.1-14 = Ezra 1) – Artaxerxes (3 Ezra 2.15-25 = Ezra 4.7-24) – Darius (3 Ezra 3.1–5.6 or 5.7-70; 6.1ff. = Ezra 2.1–4.5; 5.1ff.). The transposition of the Artaxerxes correspondence arises not only out of the interpolation of the narrative about the pages (3 Ezra 3.1–5.6), as is generally recognized, but out of a recension which unlike the Massoretic Ezra as far as possible avoids any reference to the Nehemiah memoir and the building of the wall and the city that is still to come. However, that by no means indicates that this recension is the original one.[17] The order of the text in 3 Ezra above all has against it the repeated 'foundation' of the building of the temple by Zerubbabel and Jeshua in 3 Ezra 5.46ff. (especially vv. 52, 54) = Ezra 3.1ff. in the 'second year' after the homecoming. This can no longer be the case after the foundation of the temple by an anonymous Golah in 3 Ezra 2.17f. (not Sheshbazzar under Cyrus) and the prohibition by Artaxerxes; the same is true of the stop to the building in 3 Ezra 5.63-70 = Ezra 4.1-5, which falls back behind the 'second year of Darius' that has already been reached in 3 Ezra 2.25 = Ezra 4.24, but does not mention the Artaxerxes affair at all and prepares for the new beginning in 3 Ezra 6.1ff. = Ezra 5.1ff. Only the suspicious 'two years' between Cyrus and the accession of Darius in 3 Ezra 5.70 = Ezra 4.5 seem to go to the time of Artaxerxes. Thus 3 Ezra 5.7-70 = Ezra 2.1–4, 5, apart from a few bits of retouching, do not presuppose the Artaxerxes correspondence, and are left hanging between the 'second year of Darius' in 3 Ezra 2.25 = Ezra 4.24 and 3 Ezra 6.1 = Ezra 4.24; indeed in 3 Ezra they appear as an addition between 3 Ezra 2.25 = Ezra 5.1 and 3 Ezra 6.1ff. = Ezra 5.1ff. Moreover the contradiction between Ezra 5.16 and 4.24; 5.1 is only partially removed by putting Ezra 4.7-24 first: in 3 Ezra 2.15ff. it is not Sheshbazzar who lays the ground for the building of the temple; there can be no question of any continuous building activity. The king's answer in 3 Ezra 2.22-24 no more goes into the question of building the temple in 2.17f. than does Ezra 4.8-23. In all this 3 Ezra proves to be dependent on the Massoretic version and can be understood as a further attempt to mend the breaks in the narrative about the building of the temple in Ezra 1–6 without reference to Nehemiah and the building of the walls that is still to come. But regardless of which of the two versions may be original, the Artaxerxes correspondence is in any case a late addition. In 3 Ezra it interrupts the connection between the permission to return home and the homecoming (2.1-14 = Ezra 1 and 3 Ezra 5.7ff. = Ezra 2.1ff.), and in the Massoretic text the transition from Ezra 4.5 to 4.24; 5.1ff., to which in its way 3 Ezra 5.70; 6.1ff. also bears witness.

2.5   Summary: a few resolutions on building the temple which have been brought together in the form of a protocol are the basis of the composition in Ezra 1–6; presumably they reflect the historical situation accurately but give it in their own words. They have been put in narrative form in one or two stages and elaborated into an Aramaic chronicle of the building of the temple in Ezra 5–6. Subsequently, first the retrospects of the chronicle about the building of the temple have been put in narrative form (1.1-11; 3.8abα, 10a, 12f.; 4.1-5) and the whole has been provided with a new conclusion (6.16-18); after that the prehistory has been enlarged by various additions, of which some are close to the books 1–2 Chronicles (Ezra 2; 3.1-7, 8bβγ, 9, 10b-11; 6.19-22), the others (4.6, 7, 8-23) are close to the more immediate context in language and style and thematically are close to the book of Nehemiah.

3.   The Nehemiah memoir

Literature as above on II.1, also U. Kellermann, *Nehemiah*, BZAW 102, 1967; J.L. Wright, 'Nehemiah's Account of the Judean Restoration and First Reception in Ezra–Nehemiah', Göttingen dissertation 2003.

3.1   The 'words of Nehemiah, son of Hacaliah' (Neh. 1.1a) are quickly told. Nehemiah was the cupbearer to king Artaxerxes I (465/464–425 BC), as is said twice, once at the end of the opening scene, which takes place in the month of Chislev in the twentieth year (1.1, 11b), the second time at the beginning of the narrative, which is dated to the month of Nisan in the twentieth year of king Artaxerxes (2.1). Quite contrary to custom, on one occasion Artaxerxes notes the bad mood of his cupbearer, and when the cupbearer complains to him about the sorrow he is feeling, the state of the city and walls in Jerusalem, the king grants his request to travel to Judah for a certain time (2.1-6). Hardly had Nehemiah arrived in Jerusalem when he inspected the walls and persuaded the prefects of the city and all others involved to collaborate in rebuilding the wall; they set to work without delay (2.11-18). The work went ahead rapidly (3.38), then efforts slackened a little (4.4), but when reinforcements came (4.6a) they returned to work (4.9b). After twenty-five days, on the 25th of the month Elul, the wall was completed (6.15). At its dedication two festal processions went along the wall, one to the right and the other to the left (12.27, 31f., 37, 38f.), meeting in the temple court for a sacrifice (12.40, 43).

That is the skeleton, indeed to some degree the basic substance, of the first-person report which in the present text extends from Neh. 1.1 to 7.5, is taken up again in 12.(27,) 31 after the great insertion of Neh. 7.6–12.26, and continues to the conclusion of the book in Neh. 13.31. The basic narrative has its closest parallel in the short episodes of the inscription of the Egyptian physician Udja-Hor-resenet, who was likewise in Persian service.[18] All the rest is elaboration or expansion of the action by further episodes; here we have to examine individual instances and decide what is original and what secondary.[19]

3.2   We start with the beginning and the end. There is agreement that the beginning is overloaded and has been worked over at a secondary stage. Usually scholars content themselves with deleting the prayer in 1.5-11a, but that does not remove all the problems. The two beginnings in 1.1b-3, 4 and 2.1ff. not only cause chronological difficulties but also disagree in content and terminology. In the one case Nehemiah's main concern is the fate of the population of Jerusalem and in the whole province of Judah – which evidently still exists – who have returned from captivity, or those who have escaped it, and peripherally also especially the state of the wall and the gates (1.3 from 2.13); in the other case he is interested only in the state of the city and the gates, which motivates the building of the wall and dominates the action of the memoir (cf. 2.3, 17). The simplest solution is that after the heading 1.1a, the original beginning lies in 2.1; 1.1b-11 were inserted as a preface at a secondary stage, first to explain how Nehemiah knows of the sorry state, and further in order to put the building of the wall in a wider theological context, which is served both by the extension of the object of the mission in 1.1b-3 and also by the prayer in 1.4, 5-11. The independent dating (calculated according to the Seleucid autumnal calendar?) in 1.1b is understandable only in connection with Ezra 7–10. Nehemiah 1.11 leads on into 2.1.

The first striking thing about the conclusion is the parallel of 6.15 + 12.27-43 with Ezra 6.15 + vv. 16-18, 19-22 (cf. also Ezra 3.10-13). The two scenes are certainly tuned to each other. But the consecration in Ezra 6 is secondary; in Neh. 12 it seems to be original. So if Ezra 6.16-18 has first been expanded after the model of Neh. 12, in Ezra 6 the priests and levites and other cult personnel have been added in assimilation to Neh. 12.27-30, 33-36, 41-42; they are already mentioned in the lists in Neh. 7; 11-12, which are themselves secondary, and are filled out further in 11.16f., 21-24; 12.1ff., and here in view of 12.27ff. are also settled outside Jerusalem (11.20, 36, emended text, and 12.1-26).

Furthermore there is a series of additions which extend Nehemiah's mission, the building of the walls. The model practice of the cult in 12.44-47, which recalls the foundation of the cult by David and Solomon and therefore 1–2 Chronicles, and the breaking up of the mixed marriages in 13.1-13 in accordance with Deut. 23, are generally regarded as additions which bridge the chronological and thematic gap between Neh. 1–12 and Neh. 13 and make Nehemiah's measures in 13.4ff. seem the exception to the rule. The additions depend on the 'on that day' in 12.43; 12.44; 13.1. Williamson has demonstrated that neither the second mission of Nehemiah in 13.4-31, which concerns the offerings, the observation of the sabbath and the mixed marriages, nor the resumé of Nehemiah's governorship in 5.14-19, which bridges the chronological gap, can have been part of the first edition of the memoir.[20] The characteristic commemoration formula (13.14, 22, 31), which, if it were original and typical of the memoir, would also to be expected after Neh. 6.15 or 12.43, occurs only here and in 5.19. And only here is Nehemiah equipped with comprehensive competences relating to all the interests of the people, of the kind due to a 'governor of Judah' (5.14f.; 12.26). We may leave aside here the question whether the further despatch (13.6f.) which follows from the limitation on the stay in 2.6 is historical or a literary imitation of 2.1ff. There are close connections between Neh. 12.44ff.; 13.4ff. and Neh. 10.31ff.; 2 Chron. 31. In both places, as in Neh. 11–12, the text has been supplemented with all kinds of cultic personnel in the style of the (secondary) Chronistic special material.

3.3   After the beginning and end we now turn to the body of the memoir. Scholars argue that the list of those who took part in building the city wall in Neh. 3.1-32, which has beyond doubt been composed for the context, is original and cannot have been invented. However, the duplication or triplication of the description of the building, each time followed by the reaction of the opponents, in 2.18 + vv. 19ff.; 3.1-32 + vv. 33ff.; 3.38 + 4.1ff., is a bit suspicious. In the text as it is we are to think of different stages in the building: in 2.18 the decision, in 3.1ff. the start, in 3.38 the continuation of the building work and in 6.1ff., 15ff. the completion. But the formulation does not produce that everywhere. The censure of the people of Tekoa in 3.5 is enigmatic. As in the case of the list in Ezra 2, which stands for a homecoming that is not related, we have to leave an open verdict.

Nehemiah's famous remission of debts in Neh. 5.1-13 also represents an interruption, to which the secondary resumé of Nehemiah's governorship up to the thirty-second year of Artaxerxes (cf. 13.6) in 5.14-19 is attached. The social question is presumably sparked off by the indications of the one-sided burden of work and the resultant tensions in 4.4, 6a, 9b (cf. 5.1 with 4.6a), which are now covered over by the hostile attacks and the defence against them. The remission of debts has nothing at all to do with the building of the wall, and all the more to do with Nehemiah's role as governor of Judah as in Neh. 13. So it must have been added later, before 5.14-19 or simultaneously with it.

Finally, at several points Nehemiah's controversy with his opponents, mainly Sanballat the Horonite, Tobiah the Ammonite and Geshem the Arabian, has been incorporated into the framework of the main narrative: 2.7-10, 19-20; 3.33-37; 4.1-17; 6.1-14, 16, 17-19. It, too, has something to do with Nehemiah's role as governor of Judah. In the correspondence from Elephantine from the time around 410 BC, mentioned above, Sanballat is attested as governor of Samaria under Darius II and is here represented by his sons Delaiah and Shelemiah. It is quite conceivable that he was already in office in the time of Artaxerxes I, and from the twentieth to the thirty-second year of the king (445–433 BC), and also afterwards, was still the colleague of Nehemiah, the governor of Judah. Usually the appointment of Sanballat and Nehemiah as governor is connected with the Megabyzos revolt between 449 and 446 BC. So the Sanballat pieces have an air of history, but it is no more than an air.

We know from other inscriptions, the Samaria papyri from the fourth century BC, and from Josephus that there was not just one governor by the name of Sanballat, but at least two and perhaps even three, presumably all from the same family; they held office up to the beginning of the Hellenistic era.[21] The identity of the names of both the governors and Persian kings under whom they held office could easily have led to confusion. Thus kinship with the house of the high priest of Jerusalem is reported both for Nehemiah's contemporary (Neh. 13.28) and for the Sanballat under the last Darius (III) (Josephus). It is also remarkable that according to Neh. 3.1 the high priest at the time of Nehemiah is Eliashib (according to 12.26, his predecessor Joiakim), but in 13.28 Nehemiah already has dealings with a descendant of Jehoiada, the son of Eliashib, and thus with a grandson or even later descendant of Eliashib. According to the list of high priests in 12.10f., 22f., this brings us to the generation of Jonathan/Johanan and Jaddua and with them in turn to the time of a Darius (Neh. 12.22f.); in another way Johanan is attested under Darius II (together with Sanballat in Elephantine) and Jaddua under Darius III (in Josephus). Tobias, the Ammonite servant, who according to Neh. 13.4ff. is said to be related to the high priest Eliashib (cf. further 6.17f.), has a double in Hellenistic times, the founder-father of the Tobiad family which was settled in Transjordan and the son-in-law of the high priest Onias II, the latter according to Josephus (*Antt.* XII 4.1-2) the successor of the man who was married to Sanballat's daughter. It is uncertain whether the priest Eliashib in Neh. 13.4 is identical with the high priest in the time of Nehemiah (3.1). Things are no better with the Arab Geshem mentioned in Neh. 2.19ff.; 6.1ff., whose name is often attested and widespread in ancient North Arabian inscriptions of the Persian and Hellenistic periods, so that the fact that this is the same name as that of the father of Qainu, sheikh of Qedar, at the end of the fifth century and of Lihyanite (Dedanite) kings in the fifth and third century BC has no significance.[22]

In short, the synchronization of Nehemiah and the high priest Eliashib with the governor Sanballat who is mentioned under Darius II, but at all events already under Artaxerxes I, which follows from the generation of the sons of Sanballat (Delaiah and Shelemaiah) attested in Elephantine and the high priest of Jerusalem (Johanan), and their contemporaneity with the governor of Judah named Bagohi (Bagoas) under Darius II, may perhaps be correct, but that does not mean that everything that is related of Sanballat and the other opponents of Nehemiah belongs to this time. As the names live on and remain prominent down to the Hellenistic period, later experiences can also have been embodied in them.

The literary evidence also suggests that this is the case. The dominant view is that all the passages are original, which presupposes that the memoir in Neh. 1.1–7.5 is more or less a unity. However, as there have already been indications of a later revision at other points, the differences to be noted within the Sanballat pieces gain importance. The three main enemies Sanballat, Tobiah and Geshem are introduced with an indication of their origin (some also think that this is a designation of office) in two places, in 2.10 (without Geshem) and 2.19; all the rest presuppose the introduction. Of the two introductions, 2.10 with vv. 7-9 indicates an extension of the commission to the temple mount (cf. 7.2) and 'the Israelites'. Moreover the task is already on everyone's lips even before Nehemiah has revealed himself (2.12). Consequently the original beginning of the enmity will lie in 2.19-20, where it inserts itself by a keyword connection ($\underline{t}wb$, 'the good work', Tobiah?), and the resumption of v. 18 in v. 20 ($n\bar{a}q\bar{u}m$, 'we will set out'), between 2.17 and 3.38 or 3.1 ($wayy\bar{a}q^a m$, 'and he set out'). The scene is somewhat reminiscent of the conversation between Zerubbabel and the enemies of Judah and Benjamin in Ezra 4.1-3, but does not stop the work. The theme continues in 3.33-37 with the list of those involved in the building in 3.1-32 – original or inserted later – which documents the start of the work and its state. The curse in 3.36f. sounds like a conclusion. Nehemiah 2.10 and 6.16–7.3 are connected with the extension of Nehemiah's mission in Neh. 2.7-9. The first passage inserts itself, anticipating 2.19f., between the limited authorization of Nehemiah in 2.6 and his arrival in Jerusalem in 2.11; the second passage between the conclusion of the building work in 6.15 and the dedication in 12.(27,) 31ff. Perhaps we may also connect 6.1-9 with this (cf. vv. 1, 6). The question of loyalty, which is dealt with in the letters and delegations and brought into play by the enemies, recalls Ezra 4.4f., 6-7 and of course Ezra 4.8ff. The continuation in 6.10-14 which is spun out of Neh. 6.7 and the extension of the conflict into a war with the neighbouring peoples in ch. 4 seem to me to be even later. Both passages presuppose the insertion of Neh. 5 between 4.4, 6a, 9b and 6.1ff.

3.4   The main characteristic of the Nehemiah memoir is the first-person style. Nehemiah 7.6–12.26, which manifestly interrupt the stylistic and thematic connection, are therefore generally regarded as an insertion. The inner core of the insertion comprises Neh. 8–10 and introduces Ezra and the law into the Nehemiah memoir (cf. also 12.26, 36). Its literary relationship to Ezra 7–10 is discussed below (under 4.). It presupposes the list of those coming home in Neh. 7.6-72; the transition in 7.72b/8.1 resembles that of Ezra 2 after 3.1(-7).

The external shell of the insertion comprises the list of those returning home in Neh. 7.6-72a, which is identical to that in Ezra 2, along with the register of personnel and further lists of those returning in Neh. 11.1–12.26. Here Neh. 11 is the model for 1 Chron. 9. At the beginning the insertion is linked to the context by the introduction in 7.4-5, which is in the first person, and at the end by 12.27-30. Some scholars therefore regard at least parts of the list as original. But the twofold summons of the agents to the dedication of the wall in 12.27-30 and v. 31 and the interruption of the connection between the completion and the dedication in 6.15(–7.3) and 12.(27,) 31ff. suggest, rather, that the whole question of the settlement is an addition.

The lists are not unitary. Presumably the first was 7.4, 5a, with a basic content of Neh. 11 (7.4 + 11.1f., 3ff. or 7.4, 5a + 11.3ff.), then Neh. 7.5b, 6-72 from Ezra 2, and lastly Neh. 12.1-26. At the same time the literary connection of Neh. 11.1f., 3 to 7.72a is so close that we get the impression that the reproduction of Ezra 2 in Neh. 7.6-72a through 7.5b and the addition of the list in Neh. 11.3ff. with a very similar structure through 7.4, 5a took place at the same time (cf. 7.6 and 11.3). The transition in Neh. 7.72b; 8.1ff. was either taken over contemporaneously with the list in Ezra 2 = Neh. 7.6-72a from Ezra 3.1 or is later at both points. If in Neh. 8–10 (also 12.26, 36), Ezra and Nehemiah are synchronized, and in Neh. 7 and 11–12 Zerubbabel/Jeshua and Nehemiah/Jehoiakim-Eliashib, in the additions (11.16f., 21ff.; 12.1ff.; cf. also 1 Chron 9) both pairs are made parallel with the pre-exilic conditions under David and Solomon, cf. 12.44-47.

Since Neh. 7 is dependent in literary terms, no more can be said on the origin of the list than on Ezra 2. Nehemiah 12.1-26 is a literary compilation from 1 Chron. 24; Ezra 2/Neh. 7; Neh. 11/1 Chron. 9 and Neh. 10 on the basis of the series of high priests in Neh. 12.10f., 22f. This continues 1 Chron. 5.27-41 (cf. Ezra 3.2) with some surpluses (from Joiarib, vv. 6, 19) which extend down to the Maccabean period. The principle is papponymy, that is, the identity of the names of the tribal ancestors of priests and levites at the time of Zerubbabel (12.1-9) with their successors at the time of Nehemiah and Ezra (12.12-26). Now and then a basis in sources is postulated only for Neh. 11/1 Chron 9; the proposals extend from the pre-exilic period to the Maccabean period, not least because the whole list is full of military technical terms, and the places of the tribes of Judah and Benjamin mentioned in the second part, vv. 25ff., go beyond the frontiers of the Persian province of Judah. But that can also be a programme based on tradition (for the boundary points cf. Josh. 15), knowledge and the concrete view of the author.

3.5.   Summary: the basis of the book of Nehemiah is 'the words of Nehemiah, son of Hacaliah' (Neh. 1.1a), a short report in the first person by the cupbearer at the court of king Artaxerxes (I) about the building of the walls in Jerusalem which he initiated and their dedication: Neh. 2.1-6, 11-18; (3.1-32?;) 3.38; 4.4, 6a, 9b; 6.15; 12.27, 31f., 37, 38f., 40, 43. Everything else is based on revisions. Here Nehemiah appears as the governor of Judah, sent by the Persian king and responsible for the whole commonwealth. In this function he enters into competition with Sanballat and his entourage (2.7-9, 10, 19f.; 3.33ff.; 4.1ff.; 6.1-9, 10-14, 16, 17-19). In addition, at the beginning (Neh. 1), in the middle (Neh. 5) and at the end of the book (Neh. 13), he is entrusted with regulating internal affairs in Israel. The form of the memoir arrived at in this way is very close to the narrative of the building of the temple in Ezra 1–6. Finally, the first-person report has been enriched by extensive lists and the Ezra passages in Neh. 7–12 and set against a wider horizon in the theology of history. The points of contact with the book of Ezra, and also with Chronicles and its secondary passages, increase from time to time.

4. The Ezra narrative

Literature as A. II.1 above, also H.H. Schaeder, *Esra der Schreiber*, BHTh 5, 1930; W.T. In der Smitten, *Esra. Quellen. Überlieferung und Geschichte*, SSN 15, 1973; J.C.H. Lebram, 'Die Traditionsgeschichte der Esragestalt und die Frage nach dem historischen Esra', in H. Sancisi-Weerdenburg (ed.), *Achaemenid History* I, 1987, 103-38; K. Koch, 'Esra und Jehud', in P. Frei and K. Koch, *Reichsidee und Reichsorganisation im Perserreich*, OBO 55, [2]1996, 206-307.

4.1   The Ezra narrative poses many riddles. The main problem is the distribution of the material in Ezra 7–10 and Neh. 8(–10). The demarcation in Neh. 8–10 is made more difficult by the fact that the penitential prayer in ch. 9 and the obligation accepted by the people in ch. 10 – pronounced by the Levites (cf. 9.5) – presuppose instruction in the law and are connected both by the chronology (7.72b; 8.2, 13, 18; 9.1) and also by literary references back to ch. 8. But Ezra – with the exception of 9.6 in the Septuagint – does not appear again. That in turn fits with the text of 3 Ezra, which is also the basic text for the paraphrase by Josephus (*Antt.* XI), where only Neh. 8 (half of it) immediately follows Ezra 7–10, and the mention of Nehemiah in Neh. 8.9/3 Ezra 9.49 is absent. From this it has been concluded that there was an independent Ezra narrative alongside the chronicle of the building of the temple and the Nehemiah memoir, the so-called Ezra source, comprising Ezra 7–10 + Neh. 8. This was divided into the books of Ezra and Nehemiah when the individual elements were worked together. This hypothesis is put forward in different variants – the transposition of Neh. 8 between Ezra 8 and 9f. or the addition of Neh. 9 is particularly possible. Moreover it has to reckon with extensive literary interventions, which can only be followed approximately in the text, of a redaction which breaks up, abbreviates or supplements the Ezra source and has put it in its present form. It is already very strange how on this question, probably for the sake of historicity, even exegetes who otherwise have reservations about literary criticism tend towards an accumulation of literary-critical and redaction-critical hypotheses.

However, the position of Neh. 8(–10) remains a problem, even if we do not reckon with a formerly independent Ezra narrative but with a 'Chronistic' creation, that is, a narrative which comes from the redactor responsible for the compilation of material in Ezra–Nehemiah. For the sake of simplicity Noth[23] argues for attributing not only the composition but also the positioning to the redactor (the Chronicler). However, the reasons given for the hypothesis of an independent Ezra source, especially the testimony of 3 Ezra, also allow transposition hypotheses in the 'Chronistic' context.

At all events, though, the transposition stands on a shaky basis. The evidence of 3 Ezra is unconvincing because 3 Ezra 9.37f. also translates 7.72a at the transition in Neh. 7.72/8.1 and thus already presupposes the list in Neh. 7.6-72 which has been taken over from Ezra 2 (= 3 Ezra 5.7ff.). Moreover that is also the case in Neh. 8.17, where the people is identified with those returning home from captivity. The closing note in the list, Ezra 10.44, has been smoothed over in 3 Ezra 9.36 to attach Neh. 8 to Ezra 7–10: Ezra 10.44 by no means requires the mention of the sending away of women and children but is a resumé of the list of those in debt in vv. 18ff.; the dissolution of the mixed marriages is already complete in v. 17. By contrast,

3 Ezra 9.36 makes the note about registration – corresponding to Neh. 7.72a – go over into narrative again. A further indication is the alteration of the syntax of Neh. 8.9 in 3 Ezra 9.49, which here as in 3 Ezra 5.40 = Ezra 2.63 regards the quite enigmatic designation Hattirshata, used in the Massoretic text as a title and usually translated as 'the governor', as a proper name – distinct from Nehemiah! As a result it avoids the identification with Nehemiah in Neh. 8.9 and 10.2 and turns the countless subjects of the singular 'And spoke' into objects. But the original subject in Neh. 8.9f. is Nehemiah. The conclusion in 3 Ezra 9.55, which Josephus supplements in accordance with Neh. 8, also indicates that this is an extract and not the original version of Neh. 8. The cut in 8.12 lies precisely where the first public reading of the law ends and the first festival is celebrated. The beginning of 8.13 ('And they assembled') has been supplied as a pick-up line by the epitomizer or translator himself or by the copyists in order to refer to the continuation, which is no longer necessary. For this and other reasons, those who defend the originality in 3 Ezra as well must reckon with substantial later interventions. That does not make the hypothesis any more credible. Without 3 Ezra, the only argument left is the isolated position of Neh. 8, which is not changed much even by the transposition – except for the chronological connection between Neh. 7.72b/8.2 and Ezra 7.7-9; 8.31; 10.9, 16, 17. However, the real problem lies at a completely different point: the discussion of the position of Neh. 8 goes round in a circle and cannot be ended, simply because the basic alternative 'original or Chronistic?' does not go far enough. What has so far not been seriously tested[24] is the possibility that Neh. 8(–10) has not been transposed and does not come from the same author as Ezra 7–10, but has been inserted by a later hand between Neh. 6–7 and 12 in order to synchronize the two figures of Ezra and Nehemiah, as also in Neh. 12.26, 36, and to assimilate the different enterprises to each other (cf. Neh. 8.9).

Further problems of the Ezra narrative are the break in style between the third-person and first-person reports in Ezra 7–10, the relationship between the Hebrew narrative framework and the Aramaic edict in Ezra 7–8, the authenticity of the edict in 7.12-26, the identification of the 'law in Ezra's hand' (7.14) and its relation to the Torah, the historical question whether Ezra is to be put before Nehemiah under Artaxerxes I or after Nehemiah under Artaxerxes II, and, inseparable from all this, the relationship of the Ezra narrative to the other elements of the composition in Ezra–Nehemiah (and Chronicles). None of these questions can be answered without an analysis of the literary composition of Ezra 7–10 and Neh. 8–10.

4.2   Ezra 7–10 is composed of an introduction in the third person (7.1-11), the Aramaic rescript of the so-called firman of Artaxerxes (7.12-26), the first-person narrative of Ezra's journey to Jerusalem (7.27–9.15), and the third-person narrative of the dissolution of the mixed marriages (10.1-44). The breaks which mark the striking change of style are, first, the transition from the quotation of the edict to the implementation of the instructions given there in 7.27ff., and secondly, the prayer in Ezra 9. Stylistically this belongs to the first-person report in chs 7f., but thematically it already belongs to the third-person report in ch. 10, which in 10.1 refers to ch. 9 (note the occasion of the prayer in 9.1-4 and in the prayer itself vv. 10-12, 14a). Conversely, 8.35-36 thematically reach the conclusion of the first-person narrative which opened in 7.27f.

Of the ingredients of the composition, ch. 10 (especially v. 1) presupposes ch. 9 and ch. 9 (vv. 1, 8f.) presupposes chs 7–8. If we look for a core of the tradition, it can only lie in the travel report in Ezra 7–8. The fact that here not all the instructions of 7.12-26 are carried out but only the homecoming (7.13/8.1ff., 15ff.), the bringing of the gifts and offering of a sacrifice (7.15-19/8.24-34, 35), and the handing over of the accompanying letter to the satraps (7.20-24/8.36), does not tell against this, since in Ezra 9–10 and Neh. 8–10, too, the other commissions, the investigation of the situation in Judah and Jerusalem by means of the law, and the installation of judges in Transeuphratene (7.14, 25f.) are either not carried out or are carried out in a way which does not correspond directly to 7.12-26. And there are several indications that Ezra 7–8 is in fact the literary core of the narrative, which was subsequently enriched with Ezra 9f. and Neh. 8–10. These are: (1) the twofold conclusion in 8.35, 36 (note the impersonal formulation in the third person plural); (2) the renewed change of style mediated through the prayer, for which there is no substantive reason and there are virtually no analogies – in contrast to the change from the third person to the first person in Ezra 7f.; (3) the narrative style, which is badly extended from Ezra 9, the new topic which emerges immediately and also occurs in Neh. 10 and 13, and the quite different tendency, especially in the recapitulation of Ezra 1–8 in 9.8f. or in the verdict on those returning home in 9.4; 10.6, 7f.; (4) the fact that there are additions in Ezra 7–8 which are connected with the addition of Ezra 9–10 and the continuation in Neh. 8–10 (for example, 7.6aβγ, 10, 11b).

The framework of the travel report in Ezra 7–8 is in 7.1a, 6aαb; 8.15a, 21-22a, (22b-23,) 31f. Since the transition from 7.6 to 8.15a or 8.21 cannot be original and the journey must have some purpose, the report is dependent either on the Aramaic rescript 7.11, 12-26, to which the benediction in 7.27f. reacts, or on the Hebrew narrative in 8.1-20, 24-30, 33-36, or on both. So as not to complicate things unnecessarily, I shall start from the last alternative.

The travel report is not an independent narrative, but bound up with its context in Ezra–Nehemiah in many ways. The beginning, which is the foundation of it all in 7.1a, and which one cannot separate by literary criticism either, explicitly presupposes the prehistory in Ezra 1–6: 'And after these things ... ' Now that means that the earliest Ezra narrative was already composed as a continuation of Ezra 1–6. In keeping with this, the twelve lay families in 8.1-14 are an extract from Ezra 2, reduced to the number of the tribes of Israel (8.24, 35). Moreover this is an explanation of the many linguistic and stylistic features and points of content which the rescript in 7.12-26 has in common with the documents in Ezra 4–6 with regard to the royal decree and the financing of the enterprise, and which the rescript and narrative have in common with Ezra 1–2 with regard to the homecoming, the bringing of gifts and the ensuing sacrifice. Compare only Ezra 7.13 with 1.3; 7.15-19 and 8.24-30, 33-34 with 1.4, 5, 7ff. (5.13-16; 6.5) and 2.68f.; 7.20, 21-24, 26 and 8.36 with 6.4, 8-12; 8.35 with 6.16; 7.27f.; and 8.36 with 6.22. In contrast, the Nehemiah memoir is imitated above all in the framework of the travel report. The unexpected first-person style speaks for itself; the 'hand of God' over Nehemiah (Neh. 2.8, 18) is also over Ezra in all things (7.6, 9, 28; 8.18, 22, 31, cf. also the expression 'put into the heart' in 7.27 with Neh. 2.12; 7.5); the presence of the 'hand of God' on the journey makes the military escort unnecessary (Ezra 8.22 against Neh. 2.9). Like Nehemiah, Ezra too observes an interval of three days (Ezra 8.15, 32; Neh. 2.11) and hands on instructions from the king to the satraps and governors of Transeuphratene (Ezra 8.36; Neh. 2.9). With good reason the references concentrate on the short account of Nehemiah's journey in Neh. 2.7-9, 11, which is in turn secondary. The framework of the Ezra narrative in Ezra 7–8 is developed from it, but the narrative itself imitates Ezra 1–6 and fills the gap between Cyrus and Darius in Ezra 1–6 and the twentieth year of Artaxerxes in Neh. 1 or 2ff. in terms of both chronology and content. This, and the tendency to fill out the narrative, suggests that what is in view in Ezra 7–8 is not yet the sorry situation of Neh. 1 but the original beginning in Neh. 1.1 + 2.1ff.

All this means that the travel account in Ezra 7–8 has been composed for the literary context of Ezra 1–6 and Neh. 1.1a; 2.1ff. The filling-out also attributes to Artaxerxes, after Cyrus and Darius, a marked commitment to the temple (8.36), first in order to provide a theological basis for his spontaneous agreement to Nehemiah's request, and secondly in order to put the building of the city and the wall themselves in a new light. The building of the temple and the wall are simply two sides of the same coin, namely, the basis of life for the people of Israel who have returned home from the Golah, constituted by the God of Israel in collaboration with the Persian kings. The Ezra narrative thus reinforces the connection between the building of the wall and the building of the temple which had presumably been there previously, and which the conclusions in Ezra 6.15 + 6.16ff. and Neh. 6.15 + 12.(27,) 31ff. that have been assimilated to each other are looking for. Accordingly, if we have two analogous but still different building projects divided between two eras, the oldest stage of the Ezra narrative in Ezra 7–8 presupposes the two together.

4.3   Thus far there is clarity, and all that has been said thus far applies quite independently of the question whether in Ezra 7–8 we regard the Aramaic rescript in 7.12-26 or only the Hebrew narrative without the rescript as the earlier. To this question we now turn. Because of the differences, particularly the surpluses in the rescript, it is improbable that both are equally original. If the rescript was the basis of the narrative, as is almost unanimously thought today, then the narrative framework spun out of it has been composed for the context of Ezra–Nehemiah. But that has by no means been demonstrated. With the exception of 7.27f., the narrative, including 8.25 and, if we take Neh. 2.7-9 into account, even Ezra 8.36, is quite easy to understand in connection with the introduction 7.1-6, even without the rescript. Conversely, the rescript seems quite lost without the narrative framework.

The decision depends not least on the originality of the strange and at any rate contrived list of those returning home – two priests (cf. 1 Chron. 24), a member of the house of David and twelve lay families selected from Ezra 2/Neh. 7 – in Ezra 8.1-14 and the twofold 'And I assembled (them)' in 7.28 and 8.15a. This is once connected with 7.27f. and the rescript and the other time with the list of those returning home in 8.1-14. The list is calculated on the twelve members of the priestly college of 8.24,[25] which the authors – rightly or wrongly – connected with the eleven or twelve leaders of the procession of those returning home under Zerubbabel in Ezra 2.2/ Neh. 7.7 and the twelve tribes of Israel of Ezra 8.35 (cf. 6.22), in order to stylize Ezra's journey as the second exodus.[26] But the calculation does not work out. Like the priests and levites in 8.29 and the usual three estates – laity, priests and levites – in 7.13; 8.29, who have been increased by some others in 7.7, 24 and 8.20, the twelve priests in 8.24 can very much more easily be subsumed under the 'heads' of 7.28 (and 8.15b-20). The list in 8.1-14 deviates from this terminologically ('heads of families' in 8.1) and in its selection and is therefore secondary. 'And I assembled them' in v. 15a is a resumption of 7.28, a verse which is continued in 8.15a with the indication of place 'at the river ...' With the list, the assembly of levites in 8.15b-20 also drops out; certainly like 7.28 it speaks of 'heads', but it completes the lists of 'heads of families'. After the priestly and lay families in 8.1-14, 8.15b-20 completes the three (and more) estates of 7.13 (7.7, 24; 8.20) and also gives the levites names. Ezra 7.27-28; 8.15a is thus continued in 8.21, here too with the striking 'there', coined on the detail of place in 8.15a, which because of the insertion of v. 15b-20 had to be supplied in v. 21. If we cut out both the list and the assembling of the levites, the Aramaic rescript and the transition in 7.27-28 get the priority.

The situation looks rather different if we take note of the surpluses in the rescript by comparison with the narrative. The least forced explanation is that they are a subsequent extension in order to give Ezra the priest the same status as the governor Nehemiah at Tattenai's inspection in Ezra 5–6 and to lend an official colour to his journey. Thus a superior purpose is attached to Ezra's mission: the inspection of the situation in Judah and Jerusalem in accordance with the 'law (the laws) of your God in your hand', which – with or without the 'laws of the king' in 8.36 as a support – is regarded as the 'law of the king' (7.14, 26 and Ezra's title in 17.21, the plural like 8.36 in 7.25). The theological foundation of the offering of gifts, namely, the law of God, and the official colouring come together in Ezra's remarkable title, which sounds very official, and the definition of his purpose. The bringer of the gifts becomes the state commissioner in both matters of the Jewish religion and, according to 7.25, matters under Jewish jurisdiction. The surpluses suggest more the priority of the narrative, but this is incapable of life without the transition into the first-person style in 7.27f. or 8.1-14, 15.

That leaves as the only possible way out of the dilemma the conclusion that the rescript and the narrative are after all equally original. Here, however, we must be clear that neither is a unity. In the rescript addressed to Ezra the literal quotation of the orders to the governor of Transeu-phratene in 7.21-24, who is being addressed directly, drop out of the framework. Initially the quotation embraces only 7.21f. and has been successively expanded in vv. 23, 24, 25. All the difficulties would be settled at a stroke if we might attach vv. 21f. directly to 7.11a, 12-13. That would give us in 7.21f. a fragmentary, perhaps even authentic core, of the Ezra tradition which entered the original narrative through 7.11-13 and 7.27f. as well as through 8.15a, 21ff. and 8.36 before this in turn was anchored in the rescript (7.14, 15-19, 20, 26, additions vv. 23, 24, 25) and supplemented in 8.1-14, 15b-19, 20. A direct attachment of 7.21f. to v. 12 has the syntax (copula in v. 21) against it; an attachment to v. 13 could be supported by the taut syntax in vv. 14ff. and the thematic transition in v. 20, with which vv. 14-19, 20 detach themselves from the rest. In this way the commissioning of Ezra for an inspection in accordance with the 'law of your God in your hand' would clearly prove to be secondary. Moreover this would also explain the remarkable situation that 'the law' (*dātā'*) in the existing text on one occasion means the writing itself and the 'commandments' of the king given in it (7.13, 21) – thus the plural in 8.36 and according to the meaning also 7.11a – and on the other the law of God in Ezra's hand, likewise valid as the king's law, which cannot be simply identical with the king's letter – thus in 7.14, 26 and the additions vv. 23, 25. The connection consists in the fact that the letter and the 'laws of the king' of 8.36 (especially 7.23) handed over to the satraps set in motion precisely what is decreed in 7.26: the constitutional recognition of the Jewish religion with the Jewish law as its basis. Finally, 7.27f. would also be preserved as the original caesura for the change of style. But the other possibility is also conceivable, namely that the quotation in 7.21f. is carrying out the order to Ezra and, as v. 26 attaches itself seamlessly to the second-person style in v. 20, has been inserted subsequently, after 8.36 or at the same time. In that case the question of the originality of the rescript remains open and has to be decided by the other criteria.

Within the Hebrew narrative one or the other passage is also expanded by 8.1-14, 15b-20, which have already been discussed, but that is not very important for the question of composition. The high-priestly genealogy of Ezra in 7.1b-5,[27] compiled from 1 Chron. 5.29-32, 37-40, is regularly doubted. By contrast, the syntax in 7.1a, 6aα is difficult, so that Galling emends following G and 3 Ezra 8.1. The reason why Ezra is made to descend directly from the last high priest before the exile, Seraiah, by-passing the post-exilic line of Jozadak and Jeshua (Ezra 3.2), is that he comes from nowhere, but has to have equal birth to the high priest in order to be able to play the same role alongside Jehoiakim and Eliashib together with Nehemiah under Artaxerxes as Zerubbabel and Jeshua under Cyrus and Darius. At all events, vv. 6aβγ, 10, 11b, which comprehensively reinterpret the Aramaic title 'the priest, the scribe of the law of the God of heaven' of 7.12, 21 in respect of 7.25, chs 9–10 and Neh. 8–10, so that Ezra does not institute investigations in accordance with the law (7.13f.) but himself investigates and teaches the law,[28] are secondary. Verse 6aβγ supplements the genealogy in vv. 1-6a; v. 10 – after the model of vv. 13, 14 – the homecoming in vv. 7, 8-9; v.11b the simple translation 'the priest, the scribe' in v. 11a. The anticipation of vv. 8-9 in v. 7 is also an addition, and finally the dating in vv. 8f. itself, which makes Ezra's departure on the twelfth day of a first month in 8.31 – unless here too the date has been added for a consecutive chronology up to 10.9, 17 – a (new) exodus of the people on the New Year's Day of the seventh year of Artaxerxes. In Ezra 8, as well as 8.1-14, 15b-19, 20, perhaps vv. 22b-23 and vv. 26-27 are also additions. Verses 35 and 36 again go over into the third-person style, but this can already be observed from vv. 33f. on and thus is no grounds for exclusion. Verse 35 corresponds to 6.16, v. 36 stands and falls with 7.21f.

4.4   After the analysis of the text, we now turn to the much-discussed question of the authenticity of the Aramaic rescript in 7.12-26 and the historicity of Ezra. Here, too, time and again historical analogies have been attempted, especially those of the so-called imperial authorization, that is, the sanctioning of indigenous laws or institutions by the Persian central authority.[29] Beyond doubt they bring the authenticity into the realm of the possible, but they do not do more than that. As in the case of Ezra 4–6, they mean only that the Aramaic rescript together with the expansions has been made according to the pattern of Persian documents. The opponents of authenticity are fond of bringing up the Jewish (Chronistic) colouring of the rescript and the view that a Persian king would not have bothered about the details of the Jewish commonwealth. The arguments are relativized by the historical analogies, which show precisely this. A decision for or against the authenticity cannot be made in this way.

Only the literary evidence, here the question of the originality of 7.21f. in the context of the Ezra narrative, can prove decisive. This is the only passage which can lay claim to authenticity. Everything else in Ezra 7–8, the Hebrew narrative and the Aramaic rescript, depends on the context in Ezra 1–6 and Neh. 2ff. and has been composed for it. We do not know what the historical presuppositions are. We cannot as a result dispute the historicity of Ezra, but we cannot assume it either. And as for the investigation of conditions in Judah and Jerusalem 'in accordance with the law of your God in your hand' and the identification of the royal law and the divine law, the couple of verses in Ezra 7 can hardly have been the birth of the Torah, the Pentateuch as the normative entity of Judaism; rather, they presuppose a similarly lengthy process, perhaps in fact even sanctioned or instituted by the central Persian authority. Ezra and the offering of gifts were not necessary for this. As in the case of the *Letter of Aristeas* and the Greek translation of the Pentateuch, the narrative by and large reflects the process, perhaps even with some degree of accuracy, but is not identical with it. The identification of the process with the person of Ezra and his mission corresponds to the identification of the laws of the Pentateuch with the revelation to Moses on Sinai, and is the work of legend.

As a result, the speculations about the law that Ezra is said to have brought from Babylon are also superfluous. What is meant is more or less the Pentateuch which has been handed down to us, whether or not the individual regulations in Ezra 7–8 (and 9f., Neh. 8–10) correspond to it. Despite all the respect for the tradition, even the Pentateuch acknowledged as the Torah was not an unchangeable entity but was continually adapted to current needs in copies, rewritings and interpretations, and thus also in usage. Moreover we must take into account the fact that 'the law' has a different significance at the different literary levels: first of all it is used more in accordance with the concept (thus especially in 7.12ff.), and then it is applied in accordance with its substance (Ezra 9f.); finally it is studied, read aloud, and sometimes even cited word for word (Ezra 7.6, 10, 11b, 25; Neh. 8–10; 13). However, the differences do not justify the assumption of a law fundamentally different from the Pentateuch that has been handed down to us, containing everything suggested by the Ezra narrative, or just parts of it, which contained even less.

In short: Ezra may or may not have existed, but at all events the Ezra narrative is legend. It says little about Ezra and his time, and all the more about how the Torah became established in Judaism.

4.5   Hardly have the people and the house of God been seen to in accordance with the law of the God of heaven in Ezra's hand when the leaders come and report the treachery of the people to Ezra. The laity, priests and levites, with the leaders at their head, have entered into marriages with the heathen and polluted the 'holy seed'. Ezra rends his garments, tears his beard and hair and begins to mourn. At the time of the evening sacrifice he rouses himself to offer a penitential prayer which acknowledges the sins of Israel from the days of the patriarchs and seeks to assuage the wrath of Yhwh. Meanwhile the people assemble and join in the lament. First of all the leaders pledge that they will act in accordance with the law and dissolve the mixed marriages, and force Ezra to act. After three days, on the twentieth day of the ninth month, all the men from Judah and Benjamin assemble and do the same thing. A procedure is agreed, and on the first day of the first month everything is settled. The guilty are written down in a list.

According to Ezra 7–8 this turn for the worse in Ezra 9–10 comes as quite a surprise. Those who think that Ezra 7–10 is an independent authentic Ezra source must invent all kinds of developments as a basis for the step from the one to the other. It is easier to explain it from the literary context for which Ezra 9–10 was composed. The beginning in 9.1 ('And when these [viz., the things in Ezra 7–8] had been completed ...') and also the first-person style, resumed after 8.33f., 35f., which, after the prayer of Ezra 9.5ff., in 10.1 changes into the third-person style; the ongoing chronology in 10.9, 16, 17 (cf. 7.7-9; 8.31); the retrospect on the restoration of the temple in 9.8f., here and there, especially where the text comes to speak about the Golah and the father's houses; and also the terminology and above all the implementation of the law in Ezra's hand make it clear that the text may be read a priori as a continuation of Ezra 7–8 and an elaboration of the commission to investigate the situation (cf. 10.16, emended text) and implement the law, which is given in 7.14, 25 and reflected on in 7.10. In turn, the serious differences, which relate not only to the chronological delay or the change in mood but specifically to the main passages, that is, the restoration which is narrated in Ezra 1–8 without any disturbance and even the commission to inspect the situation in accordance with the law, which is not really carried out in Ezra 7–8, lead to the conclusion that the chapters do not come from the same author but from a later one. Thus Ezra 9–10 prove to be a development of the Ezra narrative in the framework of the book of Ezra. The development does precisely what modern exegetes also do when they are convinced of the historicity of the account and want to convince others: it fills in the gaps in the text which has been handed down. Thus Ezra 9–10 make a first attempt to give a narrative elaboration of the investigation according to the law in Ezra's hand. Nehemiah 8–10 undertake a second.

The author makes use of an example which is not given in Ezra 1–8, if we leave aside the indications in 2.59ff.; 4.1-5 and 6.21, and on this occasion introduces a new theological dogmatics which is familiar to him or fits in well; scholars call it the Deuteronomistic picture of history.[30] It may be that the question of mixed marriages was in fact a topic of concern in the author's time. As with the predilection for genealogical lists in the post-exilic literature, the historical background to the topic could be that on occasion Judah had to demonstrate to the central Persian authorities that it was a separate race in order to attain the status of a province in the Persian empire.[31] But there is yet another reason why the author chose this particular example of mixed marriages for the implementation of Ezra 7–8, and in Ezra 9–10 made a theological U-turn.

The book of Nehemiah provided the occasion. The expansion of the Nehemiah memoir by Neh. 1 and Neh. 13 is presupposed. The points of contact between the prayer in Ezra 9 and Neh. 1 are obvious, in terms both of the common theological (Deuteronomistic) stamp of the two prayers and their main concern: neither the temple nor the walls but the 'rest who had escaped (from captivity)', the Jews and members of the people of Israel who had remained at home and those who had returned, are the centre of interest in both passages (Ezra 9.8, 13-15; Neh. 1.2f.). We can perhaps establish that, as I conjecture, Neh. 1 is the giving part and Ezra 9f. the taking part from the fact that the narrative framework and main topic of the prayer of Neh. 1 (the dispersal and imprisonment of the servants of God) are used in the prayer of Ezra 9 (vv. 6-9, 13-15), and are tailored to the theme of Ezra 1–8, the building and furnishing of the temple. However, the occasion is again quite a different one, into which Neh. 1, conversely, does not go. Common elements of terminology like the 'overseers' ($s^e g\bar{a}n\hat{\imath}m$) in Ezra 9.2 from Neh. 2.16, etc., and above all the new occasion for the penitential prayer itself, the mixed marriages, which Ezra 9–10 might have taken from Neh. 13.23ff., point in the same direction. Here too, of course, one can argue over the direction of the dependence, but I think a generalization from the individual scene more probable than the opposite. For both the relationship to Neh. 1 and that to Neh. 13.23ff. is characterized by this generalization in Ezra 9–10, which in turn can be derived from the perspective of all Israel already given in Ezra 1–8 (1–4; 5.17; 6.17, 21; 7.10, 11, 13, 28; 8.1ff., 35). Since Neh. 1 had put the building of the walls and the mission of Nehemiah, now divided into two phases (5.14; 13.6f), in a different theological key, Ezra 9–10 in its own way filled the gap which thus opened up at the transition from Ezra 1–8 to Neh. 1.1a from the description of the situation in Neh. 1.1b-3. According to

Ezra 9–10, the mixed marriages are the manifestation of the persistent guilt that is lamented in both prayers and the reason for the persistent wrath of Yhwh (10.14); they are therefore the reason for the desolate state of the city described in Neh. 1.1b-3 and the delay in the restoration from the seventh to the twentieth year of Artaxerxes. In short, Ezra 9–10 not only develop Ezra (1–6;) 7–8 but at the same time prepare for Neh. 1–13. This is a typical piece of updating which inserts itself into an already existing literary context and expands in both directions. Together with the new introduction in Neh. 1, which with the dating in 1.1b (cf. Ezra 7.7-9; 8.31; 10.9, 16, 17) seems to develop the book of Ezra, it replaces the earlier transition from Ezra 1–8 to Neh. 1.1a; 2.1ff.

Since the picture of the composition does not change much, we need go only briefly into the question of unity. Certainly those passages which rebuke the Golah that has just returned home for mixing with the people of the surrounding countries (the land) have been added: Ezra 9.4; 10.3, 6, 7-8; in 10.16, by contrast, the Golah is part of the commission of investigation. The additions assimilate the text to the terminology of 1.5; 4.1, where Judah and Benjamin (10.9) are identical with the homecomers. In order not to incriminate Ezra and his followers, those who make additions in 9.4 and 10.3 introduce a host of the faithful who tremble at the word of God. Galling also regards the whole penitential process in 9.3–10.1 as an addition, and combines 9.1-2 with 10.2-6 in one scene. Here the distribution of the expression 'people of the lands/the land' does not completely fit the picture, since 9.1f. goes with 9.11, 14 and 10.2 with 10.11. The expression 'foreign women' also occurs only in 10.2ff. and 10.9ff.; by contrast the introduction and prayer in 9.1f. and 9.11f., 14 speak of participation in the 'abominations' of the peoples and describe the process of marrying-in. Even if we reckon with imitation of 9.1-3 in 9.5ff. and of 10.2, 4-5 in 10.9ff., the differences between chs 9 and 10 remain. The change from the first-person to the third-person style goes with them. Does the updating therefore first end with ch. 9 as a transition to Neh. 1, and was it only subsequently expanded by 10.1ff.? We can ask whether the fact that in ch. 10 Ezra arises twice, in vv. 5 and 10, means anything, especially as the estates mentioned in 9.1 – priests, levites and all Israel – were already made to swear an oath in 10.5. Therefore perhaps not only those who return home in 10.6-8 but also the scene in 10.9-17, which elaborates the gathering of the people (cf. 10.1, 5), are secondary. The list of the guilty ones who left their foreign wives mentions a number of priests, levites, singers, gatekeepers and lay families who also occur in Ezra 2. The literary dependence cannot be demonstrated any more than in the case of 8.1-14, because no principle of selection can be recognized. Whether we therefore take the lists as common currency and may draw conclusions from them for the development of the population in post-exilic Judah may be left open.[32] It is like wanting to reconstruct the history of the ancient world by means of the lists of people in Exod. 23.23; Deut. 7.1; Judg. 3.3, 5; and Ezra 9.1. The resumption of 10.17 in vv. 18, 44 suggests that the list has been added in order to document the estates mentioned in 9.1 and 10.5, if it did not even once link up with v. 5.

4.6   The Ezra narrative continues in Neh. 8. In addition to the protagonists and their titles, scribes and priests, the dominant theme, the reading out of the Torah, is also taken from Ezra 7–10. The main points of contact are the characterization of Ezra as an expert in the Torah in 7.6, 11, which corresponds to his Aramaic title and commission in 7.12, 14, and the somewhat different task of teaching the Torah in 7.10, which corresponds roughly to the commission of 7.25. Ezra appears twice, alone and together with the levites, as one who reads out and expounds the law: the first time in Neh. 8.1-12 on the first day of the seventh month, where the reading and explanation of the book of the Torah issue in a call to go home and celebrate, and the second time in 8.13-18, where the very next day, the second day of the seventh month, the people again assemble for the reading of the law and encounters regulations for the feast of tabernacles in the seventh month; the feast is immediately prepared and, accompanied with daily readings of the law by Ezra, is celebrated on seven days and one day. Thus, as if the feast had been celebrated on the prescribed dates of the fifteenth to the twenty-second day of the seventh month,[33] in Neh. 9.1, on the twenty-fourth day of the seventh month, the people assemble for the third time for a tripartite celebration of the covenant with the reading of the Torah, a penitential prayer and the conclusion of the covenant in Neh. 9–10. The feast of the covenant, which is led mainly by the levites, takes place without Ezra, but it too shows clear references to the Ezra narrative in Ezra 7–10, especially to the penitential prayer in Ezra 9 which has a considerably heightened parallel in Neh. 9, and the twofold commitment of the people on the question of mixed marriages in Ezra 10, which in 10.3, 5 likewise foresees covenant and oath (cf. Neh. 9.2; 10.29f., 31ff.) and moreover is thematically extended in Neh. 9f. Thus the three scenes in Neh. 8.1-12, 13-18 and Neh. 9–10 are not really a seamless continuation, but more a duplication and modification, of the Ezra narrative in Ezra 7–10. That also applies to Neh. 8, where the institution of a college to deal with the question of mixed marriages in Ezra 10 is replaced by the college of levites to teach the law, in order to fulfil the task of Ezra 7.10, 25.

But Neh. 8–10 is meant to continue or imitate not only the Ezra narrative but also the book of Ezra as a whole. That is evident from the fact that the first two scenes in 7.72b/8.1-12 and 8.13-18 have been formulated on the model of Ezra 3. The beginning in Neh. 7.72b/8.1 corresponds almost word for word with Ezra 3.1 and in both cases picks up the list of those returning in Ezra 2 = Neh. 7.6-72a; the joyful feast in Neh. 8.9ff. recalls Ezra 3.12f.; the feast of tabernacles in Neh. 8.13ff. repeats Ezra 3.4. However, in Neh. 8 everything takes account of the Torah itself, whereas in Ezra 3 the Torah serves as the criterion of the action (cf. vv. 2, 4). The point of contact for the imitation was presumably the analogous goal, the consecration of the temple in Ezra 6 and the dedication of the wall in Neh. 12. Both festivals are thus prepared for by actions in accordance with the law, the building of the altar and the feast of tabernacles in accordance with the law under Jeshua and Zerubbabel in Ezra 3, the reading of the law and the feast of tabernacles in accordance with the law under Ezra and Nehemiah in Neh. 8. The continuation of Ezra 6 in Ezra 7–10 corresponds to some degree to the continuation in Neh. 9–10 and 13. In accordance with all this it is clear that Neh. 8(–10) in no case belongs to a previously independent Ezra narrative. At least the composition in Ezra 1–10 is presupposed.

But there is more than that. Like Ezra 7–10 before it, Neh. 8(–10) also presupposes the book of Nehemiah, indeed the present position in the book of Nehemiah. The beginning in Neh. 7.72/8.1 depends, like Ezra 3.1, on the repetition of the list of Ezra 2 in Neh. 7.6-72a, which in turn is dependent on Neh. 7.4f. and therefore cannot stand anywhere else but here. The celebration of the covenant in Neh. 9–10 imitates Ezra 9–10, and if the repetition is to make any sense, can also stand only in the book of Nehemiah and nowhere else. It confirms in the twentieth year of Artaxerxes the covenant of Ezra 9–10 from the seventh year of the same king. As it presupposes Neh. 8, this chapter too belongs in its present place. The argument that the chronology of Neh. 8–10, the seventh month in 7.72a/8.2, 13ff.; 9.1, would fit better the seventh year and the first day of the first month of the eighth year in Ezra 7–10 (7.7-9; 8.31; 10.9, 16, 17), and even better the fifth month of the seventh year in Ezra 7–8 (7.7-9), than the sixth month in the twentieth year of Artaxerxes in Neh. 6.15, because otherwise there would be two years between the first and second appearances of Ezra, confuses the levels of historical reconstruction and literary composition. The two must be kept strictly apart, and what is right for Nehemiah (cf. the twelve years in Neh. 5.14 and 13.6f.) should be legitimate for Ezra. Finally, the mention of Nehemiah in Neh. 8.9 can be explained only from the present position of Neh. 8. The repeated verb 'and spoke' in Neh. 8.9, 10 beyond doubt calls for only one subject. Therefore 'Nehemiah, that is the Tirshata, and ... and the levites who instructed the people' is usually deleted in v. 9, producing 'Ezra, the priest, the scribe' as subject. However, the literary-critical operation does not match the structure of the text, but only the preconceived view that Neh. 8 must be a text from the Ezra memoirs. In that case one would have to delete v. 9 completely and attach vv. 10, 12a directly to vv. 1-3 or vv. 1-6. But the most natural solution to the problem is to take Nehemiah, who is named first, as the original subject of the verbs in vv. 9 and 10. In assimilation to 10.2 he was identified with the title Hattirshata ('that is the Tirshata') from Ezra 2.63; Neh. 7.65, 69 and later was supplemented with Ezra and the levites from Neh. 8.1-6, 7f.; 9.4ff. ('and Ezra ... and the levites ...').[34] Thus the transposition hypothesis can finally be laid to rest. On the basis of the perspectives mentioned we must perhaps start instead from the fact that in connection with Neh. 7, first Neh. 8, and then, in connection with Neh. 7–8, in turn Neh. 9–10 (like the following chapters Neh. 11–12) were from the beginning composed for the position in the book of Nehemiah in which they now stand.

The only thing that needs serious discussion is the question whether the great insertion in Neh. 8–10 is a unity and how it relates to the synoecism in Neh. 7 and 11–12. This has likewise been inserted between the completion in 6.15 or 6.16–7.3 and the dedication of the wall in Neh. 12.(27,) 31ff. As Neh. 7–8 has been shaped after Ezra 2–3 and Neh. 9–10 on the model of Ezra 9–10, and Neh. 11 (12.1-26) in turn goes back to Neh. 7.4 and 7.6, 6-72, one is inclined to think of one author. But the unitary principle of imitation does not of itself prove literary unity.

Within 8–10, 8.13-18 must be a supplement to (7.72b;) 8.1-12,[35] and Neh. 9–10 a supplement to 8.1-18, in turn expanded in 10.2-28 and 10.38b-40a. At the beginning is the idea to have the synoecism organized by Nehemiah, the repopulation of the holy city (7.4, 5a; 11.1ff., 18), taking place on a day hallowed by the public reading of the Torah (Neh. 8.9-12). In the second approach in 8.13-18 the 'holy day' has become the feast of tabernacles, prescribed in the Torah for the seventh month, here dated quite vaguely, and in Neh. 9–10 the festal assembly of 8.18 has finally become the penitential ceremony – appointed precisely in accordance with the date of the feast of tabernacles prescribed in the law, drawn from Ezra 9–10 and Neh. 13 and led by the levites – together with the obligation to enter into a covenant to keep the 'holy seed' pure (cf. Neh. 9.2 in accordance with Ezra 9.2), to observe the holy sabbath and to maintain the sanctuary.

Nehemiah 7.72b/8.1-12 have been inserted either between 7.4-72a and Neh. 11 (with supplements in 11.16f., 21ff.; 12.1-26) or, contemporaneously with the list of those returning home from Ezra 2, in 7.5b, 6-72a between 7.4, 5a and 11.3ff. I think the latter more probable. The resumption of the theme of 7.4, 5a and the verbal references to 10.35ff. in 11.1f are due to this and the following insertions. The synoecism presupposed in Neh. 7.4, 5a and 11.3ff. ensures that the whole province in Judah and Jerusalem is able-bodied, with a view to the appointment of the guards in 7.3 (cf. $m^e d\bar{\imath}n\bar{a}h$, 11.3), before the core of the defensive capability of the province and its symbol, the wall built by Nehemiah, is dedicated. With Neh. 7.5b, 6ff. the province receives the foundation of its population policy in the Zerubbabel Golah (cf. $m^e d\bar{\imath}n\bar{a}h$ in 7.6), just as in (7.72b,) 8.1-12 and 8.13ff.; 9–10 it receives its theological foundation in the Torah brought by Ezra. Both give the Nehemiah memoir a new orientation before it ends in 12.(27,) 31f., 37-40, 43; and 13.4-31, and form the basis for the additions in 12.1-26, 27ff., 44-47; 13.1-3.

4.7   Summary: The earliest Ezra narrative is to be found in Ezra 7–8. The basis of it is perhaps the splinter of tradition in 7.21f., which is the only one that could be authentic. Otherwise the original travel report (say 7.1-6, 11a, 12f., 21f., 27f.; 8.15a, 21-36) is a text which has been composed for the literary context of Ezra 1–6 and Neh. 1.1a + 2ff., in order to set alongside Zerubbabel and Jeshua under Cyrus and Darius in Ezra 1–6 the two figures of Ezra and Nehemiah under Artaxerxes, and also to claim for this time the royal concern for the temple which is set down legally in a letter in 7.12ff. The travel report in Ezra 7–8 was first supplemented with Ezra 9–10, with an eye to Neh. 1 and 13, and then taken up and developed further in Neh. (7–)8 (vv. 1-12, 13-18) and Neh. 9–10. The different waves of development attracted a series of additions, for example, Ezra 7.6aβ, 7, 8-9, 10, 11b; 8.1-14, 15b-19, 20; 9.4; 10.3, 6-8; 10.9ff., 18ff.; Neh. 8.7f., 11, 12b; 10.2-28, 38b-40, etc. The basic material and the additions bring Ezra and Nehemiah ever closer together and complete the analogy with the two figures of Zerubbabel and Jeshua and the generation of those returning home from Ezra 1–6. Here the Ezra who returns home embodies the Torah, which becomes the spiritual and legal foundation of the temple rebuilt by Zerubbabel and Jeshua and its ongoing existence, and the criterion for life together under the protection of the walls of Jerusalem rebuilt by Nehemiah and in the province administered by him.

5.   Result

The books of Ezra and Nehemiah are based on two independent sources which came into being and were handed down independently of each other: the chronicle of the building of the temple in Ezra 5–6 and Nehemiah's memoir in 1.1a + 2-6 + 12. The building of the temple and the building of the walls were put in parallel by the Hebrew framework of the chronicle of the building of the temple in Ezra 1–4, which in turn grew up gradually, and the Aramaic conclusion in Ezra 6.16-18. Both building projects were realized and solemnly consecrated in the face of the vigorous resistance of the enemies of Judah and Benjamin. Lastly, Ezra and his law intervened, first with the first-person report in Ezra 7–8, which relates the two figures of Ezra and Nehemiah, and brings Ezra–Nehemiah together as one book. The controversies with Sanballat and his companions in Neh. 2–6, the synoecism in Neh. 7 and 11, Nehemiah's concern for the Israelite commonwealth and further measures in Neh. 1; 5; and 13, came partly before and partly after the books were brought together; in the course of this, further tasks of Ezra were also added in Ezra 9–10 and Neh. 8–10.

Table A.II.1

Sources	Ezra–Nehemiah	Supplements
Ezra	1.1–4.5(, 24)	3.1-7, 8b, 9, 10b, 11
		4.6-23(, 24)
Chronicle of the building of the temple		
(4.24;) 5.1–6.15	6.16-18	6.19-22
Ezra tradition		
(7.21f.?)	7.1–8.36	7.7-10, 11b, 14-20, 23-26
		8.1-14, 15b-20
		9–10
Nehemiah		
Nehemiah memoir		
1.1a	1.1b-11	
2.1-6	2.7-9, 10	
2.11-18	2.19-20	
3.(1-32,) 38	3.33-37	
4.4, 6a, 9b	4.1-17	
	5.1-13, 14-19	
	6.1-14	
6.15	6.16, 17-19	
	7.1-3	
	7.4-5a(, 5b-72a)	
		(7) 8; 9–10
	11.(1f.) 3ff.	11.(1f.), 16f., 21ff.; 12.1-26;
12.(27,) 31-32, 37-40, 43		12.27-30, 33-36, 41-42, 44-47;
		13.1-3
	13.4-31	

Notes

1 Jeshua in Ezra is identical with Joshua in Haggai and Zechariah.
2 O. Kaiser, *Grundriss der Einleitung in die kanonischen und deuterokanonischen Schriften des Alten Testaments* 1, 1992, 133.
3 G. Steins, in E. Zenger et al., *Einleitung in das Alte Testament*, Kohlhammer Studienbücher Theologie I, 1, 1995, 175f.
4 If we delete the initial 'thereupon' the narrative could have begun with 4.24 as a starting point and a protasis to 5.1. Of course the beginning in 3 Ezra 6.1 is finer ('In

the second year of King Darius there appeared as prophets ...'), but it too is presumably also connected with the prefixing of Ezra 1–4.

5   Miswritten from the Akkadian and Aramaic Shatabarzanu with a confusion of *r* and *b*.

6   Thus already the Tab'el memoir hypothesis, put forward by A. Klostermann and reinforced by H.H. Schaeder; cf. Schaeder, *Iranische Beiträge* I, SKG.G 6, 5, 1930, reprinted 1972, 14ff.; id., *Esra der Schreiber*, BHTh 5, 1930, 27f. Noth, *ÜSt*, 151f., is against this, but his own proposal, ibid., 152-4, is no less 'artificial'.

7   Cf. W.H. Kosters, *Die Wiederherstellung Israels in der persischen Periode*, 1895, 22f.

8   It is virtually impossible to decide whether the 'governor of the Jews' who disrupts the syntax of v. 7 is original or has been added in assimilation to Ezra 5.14 and in retrospect to Zerubbabel after Hag. 1.1 (cf. 3 Ezra 6.26). The regulations about implementation which follow differ from vv. 6-7 by virtue of the regular headings (cf. 6.1, 3).

9   Whether in this case we want to connect vv. 9f. with the letter to Darius in 5.6-8 or with the Cyrus history in 5.10ff. depends on how much importance we attach to the reference back in v. 9 ('those elders'), which in the framework of the letter has only the personal suffix of the expression 'in their hand' (v. 8) as a point of reference, and otherwise refers to v. 5, and whether the formulation in 5.3f., which is dependent on vv. 9f., is original or was added later.

10   With the usual expansion of the measure according to model of the temple of Solomon ('at the place where one offers sacrifices') in v. 3.

11   For the connections cf. R.G. Kratz, *Kyros im Deuterojesaja-Buch*, FAT 1, 1991, 88-90, 183ff.

12   B. Porten and A. Yardeni, *Textbook of Aramaic Documents from Ancient Egypt* 1, Jerusalem and Winona Lake 1986, 62-5, 68-79; ANET[3], 491f. See also E. Meyer, *Der Papyrusfund von Elephantine*, 1912; K. Galling, *Studien zur Geschichte Israels im persischen Zeitalter*, 1964, 149ff.; B. Porten, *Archives from Elephantine*, 1968; R.G. Kratz, *Translatio Imperii*, WMANT 63, 1991, 141, 251-3; for the dispute over authenticity cf. id., 'Die Entstehung des Judentums', *ZThK* 95, 1998, 167-84.

13   Porten and Yardeni, *Textbook of Aramaic Documents from Ancient Egypt*, 78f.

14   Ibid., 54f.

15   Cf. Galling, *Studien zur Geschichte Israels im persischen Zeitalter*, 78-108.

16   Or with Rudolph's emendation, HAT I/20, 44, 'in this way'.

17   Thus Böhler, *Die heilige Stadt in Esdras α und Esra–Nehemia*, 119f., 216ff.

18   TUAT I/6, 603-8.

19   The basic framework can also be glimpsed in Josephus (*Antt*. XI, 5, 6-8 = Neh. 1.1-6, 15 + 12.27-43 + 6.16–7.4 + 13.4ff.), who possibly had a still independent Nehemiah memorandum in front of him, but beyond doubt he offers only an extract, and not the original form. For Ezra 1–10 + Neh. 8 he bases himself on 3 Ezra (*Antt*. XI, 1, 1-5, 5). However, that does not yet prove that 3 Ezra is prior to the Massoretic composition Ezra–Nehemiah, which is older than Josephus and thus can also be older than 3 Ezra.

20   WBC 16, xxvi-xxviii.

21   Those attested are Sanballat (I), father of Delaiah and Shelemiah, under Darius II (Elephantine, TGI[3], 87, 88); Sanballat (II), father of the governor Hananiah and his brother, whose name is illegible, under Artaxerxes II and III (Samaria papyri); and a Sanballat (III) at the time of Darius III and Alexander the Great (Josephus, *Antt*. XI, 7, 2). It is usually assumed that Sanballat II was a son of Delaiah and Sanballat III a son of Hananiah. Cf. Galling, *Studien zur Geschichte Israels im persischen Zeitalter*, 209f.; Kellermann, *Nehemiah*, 166f.; H.G.M. Williamson, in *AncBD* 5, 1992, 973-5.

22   Cf. Kellermann, *Nehemiah*, 172f.; N.A. Willliams in *AncBD* 2, 1992, 995.
23   *ÜSt*, 125ff., 145ff.
24   But cf. Steins, 207.
25   Sherebiah, Hashabiah and ten brothers. In 8.18f. the first two have become levites.
26   Koch, 'Esra und Jehud', 257, regards the 'programmatic division' as original over against the 'gradual weakening' in Ezra 2/Neh. 7; Ezra 10; and Neh. 10. The presupposition of that is that it has to be proved 'that Ezra was in fact inspired by the idea of a structure of twelve for the people whom he had reunited'.
27   The names missing from 1 Chron. 5.33-36 may have fallen out as the result of a slip of the eye.
28   Cf. R. Rendtorff, 'Esra und das "Gesetz"', *ZAW* 96, 1984, 165-84.
29   Cf. Kratz, *Translatio*, 246-55; P. Frei, 'Zentralgewalt und Lokalautonomie im Achämenidenreich', in P. Frei and K. Koch, *Reichsidee und Reichsorganisation im Perserreich*, OBO 55, [2]1996.
30   See O.H. Steck, *Israel und das gewaltsame Geschick der Propheten*, WMANT 23, 1967.
31   Cf. K.G. Hoglund, *Achaemenid Imperial Administration in Syria–Palestine and the Missions of Ezra and Nehemiah*, SBL.DS 125, 1992, 236ff.
32   Cf. R. Smend, *Die Listen der Bücher Esra und Nehemia*, Basel 1881; Meyer, *Entstehung*, 94ff.; Koch, 'Esra und Jehud', 252-7.
33   Cf. Lev. 23.33ff.; the joy in v. 40 and Deut. 16.13-15; the public reading of the Torah and the reference to Joshua after Deut. 31.9ff.
34   Cf. Noth, *ÜSt*, 130.
35   The section is heavily glossed. The following are dubious: the detail of place in v. 2 ('before the assembly . . .'), which takes the word of reference from the suffix in v. 3, the hearers in v. 3aβ, the list of persons alongside Ezra in v. 4 ('and Ezra stood, and alongside him there stood . . .') and the levitical insertions in vv. 7-8, 11, 12b. The relationship between vv. 1-3 and 4-6 is problematical in other respects.

III. The Chronistic History

1. The hypothesis

The hypothesis of a unitary Chronistic history comprising the books of Chronicles, Ezra and Nehemiah arose for the first time in the first half of the nineteenth century with Leopold Zunz in his *Religious Lectures on the Jews* of 1832.[1] Since Zunz disputed the tradition that Ezra was the author of Ezra–Nehemiah, he was forced to adopt the following alternative:

But the one statement unties this Gordian knot: that we regard Chronicles and the Book of Ezra as two parts of one and the same work, which belong together. Then in the book of Ezra we likewise have the Chronicler with his accounts of gatherings of the people, festivities and readings of the law, his praises of the levites and especially the singers, his extraordinary concern for the ordering of sacrifices, his predilection for genealogies, his exaggeration of numbers, his elaborations of the Pentateuch and the psalms, his historical ignorance, his decorative style and his characteristic forms of words.[2]

The connection between style and content was then often discovered – in fact or allegedly independently of Zunz – and since then the hypothesis of the Chronistic history has been advanced by most scholars to the present day, although it has occasionally been put in question.[3]

In the meanwhile it is only the Chronicler's way of working which has come to be regarded in a more differentiated way. The author has become a redactor who wrote out the sources before him (the basic material in Genesis–Kings for 1–2 Chronicles, the Aramaic chronicle in Ezra 4–6, the Ezra narrative in Ezra 7–10 + Neh. 8(–10) and the Nehemiah memoir in Neh. 1–7 + 12–13), put them together and revised them, and in the course of this also enriched them with his own formulations. Thus the distinction between tradition and Chronistic redaction has become fundamental to the exegesis of Chronicles and Ezra–Nehemiah. Everything that is not basic material or source is regarded as the 'Chronicler's' own contribution. Even those who dispute the unity of the Chronistic work use this distinction, but divide the Chronistic redaction in Chronicles on the one hand and Ezra–Nehemiah on the other into two authors, or two phases in the life of the same author.

The strongest argument for the hypothesis is the overlapping of the text of 2 Chron. 36.22f. with Ezra 1.1-3. There is no doubt that it produces a literary connection and indicates the continuation of 1–2 Chronicles in Ezra–Nehemiah. However, this connection need not be original. Whereas Ezra 1.1-3 is indispensable for the continuation in Ezra–Nehemiah, 2 Chron. 36.22f. could be just an addition. But 2 Chron. 36.20f. already indicates the change of rule, and for this refers to the seventy years of Jeremiah for Babylon, combined with the sabbath years from Lev. 26 (Jer. 25.11f.; 29.10; cf. Zech. 1.12; 7.5). In Ezra 1.1-3 = 2 Chron. 36.22f. this provides the basis for the calculation of the first year of Cyrus (in Babylon). 2 Chronicles 36.20f. ends with a look at the future prophesied by the Torah and the prophets, for which it did not need a continuation in Ezra–Nehemiah. Ezra 1ff. in turn begins where 2 Chron. 36.20f ends, and reconstructs the post-exilic history from the Torah and the prophecies of the prophets (Jeremiah, Haggai and Zechariah and Isa. 40.1ff.). Now both 2 Chron. 36.20f. and Ezra 1; 2 Chron. 36.22f. belong to the 'Chronistic' redaction, but are evidently not on the same literary level. That means that there was not so much one person who was 'the Chronicler' as a variety of 'Chronistic' stages of redaction, some which do not take account of the connection in the Chronistic work and others which constitute it or presuppose it. Quite apart from the differences arising from the situation, that explains both the linguistic and conceptual differences between Chronicles and Ezra–Nehemiah which are time and again cited by those who dispute their unity and the common features which are emphasized by those who support this unity, down to the editorial comment in 2 Chron. 36.22f. which combines the two books (scrolls) that were handed down separately by a pick-up line. Thus the hypothesis of the Chronistic history is both true and false at the same time, depending on the level of redaction at which one is moving.

There are few proposals which not only distinguish between the sources and 'the Chronicler' but reckon with a differentiated growth more appropriate to the state of the text. In the Anglo-Saxon sphere, variants of the so-called block model are enjoying some popularity. If the literary cohesion of the Chronistic work is thought to be original, 3 Ezra offers itself as an older version of the connection between 2 Chron. 35–36 and Ezra 1–10 + Neh. 8, expanded at a second stage by the Nehemiah memoir and replaced by the Massoretic Ezra. The hypothesis stands and falls with the originality of 3 Ezra, of which I am still not convinced. In order to be able to keep Chronicles and Ezra–Nehemiah apart, H.G.M. Williamson by contrast separates Ezra 1–6 and sees it as an earlier insertion, close to Chronicles, before the associated Ezra–Nehemiah narrative in Ezra 7–Neh. 13, which was formerly independent. This proposal comes to grief simply because Ezra 7.1 is not an independent beginning. Ezra 1–6 do not imitate Ezra 7ff.; rather, conversely, Ezra 7–8 and Neh. 7–8 imitate the narrative which has emerged from Ezra 5f., which is itself coherent. In the German-language literature scholars think more in terms of literary strata. The proposal put forward by Galling, who distinguishes between two Chroniclers, is usually dismissed quickly, but never seriously examined. Not far removed from that, Steins[4] finds the stratum which combines both books in the Chronistic history only in the late cultic additions to Chronicles and Ezra–Nehemiah (1 Chron. 12; 15f.; 23ff.; Ezra 3.8-11; 6.18, 19-22; Neh. 10–13, etc.), and thus to some degree returns to Zunz. Otherwise he reckons with a separate origin, in which Chronicles (in the basic strata as also in the supplements), while largely presupposing the major composition of Ezra 1–Neh. 13 and using it as a source, does not yet have it in mind as a literary continuation. I shall go on to sketch what the development looks like after analysing all the elements of the composition in Chronicles and Ezra–Nehemiah.

2. Sources, basic writing and supplements

First come the pre-Chronistic sources, which were handed down separately. They include the basic biblical material for 1–2 Chronicles, the books of Samuel to Kings, for 1 Chron. 1–9 also Genesis–Kings, and for all the rest, in so far it cannot be found in other biblical books, the intangible 'oral tradition', that is, a mixture of knowledge and learned speculation. Further sources are the chronicle of the building of the temple in Ezra 5–6 and the basic material of the Nehemiah memoir in Neh. 1.1a + 2–6 + 12; one is at the same time the basic writing for Ezra, the other the basic writing for Nehemiah.

Next, all these sources receive a redactional revision. In 1–2 Chronicles the excerpt of the history of the Davidic kingship of Judah forms the basic writing, enriched here and there with the Chronistic special material in its original state. In Ezra 1.1–4.5; and 6.16-18 the chronicle of the building of the temple is given a new narrative framework, at the beginning written in Hebrew and at the end supplemented in Aramaic. Nehemiah's memoir is supplemented with narrative features which make the builder of the walls the governor and fighter against the external enemies of Judah, namely, Sanballat and his entourage, and the governor of Judah soon also becomes the renewer of Israel. But the redactional revision of the sources is not all on one level. Initially, the composition of the basic writing of 1–2 Chronicles and the development of the Nehemiah memoir followed each other separately. The expansion of the narrative about the building of the temple in Ezra 1–6 is different. It demonstrates relations to both sides.

With Ezra 1.1ff. the narrative takes up the prospect of Chronicles in 2 Chron. 36.20f. and reports the fulfilment of the prophecies to be read in

Jeremiah, Haggai and Zechariah, and in Isa. 40ff., that is, the end of the Babylonian exile, a second exodus and the rebuilding of the temple under Darius and Cyrus (Isa. 44.28; 45.12f.) and Darius (Haggai–Zechariah). At the conclusion in Ezra 6.16-18 the redaction has the completion of the building of the temple in 6.15, followed by a feast of consecration, so that the scene resembles the conclusion of the building of the walls in Neh. 6.15 (6.16–7.3) + 12.27, 31-43. In substance the redactional narrative framework in Ezra 1–6 comes from the earlier source Ezra 5–6 and draws on the interest in Judah of the basic writing of 1–2 Chronicles, orientated on the temple and Israel; in Ezra 1–6 this goes with an exclusive interest in the Babylonian Golah and its material concern for the building of the temple.[5] The interest in the Golah is also expressed in the exclusion of the 'enemies of Judah and Benjamin' from the building of the temple in Ezra 4.1-5; this in turn corresponds to Nehemiah's clash with the enemies of Judah over the building of the wall. In the later addition of Ezra 4.6-23 (and 6.14βγ) this interest is even more closely dovetailed with the theme of the Nehemiah memoir which follows; the redating of the building of the temple to the reign of Darius II, and of Nehemiah and the walls to the time of Artaxerxes II, agrees with this.

Thus Ezra 1–6 is the connecting link which for the first time brings into a literary relationship the two works composed and handed on independently of one another, the basic document in 1–2 Chronicles and the Nehemiah memoir. After the rebuilding of the temple, which replaces the temple of Solomon, Nehemiah restores the political sovereignty of the province of Judah, which replaces the empire founded by David, by building the walls and making a successful defence against the enemies of Judah. In David's place the Persian kings take over royal care for temple and province in Yhwh's kingdom (cf. 1 Chron. 17; Ezra 1.1ff.).

Table A.III.1		
Excerpt	Chronicle of the building of the temple	Nehemiah memoir
1–2 Chronicles	Ezra 5–6	Neh. 1.1a + 2–6 + 12
	Ezra 1–6	

Subsequently the literary connection, once restored, becomes increasingly close. The extensive expansions in 1–2 Chronicles and Ezra–Nehemiah are responsible for this. In part they reinforce the redactional emphases and connections in and between the books which are already there: the divine pragmatism in 1–2 Chronicles which apportions glory and honour to the kings of Judah depending on how they have behaved towards Yhwh and his law, and the analogy of the era of Zerubbabel and Jeshua to

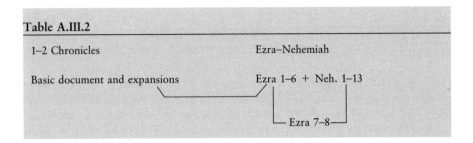

Table A.III.2

1–2 Chronicles	Ezra–Nehemiah
Basic document and expansions	Ezra 1–6 + Neh. 1–13
	Ezra 7–8

that of Nehemiah in Ezra–Nehemiah with the insertion of Ezra in Ezra 7–8, which sets the priest and scribe from the Golah alongside the governor.

But above all, in both places the expansions make the internal constitution and genealogical separation of the entity 'Israel' the dominant theme (1 Chron. 1–9, etc.; Ezra 2; 8.1-14; 9–10; Neh. 1; 5; 7 and 11; 13.4ff.). As the fate of Israel depends on keeping God's law, the didactic dissemination and the obligation to observe the Torah become the sole content of its existence (2 Chron. 17.7-9; 19.4ff.; Ezra 7; Neh. 8–10). Thus the details of the temple cult and its performance in accordance with the Torah, the priests, levites, gatekeepers and singers, the gifts, offerings, sacrifices, songs and festivals and all that goes with it, become more and more important (1 Chron. 15f.; 23ff.; 28f.; 2 Chron. 29–31; 35 etc.; Ezra 3.1-7, 8b, 9, 10b-11; 6.19-22; 8.15b-19, 20; Neh. 8–10; 11.16f., 21ff.; 12.1ff., 27[ff.], 44f.; 13). It is not always easy to say what depends on what. Among the additions are those that come from the same hand and those that arise out of reciprocal stimulation. Last of all came the editor's remark in 2 Chron. 36.22f., which indicates the context beyond the limits of the book and its anachronistic position in the canon.

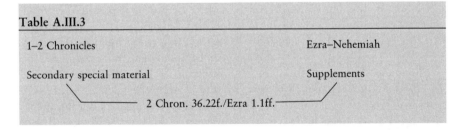

Table A.III.3

1–2 Chronicles	Ezra–Nehemiah
Secondary special material	Supplements
	2 Chron. 36.22f./Ezra 1.1ff.

3. Dating

Above, I gave the middle of the fourth century as the time of the composition of the basic document of 1–2 Chronicles, and conjectured the late Persian and Hellenistic period down to the time of the Maccabees for the additions. There is nothing against dating the sources of Ezra–Nehemiah, the basic document of the narrative of the building of the temple in Ezra 5–6 and the basic material of the Nehemiah memorial in Neh. 1.1a + 2–6 + 12, including the first mentions of Sanballat (Neh. 2.19f., etc.), as early as the Persian period. The chronicle of the building of the temple presupposes at least Darius I (522–486 BC), and the Nehemiah memoir at least Artaxerxes I (465/464–424 BC); the former must have been composed around the middle and the latter towards the end of the fifth century or in the first half of the fourth century BC. The redactional transition for the first connection between Chronicles, Ezra 5–6 and Nehemiah already presupposes the basic material of the original stratum of 1–2 Chronicles and thus belongs to the end of the fourth century, in the reign of Arses and Darius III, if not already in the early Hellenistic period. The insertion in Ezra 4.6, 7, 8-23, with the corresponding expansion in 6.14, which puts the completion of the building of the temple under Darius II and consequently Nehemiah under Artaxerxes II, leads to the same period. The occasion could have been the rebuilding of the temple on Elephantine and perhaps the foundation of the Samaritan temple on Gerizim, though we know nothing of this. At all events, a literary and theological development begins with the bringing together of Chronicles and the Nehemiah memoir in which the second Jerusalem temple, its cult and its festivals (especially Passover and Succoth) takes the place of the temple of Solomon; the province of Judah in the Persian empire takes over the heritage of the Davidic kingdom; and the 'post-exilic' exiles in Judah and Benjamin, with or without the participation of those who have separated themselves from the people of the land, are regarded as the only legitimate descendants of pre-exilic Israel and guardians of the Torah (the Pentateuch). The bringing together of Chronicles and Ezra–Nehemiah, and the further revising which arises out of this, are focused on the identity of pre- and post-exilic Israel, which is guaranteed exclusively in Judah and Jerusalem. It hardly emerges that this is disputed by others who claim the same thing for themselves (cf. Ezra 4.2). The opponents are the enemies of Judah and Benjamin.

This means that we cannot put the insertion of Ezra into Ezra 7–8 and the further literary development of the Chronistic work before the transition from the Persian to the Hellenistic era. The various developments of it must have been added in the Ptolemaean and Seleucid period, but essentially still in the time before the Maccabees, that is, in the course of the third and early second centuries BC. The problems of the priestly name Joiarib in 1 Chron. 24.7ff.; Ezra 8.16; Neh. 11.10 (1 Chron. 9.10); 12.6, 19, the description of the boundaries in the list of places in Neh. 11.25ff, and the comparison of Neh. 9 with Dan. 9 and 4QDibHam[a] (= 4Q504) show that for details we must go down to the Hasmonaean era. The *terminus ad quem* is given by the fragments from Qumran Cave 4 (4Q117), a manuscript from the first century BC, of which the fragments of Ezra 4.2-6; 4.9-11; and 6.5 have been preserved. Moreover at the seam marked by 4.5, 6 this confirms the Massoretic version and not the recension of 3 Ezra.

Notes

1   Noth, *ÜSt*, 12-34.
2   Ibid., 21.
3   For the pros and cons see S. Japhet, 'The Relationship between Chronicles and Ezra–Nehemiah', and K.F. Pohlmann, 'Zur Frage von Korrespondenzen und Divergenzen zwischen den Chronikbüchern und dem Esra/Nehemiah Buch', both in *VT.S* 43, 1991, 298-313, 314-30.
4   *Chronik*, 442f.
5   The references to Chronicles can also be taken up in word references, but most are secondary in Chronicles or Ezra or in both places, and thus already presuppose the combination. Cf. Ezra 2.68f. and 8.24ff. with 1 Chron. 29.1ff.; Ezra 3.7 with 1 Chron. 22.4; Ezra 3.8 with 2 Chron. 3.3; and 8.16; Ezra 3.8b with 1 Chron. 23.4; Ezra 3.9 with 2 Chron. 34.12; Ezra 1.5; 4.1 (Judah and Benjamin) with 2 Chron. 11.1-12.

B   The Torah and the Former Prophets

I.   The Law in the Pentateuch

1.   Survey

F. Crüsemann, *The Torah*, 1996; E. Otto, *Theologische Ethik des Alten Testaments*, ThW 3.2, 1994.

The law, the Torah, which Yhwh has given to Moses for Israel, does not appear first in ChrG, but already has a central position in the material on which it is based, the books of Samuel–Kings or Genesis–Kings. Various terms are used for it in Hebrew – mainly *tōrāh/tōrōth, mišpāṭ/mišpāṭīm, ḥoq/ḥuqqīm', ḥuqqāh/ḥuqqoth, miṣwāh/miṣwōth* – and the terminology also shows characteristic differences in its distribution over the writings of the Old Testament.[1] For example, in contrast to the 'Torah of Moses' in the books of Deuteronomy and Joshua–Kings, alongside it the very much broader expression 'Torah of Yhwh/God' has become established in ChrG. But what is meant is the same everywhere: the will of God laid down in writing, the observance of which brings life and contempt for which brings death.

Within the context of the books of Deuteronomy–Kings which Noth termed DtrG, there is a system of references which in Deuteronomy, and strikingly almost exclusively in the framework chapters, designates this itself as 'the (this) Torah', which according to Deut. 1.5 Moses presents to Israel and in 31.9ff. writes out in accordance with God's instructions; following this, in Joshua–Kings it refers to this very Torah written out by Moses, 'the (this) book of the Torah of Moses'.[2] But the system is not carried through consistently, as for example in Deut. 17.18f.; 28.58, 61; 29.19f., 26; 30.10, where it is already presupposed that the law which is still to be presented has already been written down; in 2 Kgs 22.8, 11; 23.2, 21, where the book is thought to have been hidden for a long time; or in Josh. 24.26, where Joshua writes 'all these words in the book of the law of God'. Moreover, for example, in Josh. 1.7f. or 8.34 it is by no means certain whether only Deuteronomy or the whole Pentateuch, as in ChrG, is meant. It is also remarkable that there is no reference to the Torah of Moses in Judges and Samuel (2 Sam. 7.19 means something else). In Samuel this may be connected with the material, which has in any case hardly been worked on (by the Deuteronomists), but in the framework scheme of the book of

Judges one would expect a corresponding reference. Instead of this, while there is much talk of cultic offences against Yhwh, above all of the offence against the First Commandment, which is introduced in Exod. 20 and Deut. 5 in the framework of the Decalogue, there is no talk of the law book of Moses and accordingly no talk of Deuteronomy either. The horizon extends beyond Deuteronomy.

Where, in contrast, there is an explicit reference to Deuteronomy, it should be noted that particularly in the framework chapters this is meant as an account of all that Yhwh has revealed to Moses on Mount Horeb, that is, on Sinai, in Exod. 19–Num. 10 (cf. Deut. 5). That means that in terms of content the reference to Moses' book of the law is always at the same time also a reference to the law of Sinai/Horeb. Correspondingly, at any rate in literary terms, Deuteronomy presupposes the giving of the law in Exod. 20–24 and 32–34, that is, the texts of the Sinai pericope, which according to the classical division of sources in the Pentateuch belong to the Jehovist (JE). But Deuteronomy also makes references to the other stratum in the Pentateuch, the Priestly Writing (P), for example to the food regulations in Lev. 11 (cf. Deut. 14), and to the so-called Holiness Code in Lev. 17–26, which like Exod. 20.24-26 and Deut. 12 begins in Lev. 17 with regulations about the place of the cult and like Exod. 23 and Deut. 28 ends in Lev. 26 with the announcement of blessing and curse. The covenant of Yhwh with Israel is most closely bound up with the law. It runs like a scarlet thread through the whole, and is especially prominent in the scenes of the covenant-making with Noah (Gen. 9), with Abraham (Gen. 15 and 17, cf. also Exod. 6.2ff.; 25.8; 29.45f.; 40.34f.; Lev. 26.11ff., 42ff.), on Sinai (Exod. 19–24 and 32–34), in Moab (Deut. 26–30), in Shechem (Josh. 23–24), and with Josiah (2 Kgs 22–23).

In addition there are connections on the narrative level both in Deuteronomy itself, for example, in Deut. 1–11, mirroring the wandering through the wilderness into the land of Moab (Num. 10–36), with the stay on Sinai (Exod. 19–Num. 10), and also in the subsequent books, which go back beyond Deuteronomy right into the Pentateuch. The (few) allusions to the patriarchs and the (many) allusions to the Exodus are particularly significant; at least the historical retrospect beginning with Abraham in Josh. 24 and the relationship between the Moses narrative in Exod. 1f. and the forced labour under Solomon in 1 Kgs 9 and 11f., or between the story of the golden calf in Exod. 32 and the setting up of the bulls in 1 Kgs 12, imply a literary connection. The same is true of the angel who accompanies Israel on its way from Sinai to the promised land, cf. Exod. 23.20ff.; 32.34; 33.2f.; Judg. 2.1-5. If one wanted to take things to extremes, the chronology of the 4000 years from the creation of the world until around Hanukkah in the year 164 BC[3] could also be cited for the connection.

So it is clear that if we begin from what is given, Genesis–Kings form a consecutive narrative. In it the history of Israel is reconstructed and judged in accordance with the criterion of the law, which is revealed to Moses in Exod. 19–Num. 36 by Yhwh on Sinai (Exod. 19–Num. 10) and in part also still in the wilderness (Num. 10–36), and in Deuteronomy is proclaimed by Moses to the people in the land of Moab, immediately before they cross over to the promised land. The hinge is Deuteronomy, which looks both backwards and forwards. Borrowing from the designation 'Deuteronomy', scholars call the historical narrative constituted by the law, the language and content of which is influenced by it, the 'Deuteronomistic history' (DtrG). To begin with, we should assume that it extends from Genesis to 2 Kings.

1.2   Although the law in the Pentateuch shapes the whole literary context from Genesis to Kings, scholars are agreed that in literary terms it is secondary. We must be clear that accordingly around half the text in the Pentateuch has been added, and in the area of Exodus–Deuteronomy, from where the law dominates, this figure rises to a good two-thirds. In view of the undisputed consensus on this question, one is sometimes surprised at the fashionable scepticism about literary and redaction criticism in the Old Testament.

Within the great block of the lawgiving, in turn a distinction is made between three highly complex corpora: (1) the Priestly law (Exod. 25–31; 35–40; Lev. 1–Num. 10 and parts in Num. 10–36); (2) Deuteronomy (Deut. 1–34); (3) the Book of the Covenant (Exod. 20–23), so called after Exod. 24.7, a law book enacted and publicized for the first time in the framework of Exod. 19–24 and renewed in Exod. 32–34. Since Wellhausen's *Prolegomena*, the relative chronology has also been by and large clear: (1) is the latest law, (3) the earliest and (2) stands between (1) and (3).

The question that will occupy us is how the individual corpora became parts of the whole, that is, in what way they found their way into the composition of Genesis–Kings and what preceded them in each case. Only thus is it possible to get on the track of the original form of the narrative books and the earlier versions of the composite work in Genesis–Kings. And only thus is it possible to check the classical hypotheses, the division of sources in the Pentateuch, and the limitation of the Deuteronomistic history to Deuteronomy–Kings by Noth.

In the framework of the classical hypotheses the situation presents itself as follows:

The Book of the Covenant under (3) is a secondary element of the pre-Priestly narrative source JE (Jehovist) in Genesis to Numbers and has often been expanded by the redactor R or R^P, both before and after being worked together with the other source P (Priestly Writing).

The Priestly law under (1) is an element of the independent narrative source P in Genesis–Numbers; not, however, the basic writing P^G but the supplementary (secondary) material P^S. Here there is some dispute as to whether P^G consisted only of narrative or also contained law. Moreover there is no dispute about the independence of P, that is, about whether throughout, or at least in parts of P, P^S was composed as a redactional stratum for the literary context in Genesis–Deuteronomy and thus to some degree is to be identified with the so-called final redaction R or R^P.

The law under (2), Deuteronomy, is regarded as an entity in itself, which has been given a secondary framework and in Deut. 1–3 has been built up by Noth's Deuteronomist at the beginning of the Deuteronomistic history work in Deuteronomy–Kings, before at some point the Tetrateuch in Genesis–Numbers (JE + P = R) was combined with DtrG and then divided into the two parts of the canon, the Pentateuch (Genesis–Deuteronomy) and the Former Prophets (Joshua–Kings).

In what follows I shall start from the overall context in Genesis–Kings and gradually strip away the strata.[4]

2. The Priestly law

T. Nöldeke, *Untersuchungen zur Kritik des Alten Testaments*, 1869, 1-144: 50f.; Wellhausen, *Composition*, 81f., 96-116, 134-86, 335ff.; Noth, *Überlieferungsgeschichtliche Studien*, 190ff.; id., *Überlieferungsgeschichte des Pentateuch*, 7-9, 18-19; R. Rendtorff, *Die Gesetze in der Priesterschrift*, FRLANT 62 (1954), [2]1963; K. Koch, *Die Priesterschrift von Exodus 25 bis Leviticus 16*, FRLANT 71, 1959; id., 'Die Eigenart der priesterschriftlichen Sinaigesetzgebung', *ZThK* 55, 1958, 36-51; D. Kellermann, *Die Priesterschrift von Numeri 1, 1 bis 10,10*, BZAW 120, 1970; V. Fritz, *Tempel und Zelt*, WMANT 47, 1977; E. Blum, *Studien zur Komposition des Pentateuch*, BZAW 189, 1990, 287-332; T. Pola, *Die ursprüngliche Priesterschrift*, WMANT 70, 1995.

Commentaries

M. Noth, *Exodus*, OTL, 1962; id., *Leviticus*, OTL, 1977; id., *Numbers*, OTL, 1968; K. Elliger, *Leviticus*, HAT I/4, 1966; W.H. Propp, *Exodus*, AB, 1999; J. Milgrom, *Leviticus*, AB, I, 1991; II, 2000; B.A. Levine, *Numbers*, AB, I, 1993; II, 2000.

Research

E. Otto, 'Forschungen zur Priesterschrift', *ThR* 62, 1997, 1-50.

2.1   The Priestly legislation begins with the arrival of the Israelites in the wilderness of Sinai and Moses' ascent of the mountain in Exod. 19.1; 24.16-18a.

In the third month after the people of Israel had gone forth out of the land of Egypt, on that day they came into the wilderness of Sinai. And the glory of Yhwh settled on Mount Sinai, and the cloud covered it six days, and on the seventh he called to Moses out of the midst of the cloud. Now the appearance of the glory of Yhwh was like a devouring fire on the top of the mountain in the sight of the people of Israel. And Moses entered the cloud, and went up on the mountain.

Three long sections follow this: (1) the instructions for building and establishing a sanctuary, the tent of meeting, and the literal implementation of this in Exod. 25–31 and 35–40; (2) the legislation 'from the tent of meeting' (Lev. 1.1) and/or on Mount Sinai (Lev. 7.37f.; 26.46 and 27.34) in Lev. 1–27; (3) the instructions and laws for 'setting out in the wilderness of Sinai in the tent of meeting', Num. 1–10, the setting out itself in Num. 10.11ff., and afterwards further laws on the way from the wilderness of Paran to the wilderness of Zin in Num. 10–20 (chs 15 and 18–19) and in the fields of Moab in Num. 26–36 (36.13).

After the instructions and the report on how they are carried out under (1), in Exod. 40.1-15 the command is given to set up the tabernacle: 'Yhwh said to Moses, "On the first day of the first month you shall erect the tabernacle of the tent of meeting ..."' In 40.16-33a the work is carried out, and in 40.33b it is completed: 'Thus did Moses; according to all that Yhwh commanded him, so he did. And on the first month in the second year, on the first day of the month, the tabernacle was erected ... So Moses finished the work.'

The legislation which begins in Lev. 1.1 under (2) is connected through Exod. 40.34-35, the fulfilment of Exod. 25.8; 29.45-46, with the building of the sanctuary. Exodus 29.45f.: 'And I will dwell among the people of Israel, and will be their God. And they shall know that I am Yhwh their God, who brought them forth out of the land of Egypt that I might dwell among them; I am Yhwh their God.' Exodus 40.34f. after the erection of the tabernacle in 40.16f.: 'Then the cloud covered the tent of meeting, and the glory of Yhwh filled the tabernacle. And Moses was not able to enter the tent of meeting, because the cloud abode upon it, and the glory of Yhwh filled the tabernacle.' Leviticus 1.1f.: 'Yhwh called to Moses, and spoke to him from the tent of meeting, saying: "Speak to the people of Israel, and say to them ..."' The lawgiving comprises the following parts: (a) the sacrificial laws of Lev. 1–7; (b) the appointment of Aaron as priest, the first sacrifice with a first incident and further priestly laws in Lev. 8–10; (c) the laws of cleanness in Lev. 11–15 and the Day of Atonement in Lev. 16, which in 16.1 takes up Lev. 10.1f.; (d) the laws about the holiness of cult and people, the so-called Holiness Code, in

Lev. 17–26, with an appendix in 27. The location of the revelation 'on' Mount Sinai in Lev. 7.37f.; 26.46; 27.34 clashes somewhat with Lev. 1.1; or is the thought simply of being physically close 'on' Mount Sinai?

The legislation in the wilderness which follows under (3) is combined with the account of the building of the tabernacle in Exod. 25–40, first by the heading in Num. 1.1 and secondly with the reference forward to the role of the cloud as a signal for setting out or stopping in Exod. 40.36-38 = Num. 9.15ff.:

Yhwh spoke to Moses in the wilderness of Sinai, in the tent of meeting, on the first day of the second month, in the second year after they had come out of Egypt, saying ... (Num. 1.1)

Whenever the cloud was taken up from over the tabernacle, the people of Israel would go onward, but if the cloud was not taken up, then they did not go onward till the day that it was taken up. For throughout all their journeys the cloud of Yhwh was upon the tabernacle by day, and the fire was in it by night, in the sight of all the house of Israel. (Exod. 40.36-37, 38)

On the day that the tabernacle was set up, the cloud covered the tabernacle, the tent of the testimony; and at evening it was over the tabernacle like the appearance of fire until morning. So it was continually; the cloud covered it [the tabernacle] by day, and the appearance of fire by night. And whenever the cloud was taken up from over the tent, after that the people of Israel set out, and in the place where the cloud settled down, there the people of Israel encamped ... (Num. 9.15ff.)

In the second year, in the second month, on the twentieth day of the month, the cloud was taken up from over the tabernacle of the testimony (that is, of the law), and the people of Israel set out by stages from the wilderness of Sinai, and the cloud settled down in the wilderness of Paran. (Num. 10.11f.)

The story of the spies in Num. 13f.[5] and, in so far as nothing else is said (Num. 14.45), the rest of Num. 15–19, the stories of the priests in Num. 16–17 and the lawgiving in Num. 15 and 18–19, taken account of in Num. 13f. and 16–17, is set in the wilderness of Paran, before in 20.1 the whole community reaches the wilderness of Zin, and in the present text Meribath-kadesh (cf. 20.13; 27.14). After that Israel has to go from Kadesh in the wilderness of Zin to Moab in Transjordan (Num. 2–24; 25.1), where again some laws are presented in Priestly style among all kinds of narratives and lists in Num. 25–36: Num. 28–30; 34–36. Numbers 36.13 concludes the whole section: 'These are the commandments and the ordinances which Yhwh commanded by Moses to the people of Israel in the plains of Moab by the Jordan at Jericho.'

2.2   The Priestly legislation in Exod. 19–31; 35–40; Lev. 1–27 and Num. 1.20; 25–36 is secondary in the framework of the overall text of Exodus–Numbers, but it is also by no means a unity in itself.

The assumption that – after the conclusion in Exod. 29.45f. – the further instructions in Exod. 30–31, the account of their implementation in Exod. 35–39 and great parts of Exod. 40 are additions is more or less undisputed. The main reason for this is the golden altar of incense which is added in Exod. 30–31 and presupposed in 35–40 (and Lev. 4f.), but at other points is absent or even unnecessary. In addition the secondary passages contain strikingly clear references back to Gen. 1, the beginning of the Priestly Writing: cf. Exod. 31.12ff.; 35.1ff., the sabbath (with Exod. 20.11); Exod. 39.42f., the concluding contemplation of the work and the blessing of the Israelites; Exod. 39.34 and 40.33, the completion of the work. That could be an indication that the Priestly Writing once ended at this point and on Sinai – in quite deliberate contrast to Exod. 20–24; 32–34 and Deuteronomy – originally contained no law but only the building of the sanctuary. The most radical solution is to reduce the text to the framework in Exod. 19.1; 24.16-18a; 25.1, 8f.; 40.16f., 33b and assign everything else to the secondary material.[6] If that is too radical, something may be added from Exod. 25–29. In that case the basic writing could have ended in Exod. 40.16f., 34 and has perhaps already been filled out in Exod. (25–29;) 30f. and 35–40, before in Leviticus–Numbers the law on Sinai and in the wilderness was attached as a continuation (Exod. 40.35 + Lev. 1.1ff.; Exod. 40.36-38 = Num. 9.15ff.) That at any rate the core of the Priestly Sinai pericope is to be found in Exod. 25–40 emerges from the fact that the law in Leviticus–Numbers everywhere presupposes the sanctuary and the indwelling of God, which fulfils the promise of God's being there for Israel.

As for the continuation in Leviticus–Numbers, following the analysis of Wellhausen and Noth, the pure legal texts, which have only a loose connection with the narrative or no connection at all, are excluded. These are Lev. 1–7; 11–15; 17–26 with an appendix in 27, the legal parts of the ordering of the camp in Num. 1–9 (5–6; 8.1-4; 9.1-14), the insertions in Num. 15; 18–19; and 28–30 and the narratives dependent on the law and the many lists in Num. 16–17; 25–26; and 31–36. To the basic writing called P[G] are assigned the appointment of Aaron as priest and the first sacrifice in Lev. 8–9, or even just the sacrifice in Lev. 9 (with or without the continuation in Lev. 10 and 16); with some exceptions also the departure in Num. 1.1–10.28, chiefly 10.11f.; the story of the spies in Num. 13–14; the narrative about the water of strife in Num. 20.1-13 and Aaron's death in 20.22-29; after that some notices about the journey which have been put together (for example, 21.4, 10f. and 22.1); the announcement of the death of Moses and the appointment of Joshua in Num. 27.12-23; and finally the death of Moses in Deut. 34.1, 7-9. The presupposition of this analysis is that P[G] was a purely narrative work and that everything to do with the law, the laws themselves and the model narrative for the law are to be attributed to the supplements called P[S]. Other scholars also include parts of the legislation in Leviticus in the original stratum of P and regard the interweaving of history and law in P as original. Recently, there has even been a desire to declare that everything is a unity through some overarching structures and word-links, like the covenant formula in Gen. 17; Exod. 6; 29.45-46; Lev. 11.44f.; 19.2; 20.26; 22.31-33; 25.38; 26.11f., 42-45; Num. 15.40f. or echoes of the regulations about clean and unclean animals in the instructions about food in Gen. 1 and 9. 'And what different complexes of tradition fit together into a closed compositional whole under this "world-historical" horizon!'[7] However, the problem lies in the need to explain, over and above a superficial description of the text, how such different complexes of tradition found a place 'under this "world-historical" horizon' and also why the 'horizon' is not the same everywhere.

The problem is best approached by the redactional juncture in Exod. 40.34-38, which combines the conclusion of the account of the building in 40.16f. with its continuation. As we have already seen, 40.34-35 serves as a hinge between Exod. 25–29 (25.8; 29.45-46) and the revelation of the laws to Moses in Lev. 1ff.; by contrast, Exod. 40.36-38 serves as a hinge between Exod. 25–40 and the setting out from Sinai and further wandering through the wilderness in Num. 1ff. or 9.15ff. Both the premature reference to Num. 9–10 in Exod. 40.36-38, which interrupts the connection between 40.35 and Lev. 1.1 and the resumption in 9.15ff., which repeats and extends Exod. 40.34-38, indicate that considerable work has been done at the transition from Exod. 40.16f. to Num. 10.11f. Two possibilities arise from this: either the continuation of the account of the building (with its conclusion in Exod. 40.16f., 34) initially contained only the law (Exod. 40.35 + Lev. 1–26) and was then supplemented in Num. 1ff. by the wandering in the wilderness (in the course of this also by Exod. 40.36-38 and Num. 9.15ff.), or the wandering in the wilderness in Num. (1ff.), 10; 11f.; and 13ff. is the earlier continuation of Exod. 40.16f., 34 and has been interrupted by the insertion of the laws in Exod. 40.35/Lev. 1.1ff. (and Numbers) and therefore also has been once again announced by way of an addition in Exod. 40.35-38.

The first possibility is supported by the fact that with Lev. 26 a certain conclusion is reached after the first break in Exod. 40, which moreover resembles Exod. 23 and Deut. 28. The second is supported by the fact that the law from Lev. 18 on clearly focuses on the imminent settlement and thus precisely on what begins with the departure from Sinai in Num. (1ff.;)10; 11f. and is referred to by the introductory formulae in Num. 15.2,17. Only there is no real end for the wandering in the wilderness in the Priestly text, whereas Lev. 26 (27) with the prospect on the imminent settlement, the loss of the land and God's renewed care can stand by itself. Therefore the assumption that the account of the building in Exod. 25–40 has been initially expanded by the law in Lev. 1–26(; 27) and afterwards by the accounts of the settlement and various other laws in Num. 1–36 is more probable.

2.3   However, neither the law nor the narrative is a literary unity. First of all the law: Lev. 1–7 focus on the priestly ordination which follows and the first properly performed sacrifice in Lev. 8–9, but offer only a very much more extended repetition of the regulations for sacrifice that have already been given and thus interrupt the context of the implementation in Lev. 8–9 with the instructions in Exod. 29 and 40.1-15. Leviticus 10 is a secondary appendix to Lev. 9 and is taken further in 16.1ff. Leviticus 11–15, where Moses and Aaron or Moses alone are addressed, are pushed in between Lev. 10 and 16 and evidently seek to be understood with Lev. 16 as a prelude to Lev. 17–26 (27) under the overriding theme of 'sanctification', the condition for Yhwh's being God for Israel. In particular the various forms of the acceptance and variation of the covenant formula from Gen. 17.7f. and Exod. 6.7 show that each time the promise is set against new literary 'horizons' though, as is usual in developments, the different 'horizons' do not of course exclude one another but fuse with one another. If the covenant promise originally finds its goal in the indwelling of God in the sanctuary in Exod. 25–40 (Exod. 25.8; 29.45f.; 40.34), in the Holiness Code (Lev. 20.26; 22.31-33; 25.38, 55; 26.11f., 42-45) it is combined with paraenesis. Again the anticipation of holiness (paraenesis) and covenant in the framework of the laws of cleanness in Lev. 11–15 (11.44f.) opens up a new 'horizon'; the resumption in Num. 15.40f. makes its own way – it is very inappropriate after the conclusion in Lev. 26 and therefore mostly goes by the board – to conclude the reminiscences of Lev. 17–26 (and Lev. 4), which in future are to be recalled by the tassels from Deut. 22.12 (Num. 15.37ff.), on the occasion of the failed attempt at settlement in Num. 13f.

If we leave the interludes out of consideration, only the priestly ordination of Leviticus and the first sacrifice in Lev. 8–9 or the Holiness Code in Lev. 17–26 qualify as the original stratum of Leviticus and the continuation of the account of the building in Exod. 25–40. In both cases we have further developments of the account which in Exod. 29.42-46 expand, and at the end each in their own way take up, the conclusion of the account of the building in Exod. 40.34 (Lev. 9.23f.; 26.11f., 42-45). The report of the implementation in Lev. 8 relates to the instructions in Exod. 29 – for their part added in Exod. 25–29 – as Exod. 35–39 relate to 25–31, and is thus secondary.[8] With the date in v. 1, Lev. 9 is dependent on the seven days of Lev. 8 and introduces the interests of 'the people' in the immediate cultic event, which are hardly taken note of either before or afterwards. It thus mediates the presence and inaccessibility of the glory of Yhwh in the tent (Exod. 40.34f.) to the people with the presence and appearance (Exod. 9.42-46).[9] Leviticus 17–26 adds to the sanctification by God himself (Exod. 29.43f.) the demand for holiness, that is, paraenesis; as is generally conceded, it is recognizable as a special piece in P by that alone. As the sacrificial regulations given in Lev. 17 for Aaron, his sons and all the

Israelites do not yet seem to know anything about the first sacrifice in Lev. 8–9, the Holiness Code in Lev. 17–26 gets the priority. Leviticus 17.1 attaches seamlessly to Exod. 40.34, unless originally the Holiness Code was headed with Exod. 40.35/Lev. 1.1 instead of Lev. 17.1.

2.4   After the law, we turn to the narrative. Numbers 1.1–10.10 prepares for the departure in 10.11f., 13-28. The original stratum of this chapter is to be found in the ordering of the camp and the Levites in Num.1–4; 7; 8.5ff. Unlike previously, the people of the Israelites goes to the camp, and the tribe of Levi and the levites are distinguished from the Aaronide (and therefore levitical) priests as a separate group of temple servants. Really the book of Numbers should have been called 'Leviticus'. These differences already prove sufficiently that Num. 1–9 is later than the account of the building in Exod. 20–25 and the law in Leviticus. Mixed laws are interspersed, which perhaps only repeat and vary what is already in Leviticus, but presuppose the ordering of the camp, that is, the present context. There are also many repetitions and explanations within the original ordering of the camp and the levites; these seem to have been added in stages: compare only the list of the tribes in 1.4-16 with the more extended one in 1.17-47, which deviates in its order and competes with Num. 2, especially in 1.44-47 (with a corresponding addition in 1.48-54); and 2.32-33, or the call of the levites in 3.5-13, with the extended taking down of the camp first in 3.14-51, then in ch. 4. Numbers 7 and 8.5ff. are dependent on chs 1–4, but – anticipating 9.15 – are chronologically out of order (7.1) and direct attention back to the setting up of the sanctuary in Exod. 40. Numbers 8.5ff. imitates the priestly ordination in Lev. 8 for the levites. The reference back to Exod. 40.34f.(, 36-38) in Num. 9.15-23 is likewise secondary, but older than the appendices in Num. 5–9; it is pushed between the inspection of the people in Num. 1–4 and the departure in 10.11ff., in order also to explain the leading by the cloud as the rule for obedience to the law. The trumpets of 10.1-10 as a signal for departure compete somewhat with the cloud of 9.15-28. Finally, 10.13-28 are a supplement to 10.11f., which is dependent on Num. 2 and makes one think that the taking down of the camp in Num. 1.1–10.10 as a whole could be secondary by comparison with the simple notice about setting out in 10.11f.

The way of the cloud and with it of the Israelites after their 'departures' (cf. Exod. 40.36-38/Num. 10.11f.) initially leads from the wilderness of Sinai into the wilderness of Paran. In Num. 10.29–12.16, the cloud makes a detour of three days' journey far from Sinai into the wilderness (10.33f.), and via Tabera (11.3) the people reach Kibroth-hattaavah and Hazeroth in the wilderness of Paran (11.35; 12.1, 16). The detour interrupts the original connection between Num. 10.11f. and Num. 13f., and is evidently an insertion. The original Priestly stratum of the story of the spies in Num.

13f.[10] indicates a settlement directly from the south towards Judah. However, this is unsuccessful; it comes to grief on the bad reports about the land from the spies and the lack of faith on the part of the Israelites. This failure, which seems very surprising after all that has gone before in Exod. 25–Num. 10, has largely been interpreted as a warning against similar voices in the Diaspora and a desire to return to the land. But what kind of an appeal would it be that punishes the hesitation and doubt of the dispersion with the death penalty? One only has to set Isaiah 40–66 or the text about giving in Ezek. 36.1-15 against this to recognize very quickly that this can hardly have been the original intention. Rather, the generation of Moses must commit a grave sin and be punished, and in the end even die; it belongs among the calumniators of Ezek. 36 only because according to the existing narrative of the settlement in Num. 20–24 and Joshua it enters the land without Moses and not on the direct way from the south, which lies closest to post-exilic Judah, but from the East. Even if the explicit reason for the detour by the Sea of Reeds and the east is given only in supplements (14.25, 39-45), the original stratum in Num. 13f., which counters the story of the spies in Josh. 2, is comprehensible only in the light of the continuation of the wilderness wandering in the non-Priestly text of Num. 20–24. The theme of the settlement has prompted the communication of corresponding laws in Num. 15 (15.1f., 17f.).

Before the continuation of chs 13–14 (and 15) follows in Num. 20, in Num. 16–19 we have the story of Dathan and Abiram and its developments, which increase the sin of Num. 13f. It is told in three versions which build on one another, that is, by successive accumulation: (1) Dathan and Abiram rebel against Moses' leadership, heighten the opposition of the people in Num. 13f., and are severely punished for this (vv. 12-15, 25-34); (2) (Korah and) Dathan and Abiram and the Reubenite On take 250 leading men and protest against the sole priesthood of Moses and Aaron; they lose the test over the sacrifice (vv. 1-7, 16-24, 35); (3) Korah and the levites rebel against the priesthood of Aaron (additions in vv. 5, 6, 7b-11, 16-24, 32, 33).[11] The story has been given further additions in Num. 17–18 which confirm the authority of Moses and the priesthood of Aaron and again regulate the rights and duties of priests and levites. By contrast, Num. 19 looks rather to Num. 20.1, 22f., the death and burial of Miriam and Aaron, and therefore at this point introduces some rites of purification, especially in the case of contact with a dead body.

Like Num. 13–14, the original continuation of the wandering in the wilderness in Num. 20.1-13 is not independent. From the wilderness of Paran (or Hormah, 14.45) it goes into the wilderness of Zin. Here the rebellion against Moses and Aaron of Num. 13f. (and 16?) is repeated, this time on the model of Exod. 17.1-7, in connection with the lack of water. Again the reason why Moses and Aaron may not enter the land (v. 12) is perhaps secondary. But whether one sees the basic version ending in v. 12 or v. 13, here too it already presupposes the non-Priestly text and therefore the detour by Transjordan in Num. 20.14ff. For the goal of the narrative, the demonstration of the 'holiness' of Yhwh (*qdš*, hiphil or niphal) at the waters of strife ('waters of Meribah') in 20.12-13, is quite simply a theological aetiology of the oasis of Kadesh, where according to the existing non-Priestly text 20.1aβb, Israel camps, Miriam dies and is buried, and from where in 20.14ff. Moses sends the messengers to the king of Edom. Similarly the death of Aaron in 20.22-29 presupposes the topographical note in 20.1aβb and the non-Priestly connection in the text, which originally led directly from Kadesh, going round Edom (20.14-21), to the region between the Arnon and the Jabbok (21.21ff.), and is now interrupted by the detour via Mount Hor in 20.22ff.; 21.4ff. (with a resumption of 20.21 in 21.4 corresponding to 14.25) and the list of stations in 21.10-20, which geographically goes much too far.

Finally, the change of place of Num. 20–24 is also presupposed by 27.12-23, originally perhaps only vv. 12-13a, the germ of the whole section in Num. 25–36, which is located in the fields of Moab, reached in Num. 20–24. The announcement looks forward to the death of Moses in Deut. 34 and introduces the farewell discourse, Deuteronomy. The geography (the indefinite hill-country of Abarim) and the scene in 27.12f. form a link between 22.1; 23.14; 25.1 (the summit of Pisgah in the fields of Moab by Shittim); and Deut. 34.1, 6 (the summit of Pisgah in the fields of Moab in the valley opposite Beth-peor). The continuation in Num. 27.13f. forms a link beyond Num. 20–24 between Num. 20.1-13, 22-29 (vv. 12, 24) and Deut. 34. Finally, like Deut. 31 (vv. 3b, 7f., 14f., 23), Num. 27.15-23 is already thinking beyond Moses' death to his successor. It is no coincidence that after some material has been inserted in Numbers, this passage is picked up twice: the recollection in Deut. 3.21f., 23-29 assimilates it to Deut. 31–34; the repetition in Deut. 32.48-52, shortly before the beginning of the scene of Moses' death, assimilates this in Deut. 31–34 to Num. 27.12f.

Moreover the mention of the gift of the land and the appointment of Joshua as successor in Num. 25–36 has set in motion an enormous avalanche of development. Even the most dogged critics of literary criticism and defenders of a unitary Priestly redaction in the Pentateuch, or at least a redaction which is treated as a unity, are overwhelmed by it. In other words: there is more or less a consensus that the material in Num. 26–36 is secondary. In ch. 26 the development presents a new inspection of the people (cf. Num. 1f.) for the purpose of dividing out the land (vv. 52-56); to this the special case of the daughters of Zelophehad in 27.1-11, which already presupposes Num. 16 (v. 3) – added on the basis of 26.33 – meaningfully attaches itself. After the invitation to view the land and the appointment of Joshua in 27.12-23, accordingly there follow in Num. 33.50-

56 + Num. 34–36 the instructions to divide the land, again in ch. 36 with the special case of the daughters of Zelophehad of the tribe of Manasseh, from 27.1-11. The information is for the most part taken from the book of Joshua. After an appropriate question, Num. 32 (and 34.13-15) add a further special case, the distribution of the land east of the Jordan to the two and a half tribes; here in vv. 7ff. there is a recollection of Num. 13f., as there is in 27.1f. of Num. 16. Whether this special tradition, which deviates in some respects, is older, as most assume, or perhaps after all younger than its parallels in Num. 34.14f.; Deut. 3.12ff.; Josh. 1; 13 and 22.1-6, is not settled. The list in Num. 33 does not yet seem to be known by the summary list of stages in Num. 33 drawn up by Moses himself, which recapitulates the route from Exod. 12 to here before the distribution of the land. Finally, the episodes in Num. 25 and 31 also have to do with the settlement and Joshua's wars. In the apocryphal passage 25.1b-5, in combination with 23.28 (Peor), the camp of Shittim in 25.1a, from where in Josh. 2.1; 3.1 Israel crosses the Jordan to the promised land, quite surprisingly becomes a place of sin. The mixing with the Moabite women, which results in the downfall of Baal-peor and thus the transgression of the first commandment in the fields of Moab, vividly shows the danger posed by the situation after the settlement (cf. Deut. 12.8ff.) that is urgently warned against by Exod. 23.20-33; 34.10ff. and Deuteronomy at many points, especially Deut. 7.1ff. This again becomes the problem in Judg. 3.5f. Because it may not burden the settlement, the sin must be obliterated before the inspection of the people and the instructions about dividing the land in Num. 26ff. The development in 25.6ff., which expands 25.1-5 and with 25.1-9 also comes to stand clearly before this inspection, and the development of the theme in Num. 31 (with 25.16-18), which already presupposes 27.12ff. (cf. 31.1f.), transfer the conflict – for whatever reasons, perhaps on the basis of an association with Jerubbaal in Judg. 6–8 – to the Midianites. It is hard to say whether or not Num. 31 already knows the insertion of the laws in Num. 28–30: 31.1f. immediately picks up 27.12f.

To recapitulate: the original thread of P, interwoven with a wealth of expansions, runs from Num. (1ff.;) 10.11f. through chs 13f. and 20.1-13 to 20.22-29 and 27.12-13, but is already secondary by comparison with the account of the building in Exod. 25–40 and the law in Lev. 1–27 (originally 17–26), and always presupposes as a literary context the non-Priestly wandering through the wilderness in Num. 20–24; and in 27.12ff. also Deuteronomy (and Joshua) which follows. Everything else consists of later and very late additions in the framework of Genesis–Kings or the Pentateuch.

2.5   The result of the analysis – which of course has been far too summary – implies an answer to the questions discussed by scholars as to where the original end of the Priestly Writing lies and how far we may reckon with an independent Priestly Writing.

There is controversy over the end of the Priestly Writing. Some scholars still find it in the book of Joshua, for example, in Josh. 4.19; 5.10-12; 14.1f.; 18.1; 19.51,[12] in order to preserve a complete narrative thread. Noth[13] made the necessary objections to that view and demonstrated that these are additions in the Priestly style which presuppose the bringing together of P and the non-Priestly text in Genesis–Numbers and the combination of Genesis–Joshua. So for a long time the death of Moses in Deut. 34.1, 7-9 was regarded as the end of P. However, this assumption, too, has proved false. Here likewise we have additions which mix Deuteronomic-Deuteronomistic and Priestly material and presuppose or constitute the finished Pentaeuch.[14] That leaves only the three possibilities indicated: (1) the conclusion of the founding of the sanctuary on Sinai in Exod. 40; (2) the conclusion of the legislation on Sinai in Lev. 26(; 27); (3) the conclusion of the wilderness wandering somewhere in the wilderness of the book of Numbers: in the wilderness of Paran (Num. 10.11f.; 13f.); in the wilderness of Zin (Num. 20.1-13, 22-29); or in the fields of Moab (Num. 25–36). It has proved that (1) is a first, (2) a second, and (3) not a proper conclusion.

The position has to do with the fact that the Priestly Writing forms a literary unity with the non-Priestly text in Genesis–Numbers. It is beyond dispute that this unity is secondary, but there is a dispute as to whether the Priestly Writing was composed a priori for the non-Priestly context or came into being separately and was worked together with it only later. The conclusion under (1), the end of the foundation of the sanctuary on Sinai in Exod. 40, together with the secondary additions in Exod. 25–40, can immediately be imagined in a separate writing which, while it knows the non-Priestly covenant on Sinai in Exod. 20–24 (and 32–24) and presumably also its renewal in Moab in Deuteronomy, quite deliberately replaces it by the story of the foundation of the sanctuary. I see the end of the basic document P[G] here.

The secondary extension of the law by Lev. 1–27 with the conclusion in Lev. 26 (and appendix in ch. 27) is also immediately conceivable in a separate writing. Granted, the knowledge of the revelation of the law on Sinai (Exod. 20–24; 32–34) and in Moab (Deut.) is presupposed, this is now also received positively in a Priestly way and combined with the foundation of the sanctuary on Sinai – which for the first time competes with it. Just as Deuteronomy is a novella of the Book of the Covenant in Exod. 20–23 (more on this below), so the Priestly law in Leviticus is a novella of Deuteronomy.

That is the case particularly with the Holiness Code of Lev. 17–26,[15] which reformulates Deuteronomy in the spirit and style of the Priestly writing and in my view stands at the beginning of the literary development in Leviticus. Until recently the strange mixture of P and Deuteronomy has been explained by saying that the Holiness Code is an originally independent collection of the law which was subsequently taken into the Priestly narrative and in the course of this was heavily revised. The correct insight here is the observation of the special position of Lev. 17–26 (27) by comparison with the basic writing of P: the assumption of former independence is wrong. The Holiness Code lacks an independent beginning; the historicization, that is, the projection back into the time of Moses and the tent of meeting, is already given in the basic material of Lev. 17 (cf. 19.21; 24.3); and the equally well-established differences and common features with P, which cannot be resolved by literary criticism, are explained much better with the supplementary hypothesis proposed by Karl Elliger.[16] This assumes that Lev. 17–26 (27) were conceived a priori for the context of the Priestly Writing, regardless of earlier legal material which may have found its way in here, and later additions. Moreover the same goes for the laws in Lev. 1–7 and 11–15. They too have their own prehistory and go back to earlier rituals, perhaps also smaller collections. But the sacrificial laws also presuppose the historicization and show the stylizing of sacrifice throughout as a sin offering, which is typical of P. The laws of cleanness are linked with the context above all by headings and endings (cf. the announcement in 10.10 and the brackets 11.44f.; 15.31) and by the concept of the 'camp', but as a whole seem less touched by P than Lev. 1–7 and to have grown either before or after their acceptance. Here too there are isolated parallels with the Book of the Covenant in Exod. 20–23 and Deuteronomy, cf. Lev. 11 = Deut. 14.

Precisely because of the orientation on Deuteronomy and the parallel endings in Exod. 23; Lev. 26 and Deut. 28, we can of course ask whether the Holiness Code in Lev. 16–27 and everything else in Lev. 1–15 was not after all already conceived for the literary combination of P^G in Exod. 25–40 with the non-Priestly text in Exod. 19–24 (+ 32–34) + Deuteronomy. Beyond doubt, as a provisional revelation of the law, together with Exod. 19–40 located on Sinai and then proclaimed publicly in Moab in Deuteronomy, it fits admirably into the narrative context and was also doubtless once used in that way. But since the narrative links are made only in Numbers, namely, through Num. 10.11f. and 27.12ff., I think it more probable that the insertion into the narrative context of the Pentateuch of the Holiness Code, which came into being within the framework of the Priestly Writing, took place only at a second stage. This could also be supported by the fact that at least in Exod. 35–40; Lev. 8f.; 16.34; 21.24; 23.44; and 24.23 the view prevails that Moses first gave the Israelites the instructions and laws revealed to him by God (as in Exod. 24.3-8; 34.31f.) at a particular place, that is, on Sinai, and not first in the land of Moab. Thus Leviticus 26 (27) marks the end of an expanded Priestly Writing which is still independent but, in Exod. 25–40 and Leviticus, is expanded by the law, among other things with details of the cult, above all the notion of atonement which is now dominant, that is, the end of P^S.

The original stratum and the expansions in Numbers are different. Here it has been proved that the earliest narrative thread of P in Num. (1ff.;) 10; 11ff; 13f.; 20.1-13, 22-29; and 27.12-23 already presupposes the non-Priestly context of Num. 20–24(; 25.1a) + Deut.(; Josh.; Judg.). Here P is clearly a redactional stratum which was not viable at all without the context and ended in nothing. Expressed in sigla, that means that the Priestly Writing in Numbers is something like R or even R^P. In its footsteps follow the many supplementers who gradually fill out the narrative context in Numbers with further stories of sins which have a Priestly-Deuteronomic tone (Num. 11f.; 16–18; 25; 31), lists and instructions in the context of the settlement (Num. 1–10; 26.1-27.11; 32; 33; 33.50-54[2] + 34–36), and further legislative material (Num. 5–9; 15; 19; 28–30). For the sake of simplicity, in what follows I shall not distinguish between the first redaction and the supplements in R, but characterize with superior letters only the literary environment from which the many different supplements come.

The fillings-out do not immediately fit into the existing system, according to which Moses in Deuteronomy recapitulates the stories and laws of Exod. 19–Num. 24 (in the supplements Deut. 3.12-20, also Num. 32; 34.13-15). The legislation 'in the wilderness' between Sinai and Zin (Num. 1–19; cf. 1.1; 15.40f.) and in the fields of Moab (Num. 25–36, cf. 36.13 after Lev. 26.46; 27.34), that is, where the proclamation of the law of Sinai/ Horeb is also located in Deuteronomy, tends rather to compete with them, especially as it reaches out beyond the death of Moses to Josh. 13ff. (and Judg. 6–8). At the same time, the laws in Numbers are always given only to Moses to hand on to the Israelites, and are not published either here or in Deuteronomy. That means one of two things. Either the supplementers regarded Deuteronomy (implicitly) also as a proclamation of the laws that they had added in Numbers. This could be supported by the complicated and over-full heading in Deut. 1.1-5, which surveys the whole stretch of the way from Horeb (the mountain and wilderness of Sinai) via Kadesh (the wilderness of Zin) to the land of Moab, that is, all three eras of the lawgiving (Sinai, wilderness, Moab). Or they thought that the individual stages of the revelation of the law (at Sinai, in the wilderness, in the fields of Moab, supplemented from Horeb in the land of Moab) added up to a totality of the Torah which was revealed by God to Moses and communicated by him to the Israelites on various occasions. The recapitulation of Exodus–Numbers in Deut. 1–3 and the repetition of Num. 27.12ff. in Deut. 32.48ff, which together with the supplements in Num. 26–36 constitute the limits of the book, could support this. Probably some thought the former and others the latter. The (pre-Qumran) Temple

Table B.I.1

P^G	P^s	R^P	
Genesis–Exodus P		Genesis–Exodus PJE	
Exod. 25–29			
	30–31	JE 32–34	
	35–39		
40.16-17, 33b, 34	40.1-34		
	40.35	40.36-38	
Lev.	1–7		
	8–10		
	11–15		
	16		
	17–26; 27		
Num.		(1ff.)	1.1–10.10
		10.11-12	10.13-28
		10.29–12.16	
		13–14	
		15	
		16–18	
		19	
		JE 20.1	
		20.1-13	
		JE 20.14-21	
		20.22-29	
			21.1-3
		21.4a	21.4b-9
			21.10-20
		JE 21.21-24	21.25-35
		JE 22.1–25.1a	
		25.1b-5, 6ff.	
		26.1–27.11	
		27.12-23	
		28–36	
		Deuteronomy	

Scroll, which demonstrably underwent a lengthy process of redaction,[17] has solved the problem only a little later, or more or less contemporaneously, in its own way: it transforms Moses' speech in Deuteronomy into a speech by God and puts it after Exod. 34 as a revelation on Sinai, together with instructions for the building of the temple which to some degree replace the Priestly account of the building in Exod. 35–40, and other laws from Leviticus–Numbers, which with Deuteronomy flow into one.

2.6   Summary: P^G (the independent basic writing) can be found in the original stratum of Exod. 25–40, P^S (additions within the framework of the still independent Priestly Writing) in the addition of the law in Lev. 17–26 and the supplements in Exod. 25–40; Lev. 1–16; and 27, R^P (supplements in the literary context of Genesis–Kings and the Pentateuch) in Num. 10.11f.; 13f.; 20.1-13, 22-29; 27.12-23 and the elaborations in Num. 1–10(; 11–12); 15–19; 25–36.[18] As in the case of the distinction between the first and second Chronicler, I regard a summary of the many expansions in the collective designations of the main stages as practical, but think that there is no point in increasing the number of sigla, provided that it is made clear that the secondary strata (here P^S and R^P) do not come from the same hand but from many hands and have grown up over generations. The *terminus a quo* must, however, be the Second Temple, for which the basic writing provides the theological programme – transcending the actual circumstances.

3.   Deuteronomy

Wellhausen, *Composition*, 186-208, 353-63; G. Hölscher, 'Komposition und Ursprung des Deuteronomiums', *ZAW* 40, 1922, 161-255; Noth, *Überlieferungsgeschichtliche Studien*, 12-18, 27-40; T. Veijola (ed.), *Das Deuteronomium und seine Querbeziehungen*, SESJ 62, 1996; J.P. Sonnet, *The Book within the Book: Writing in Deuteronomy*, BIS 14, 1997; E. Otto, *Das Deuteronomium*, BZAW 284, 1999; id., *Das Deuteronomium im Pentateuch und Hexateuch*, FAT 30, 2000; R.G. Kratz and H. Spieckermann (eds), *Liebe und Gebot: Studien zum Deuteronomium (FS L. Perlitt)*, FRLANT 190, 2000.

Commentaries

C. Steuernagel, HKJ I/3,1, ²1923; Braulik, NEB 15, 1986; NEB 28, 1992; E. Nielsen, HAT I.6, 1995; L. Perlitt, BK 5, 1990ff.; M. Weinfeld, AB, 1991.

On research

H.D. Preuss, *Deuteronomium*, EdF 164, 1982; id., 'Zum deuteronomistischen Geschichtswerk', *ThR* 58, 1993, 230-45; C. Houtman, *Der Pentateuch*, Contributions to Biblical Exegesis and Theology 9, Kampen 1994, 279-342; T. Veijola, 'Deuteronomismusforschung zwischen Tradition und Innovation (I)', *ThR* 67, 2002, 273-327.

3.1   The 'Second Law', as the fifth book of the Torah is called after the
translation of Deut. 17.18 in the Septuagint and the Vulgate, is the key to
the solution of the literary problem of the bracketing together of the books
of Genesis–Numbers, the Tetrateuch or Pentateuch, with the Former
Prophets, the books of Joshua–Kings, which after the dissection by Noth
are said to form an independent historical work. If we remove the Priestly
law in Exodus–Numbers (above, 2), the structure of the text is as follows.
After their exodus from Egypt in Exod. 1–14, on their wandering through
the wilderness (Exod. 15–18), the Israelites reach Sinai, where Moses
receives the law from Yhwh and twice obliges Israel to observe it (Exod.
19–24 and 32–34). Further stations are Kadesh, where Miriam dies and is
buried (Num. 20.1aβb), and, after some forced detours, lastly Shittim in the
fields of Moab (Num. 20.14ff.; 21.21ff.; 22–24; 25.1a). There is a
widespread view that here the old pre-Priestly thread, the 'glorious
narrative book' of the Yahwist (J) and the narrative of the Jehovist (JE)
expanded by E (the Elohist or supplements), breaks off.[19] However, the
thread does not break off, but is spun further, not in Numbers or even in
Deuteronomy, but in Josh. 2.1; 3.1, where Joshua sends out spies from
Shittim into the promised land and Israel crosses the Jordan. Deuteronomy
stands in between. On various occasions Deut. 1–11 looks back to the
history in Exodus–Numbers, and with the appointment of Joshua and the
death of Moses elements in Deut. 31–34 prepare for the continuation of the
history in Joshua–Kings. In Deut. 12–30 the law – which is in literary
dependence on Exod. 20–23 – is finally proclaimed publicly once again and
the people are obliged to observe it by the conclusion of a covenant. I
pointed out in the introduction to this book that one cannot simply attach
Deuteronomy to one side or the other. Thus the question arises where it
originally belongs and how it has come into its present literary position as a
bridge between Numbers and Joshua in the framework of the Enneateuch
(Genesis–Kings).

In his 1805 dissertation de Wette[20] demonstrated, at the same time as
Johann Severin Vater, that Deuteronomy is to be separated from the
preceding books of the Pentateuch and is the work of another, later author.
In so doing he disputed its Mosaic authorship, and only a little later, for
this and other reasons, concluded that Deuteronomy is not only identical
with the law rediscovered and applied by 2 Kgs 22–23 but belongs in this
period. De Wette already conceded that the book which was found need
not have been the existing Deuteronomy in its full extent. Wellhausen went
in search of the literary core and distinguished between the law in Deut.
12–26 and a twofold framework in Deut. 1–4/27 and Deut. 5–11/28–30.
With Vater he found the original law, which he designated Ur-
Deuteronomy, in Deut. 12–26.[21] These are the two essential points with
which scholars are still concerned: the separation out of Ur-Deuteronomy

and its relation to the so-called Josianic reform. In addition there is the question of the literary incorporation of Deuteronomy into the Pentateuch, which is usually neglected.[22]

3.2   The distinction between the framework and the law is fundamental to the analysis of Deuteronomy. It arises out of a simple observation. Deuteronomy is stylized as a speech of Moses in the land of Moab. The repeated headings in 1.1-5; 4.44–5.1 (4.1; 6.1; 12.1 differ), the concluding sentence in 28.69, the new beginnings of the speech in 27.1, 9, 11; 29.1, and the narrative parts in 4.41-43; 31–34 (with further parts of the speech) fall out of this stylization. With the reference to the written book 'of this Torah' in 28.58, 61; 30.10 (17.18 is similar), sometimes a standpoint is also adopted within the discourse which clearly lies outside the stylization as a speech of Moses and presupposes the narrative note in 31.9. With the expression 'this Torah', which occurs only here and in chs 1–4 but not in chs 5–26, like chs 28f., ch. 27, too, looks back on the preceding speech. Thus the speech of Moses is clearly demarcated backwards by the narrative which begins again in ch. 27, the introductions to the speech and the narrative style in 27–28; 29–30; 31–34, and ends once at 26.19. The situation in the earlier part, where the stylization as a speech is consistently maintained only from ch. 5, is similar. Here, however, it should be noted that as already in chs 1–4, so also in chs 5–11 Moses constantly only announces the presentation of the law, and in constant admonitions to obedience prepares for a law which has not yet been communicated, but only materializes in ch. 12. So within the speech of Moses in Deut. 5–26 we must once again distinguish between the preliminary discourses in chs 5–11 and the corpus of the law in chs 12–26; here, in the corpus of the law, Moses is not explicitly mentioned as the speaker.

After all this the core of the Deuteronomic law is to be found in chs 12–26. The framework in chs 1–11 and 27–34, which consists in 1–11 of prior speeches, in 27–34 in further speeches and narrative, stands apart from this. With the further speeches in chs 27–30 and the narrative in chs 31–34 the closing passages indicate an internal and an external framework. In substance, but not in style, the historical retrospect in Deut. 1–3 has points of contact with the narrative parts of the external framework in chs 31–34; the legal paraenesis of Deut. (4;) 5–11 with the further speeches of the inner framework in chs 27–30.

The core and the framework are in some respects related to each other; here the law in its substance, that is, apart from traces of secondary revision, makes sense without the framework, but the framework does not make sense without the law. That allows the conclusion that the framework is secondary to the law in literary terms. The difference between the internal and external framework already indicates that the expansion did not take place all at once. Wellhausen and others reckoned with different editions of Deuteronomy which came into being independently of one another. By contrast, Gustav Hölscher made it clear that both the relationship between the core and the framework and also the internal stratification of the law and the framework are most easily explained by the supplementary hypothesis, that is, the assumption of a gradual literary extension of the core from the inside outwards.

3.3   If we look more closely, it very soon proves that the literary core in Deut. 12–26 also combines much that did not originally belong together. No one has yet found a meaningful order in the present material, nor can one probably be found. All that is clear is the caesura in 16.17, 18, which separates the cult and the law from one another; in addition there is a certain preponderance of family law in chs 21–25. After that we can very roughly speak of a division into three: 1. 12.1–16.17, laws about the cult; 2. 16.18–21.9, laws about offices; 3. 21.10–25.19, family laws and a mixture of laws. Deuteronomy 26 spans an arch back to the laws about the cult at the beginning, and to the regulations about the tithe in 14.22ff. The conjecture which has often been made that the sequence of laws or blocks of laws follows the structure of the Decalogue has to reckon with too many exceptions, and arises, if at all, only for a late edition and not for the basic state of the material. However, opinions differ as to whether Deuteronomy came into being by strata or blocks. Some reckon with basic material running right through which has been successively expanded and filled in; others think that only the cultic legislation in 12.1–16.17 is original, and all the rest has been added. In fact both views are right: a basic writing has been successively enlarged and expanded with additions.

One can use three quite clear and widely recognized criteria provided by the text itself for separating out the basic writing, Ur-Deuteronomy. These are:

1. The change of number in the form of address.[23] The address in the second person singular is primary by comparison with the address in the second person plural, but not every second person singular is original. The original stratum in the singular has been expanded by additions both in the plural and in the singular.

2. The relationship to the Book of the Covenant in Exod. 20.22–23.33, which served Deuteronomy as a literary model.[24] However, the Book of the Covenant has a history of its own, indicated not least by the change in number which can also be encountered here. It may have been available to Ur-Deuteronomy, written in the singular, in the form of a second-person-singular revision which is the framework in Exod. 20.24-26 and

22.20–23.19 to the earlier collection of *mišpāṭîm* in Exod. 21.(1,) 12–22.19. The secondary additions to the Book of the Covenant already shape the basic stratum in Deuteronomy. Subsequently both corpora received additions in the second person plural and the second person singular (Exod. 20.22f.; 23.20-33). Therefore at this point the qualification applies that not every allusion to the Book of the Covenant is original, and conversely Ur-Deuteronomy can also have contained laws which were not present in its model. So neither the change of number nor the comparison with the Book of the Covenant brings final clarity. For this we depend on 3.

3. Dependence on a criterion of tendency criticism, the notion of the centralization of the cult which dominates everything.[25] In particular by comparison with the Book of the Covenant (especially Exod. 20.24), and also the rest of the ancient Near Eastern legal tradition, the demand made programmatically in Deut. 12 that sacrifice shall be offered only at the one place chosen by Yhwh proves to be the specific feature of the Deuteronomic law. The demand for centralization is the motif which is the impetus towards the amendment of the older book of the law and in fact governs the changes. It is the main law of Ur-Deuteronomy and as such a positive criterion for literary division superior to all other possibilities.

Therefore what belongs to Ur-Deuteronomy and what does not is not decided either by reconstructed pre-Deuteronomistic collections in Deut. 12–26 or by the supposed external evidence from Hittite and Assyrian treaty texts, which can always have had an influence everywhere, but by these three criteria: the change of number, the relationship to the Book of the Covenant, and the law of the centralization of the cult.

If we use these criteria as a basis, the following laws prove to belong to the basic material: 12.13-28, the main law, that is, the centralization of the cult; 14.22-29, the tithe; 15.19-23, the firstborn; 16.16f., the festivals; 16.18-20 + 17.8-13, the appointment of judges and the central court; 19.1-13, the cities of refuge. In the nearer vicinity of this we also have: 15.1-18, the year of release and the freeing of slaves; 16.1-15, the extended festal calendar; 18.1-8, provisions for the Levites; 19.15-21, the rule about witnesses; 21.1-9, trial without witnesses. All the laws have a parallel in the Book of the Covenant: cf. Exod. 20.24-26; 22.28f.; 23.14-19 on the cultic laws; Exod. 23.1ff. on judgment; Exod. 21.13f. on refuge; Exod. 21.2ff.; 22.25f.; 23.10ff. on the social laws in Deut. 15.1ff.; 18.1ff. And above all, all the laws stand under the sign of the centralization of the cult. That is a matter of course in the cultic laws in 12.13–16.17, but it is also the case with the laws on the practising of justice. The centralization excludes priestly legal decisions at the local sanctuaries and the function of asylum, but to compensate for this judges are to be sent to localities, and accessible cities of refuge are to be instituted.

Everything else in Deut. 12–25 falls outside the framework in terms of style, composition and theme and therefore proves to be secondary. Deuteronomy 12.1-7 (second person plural, supplemented in the singular in vv. 1, 5, 7, 9) and 12.8-12 (second person plural) are two earlier variants of the main law in 12.13-28, which not only fill out the formulation of the earlier writing from vv. 13f. in vv. 4-7, 11, but link it with new conditions. After 12.1, everything that follows is based solely on the premise of the impending settlement, which is only hinted at in vv. 13ff., 20. Accordingly, the version in vv. 8-12 poses the choice between what had been right in the people's own eyes before crossing over into the land (v. 8) and what subsequently is right in the eyes of Yhwh (vv. 25, 28). The latter can really only be the state of rest first achieved under David and Solomon after the occupation of Jerusalem and the building of the temple (cf. 2 Sam. 7.1, 11; 1 Kgs 5.18; 8.16ff., 56); but the addition in the singular in 12.9 is also already thinking of the time under Moses and Joshua. Verse 12a imitates v. 18. Verse 12b also presupposes v. 19. The variants in vv. 2-7 go one step further. Here the 'before' and 'afterwards' become an alternative in the land itself between Israel and the other nations. The consequence of the demarcation from the outside is that the sanctuaries outside the place mentioned are not only to be profaned but also to be destroyed. For they represent a danger of infiltration by alien cultic usages (vv. 4f.). The requirement of cultic unity is here connected with the ideal of cultic purity. The conclusion of the regulation in v. 7 again imitates v. 18 or v. 12a. If we are to describe the situation in handy formulae, in vv. 1, 8-12 we can speak of a historicization and in vv. 2-7 of a theologization of the main Deuteronomic law. Both are secondary by comparison with the simple law of the centralization of the cult itself and the differentiation between profane slaughter and sacrifice in vv. 13ff., and both are bound up in some way with the historical and paraenetic framework of Deuteronomy. Scholars like to connect both with the Deuteronomic history and therefore designate them 'Deuteronomistic' as distinct from the 'Deuteronomic' law.

In 12.29–13.19 and 14.1-21 extensive elaborations, which of course have also grown up independently, follow under the sign of cultic purity. These interrupt the laws about centralization in 12.13-28 and 14.22f. The same goes for 16.21–17.7, where, interrupting 16.18-20 and 17.8ff., the jurisprudence and justice in the communities is applied to the observation of cultic purity: if there are cultic transgressions, one need not go to the central court but can eliminate the evil on the spot. The law of the king, provisions for the levites and the law of the prophets in 17.14-20; 18.1-8;

and 18.9-22 interrupt the ordering of the law in 16.18-20 + 17.8-13 + 19.1ff., and make a comprehensive law about offices out of it. Of the additions, only the provision for unemployed country levites has anything to do with the centralization. Likewise the laws about war in Deut. 20 drop out; 21.1ff. follow on from ch. 19 (cf. 21.9 with 19.13, 19 and 12.25, 28).

Finally, all the rest in 21.10–25.19 is an appendix which, following the example of 21.1-9, goes over into the discussion of individual cases in law and, as has already been said, considers above all family law. The points of contact were provided by the act of purification in 21.1-9 and the interpretation of the ordering of the court in 16.18–19.2 as an instrument for creating cleanness (cf. 16.21–17.7; 17.12f.; 19.13, 19f., 21; 21.9; see also 13.6). In this sense, first the family law is attached, which leads on broadly from the original in Exod. 22.15f., 18 and forms the framework of the whole appendix: Deut. 21.(10-14,) 15-17, 18-21 (esp. v. 21); 22.13–22.29 (esp. 22.21f.); 24.1-4; 25.5-10. Different pieces of material have been incorporated into the framework, which put the disposition completely out of joint: the block 21.22–22.12 has been inserted through 21.22f.; the block 23.1-26 through 23.1; the block 24.5–25.4 through 24.5; the appendix 25.11-19 has been attached through 25.11-12. The blocks introduce laws of mixed content, which pursue notions of purity further (21.22f.; 22.5; 23.2-15, 18-19; 24.7, 8-9; 25.11f., 16, 19) and – taking account of the brotherly ethic in ch. 15 and 19.18f. – mix the social and the cultic. The introduction of the notion of cultic purity in chs 12–14 and 16.2ff. is presupposed everywhere. With the additions, Deuteronomy comes closest to the Holiness Code and the laws relating to cleanness in Lev. 11–27. The dependence is not one-sided only in the Holiness Code (cf. Deut. 14/Lev. 11 and 19).

3.4   The original stratum of the laws of centralization is also by no means a unity, as is already evident from the insertion of the laws about humanity in Deut. 15.1-18 between 14.22-29 and 15.19-23 and the long version of the calendar of festivals in Deut. 16.1-15 by contrast with vv. 16f. In detail the situation is as follows.

The basic demand is made in Deut. 12.13-14a and is explicitly directed against the law of the altar in Exod. 20.24 that runs: 'An altar of earth you shall make for me and sacrifice on it your burnt offerings and your peace offerings, your sheep and your oxen; in every place[26] where I cause my name to be remembered I will come to you and bless you.' By contrast, Deut. 12.13-14a says: 'Take heed that you do not offer your burnt offerings at every place that you see; but at the place which Yhwh will choose in one of your tribes, there you shall offer your burnt offerings.' However, Yhwh's blessing does not remain denied to the places. Therefore in Deut. 12.15-18 the slaughter in the localities is made profane and distinguished from the cultic meals at the central sanctuary: 'However, you may slaughter and eat flesh within any of your towns, as much as you desire, according to the blessing of Yhwh your God which he has given you.' But this is no longer to be a sacrifice for Yhwh. Therefore like all other offerings and gifts, it may not be consumed within the gates: 'But you shall eat them before Yhwh your God in the place which Yhwh your God will choose, you and your son and your daughter and the levite who is within your towns, and you shall rejoice before Yhwh your God in all that you undertake.' Deut. 12.19 begins again ('Take heed that you do not') and gives a special role to the levites who have been deprived of a living by the centralization of the cult but are already taken note of in v. 18. Verses 20-28 consider the case when the central place of worship is too far away, and as in v. 14a ('in one of your tribes') b adds further details. Here v. 20 anticipates v. 21 and makes the profane slaughter in the remote places dependent on gaining the land. Verses 25, 28 generalize the precept as a 'do what is (good and right) in the eyes of Yhwh' and make the prosperity of the generations dependent on this. Deut. 12.19-28 are throughout additions to the original text in vv. 13-18.

In connection with 12.17f., 14.22-27, 28-29 deal with the tithe, which replaces the vegetable offerings of Exod. 22.28 and 23.19: it is not the surpluses or the best, but the tithe of the produce of the field which is to be given year by year and either consumed as such at the place which Yhwh will choose or, if the journey is too long and the burden too heavy, sold beforehand. The proceeds are to be used to have a joyful feast before Yhwh at the chosen place. Verse 26 ends like 12.18. Like 12.19, v. 27 adds the special role of the levite; originally it is at best 'the levite who is within your gates' who as in 12.18 may have concluded the abbreviated list of those taking part in the cult in v. 26b, but cf. 15.20 and here 14.29. The additional regulation in 14.28-29, which was probably added later, is a consequence of the centralization of the offerings. Since these always also served as provisions, the whole tithe is to be left at intervals of three years to the poor in the localities, who now also include the levites. But they lose their cultic character here. The text is expanded not only in v. 27 but also in vv. 23f., 29b.[27]

After the interruption by the laws of humanity in Deut. 15.1-18, which have been attached to the tithes for the poor of 14.28f. and in turn have been expanded by the brotherly ethic (cf. also 19.18f., etc), 15.19-23 continue the cultic legislation of 12.13-18 and 14.22-29. The tithe from the produce of the field is followed by the offering of the firstborn from the animals (cf. Exod. 22.28f.). Like Deut 14.22, 15.19 also refers back to 12.17f.: all (male) firstborn of oxen[28] and sheep are to be consecrated to Yhwh and year by year consumed at the place which Yhwh will choose. With the words of 12.15f. animals with a blemish which are therefore not suitable for the cult are released for profane slaughter.

If 14.22-29 and 15.19-23 deal with the offerings, 16.1-17 deal with the dates on which they are to be offered. The texts are directly connected in terms of content and literary form. Deut. 16.16f. offers the shortest version of the calendar of festivals, in which Exod. 23.14-17 is cited and the notion of centralization is applied. The three agricultural festivals already mentioned in Exod. 23.17 for pilgrimages to presumably local sanctuaries which are not specified more closely become pilgrimages to the place which Yhwh will choose. Here some of the names change: the feast of unleavened bread remains, the 'harvest festival' becomes the 'feast of weeks', and the 'feast of ingathering' the 'feast of tabernacles'. I cannot recognize a deeper significance for the change of names. Perhaps the festivals are to be deprived of their localized character for the sake of the idea of centralization. The historicizing additions in Exod. 23.15 are not taken note of in Deut. 16.16f. and were presumably not even there previously. This is the first original version of the calendar of festivals in Deuteronomy. It was the occasion for further elaborations in 16.1-15 which give the festivals a new sense and have therefore been prefixed to them. All three festivals get back their agricultural character and are fixed in a rhythm of seven days: vv. 1, 3f., 8; vv. 9f.; vv. 13, 15. The feast of unleavened bread is combined in vv. 1-7 with the Passover and in v. 8 with the sabbath; in vv. 1, 3, 6, like the feast of weeks in v. 12, it is explained in terms of the exodus from Egypt, in other words historicized. In vv. 11-12 and 14-15 the feast of weeks and the feast of tabernacles take on a social emphasis. The 'joy' and the lists of those participating in the cult are salvaged from ch. 12; the choice of the place of worship is expressed in two of three cases, vv. 2, 5f., 11, with the secondary long form of the centralization formula.[29] In short, 16.1-15 is a later elaboration of the centralized laws about the festival in 16.16-17, which from there on serve as a summary of vv. 1-15. I cannot find an old, pre-Deuteronomic calendar of festivals in vv. 1-15. The verses do not arise for the basic Deuteronomic version simply because the combination of Passover and exodus, which has its closest parallel in the Priestly Writing and the post-Priestly expansions in Exod. 12–13, is no part of Ur-Deuteronomy, and if it is taken by itself, the feast of unleavened bread in Deut. 16.1aα, 3a lacks the clause about centralization.

The new legal order inspired by the idea of centralization begins with 16.18. The judgment at the gate exercised by the elders and the priestly legal decision at the local sanctuaries (cf. Exod. 22.7) are replaced by a professional college of judges which wholly takes the place of the elders and priests or only the priests alongside the elders. In v. 19 the subject of the practice of the law changes; the judges are not addressed, but the passage has the second-person-singular form of address of Deuteronomy: in other words it is addressed to the people itself. The general admonitions which are drawn from Exod. 23.6-8 must be an addition. The original continuation of Deut. 16.18 (without 'your tribes') is in 17.8ff. The priestly exercise of justice is shifted from the local sanctuaries to the central sanctuary, for those cases (profane and cultic) which cannot be decided by the local college of judges. It is unclear who is responsible, the (levitical) priests or the judges. As the verbs are in the plural, the priests must be original: the 'judge who is there in these days' (v. 9) is a supplement assimilated to v. 12 (cf. 19.17b-18a). Deuteronomy 17.10b-13 are late additions: v. 10b duplicates v. 10a, v. 11 repeats v. 10 and adds the nomistic precision 'deviate neither to the right nor to the left' (cf. Deut. 2.27; 5.32; 17.20; 28.14; Josh. 1.7; 23.6; 2 Kgs 22.2); vv. 12f. put the central court at the service of cultic purity.

After the insertion of the provision in 18.1-8 (originally only vv. 3f., 6-8) for the (levitical) priests who have become unemployed as a result of the centralization, the reordering of justice continues in 19.1ff. with the establishment of cities of refuge (after Exod. 21.13f.), on which in turn the rule about witnesses in 19.15ff. and the procedure without witnesses in 21.1-9 depend. The refuge is not centralized but to some degree secularized and detached from the sanctuaries. Therefore the main sanctuary does not appear as a place of asylum. Original passages here are: 19.2-7 (without vv. 2b, 3a), 11-12; 19.15, 16-17a, 18bα, 21b (the *lex talionis* after Exod. 21.23f.); 21.1-4, 6-7, 8b; the very similar conclusions in 19.13, 19b-21a and 21.9, which also occur in 17.12f. and in other secondary passages, fit the subject of the regulations. They seem to have been added, but they could have their origin here.

3.5   Two questions are important for finding a place in the literary history for an Ur-Deuteronomy[30] which has been demarcated in this way: first the historicization of the law and secondly the beginning and end of the legal corpus.

The imminent choice of the place of worship (Deut. 12.14, 18, 21, 26; 14.23-25; 15.20; 16.16; 17.8, 10a), the gift of the land (16.18 and 15.4, 7; 16.20; 19.2f., 10; 21.1, enlargement 12.20; 19.8), and the 'I' which refers to Moses (12.14, 21, 28; 15.5, 11, 15; 19.7, 9) occur as historicizations of the laws. Even if the majority of the characteristics appear in additions, for the original stratum there remains at least the strange formulation of the giving of 'gates' (places) in 16.18, which is imitated in 16.5 and 17.2, and above all the choice of the place: in the Hebrew this is in the imperfect and with the best will in the world cannot be deleted from the laws about centralization. But the choice of the place which is announced clearly points to the situation shortly before the settlement and thus to the literary context in which Deuteronomy has been handed down. So it is also perhaps no coincidence that it was the Book of the Covenant in Exod. 20–23 in particular which served as the basis for Ur-Deuteronomy. The historicization and the literary dependence raise the question whether Deuteronomy came into being separately or for the context between Numbers and Joshua.

Nor do the beginning and the end particularly support an original independence. Deut. 12.13 is not an independent beginning: 19.12 or 19.21 or 21.8 are not a real end unless the concluding formulae in 19.13, 19b-21 and 21.9, which in 21.9 form an inclusion with 12.25, 28, belonged to it. But all the passages fall under the suspicion of being later additions; moreover the 'I' in 12.28 presupposes a knowledge of who is speaking to whom. That, too, is not stated anywhere in the original stratum of Deuteronomy. It is impossible for Yhwh to be the speaker, as he is spoken of in the third person, and the supposition that Deuteronomy was originally a divine speech is pure speculation. By contrast it is completely clear from the literary context that only Moses can be considered the speaker and the people those whom he addresses.

Many people regard the 'Hear, Israel' in 6.4-5 as an old beginning. Here the unity of Yhwh is derived from the unity of the place of worship in 12.13ff., initially in the sense that there are no longer to be different, locally differentiated manifestations of Yhwh (the Yhwh of Samaria, the Yhwh of Teman, the Yhwh of Jerusalem, etc.), as in the pre-exilic period, but only the one and only Yhwh, the God of the chosen place Jerusalem. Here at least the audience is mentioned; the speaker remains anonymous, and taken by itself the text could even have been the introduction to an independent Deuteronomy were there not other reasons, above all the formula of election and, if we add v. 6, even the first person of the speaker,[31] which tell against it.

The pendant to the 'Hear, Israel' in Deut. 6 is to be found in Deut. 26.16. Ur-Deuteronomy could once have ended with this verse. If it was originally independent, the 'today' must have referred to the day of the proclamation of the law (which was repeated). But the conclusion in 26.1-15 is preceded by a kind of appendix to the laws of centralization which draws on 14.22f. As soon as Israel has entered the land at the gates of which it stands, it is to observe the rule and offer the first produce at the place of worship chosen (vv. 1-2, 11). Here the historicization is beyond doubt presupposed, and accordingly the 'today' of 26.16 refers to the situation shortly before the entry into the land, that is, to the scene in the literary context between Exodus–Numbers and Joshua. It is almost impossible to decide which of the two conclusions in Deut. 26, vv. 1-2, 11, or 16, is the older.

For the moment I shall leave open the question of original independence, but maintain that the basic material of the laws in Deut. 12–21 with the election formula at least contains a historicizing element; moreover the earliest paraenetic framework in 6.4-5 and 26.16, while not dependent on the literary context, does fit into it well, and with the 'I' in 6.6 and the invitation to offer the first fruits in 26.1-2, 11 also presupposes it. The 'Hear, Israel' in

6.4 can easily be connected with Num. 25.1a through the beginning of the internal framework, the introduction to the speech in Deut. 5.1aα[1] ('And Moses called all Israel and spoke to them' with the following 'Hear, Israel'); the continuation of the narrative thread in Josh. 2.1; 3.1 fits seamlessly with Deut. 26.1f.,11, 16 and the death of Moses in Deut. 34.1, 5f. The later additions and appendixes to the basic writing of Deuteronomy in chs 12–26 everywhere presuppose the historical garb, and with it the incorporation into the literary context of the Pentateuch and the Former Prophets. That is also the case in the framework at the beginning and the end of Deuteronomy which has put itself successively round the core in chs 12–26, and the germ of the framework in 6.4-5 and 26.1-2, 11, 16.

The death of Moses in 34.5f., around which narrative and speeches in chs 31–34 cluster, is a special case. The death intrinsically has nothing to do with the legislation. It has therefore always been denied to the original Deuteronomy and distributed among the 'old sources' in the Pentateuch (J, E, JE and P). The correct insight here was that Moses was already dead, or at least had to die at the moment when Deuteronomy and its framework were inserted into the Pentateuch. But there is nothing to divide. Moses dies only once, and everything else that announces or elaborates his death (Num. 20.12; 27.12f.; Deut. 1.37; 3.23ff.; 4.21f.; 31.1f.; 32.48ff.; 34.7ff.; Josh. 1.1f.) is dependent on that. And as Moses can die without the law, but the law cannot have found its way into the context before the death of Moses, the death of Moses is older than the law. This is also suggested by the narrative thread, which leads from Num. 25.1a to Josh. 2.1; 3.1 and presupposes the death of Moses but not necessarily the Deuteronomic law. If we take out Deuteronomy and put Num. 25.1a and Deut. 34.5-6[32] together, we get a death notice which resembles that of Miriam in Num. 20.1aβb. Moses dies in Shittim in Moab and is buried – by whoever – nearby, in a valley in the land of Moab opposite Beth-peor. That this is the original text, and that the death was not first inserted with the insertion of Deuteronomy, is shown by the changes which the insertion caused. As a testament of Moses for the time after the settlement, Deuteronomy has a place only between the arrival in Shittim in Num. 25.1a and the onset of Moses' death in Deut. 34.5f. Thus Moses gathers the people in Shittim (Num. 25.1a) and delivers his speech: Deut. 5.1aα[1] + 6.4–26.16. The 'there' in Deut. 34.5 lost its point of reference through the insertion of the farewell speech. So now Moses ascends from the fields of Moab (cf. Num. 22.1) to the summit of Pisgah, like Shittim opposite Jericho (cf. Num. 23.14), there to die (Deut. 34.1a, 5f.).

The importance of the textual links just disclosed can hardly be overestimated. First, they indirectly confirm the analysis of the Priestly Writing and its conclusion that the parts in Numbers which make Israel set out into the wilderness after the stay on Sinai are made for an earlier narrative connection leading from the wilderness into the promised land. The earlier narrative thread cannot be divided up into different source writings, but is the literary framework into which everything else has subsequently been incorporated. Secondly, they offer proof for the conjecture that Deuteronomy originally neither closed the Pentateuch nor opened the Deuteronomistic history but likewise was inserted into the basic text which runs from Num. 25.1a through Deut. 34.5f. (without the additions) to Josh. 2.1; 3.1 – it is pre-Priestly and pre-Deuteronomic and therefore also pre-Deuteronomistic. This text can only be the old Hexateuch (Genesis–Joshua), which Noth has caused to be forgotten; under the influence of the growing Deuteronomic law it then gradually grew into the Deuteronomic Enneateuch (Genesis–Kings). I shall be returning to that.

3.6   I distinguished above between an internal (more paraenetic) and an external (more historical) framework: chs 5–11/27–30 and chs 1–4/31–34. Both shells have grown up from the inside outwards, and from the earliest framework in Deut. $5.1a\alpha^1$ + 6.4-5/26.1f., 11, 16 + 34.1, 5f., which includes the corpus 12.13–21.9 and connects it with the context.

The germ of the earlier framework is the 'Hear, Israel', in 6.4-5. This was either originally handed down as a slogan for the one God in the sense of vv. 6-9, and through v. 5 and the relative clause in v. 6 was put secondarily before 12.13ff. as an introduction to Deuteronomy; or, as I think more probable, a priori formulated as a protasis to 12.13ff. and subsequently isolated after the insertion of chs 7–11 into 6.6-9 and stylized into the confession of faith to which its use in Judaism still bears witness today.

The paraeneses in chs 6–11 (12.1ff.) have inserted themselves between the beginning in 6.4-5 and 12.13ff.; they interpret the 'Hear, Israel' and the Decalogue which is put in front of this in Deut. 5.1–6.3.[33] Deuteronomy 6.6 may have still related to the whole law which follows; however, as I have said, vv. 7-9 make the introduction into a quotable summary of the law and declare it to be the object of religious instruction and the practice of personal prayer, that is, the foundation of the pious life: the confessional statement and with it the whole law is to be taken to heart, inculcated in children and worn on the body. The instruction is repeated in 11.18ff. The paraeneses in 6.10ff. and the question for the children in 6.20ff., along with the further exposition of 'Hear Israel' in 10.12ff., say what is to be recalled here. In all these passages the commandment to love is bound up with the exodus creed and understood in the sense of the first commandment.

This understanding is more clearly expressed where there is an explicit recollection of the revelation on Horeb, as the wilderness and Mount Sinai are called in Deuteronomy, by assimilation with Exod. 3.1,[34] and the whole Decalogue or only the First Commandment is cited: Deut. 5.1–6.3 and Deut.

7–11. Deuteronomy 5.1–6.3 is the Deuteronomic version of Exod. 20, which can easily be recognized as an addition by the second person plural. The question which of the two versions of the Decalogue is the older is now often decided in favour of the priority of Deut. 5, but given the state of the synoptic text that is quite improbable.[35] Just as Deut. 12–26 is a novella of the Book of the Covenant in Exod. 20–23, so Deut. 5 is a new edition of the scene in Exod. 19–20, which can be seen originating in Exodus and in Deut. 5 appears as a smooth narrative context. In the framework of Deuteronomy, Deut. 5 shifts the revelation of the law communicated here forward to Sinai in Exodus and in so doing further assimilates the two scenes. Just as in Exod. 20–23 the Decalogue and the Book of the Covenant follow one another, so too in Deuteronomy the Decalogue in ch. 5 is followed by the proclamation of the revised Book of the Covenant in Deut. 6–26. The idea of the retrospect is a new addition to the historical garb of Deuteronomy as a farewell discourse of Moses before the settlement. The continuation thus becomes the repetition and public communication of the law revealed partly publicly on Sinai and partly only to Moses.

With the insertion of the Decalogue, the following 'Hear, Israel' in Deut. 6 (cf. 5.1/6.4) and the Deuteronomic law take on a new significance. The unity of Yhwh is interpreted in the sense of uniqueness and exclusiveness: Yhwh is not only one God but the one and only God for Israel. At the same time this is the basis for a unique relationship with God. It goes back to the unique historical act of Yhwh, the liberation of Israel from Egypt. Whereas the Deuteronomic law had hitherto been a matter of showing the love of God called for in the 'Hear, Israel', from now on both the love of God and the law stand under the sign of Yhwh's claim to exclusiveness. That is also the reason why the Deuteronomic law is bound back to the revelation on Sinai in Exod. 19–24 through Deut. 5. Thus various paraeneses attach themselves in chs 7–11 which – with or without a historical reminiscence – develop the first commandment in many ways and now and again explain more clearly the connection between the election, testing and disobedience of the people in the exodus story (especially Exod. 23 and 34 in Deut. 7; Exod. 16 and the forty years of Num. 14.34, etc. in Deut. 8; Exod. 32–34 in Deut. 9–11) and the history of the people after the settlement from Joshua on. It is not the ordering of the commandments in the Decalogue but the first commandment that governs the redaction history of Deuteronomy.[36]

In contrast, the external framework in Deut. 1–3 and – after the interruption through ch. 4 – once again in 4.45-49 depicts the historical course to the recapitulation of the Sinai revelation in the land of Moab in Deuteronomy which lies in the background. The way from Sinai through the wilderness to the place of the proclamation of the law is described on the basis of Num. 10–36, above all with the use of earlier texts in Num. 20.14ff.; 21.21ff. in Deut. 2–3 (without Balaam, Num. 22–24, but cf. Deut.

23.5f.), and also of Num. 11 and Exod. 18 in Deut 1.9ff.; Num. 13f. in Deut. 1.19ff.; Num. 32; 34.13-15 (and Josh 1.12ff; 12f.) in Deut. 3.12ff.; Num. 20.12 and 27.12ff. in Deut. 3.21f., 23f., that is, with recourse to texts which, to put it cautiously, do not belong in the earliest strata of all in the Pentateuch and which, to put it more plainly, in part presuppose the incorporation and further writing of the Priestly Writing in Numbers. Certainly Deut. 1–3 are also glossed on a number of occasions (second-person-singular form of address, archaeological glosses, etc.) and for example, in 1.9-18 are also expanded by larger passages, but the references to the book of Numbers are integral to the substance. In Deut. 1 and 3.23ff. they are to explain with Num. 13f. and 20 why the wilderness generation may not enter the land. In Deut. 2–3 the way through the wilderness of Num. 20–21 turns into a first act of settlement along the lines of Num. 32 (and 34.13-15). As Noth[37] has made clear, the selection follows the plan, dictated by the theology of history, that only the later Israelite areas will be fought over and conquered (Sihon and Og), whereas the territories which did not later belong to Israel (Edom, Moab and Ammon) do not need to be conquered and therefore offer no resistance.

The recapitulation is not meant to replace the preceding history but, as above all the fiction of the discourse of Moses shows, to link up with it. This is in order once again to keep in view the way from Sinai to Moab with new emphases adapted to its own interests in the farewell speech inserted between Num. 25.1a (27.12f.) and Deut. 34.1, 5f., and to serve as a paraenesis for the people before the settlement depicted in Joshua. In accordance with the content and in the literary allusions, the law of Sinai as revealed in Exodus–Numbers and in Deut. (4;) 5–28 is presupposed. Even if the connection between history and law in Deut. 1–3 is nowhere made explicit, with the exception of the heading in 1.1-5, which explains the historical retrospect on the Torah, that does not mean that the historical retrospect is older than the law, as some scholars think; on the contrary, it is an indication that history has in itself become a paradigm of the law. As such, it serves to prepare for the paraenesis in Deut. 5–11 and the proclamation of the law in Deut. 12ff. The earlier narrative transition in 5.1 is integrated into the speech of Moses in 4.1 (cf. 6.1; 12.1), and there is a narrative bridge over it in 4.41-43, 44-49. The prior insertion of Deut. 1–3 (4) before chs 5ff., like the introduction to the farewell scene in Num. 27.12f. and the filling out of the book of Numbers in the realm of Num. 25–36, contributes to the demarcation of the books. The fiction of the retrospect, which merely repeats what is there in Exodus–Numbers, creates the presupposition for regarding Deuteronomy in Deuteronomy itself (31.9ff., etc.) and in what follows (Joshua–Kings) as an independent, normative book of the law (cf. Deut. 1.5); it was finally added to the Pentateuch as a fifth book and the embodiment of the Torah of Moses.

3.7   The germ of the underlying framework is the conclusion of the corpus of law, chs 12–26, in 26.1-2, 11, 16, which ends with the pendant to 'Hear, Israel' and the death of Moses in Deut. 34.5f. Both have become the starting point for extensive further writing. In 26.17-19 the legal paraenesis in 26.16 goes over into a scene about the concluding of the covenant. The closest connections to it, and in content to 26.1-11, are the curse and blessing in Deut. 28 and the concluding paraenesis in 30.15-20. Both are additions which stylize Deuteronomy as a whole as a treaty or covenant document in the style of Hittite and neo-Assyrian state treaties. Instead of a treaty between two states with the gods as witnesses, here we have the covenant of God with his people, and heaven and earth are summoned as witnesses. The covenant is not two-sided but one-sided, and makes the law and obedience to the law the content of the relationship with God. The covenant formula arrived at in this way (the demand for the love of God in Deut. 5–6 – the communication of the law in Deut. 12–26 – the making of the covenant in Deut. 26 – the blessing and curse in Deut. 28 – the summoning of witnesses in 30.15-20) is not at the beginning of the literary historical development of Deuteronomy but right at the end and presupposes the First Commandment. The formulary is further expanded in Deut. 27.9f., 15ff. by a series of curses and the people's entering into an obligation (cf. Exod. 24.3f.), and in 27.1-8, 11-14 by the preparation of Josh. 8. The passages can be recognized as additions by the renewed introductions to speeches in 27.1, 9, 11. Likewise, the part-heading 28.69, which differentiates between the Horeb covenant and the Moab covenant and relates the two, indicates the next stimulus to further writing in Deut. 29f., another legal paraenesis which envisages the situation, after the entry, of blessing and curse, the exile, and calls for repentance and conversion to God. Here the singular in Deut. 30.1ff., 15ff., may initially have followed immediately after ch. 28, before ch. 29 was inserted with 28.69. Against the background of the covenant which has long since been broken, chs 26–28 maintain the fiction of the covenant which has just been made. Chapters 29f. begin explicitly from the breach of the covenant and punishment and call for a return to the covenant. In short, 26.16 was initially developed further in 26.17-18, 19 + Deut. 28 + 30.15ff., then in Deut. 27 and 30, and finally in Deut. 29.[38] There are also covenants and paraeneses of this kind in Exod. 24; 34; Josh. 23–24 and 2 Kgs 23 in the framework of the (Deuteronomistic) history in Genesis–Kings.

The narrative thread focused on the impending settlement, which keeps appearing in 26.1ff.; 27.1ff; 28.69 and 30.15ff. is continued up to the death of Moses in chs 31–34. Here the poetic passages in Deut. 32 with an introduction in 31.16ff. and a conclusion in 32.44ff. (song of Moses) and Deut. 33 (blessing of Moses) automatically stand out from the context. Wherever they come from, they have been inserted or written in later in order to give Deuteronomy and the Pentateuch a worthy conclusion, similar to the blessing of Jacob in Gen. 49. In other respects there are variants of the same scene in which Moses prepares for his death – indicated by the tradition in 34.1, 5f. – and bids farewell. On the one hand they are a transition to the Joshua narrative in Josh. 1ff.; on the other they are meant to conclude the book of Deuteronomy and the Pentateuch. On the basis of the architecture of the text they can be grouped as follows. Around the death of Moses in 34.1-6 (originally without his looking over the land in vv. 1b-4), on which everything else depends, first the bracket in Deut. 31.1-8 (originally only vv. 1-2a, 7f.) and Josh. 1.1-6 (originally without 3-4) formed, along with the commissioning of Joshua by Moses and the recapitulation of this in the mouth of Yahweh. Next, the writing down of the law in 31.9-13, 24-26a with a postscript in 32.46f. was inserted between 31.1-8 and 34.1ff.; this likewise serves as a bracket (cf. Josh 1.7, 8f.). Between them in turn came the consecration of Joshua in 31.14f., 23. Finally, between 31.1–32.47 and 34.1ff. there was the resumption of Num. 27.12ff. (Deut. 3.23ff.) in Deut. 32.48-52, which like the additions in 34.7-12, the song of Moses together with accompanying texts in Deut. 31–32 (31.16-22, 26b-30; 32.1-45), and the blessing of Moses in Deut. 33 sealed the conclusion of the book and encouraged the separation of the Pentateuch as the Torah.

Thus the transition from Deuteronomy to the Joshua narrative in Deut. 26–34 is prepared for at a number of levels: at the beginning there is the transition through the historical garb of the law in 26.1f.,11 and the paraenesis in 26.16 corresponding to Deut. (5.1aα^1;) 6.4-5 before the death of Moses in 34.1, 5f., to which Josh. 2.1ff.; 3.1ff. attach themselves (following Num. 25.1a). To some degree the conclusion in 30.15-20 is a doublet to 26.1-16, with the important difference that this text presupposes the making of the covenant, the curse and the blessing, and the paraenesis in Deut. 26.16ff. and 27-30. This conclusion has formed under the influence of the Decalogue and the First Commandment, which also dominates the introductory paraeneses in Deut. (4;) 5–11. Alongside or soon after the building up of Deut. 27–30 came the narrative shaping of the death scene in Deut. 34.1-5f. in chs 31–34, which picks up the narrative thread of Numbers recapitulated in Deut. 1–3. This both forms a transition to Joshua and – like Josh. 1 – marks the division of books between Deuteronomy and Joshua.

3.8   Summary: the basic document of Deuteronomy, so-called Ur-Deuteronomy, is a novella of the Book of the Covenant in Exod. 20–23 and originally contained only the centralization laws in Deut. 12–21, which limit the cult to the one place of worship chosen by Yhwh in the imminent future and draw consequences from this for the organization of the administration of justice. Deuteronomy 6.4-5 and 26.16 formed a more or less independent framework around Ur-Deuteronomy. Through the historicization of the Deuteronomic law in the formula about election and the gift of the land, the heading 5.1aα[1] and the first person used by Moses in 6.6, the concluding paraenesis in 26.1f., 11 and the transition in 34.1a, from the start, or very soon, Deuteronomy was included in the earlier narrative, which runs from Num. 25.1a through Deut. 34.5f. to Josh. 2.1; 3.1. The original framework puts the law about the one place of worship under the sign of the love of God for the one Yhwh and explains that love of God is identical to obedience to the law. Both the legal corpus in chs 12–26 and the framework passages were then developed in many ways under the aspect of the Decalogue and the First Commandment; here the links to (Genesis–)Numbers on the one hand and Joshua(–Kings) on the other were increasingly deepened; the book of Deuteronomy as a recapitulation of Genesis–Numbers became something that could be quoted within Joshua–Kings, and as the embodiment of the Torah ultimately encouraged the demarcation of the Pentateuch.

Finally a word on the dating. Since de Wette, scholars have been fond of connecting Deuteronomy with the discovery of the book, the making of the covenant and the reform of the cult under Josiah in 2 Kgs 22–23. This connection is true of the last form of the text, but in the original stratum these things have little to do with one another. The content of Ur-Deuteronomy is the idea of centralization; the Josiah pericope in 2 Kgs 22.1-2; 23.11f.,[39] 28–30 originally reported in connection with Josiah's military engagement against the Pharaoh Necho, who wanted to support the Assyrian rump state as a bulwark against Babylon, only the removal of a few signs of Assyrian supremacy in Jerusalem which had become superfluous, and in 22.3-7, 9 a renovation of the temple (with a transition to the note about reform in 23.4a). The discovery of the book, the making of the covenant and the report of the reform which is carried out derive from later additions and are inspired by Deuteronomy, which has been developed in a corresponding way. Consequently the centralization of the cult in Deuteronomy, which doubtless refers to Jerusalem as the one and only legitimate place of worship, though it is never mentioned by name, must be explained and dated from this.

Political reasons and analogies from the history of religion have been cited for this; they are meant to rescue the dating of Ur-Deuteronomy under Josiah independently of 2 Kgs 22–23. But neither of these says much. The reduction of Judah to the rump state of Jerusalem after 701 BC doubtless brought with it a concentration of political forces and thus also of worship on the capital, but I see no occasion and no necessity for the kings of Judah and especially Josiah to have adopted the limitation forced on them by the Assyrians as a power-political goal and to have elevated it to a theological programme in a divine law like Deuteronomy. As a sign of the regaining of self-confidence in Judah against the background of the decline in the pre-eminence of Assyria towards the end of the seventh century, one would rather expect the opposite, the extension and powerful encouragement of the local cults throughout the country. This can in fact still be recognized in the annalistic notice about the campaign against Necho and the report of the reform carried out, in a pious reversal of the actual circumstances. Similarities to the Assyrian state treaties and especially to the much-quoted vassal treaty of Esardaddon with the princes of Media[40] occur at various literary levels which are recognized as being late, so that the Neo-Assyrian period gives us a *terminus a quo* for Deuteronomy, but no more than that. If we went only by the parallels from the Near East, we would have to date Ps. 104; Prov. 22.17–23.11 or the Job poem towards the end of the second millennium BC.

So there is nothing for it but to date Deuteronomy according to the criterion given by the basic text itself, the theological programme of centralization of the cult. This notion is so special and singular in the world of the ancient Near East that there must be special reasons for it. I see two possibilities. Either the idea of centralization and the no less unusual 'Hear, Israel' in Deut. 6.4f., which is directed against the local differentiation of Yhwh, is a reaction to the downfall of Samaria and is meant to bind the northern Israelites, who have lost a political and religious home, to Judah and Jerusalem. Or the programme is a reaction to the downfall of the kingdom of Judah, the loss of the political and ideological centre of pre-exilic Judah connected with it, and the deportation, and has the purpose of warning against the decentralization threatened as a result, like that which took place earlier in the North (cf. 2 Kgs 17 and the remnants of Israelite paganism in Elephantine), creating a substitute for the one place of worship chosen by Yhwh. The natural centre is replaced by an artificial centre, and the state cult is replaced by the cultic claim of the deity himself, who calls for a centralization, but in so doing does not ignore the social and legal needs of the local communities. Because I find it difficult to explain why the Judahites in the pre-exilic period would voluntarily have dispensed with their ancestral local sanctuaries and conversely why the Israelites who had become homeless would have limited themselves to the one place of worship, I regard the second possibility, an early exilic dating of Ur-Deuteronomy as a response to the threatening downfall, to be more plausible. But not a great deal depends on this. At all events the address to Israel in Deut. 6.4f. presupposes a common consciousness of Israelites and Judahites.

Table B.I.2

Hexateuch narrative	Ur-Deuteronomy	Supplements
Num. 25.1a ─┐		25–36
Deuteronomy ┐		1–4
5.1aα¹ ──┐		5.1–6.3
	6.4-5	6.6-9, 10ff.
		7–11
		12.1-12
	12.13-28	12.14b, 19-28
		12.29–13.19
		14.1-21
	14.22-29	14.23f., 27-29
		15.1-18
	15.19-23	
		16.1-15
	16.16-17	
	16.18-20	16.19-20
		16.21–17.7
	17.8-13	17.9aβ, 10b-13
		17.14-20
		18.1-8
		18.9-22
	19.1-13	19.1, 2b-3a, 8-10, 13, 14
	19.15-21	19.17b-18a, 18bβ-21a
		20.1-20
	21.1-9	21.5, 8a, 9
		21.10–25.19
	26.1-16	26.5-10, 12-15, 17-19
		27–30
		31–33
34.1a ──┘		34.1b-4
34.5-6 ──┘		34.7-12
Joshua		
2.1, 3.1		

4. The Decalogue and the Book of the Covenant

Wellhausen, *Composition*, 81-98, 329-55; Noth, *History of Pentateuchal Traditions*, 31, 36, 59ff., 144ff.; id., *Exodus*, OTL, 1962; L. Perlitt, *Bundestheologie im Alten Testament*, WMANT 36, 1969, 156-238; L. Hossfeld, *Der Dekalog*, OBO 45, 1982; E. Aurelius, *Der Fürbitter Israels*, CB.OT 27, 1988, 57-126; E. Blum, *Studien zur Komposition des Pentateuch*,

BZAW 189, 1990, 45-99; C. Levin, 'Der Dekalog am Sinai', *VT* 35, 1985, 165-91; id., *Der Jahwist*, FRLANT 153, 1993, 362-9; E. Otto, 'Die nachpriester-schriftliche Pentateuchredaktion im Buch Exodus', in M. Vervenne (ed.), *Studies in the Book of Exodus*, BEThL 126, 1996, 61-111; E. Zenger, 'Wie und wozu die Tora an den Sinai kam. Literarische und theologische Beobachtungen zu Exodus 19–34', in Vervenne (ed.), *Studies in the Book of Exodus*, 265-88; W. Oswald, *Israel am Gottesberg*, OBO 159, 1998.

Research

W.H. Schmidt, *Exodus, Sinai und Mose*, EdF 191, 1983, 71-90; W.H. Schmidt, with H. Delkort and A. Graupner, *Die zehn Gebote im Rahmen alttestamentlische Ethik*, EdF 281, 1993.

4.1   If we remove the Priestly element from the Sinai pericope and Deuteronomy, what remain as law in the Pentateuch are the Decalogue and the Book of the Covenant in Exod. 20–23; these are filled out by parts of the Sinai pericope in Exod. 19–24 and 32–34 which precede and follow them. In substance the Sinai pericope is pre-Priestly and pre-Deuteronomic, and therefore pre-Deuteronomistic. But it is not a literary unity and also contains a series of later expansions influenced by Deuteronomy, the Deuteronomists and the Priestly writing.

Fundamental to analysis is the simple observation that Exod. 32–34 represent a renewal of the covenant of Exod. 19–24. Exodus 32.1-6 take up the narrative threads which have been dropped in 24.15a, 18b. Exodus 34.28 comes back to them: Moses stays with God on the mountain for forty days and forty nights. In the interim he descends from the mountain and shatters the two tablets which he has received from God in 24.12b and 31.18 and the golden calf (32.7f., 15f., 19f.); then he is again summoned up the mountain and has the second version dictated to him (34.1-4, 27f.). What is written on the tablets (34.10-26) is simply a brief summary of what has already been said in Exod. 20–23, especially 23.20ff. (34.10-16) and 23.10ff. (34.18-26). According to 24.4, 7 this has been written by Moses in the Book of the Covenant, and according to 24.12 it stood on the first tablets. The renewal of the covenant and the tablets has been necessitated by the interlude with the golden calf, which prefigures the sin of Jeroboam in 1 Kgs 12 (cf. v. 28 in Exod. 32.4), so important for 1–2 Kings. The interlude separates Moses and the people; as a consequence the revelation scene in Exod. 19–24 is to some degree repeated for Moses alone, excluding the people (cf. 34.2f. with 19.10-13).

According to Exod. 19–24 the fall comes about so suddenly that one cannot avoid regarding the whole of Exod. 32–34 as a secondary addition to the earlier Sinai pericope. The attempt made time and again to discover some ancient nucleus in Exod. 34 and in it the core of the Sinai pericope as a whole has the narrative strategy in Exod. 19–34 and the literary dependence against it all along the line.[41] It is meant to demonstrate that what is called Yhwh's privilege law, a kind of First Commandment, is older than the First Commandment. This can hardly be demonstrated successfully unless one reduces the text to the state of Exod. 23.14-17, but that rules out a comparison and does not explain the doublet. Conversely, we would be rid of all the difficulties, but would make things too simple, if we were simply to declare the addition to be post-Priestly and to foist it all on the 'final redactor'. Beyond doubt individual passages, for example, 33.7-11,[42] display relations to the Priestly building of the sanctuary in Exod. 25–31; 35–40, but these are likewise quite certainly additions. One might expect just about anything from a post-Priestly insertion, but not Exod. 34 as a response to Exod. 32–33 and a transition to Exod. 35ff. It is not enough to replace one unknown core, the ancient primal Israelite core, by another unknown, the cipher of the 'final redactor'.

Two narrative strands are in competition within the addition in Exod. 32–34. One circles around the golden calf (Exod. 32), the other around the theme of leading the people through the wilderness (Exod. 33); both come together in the introduction to the golden calf in 32.1 and the renewed making of the covenant in Exod. 34: compare here vv. 9, 17. However, both strands have been covered over by a variety of secondary additions: for example, vv. 1-6, 7f.,[43] 15aα, 20 belong to the original material in Exod. 32; vv. 12-17 to that in Exod. 33. The literary break comes in 32.30-34, 35; and 33.1a. Like the golden calf in Exod. 32, Yhwh's being with the people and the 'rest' of Exod. 33.14 have a broad literary horizon and point forward to the imminent wandering in the wilderness, the land and the temple. The analysis of Exod. 34 depends on whether one regards as original the motif of the tablets in 24.12b; 31.18; 32.15f., 19; 34.1-4, 28b, 29, which interrupts the connection of 33.18-23 and 34.5ff. in 34.1-4 and can be neglected without further ado, and whether one accords priority to the golden calf (34.17) or the motif of guidance (34.9). Internally, the address to the people in 34.11-26 drops out of the scenic framework demarcated by vv. 10 and 27f.

Usually the dominant theme of the breaking and renewal of the covenant in chs 32 and 34 is said to be original, and the motif of Yhwh's being with the people in 33.12-17 is said to have been added on the basis of 32.1, 34 or to be equally original. Exodus 32.30-34, or 32.35 is then connected with 33.12ff. or 34.1ff. A direct connection of 34.9ff. to 32.30, which picks up the two themes of 32.1, the question of Yhwh going with the people and the breaking of the covenant, would also be conceivable. But we can also reverse the relationship and find the earlier motif in the question whether

Yhwh goes with the people, that is, in 33.1a, 3a, 12-17(; 33.18f.; 34.5-8); 34.9a (with a conclusion in 34.28a), and regard the breaking of the covenant in ch. 32, which makes the confirmation of Exod. 20–23 in the making of the covenant in 34.10ff. a new covenant or first provokes the renewal of the covenant, as a second motivation of the conversation in 33.1, 12ff. It is not easy to decide between the two possibilities, as is customary in identifying the textual strata which develop the writing. The occurrence of Aaron in 32.1-6, which already led Noth to make bold speculations about the history of the tradition in his Exodus commentary and is more simply explained by saying that not only Aaron but also the whole scene has been added later, as also was Exod. 17.8ff. (cf. 24.14, Aaron and Hur), tells against the first variant and supports the second. Furthermore, the command to set out and the postponement of the punishment to later (2 Kgs 17) is more easily understood in Exod. 32.34 in the framework of Moses' intercession in 32.30-34 as an anticipation of 33.1a than vice versa. Exodus 33.1ff. seem to know nothing of the punishment which has been announced (32.34b) or even inflicted (32.35) in the meantime (cf. 33.3); linguistically the question in 33.12 picks up 33.1a more than 32.34. However, against the second variant it can be objected that the circumstantial negotiations in 33.12ff. need an occasion which makes Yhwh's going with the people a problem (cf. Exod. 32.1; 33.3). Without Exod. 32 the cause would simply be that if we leave aside the additions to the Book of the Covenant in 23.20-33 (dependent on 32.34aβ; 33.2), there had as yet been no mention of it in Exod. 19–24. Furthermore one misses an appropriate answer after 34.9a. The answer given in 34.10, 11ff. presupposes the breach of the covenant in Exod. 32 and 34.9b.

I leave the question open, because I myself am still hesitant, and fundamentally it does not change anything. However one decides, at all events the scene in Exod. 32–34 repeated between 24.18b and 34.28a presupposes the stay of Moses on the mountain and its shaping into a revelation scene in Exod. 19–24, including the Decalogue and the Book of the Covenant in Exod. 20–23, and tightens the ties which in any case exist between Exodus–Numbers and Joshua–Kings.

4.2   Moses' original stay on the mountain of God in the wilderness of Sinai begins in Exod. 19.2[44]-3a and ends in 24.18b. The Israelites come into the wilderness of Sinai and camp in the wilderness opposite the mountain of God. Moses climbs up to God and remains on the mountain forty days and forty nights. Meanwhile the following things take place:

> 1. The theophany. After a first commitment by the people to the covenant, in which Moses hands on the words of God and the responses of the people, but does not descend and ascend

(19.3b-9), Yhwh finally sends Moses down to the people to prepare them for the imminent theophany in which he appears with thunder and lightning and with fire and smoke. Moses speaks, and God answers in the thunder (19.10-19). At the end Yahweh descends on Sinai, on the summit of the mountain, and calls Moses up the mountain (19.20), immediately to send him down again so that he can communicate further precautionary measures to the people and return to the mountain together with Aaron (vv. 21-25).

2. The communication of the Decalogue. According to 19.25, Moses is down with the people when God prompts the revelation of the law and first of all proclaims the Decalogue. The communication of the Decalogue is accompanied by thunder and lightning. Moses stands with the people and calms them down; he then approaches the dark cloud (on the mountain) in which God is (20.18-21).

3. The communication of the book of the covenant. In the conversation between Yhwh and Moses, Yhwh communicates to Moses the law that he is to present to the Israelites (20.22–23.33 with headings in 20.22; 21.1).

4. The making of the covenant. Lastly, Moses is reminded once again that he is to approach Yhwh together with Aaron and now also with Nadab, Abihu and seventy elders (24.1-2). Thereupon Moses comes down from the mountain, communicates the law to the people ('all the words of Yhwh and all the statements of the law' from 20.1; 21), the people say the 'Amen', Moses writes down the law, and the next day once again commits the people to the Book of the Covenant and seals the making of the covenant with the blood of the covenant (24.3-8). After that Moses climbs the mountain three more times: once with Aaron, Nadab and Abihu and the seventy elders in order to celebrate a meal in the presence of the God of Israel (24.9-11 after 24.1-2); the second time together with his servant Joshua in order to take away the tablets inscribed by Yhwh (24.12-14); and the third time to be with God on the mountain for forty days and forty nights (24.12a, 15a, 18b).

It has long been clear that this complex of texts brings together things which did not originally belong together. That is hardly disputed by anyone. The many toings and froings, Moses' repeated ascending and descending, alone make it clear that many interests and hands have been at work on the present composition. Moreover a good deal of acuteness and paper has been used in analysing the text. However, this has suffered from the fact that people have wanted to distribute the verses between the two sources J and E at any cost. Even modern readers of the final text are still completely under the spell of the source hypothesis when they think that they have to forego any attempt at reconstructing the growth of the text – which is usually conceded – and content themselves with a description of the present Massoretic version of the text, because the division of the sources leads nowhere. Here Lothar Perlitt[45] already put an end to the fruitless 'JE game' and paved the way for an unprejudiced analysis orientated on the text itself. This did not make the literary-critical differentiations of the source hypothesis otiose, but as always the supplementary hypothesis proved to be superior. On this presupposition the compositional fabric can relatively easily be untangled.

Certainly in Exod. 24 the making of the covenant in vv. 3-9 interrupts the context of the vision of God in vv. 1-2 and 9-11, but vv. 9-11 in their turn interrupt the connection of the descent and re-ascent of Moses in vv. 3-8 and vv. 12-15a, 18b. Moreover vv. 1-2, 9-11, recognizable as an addition by the introduction to the speech in v. 1, represent a subsidiary idea, and in the light of the persons involved already drop out of the overall context of Exod. 19–24. This is a repeated implementation of Exod. 19.23, which brings the persons admitted in line with the situation in Num. 11. Furthermore the motif of the tablets in Exod. 24.12b is connected with the addition in Exod. (31.18;) 32-34 and is thus likewise secondary. Joshua and the elders come on the scene very abruptly; the trio of Joshua, Aaron and Hur is added from Exod. 17.8ff. (cf. Exod. 32.1ff.,17f.). Thus the twofold communication of the law, which is probably secondary, and the making of the covenant in vv. 3 and 4-8, can be extracted as the earliest element of the text in Exod. 24. Exodus 34.27 and Deut. 26.17-19 + Deut. 27–30; 31.9ff. also had it in view.

The making of the covenant in Exod. 24.3-8 presupposes the communication of the law in Exod. 20–23. And certainly 'all the words of Yhwh and all the precepts of the law' in v. 3 points both to the Decalogue (20.1, 2-17) and also the Book of the Covenant in Exod. 20–23 (21.1). It has been concluded from the lack of 'precepts' in 24.4, and the old observation that they are also lame in v. 3 and could thus be secondary, that the whole scene of accepting the obligation with the covenant document and the blood of the covenant in vv. 3, 4-8 originally referred only to the Decalogue in Exod. 20.1-17 and not to the Book of the Covenant in Exod. 20.22–23.33, so-called after 24.7. But the indications are anything but compelling. Even if the 'precepts' in 24.3 were to be secondary, it is by no means clear whether the 'words of Yhwh' in vv. 3 and 4 mean the Decalogue, the Book of the Covenant, or both. The heading in 20.1 could originally have referred only to the Book of the Covenant or have been added together with the Decalogue, and formulated on the basis of 24.3, 4. Moreover the building of the altar in 24.4-8 probably presupposes the law of the altar of the Book of the Covenant in 20.24-26, which is thus included in the 'words of Yhwh'. In short, the question of the sequence of the incorporation of the Decalogue and the Book of the Covenant cannot be decided on the basis of the designations of the law in 24.3, 4.

Within Exod. 19–23 three entities have been interwoven: the theophany, the Decalogue and the Book of the Covenant. All three are dependent on Moses' ascent of the mountain in 19.3a. It is the presupposition for the command to come down in 19.10ff., which is separated from its original connecting point by the anticipation of the making of the covenant of 24.3-8 in 19.3b-8, 9, written in subsequently; again, 19.20ff. presupposes the descent in 19.10ff. But the ascent in 19.3a also forms a good basis for the introduction to the speech in 20.1, which does not mention the theophany, but together with the Decalogue interrupts the connection between Exod. 19.10-25 and 20.18ff. Finally, the introduction to the speech in 20.22a presupposes the ascent, and the beginning of the speech in 20.22b-23, formulated in the second person plural, presupposes the theophany and the Decalogue, before the law with the address in the second person singular begins in 20.24. Throughout, this means the people, and only in 21.1, as in 20.22a, Moses himself as distinct from the Israelites. That raises the question which of the three connections in 19.3a-10ff. or 20.1 or 20.22ff. is original. On this in turn depends whether the theophany came into the text before the law or the law before the theophany, and which of the two laws was the first.

The classical source hypothesis posits the following sequence: first the theophany (with some conclusion in Exod. 24), then the law; here first the Decalogue (Exod. 20 in E; Exod. 34 in J) and last, mediated through 20.18-21, the Book of the Covenant. There are many objections to this reconstruction, above all the fact that neither in Exod. 19 nor in Exod. 24 did it produce a coherent text, but always only fragments of individual threads of sources. It has therefore been proposed that the relationship should be reversed and that the theophany, which in itself says very little – with all due respect for the original character of pre-exilic Israelite religion, which was not yet dominated by the law – should be put after the law and, now again following the classical documentary hypothesis, the Decalogue. The correct insight here is that the law can do without the theophany but the theophany can hardly do without the law and the circumstances accompanying the communication of the commandment. These are elaborated in a very dramatic way and spun out of the reservoir of ideas about the mountain God. They must therefore be secondary. However, all this does not yet decide the question which of the two laws Moses heard first, the Decalogue or the Book of the Covenant.

In the light of the decisive connecting point in 19.3a, both are possible.

But what tells against the priority of the Decalogue (19.3a + 20.1, 2-17 + 24.3-8 + 24.12a, 13b, 18b)[46] is that in literary terms it is dependent on the Book of the Covenant and that the in any case very compact and well rounded passages must be broken up considerably to free it from this dependent relationship. Moreover the sequence of the Book of the Covenant, Deuteronomy and Decalogue in the history of development tells against this. It would be quite remarkable if the latest law had found its way into the Pentateuch first and the two older corpora of law subsequently and quite independently of each other, although they were dependent on one another in literary terms, initially without taking account of the Decalogue in the Pentateuch. Therefore the other possibility seems more probable, namely that 19.3a was first followed by the Book of the Covenant in 20.24–23.33, whether under the heading of 20.1 or of 20.22a, with or without the attached obligation in 24.3, 4-8 and the further ascent in 24.15a before the closing note in 24.18b. Then the theophany would have been written in between Moses' ascent and the communication of the commandment and the Decalogue finally between the theophany and the Book of the Covenant. Depending on which heading one prefers for the Book of the Covenant, this would produce the following links in the text: (a) the theophany 19.10-20 before 20.1, 24ff.; 21.1, 2ff., the Decalogue 20.2-17 + 20.22a between 20.1 and 20.24-26; 21.1, 2ff.; (b) the theophany 19.10-19 + 20.18, 21 before 20.22a, 24ff.; 21.1, 2ff.; the Decalogue 20.1-17 between 19.10-19 and 20.18, 21, 22a, 24ff. In the case of (a) the Decalogue and the Book of the Covenant are communicated to Moses on the mountain, which the conclusion in Exod. 24.3, 4-8 (with the return ascent in 24.12a, 15a) fits better; in the case of (b), during the communication of the Decalogue in the storm Moses is still with the people and then approaches God again. At all events 19.3b-8, 9, 11b-13, 15b, 17-18, 21-25; 20.19f., 22b-23 are later additions.

4.3   The Book of the Covenant and the Decalogue each have their own prehistory. The core of the Book of the Covenant[47] in Exod. 20.22–23.33 is a collection of legal precepts, *mišpāṭîm*, in Exod. 21--22. The collection contains two kinds of precepts: the casuistic legal principle formulated impersonally with a condition ('If a ...'), sub-condition ('and if ...') and a conclusion ('then ...') in the imperfect or consecutive perfect and the apodeictic death sentence, which identifies the crime committed in the participial sentence with the perpetrator ('Whoever ... does') and imposes the death penalty ('he is worthy of death'). The first appears in Exod. 21.18--22.16 with various legal cases, especially bodily injury inflicted by one man on another and by an animal on a man (21.18ff., 28ff.), and claims for compensation in matters pertaining to the law of property and family law (21.33ff.); the second appears in Exod. 21.12, 15-17 and 22.18-19. The death sentences relating to the basic values of life are to some degree put as a protective framework around the casuistic legal statements taken from everyday life. In contrast to the general Near Eastern casuistic legal statements, the apodictic law was regarded as originally Israelite until Near Eastern analogies were found for it too. The different kinds of legal statements are not the basis for any distinction between Israel and Canaan, but come from different spheres of law (the clan, the family, the gate, the sanctuary).

Moreover this collection made for practical or didactic purposes, which still moves completely within the framework of the pre-exilic history of law, state and religion, was developed in various ways and in the course of this built up into divine law. The expansions can be recognized by the style, which falls into an address in the second person singular and in places also the second person plural, and makes the *mišpāṭīm* with their anonymous formulation into a divine speech to each individual in the people or the people as a whole. Apodictic admonitions are also formulated in the second person singular, the prohibitive (negation *lō'* + imperfect imperative, 'You will not ...') and the vetitive (negation *'al* + jussive 'You shall not ... '), and positive commands which lack the characteristics of legal statements. The second-person-singular additions are above all made at the end of the Book of the Covenant, a first appendix in Exod. 22.20--23.19, a second in 23.20-33; there are others in Exod. 20--21.

The additions are not all on the same level. Some of the laws in the second person singular merely complete the earlier *mišpāṭīm*, like the laws about slaves in 21.2-11 (with the second person singular only in 21.2), the *lex talionis* in 21.23, 24f. and the apodictic statements in 22.17, 27. Others have a social emphasis: 22.20--23.9 and 23.10-12. Here it is specifically a matter of protecting unfortunates, strangers and debtors from the people (the second-person-plural stratum adds widow and orphan) and alongside it the legal security and right of the weaker one before the court, the care of the poor, showing consideration to the workforce through a fallow year, and a day of rest in the rhythm of seven years of days (as in the case of the slave laws in 21.2-11). Here the passage 22.22, 26 is particularly illuminating, where it becomes clear that God himself is the speaker and is taking up the cause of the weak. The social laws draw a distinction between law and justice which also gives rights to those without rights. Both are balanced in the same codex in that Yhwh watches over both. Thus law comes to approximate to paraenesis. This may be understood as a differentiation of ethics from law or as an integration of ethics into law. In fact both amount to the same thing: the expansion of the law by the ethical norm set by God. However, the most important changes in the second-person revision relate to the deity himself, who demands their tribute. The whole of the Book of the Covenant is given a new framework by cultic regulations, which thus become part of the law decreed by the deity: the law of the altar in 20.24-26;[48] the sanctuary and altar as places of asylum in 21.13f.; the offering of the first fruits in 22.28f.; and the festival calendar in 23.14-16[49] with instructions for carrying out the sacrifices in 23.18-19 (which have been added later).

The theologizing of the law begins with the second-person-singular revision of the Book of the Covenant. It is marked less by novelty of content than by the fact that it presents the juristic, social and cultural regulations which were more or less taken for granted in the pre-exilic period as the law of God, laws proclaimed and authorized by Yhwh himself, and impresses the observance of the laws on every individual member of the people. The presupposition for this is that the regulations have lost the natural *Sitz im Leben* from which they drew authority and validity. The *terminus post quem* for this development in the history of the law is the downfall of the state of Israel around 720 and the Assyrian crisis in Judah up to 701 BC. Here for the first time the legal and cultic norms and institutions guaranteed by the state collapsed in the north and were acutely endangered in the south and therefore needed a special foundation and divine sanctions. The Book of the Covenant takes up the shattering of everything that had been taken for granted, which the prophets of the late eighth and early seventh century lamented and subsequently declared to be God's judgment on a people that had become godless, in such a way as to derive a positive divine law from the lament and complaint of the prophets.

The second addition in Exod. 23.20-33 and the second-person-plural additions in 20.22f.; 22.20–24.30; 23.9, 13 go one step further. Here the positive law of God derived from the criticism or negation of the prophets, Yhwh's claim to things taken for granted which have been lost and asked (back) by him, has itself become the law. It is not directed inwards but outwards, against the peoples and their gods. The sole purpose of the observance of the legal, social and cultic regulations decreed by God in the Book of the Covenant is the observance of the First Commandment, that is, the observance and attestation of the exclusiveness of Yhwh. This is also served by the salvation-historical connection of the Book of the Covenant, which bases the observance of the law on the exodus and settlement as a sign of the election of the people. The development presupposes the downfall of the state of Judah in 587 BC. After the complete collapse of pre-exilic conditions and in opposition to the occupation of the land by foreign powers, the exclusivity of Yhwh and his elect people becomes the sole dogma – continuing the idea of centralization relating to the place of worship and the deity in Deuteronomy.

This development comes to be concentrated in the Decalogue of Exod. 20.2-17.[50] It draws on two sources: the Book of the Covenant and the prophetic accusation in Hos. 4.2.[51] Both are summed up in the Decalogue

Table B.I.3

Hexateuch	Mišpāṭîm	+ second person sing.	Theophany	Decalogue	Supplements
Exodus 19.3a					19.3b-9
		(a) 19.10-20	(b) 19.10-19		19.21-25
		(a) 20.1———┘		(b) 20.1 20.2-17	
			20.18, 21		20.19-20
		(b) 20.22a——————┘		(a) 20.22a	20.22b-23
		20.24-26			
		21.1, 2-11			
	21.12	21.13-14			
	21.15-17				
	21.18-22	21.23-25			
	21.26-37				
	22.1-16	22.17			
	22.18-19				
		22.20-9			22.20b, 21, 23, 24b, 30
		23.1-19			23.9b, 13 23.20-33
				24.3, 4-8	24.1f., 9ff.
24.18b					
					32–34

and brought under the same heading: cultic and non-cultic, apodictic and casuistic legal regulations are related and proclaimed as God's basic demand with the help of the prophetic accusation, which is transformed into apodictic law. After the heading in Exod. 20.2-6 this basic demand in Exod. 20.2-17 embraces divine law (vv. 7-10) and human law (vv. 12-17). Both the cultic obligations towards fellow men and women (parents – the triad of killing, committing adultery and stealing – neighbour) stand under the demand for exclusivity which is connected with the act of the exodus and are to be understood as a development and practical implementation of this claim. And just as vv. 7-10, 12-17 develop the heading in vv. 2-6, so in the literary context of Exod. 20–23 the Book of the Covenant develops the basic demands of the Decalogue.

The literary borrowings in the Book of the Covenant show that the Decalogue was not just used later in this sense but came into being for its literary context, to some degree as the preface to the Book of the Covenant.

In it the formulation which categorically demarcates Yhwh, the God of Israel, from the 'other gods' appears for the first time. The strange, very general designation for the gods alongside Yhwh is the counterpart to the 'one' Yhwh in the 'Hear, Israel' of Deut. 6.4. If here, on the basis of the idea of centralization, the local differentiation of Yhwh is done away with in favour of the one manifestation of the deity in one place of worship and one people, in the prelude to and first commandment of the Decalogue the one becomes the only God alongside the 'other gods' for Israel and the other the only people of Israel, brought out of Egypt, alongside the other peoples for Yhwh. The twofold obligation to the whole law introduced by 'Hear, Israel' in Deut. 26.16, 17-19 is matched by the twofold obligation to the law introduced by the Decalogue in Exod. 24.3, 4-8, which perhaps was even added only with the Decalogue. The Decalogue crowns the development which starts from the theologizing of the law in the Book of the Covenant and leads through the idea of centralization in Deuteronomy to Yhwh's claim to exclusiveness which from now on governs the law in the Pentateuch and in the Former Prophets and, supplemented with the monotheistic confession of Isa. 40–48 and Deut. 4, the whole of the Old Testament.

4.4   The 'Book of the Covenant' (20.1 or 20.22a + 20.24–23.19 with an interim heading in 21.1), theophany (19.10-20 or 19.10-19 + 20.18, 21), Decalogue (20.2-17 with a transition in 20.22a or 20.1) and making of the covenant (24.3, 4-8), and lastly the renewal of the covenant (Exod. 32–34) are the main stages of the literary development of the Sinai pericope in the book of Exodus: in substance it is pre-Priestly and pre-Deuteronomic, and subsequently pre-Deuteronomistic. It gradually found its place between the arrival in the wilderness of Sinai in 19.2 and Moses' forty days' stay on the mountain of God in 19.3a and 24.18b (= 34.28a). The Book of the Covenant, stylized as a speech of God and supplemented with the address in the second person singular, was followed by Ur-Deuteronomy, framed with the 'Hear, Israel' in Deut. 6.4-5 and 26.16. Ur-Deuteronomy was followed by the Decalogue with the making of the covenant in Exod. 20 and 24; the Decalogue and making of the covenant in Exodus were followed by the making of the covenant in Deut. 26.17f. and the further successive literary elaboration of Exod. 19–24; 32–34 and of Deuteronomy under the influence of the First Commandment.

Over large stretches this literary-historical development – including law and theology – took place within the Pentateuch. From the Decalogue in Exod. 20 on, which gives the Book of the Covenant a new preamble to match the 'Hear, Israel' in Deut. 6.4-5 and expressly settles where it is now with the previous statement 'I am Yhwh, your God, who has brought you out of the land of Egypt, out of slavery', and in all the phases of development attached to the Decalogue in Exod. 20–24; 32–34 and Deuteronomy, the literary connection of the Book of the Covenant and Deuteronomy is presupposed. Before the Decalogue has been taken over from Exod. 19–20 after Deut. 5 it is not said explicitly how the two legal corpora and the twofold publication of the law and commitment to it in the wilderness of Sinai and in the land of Moab, the Sinai covenant and the Moab covenant, are related in the narrative context. The different addressees give some indication. In the wilderness of Sinai Moses hears the law from the mouth of God and hands on 'the words of Yhwh' on God's instructions; in the land of Moab he speaks of his own accord and inculcates the law on the people with a view to the imminent settlement, as his testament in the form of legal paraenesis. In the view of the Pentateuch – and not entirely wrongly – this is one and the same law, which is proclaimed twice and to which the people commits itself twice, the first time in principle, and the second time on a given occasion. Since a number of things have happened in between, not least the prospect of the settlement in Exod. 23.20ff. with the blessing as a conclusion as in Deut. 28 and the fall and the renewal of the covenant in Exod. 32–34, after which the law is again written out but not promulgated (34.27f.), Deut. 5 makes a distinction between the Decalogue, proclaimed to all the people in the thunder of the theophany, and the law given only to Moses on the mountain in the wilderness of Sinai, which he proclaims publicly for the first time in the land of Moab. All the further developments in writing in both passages, up to and including the incorporation of the Priestly law, live by this construction, which relates the Sinai/Horeb covenant and the Moab covenant. The preceding scene, in which the people accept the obligation, and the covenant document of Exod. 24 are not forgotten here, but with the help of the motif of the tablets – which has already been introduced in Exod. 34 in order to communicate the repeated revelation of the law – are exclusively related to the Decalogue (Deut. 5.22 and Exod. 34.28; Deut. 4.13; 10.4). The independence of the Decalogue does not stand at the beginning but at the end of the tradition, and this is also supported by the extract in the Nash papyrus.

But even without the Decalogue, the Book of the Covenant and Deuteronomy are related by the fact that one is the literary basis of the other. The only question is whether the new version of the Book of the Covenant came about in Ur-Deuteronomy when it was outside or inside the Pentateuch, and whether the two legal corpora found their way into the Pentateuch independently of one another or at the same time, or even, as is usually assumed, in the reverse order, that is, first Deuteronomy and last the Book of the Covenant. As the new version in Deuteronomy presupposes the cultic second-person-singular revision of the Book of the Covenant and in Deut. 12 the position of the law of the altar in Exod. 20.24-26, but in the

Book of the Covenant itself both are connected with the literary incorporation into the Sinai pericope through one of the historicizing headings in 20.1 or 20.22a (and 21.1), it seems to me certain at least that the Book of the Covenant – previously handed down separately and perhaps expanded by one or other of the second-person-singular laws[52] – already stood in its present literary context when it was taken up and interpreted by Ur-Deuteronomy. Whether Ur-Deuteronomy for its part arose as a paraenetic repetition of the Book of the Covenant in the land of Moab or initially outside the Pentateuch depends on the question of the historicization of Deuteronomy. Perspectives arose above (under B.II.3, 4) which support the originality of a historicization that was gradually reinforced. In this case the literary-historical development agrees with the redactional development. The separate origin and the secondary insertion of the Book of the Covenant into the literary context of the Pentateuch was followed by the origin and development of Deuteronomy in the literary context. Otherwise in the case of Deuteronomy we would have to reckon with a separate origin and subsequent insertion.

It is hard to say why the Book of the Covenant (before Deuteronomy in the land of Moab) was set on the mountain of God in the wilderness of Sinai and not, say, in Moab before the crossing of the Jordan, because apart from the later appendix in 23.20-33 there are hardly any references to the historical situation of the literary context. The only ones there are appear in the second-person-singular revision and have the exodus as their theme (22.20 = 23.9; 23.15); however, they are certainly secondary in 22.20; 23.9 (second person plural) and presumably also in 23.15. The point of contact can therefore really only have been the 'mountain of God', which offered itself as an appropriate place on the way between the sea (Exod. 14–15) and the settlement (Num. 20.1–25.1a + Deut. 34.5f. + Josh. 2.1; 3.1). Here the deity could make himself known and communicate the conditions for the life of his people. As the immediate link between Josh. 2.1; 3.1 and Num. 15.1a + Deut. 34.5f. shows, a stay in the land of Moab was originally not foreseen and had to be invented in order to locate the repeated (or, if the scene of the commitment of the people in Exod. 24.3, 4-8 was not yet there, the first) promulgation of the law, that is, the new theological version of the Book of the Covenant in Ur-Deuteronomy, Deut. 6.4–26.16, in the narrative context. Therefore in contrast to the Book of the Covenant, in Deuteronomy the selection of laws, the direction of the speech with Moses as speaker and the people as audience, and the historical location of the legal paraenesis shortly before the settlement correspond admirably from the beginning.

Accordingly the presupposition for the first insertion of the law into the narrative context was Moses' forty-day stay with God on the mountain of God in Exod. 19.2-3a and 24.18b. That may once have been the only thing that happened in the wilderness of Sinai before the law intervened. [53] Now even the ascent of Moses to God seems to be secondary by comparison with the stay of Israel in the wilderness of Sinai, as is suggested by the link to Exod. 19.2a ('And they camped in the wilderness of Sinai') in v. 2b ('And they camped there opposite the mountain'), which prepares for the ascent in 19.3a; 24.18b. The itinerary of Exod. 19.2a continues in Num. 20.1aβb, with or without this short episode: 'And they camped in the wilderness of Sinai and the people settled in Kadesh.' Accordingly Miriam died in Kadesh in the wilderness of Sinai before the mountain of God separated the arrival in the wilderness of Sinai and the settlement in Kadesh from each other. If we want, we can also think of an 'and they set out from the wilderness of Sinai' after Moses' stay on the mountain in Exod. 19.3a; 24.18b (cf. Num. 10.12a), but that is not necessary. Numbers 10.11f. and 10.33 already indicate (post-)Priestly terminology; in Num. 20.1aα after the various detours in Num. 10–19 the wilderness of Sinai becomes the wilderness of Zin.

But even the stay in the wilderness of Sinai is a secondary detour on the way of Israel from the sea in Exod. 15 to Kadesh in Num. 20.1. The itinerary of Exod. 19.2a was originally attached to Exod. 16.1aα: 'And they set out from Elim ... and came into the wilderness of Sinai, and they camped in the wilderness of Sinai.' The material introduced into Exod. 16–18 in the meantime is governed by the (post-)Priestly itinerary in 16.1aβb (into the wilderness of Sin, an artificial duplication of the wilderness of Sinai), 17.1 (from Sin to Rephidim) and 19.2aα (from Rephidim), and has thus been inserted subsequently. Exodus 16.1aα ('And they set out from Elim') and 19.2a (from 'and they came into the wilderness of Sinai') are in turn dependent on the brief episodes in the wilderness in 15.22-25a, 27. They too have been inserted between the departure and exodus after the wilderness of Shur in Exod. 15.22a and the settlement in Kadesh in Num. 20.1, though earlier than Exod. 16–18. The continuity of the action indicates that here we have the original join in the text: in Exod. 15.20f. Miriam sings her song of victory, which is a reaction to the miracle at the sea of Exod. 14; after the departure in Exod. 15.22a and the arrival in Kadesh in Num. 20.1 she dies and is buried. Genesis 16.7, 14; 20.1 should be compared for the geography.

5.   Result

Before the law came into the Pentateuch, Israel first had to reach the mountain of God in the wilderness of Sinai. From Kadesh in the wilderness of Shur (Exod. 15.22a/Num. 20.1) thirst drove them first of all to Marah, from Marah to Elim, and from Elim 'back' into the wilderness of Sinai to

Kadesh (Exod. 15.22-25a, 27; 16.1aα; 19.2a, 'and they came'; Num. 20.1aβb). Before the people settled in Kadesh and Miriam died, Moses climbed the mountain of God (Exod. 19.2b, 3a; 24.18b). Here the law intervened, first the Book of the Covenant (Exod. 20.1 or 20.22a + 20.24–23.19), after the theophany in Exod. 19–20 then the Decalogue (Exod. 20.2-17 with 20.1 or 20.22a) and the making of the covenant (Exod. 24.3, 4-8), and lastly the renewal of the covenant in Exod. 32–34. From here the law has been carried forward into the wilderness episodes of Exod. 15 (vv. 25b-26), but above all has been developed further in a backward direction.

The Book of the Covenant is the original literary basis of Ur-Deuteronomy (Deut. 5.1aα[1]; 6.4-5 + 12-21 + 26.1f., 11, 16; 34.1a, 5f.), which inserts itself after the wandering in the wilderness in Num. 20.1-25.1a between the arrival in Shittim in Num. 25.1a and the death of Moses in Deut. 34.5f. (with a continuation in Josh. 2.1; 3.1), and recapitulates the Book of the Covenant in terms of the idea of centralization. The paraenetic framework of Ur-Deuteronomy, the 'Hear, Israel' in Deut. 6.4-5 and 26.16, provokes the formation of the Decalogue in Exod. 20 and becomes the starting point both for the extensive elaboration of the Sinai pericope in Exod. 19–24; 32–34 with its many strata, and for the further legislation and legal paraenesis in Deuteronomy, all this under the sign of the First Commandment in the framework chapters Deut. (4;) 5–11 and 26–30. The historicizing connecting passages in Deut. 1–3 (4) and 31–34 are even later; on the one hand they reinforce the narrative connection with (Genesis–) Numbers and Joshua(–Kings) and on the other they contribute towards marking out Deuteronomy as the Torah of Moses.

In Exod. 25–40 the Priestly Writing shifts the foundation of the sanctuary to Sinai, where God takes up his dwelling in the midst of Israel and thus makes it possible for God to be God for Israel. This is resolved in Gen. 17 and endorsed for Moses in Exod. 6 as a counter-scheme to the law and covenant in the Sinai pericope and in Deuteronomy. The covenant with Abraham takes the place of the covenant on Sinai and the covenant of Moab. But here too the law soon makes its way in. On the basis of Deuteronomy the basic writing (P^G) is expanded with the Holiness Code of Lev. 17–26 (27) and further laws in Lev. 1–16 (P^S). Lastly, the non-Priestly and the Priestly law are worked together (R^P), which brings with it the filling-out of the wilderness wandering in Numbers with Priestly and non-Priestly narrative material, the demarcation of Deuteronomy as the law of Moses marked by Num. 27.12ff., the division of the lawgiving into three stages (on Mount Sinai (Exod.–Lev.), in the wilderness of Sinai (Num. 1–25) and in Moab (Num. 26–36 + Deut.), and finally the separation of the Pentateuch as Torah.

If we peel off the strata of the law one after another, a literary narrative thread appears which extends from Genesis to Exodus at least as far as

Joshua. The law does not belong only in the Tetrateuch (Genesis–Numbers) or Pentateuch (Genesis–Deuteronomy), nor does it stand at the beginning of a historical work that is separated from it (Deuteronomy–Kings); but from the beginning it presupposes the Hexateuch (Genesis–Joshua), which under the influence of the law grows into the Enneateuch (Genesis–Kings). Whereas the law in Genesis–Numbers + Joshua interrupts an earlier redactional connection, in Joshua–Kings it is the stimulus towards the composition and collecting of the books. We can make clear the difference from the older narrative in Genesis–Exodus by means of the Book of Jubilees,[54] which, as already happens here and there in Genesis–Exodus itself, introduces the law back into the history of creation, the patriarchs and the exodus as far as Exod. 14.

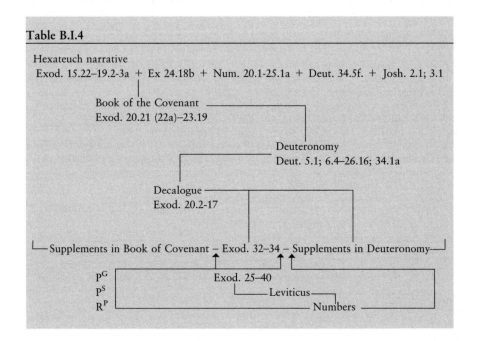

Table B.I.4

Hexateuch narrative
Exod. 15.22–19.2-3a + Ex 24.18b + Num. 20.1-25.1a + Deut. 34.5f. + Josh. 2.1; 3.1

Book of the Covenant
Exod. 20.21 (22a)–23.19

Deuteronomy
Deut. 5.1; 6.4–26.16; 34.1a

Decalogue
Exod. 20.2-17

Supplements in Book of Covenant – Exod. 32–34 – Supplements in Deuteronomy

P^G
P^S Exod. 25–40
R^P Leviticus
                    Numbers

Notes

1   There is a survey in G. Liedke, *Gestalt und Bezeichnung alttestamentlicher Rechtssätze*, WMANT 39, 1971, 13-17. M. Weinfeld, *Deuteronomy and the Deuteronomic School*, 1972 (reprinted 1992), 332ff., is more detailed on Deuteronomism.
2   Cf. Deut. 1.5; 4.8, 44; 27.3, 8, 26; 28.58, 61; 29.20, 28; 30.10; 31.9, 11, 12, 24, 26; 32.46; 33.4, 10; within the legal corpus only 17.11, 18f.; also Josh. 1.7, 8; 8.31, 32, 34; 22.5; 23.6; 24.26; 1 Kgs 2.3; 2 Kgs 10.31; 14.6; 17.13, 34, 37; 21.8; 22.8, 11; 23.24, 25.

Also R.G. Kratz, 'Reich Gottes und Gesetz im Danielbuch und im werdenden Judentum', in A.S. van der Woude (ed.), *The Book of Daniel in the Light of New Findings*, BEThL 106, 1993, 435-79: 458 with nn. 69, 70.

3   Two thousand, six hundred and sixty-six years from the creation to the exodus + 480 years up to the building of the temple + 430 years up to the destruction of the temple in 587 BC + the remaining 424 years.

4   I know that the procedure of subtraction is often criticized today, but I do not understand the criticism. If someone has a better procedure I would like to know.

5   Cf. Num. 13.3, 26 (without 'to Kadesh') and the resumption of 10.12 in 12.16 after the wanderings in 10.29–12.16.

6   Pola, *Die ursprüngliche Priesterschrift*, 343 n. 144.

7   Blum, *Studien*, 326. But cf. in ibid., 224, the concession 'that the Priestly material in particular has "grown" in a lengthy process – probably of generations – into the breadth which we have now'. We are not told what the quotation marks mean and what is to be said against the attempt to make an approximate reconstruction of this process – which Blum presupposes throughout in his compositional demarcations, 225ff.

8   Cf. Wellhausen, *Comp.*, 142-4; Noth, *Leviticus*, 68f.

9   Cf. Pola, *Die ursprüngliche Priesterschrift*, 221 n. 22.

10 Cf. C. Levin, *Der Jahwist*, FRLANT 157, 1993, 375-7; also N. Rabe, *Vom Gerücht zum Gericht. Die Kundschaftererzählung Numeri 13–14 als Neuansatz der Pentateuchforschung*, ThLI 8, 1994.

11 Wellhausen, *Comp.*, 34-2; Noth, *Numbers*, 121f., point in the right direction.

12 N. Lohfink, *Die Priesterschrift und die Geschichte*, VT.S 29, 1978, 198 n. 29.

13 *ÜSt*, 182ff.; cf. also Pola, *Die ursprüngliche Priesterschrift*, 107f.

14 Cf. the demonstration in L. Perlitt, 'Priesterschrift im Deuteronomium?' (1988), in id., *Deuteronomium-Studien*, FAT 8, 1994, 123-43. For more recent discussion cf. C. Frevel, *Mit Blick auf das Land die Schöpfung erinnern: Zum Ende der Priesterschrift*, HBS 23, 2000.

15 Cf. A. Cholewinski, *Heiligkeitsgesetz und Deuteronomium*, 1976.

16 HAT I/4, 14ff.; also Cholewinski, *Heiligkeitsgesetz*, 338; A. Ruwe, 'Heiligkeitsgesetz' und 'Priesterschrift', FAT 26, 1999.

17 J. Maier, *Die Tempelrolle vom Toten Meer*, UTB 829, 1978; id., *Die Qumran-Essener: Die Texte vom Toten Meer* I, UTB 1862, 1995, 370ff.; F. García Martínez and E.J.C. Tigchelaar (eds), *The Dead Sea Scrolls, Study Edition*, Vol. 2, 2000, 1228-89.

18 Pola, *Die ursprüngliche Priesterschrift*, 51-146, 213ff., cf. esp. 89f., 146, arrives at a similar result in a different way. I do not understand what his 'being' categories mean.

19 Wellhausen, *Comp.*, 116.

20 See in the Introduction, n. 5.

21 Wellhausen, *Comp.*, 189, 191, 193.

22 See R.G. Kratz, 'Der literarische Ort des Deuteronomiums', in R.G. Kratz and H. Spieckermann (eds), *Liebe und Gebot*, 101-20.

23 See G. Minette de Tillesse, 'Sections "tu" et sections "vous" dans le Deutéronome', VT 12, 1962, 28-87; id., 'Tu et Vous dans le Deutéronome', in Kratz and Spieckermann (eds), *Liebe und Gebot*, 156-63.

24 See B.M. Levinson, *Deuteronomy and the Hermeneutics of Legal Innovation*, New York and Oxford 1997.

25 See E. Reuter, *Kultzentralisation*, BBB 87, 1993.

26 M can also mean 'at the whole place'. The ambivalent determination offered a point of contact for the reinterpretation in Deut. 12 or is an orthodox correction.

27 Verse 23 'to make his name dwell there', 'and the firstborn of your cattle and your

sheep', v. 24aα²βγ (from 'for the place is too far ... '), perhaps also the list of kindnesses in v. 26a (from the oxen) and vv. 23b, 24b, 29b. Thus most scholars. But perhaps all of vv. 23f. were also added later, so that originally v. 25 was directly attached to v. 22. The repetitions of 12.17f., 19, 21 and the anticipation of 14.26b and 15.19ff. in vv. 23a, 24a, 27 would thus be on one and the same redactional level. Cf. Reuter, *Kultzentralization*, 161f.

28   'Among your cattle and your livestock', after Deut. 12.17, 'the firstborn of your bulls and the firstborn of your small cattle', after Exod. 22.29.

29   The original formula runs: 'The place which Yhwh (your God) will choose' (thus 12.14, 18, 26; 14.25; 16.7, 13f.; 17.8, 10; 18.6; 31.11). The long form adds that Yhwh makes his name dwell at this place or puts it there (thus 12.5, 11, 21; 14.23f.; 16.2, 6, 11; 26.2).

30   After removing all the additions: Deut. 12.13, 14a (up to 'Yhwh'), 15-18; 14.22, (23a, 24a,) 25-26; 15.19-23; 16.16f.; 16.18 (without 'your tribes'); 17.8-9aαb, 10a; 19.2a, 3b, 7, 11-12, 15-17a, 18abα, 21b; 21.1-4, 6-7, 8b.

31   Cf. Deut. 12.14, 21, 28, 35, etc., but the formula of the command in the first person (Moses) as the lawgiving authority is secondary everywhere. Only 26.16, according to which Yhwh himself has commanded the law, is different.

32   Of course without the insertion 'the servant of Yhwh in the land of Moab at Yhwh's command' in Deut. 34.5 and presumably also without v. 6b. Cf. Kratz, in Kratz and Spieckermann (eds), *Liebe und Gebot*, 102 n. 5, 119 n. 73; Kratz, 'Der vor- und der nachpriesterschriftliche Hexateuch', in J.C. Gertz et al., *Abschied vom Jahwisten*, BZAW 315, 2002, 295-323: 321.

33   Cf. H. Spieckermann, 'Mit der Liebe im Wort', in Kratz and Spieckermann (eds), *Liebe und Gebot*, 190-205.

34   Thus, however, only in the (late) framework chapters Deut. 1–4 (1.2, 6, 19; 4.10, 15); 5.2; 9.8; 28.69 and once in an addition in 18.16. This is an identification of the mountain of God 'in the desolate land' (Horeb) of Exod. 3.1ff. with the mountain 'in the wilderness' of Sinai of Exod. 19ff., which has also been taken over in Exod. 17.6; 33.6.

35   For the relationship between the two versions cf. R.G. Kratz, 'Der Dekalog im Exodusbuch', *VT* 44, 1994, 205-38.

36   Cf. C. Levin, *Die Verheissung des neuen Bundes*, FRLANT 137, 1985, 83ff.; T. Veijola, 'Bundestheologische Redaktion im Deuteronomium', in Veijola (ed.), *Das Deuteronomium und seine Querbeziehungen*, 242-76.

37   Noth, *ÜSt*, 33f. [ET, 53ff.].

38   Cf. ibid., 17 [ET, 33].

39   The germ of the account of the reform is either the notice about the high places in 2 Kgs 23.8f. (though here it is used in a positive way, already dominated by the idea of cultic purity) or the note in 23.11f. The former is supported only by the general consensus, which here as elsewhere confuses the Deuteronomistic historian's interpretation of history with history, the latter by the agreement with the historical and religious situation which is also documented in 23.28f.

40   Cf. *ANET*³ (Suppl.), 534ff.

41   Cf. E. Blum, 'Das sogenannte "Privilegrecht" in Exodus 34.11-26: Ein Fixpunkt der Komposition des Exodusbuches?', in M. Vervenne (ed.), *Studies in the Book of Exodus*, BEThL 126, 1996, 347-66; Otto, 'Die nachpriesterschriftliche Pentateuch-redaktion im Buch Exodus', 99f., etc., differs. For discussion see recently H.G. Schmitt, 'Das sogenannte jahwistische Privilegrecht in Exod. 34, 10-28 als Komposition der spätdeuteronomistischen Endredaktion des Pentateuch', in J.C. Gertz et al., *Abschied vom Jahwisten*, BZAW 315, 2002, 157-71.

42   That the idea of the tent does not fit the Priestly Writing's tent here, as it still does in Num. 11f. and Deut. 31.14f., is not sufficient reason for regarding it as pre-Priestly, indeed as very old indeed. That the tent is to be put up outside the camp follows from Exod. 32.30, the sin in the camp (cf. 32.17, 19, 26f.), and represents an assimilation to the sanctuaries of the land (cf. 1 Sam. 2.22; 2 Sam. 6.17), which in 2 Chron. 3.1, 13 also include the tent of meeting from the time in the wilderness. The iteratives point beyond Exod. 33.12ff. and 34 to the erection of the tent in Exod. 36ff. and its constant use.

43   Before Moses destroys the calf (Exod. 32.20), his attention has to be drawn to it. That happens in vv. 7f. and 19. Verses 7f. take up vv. 1-6. Verse 19 is connected with vv. 17f. and vv. 15f.

44   The usual assignation of Exod. 19.2a to P and its transposition before v. 1 robs the non-Priestly text of its beginning and foists a doublet on P. That need not be the case. The detail 'and they set out from Rephidim', which continues the itinerary of 16.1; 17.1 and shows Priestly influence, is the only problem. More on this below.

45   *Bundestheologie*, 156-203.

46   Thus Levin, *Dekalog*.

47   See E. Otto, *Wandel der Rechtsbegründungen in der Gesellschaftsgeschichte des antiken Israel: Eine Rechtsgeschichte des 'Bundesbuches' Ex.20.22–23.13*, StB 3, 1988; L. Schwienhorst-Schönberger, *Das Bundesbuch (Ex.20.22–23.33)*, BZAW 188, 1990; Y. Osumi, *Die Kompositionsgeschichte des Bundesbuches Ex 20, 22b–23*, 3, OBO 105, 1991; C. Houtman, *Das Bundesbuch*, DMOA 24, 1997.

48   The basic definition in Exod. 20.24aα(β) is taken further in v. 25 with a first sub-definition. Verse 24b is a later interpretation which is perhaps connected with the prefixing of the law of the altar and the redactional incorporation of the Book of the Covenant into the context of the Sinai pericope. The position of the law of the altar and the interpretation are most easily explained from the correspondence with the festal calendar in 23.14-17 which applied at all the sanctuaries (high places) in the land.

49   In Exod. 23.15 only: 'You shall observe the feast of unleavened bread at the date in the month of Abib', that is, without the regulation about carrying it out and the historicization in v. 15a and the syntactically clumsy gloss in v. 15b. The version of the original ordinance for the festival in vv. 15f. as pilgrimages in vv. 14, 17, in v. 14 with Yhwh in the first person, is not later but earlier than the historicization in v. 15a and has arisen as a result of the second-person-singular revision which put the cultic laws in the Book of the Covenant and the Book of the Covenant in its literary context.

50   See Kratz, *Dekalog*. I now think that the dependence of Exod. 34 rests on an addition in Exod. 20.5b-6. The references to the Book of the Covenant are sufficient for everything else (alongside Hos. 4.2).

51   Jer. 7.9 presupposes the First Commandment and therefore the finished Decalogue.

52   That the first person is Yhwh becomes clear only from the context: however, it is not Moses who is addressed in the second person but every individual in the people.

53   Levin, *Yahwist*, 364f.

54   K. Berger, *Das Buch der Jubiläen*, JSHRZ II, 3, 1981; R.H. Charles, *APOT* II, 1-82.

II   The Revision of the Former Prophets under the Influence of the Law

1.   The Deuteronomistic redaction

Wellhausen, *Composition*, 116-34, 208-301, 363ff.; id., *Prolegomena*, 245-96; Noth, *Deuteronomistic History*; A.D.H. Mayes, *The Story of Israel between Settlement and Exile*, London 1983; M.A. O'Brien, *The Deuteronomistic History Hypothesis: A Reassessment*, OBO 92, 1989; A. de Pury et al. (eds), *Israël construit son histoire: L'historiographie deutéronomiste à la lumière des recherches récentes*, MoBi 34, 1996 (ET JSOT.S 306, 2000); J. Pakkala, *Intolerant Monolatry in the Deuteronomistic History*, Publications of the Finnish Exegetical Society 65, Helsinki and Göttingen 1999; G.N. Knappers and J.G. McConville (eds), *Reconsidering Israel and Judah: Recent Studies on the Deuteronomic History*, Sources for Biblical and Theological Study 8, 2000; T. Römer (ed.), *The Future of Deuteronomistic History*, BETL 137, 2000; A.F. Campbell and M.A. O'Brian, *Unfolding the Deuteronomic History: Origins, Upgrades, Present Text*, 2000.

Research

E. Jenni, 'Zwei Jahrzehnte Forschung an den Büchern Josua bis Könige', *ThR* 27, 1961, 1-32, 97-146; A.N. Radjawane, 'Das deuteronomistische Geschichtswerk: Ein Forschungsbericht', *ThR* 38, 1974, 177-217; H. Weippert, 'Das deuteronomistische Geschichtswerk: Sein Ziel und Ende in der neueren Forschung', *ThR* 50, 1985, 213-49; H.D. Preuss, 'Zum deuteronomistische Geschichtswerk', *ThR* 58, 1993, 229-64, 341-95; A. de Pury and T. Römer in de Pury et al. (eds), *Israël*, 9-120 (ET 24-141); T. Veijola, 'Deuteronomismusforschung zwischen Tradition und Innovation (II)', *ThR* 67, 2002, 321-424 (to be continued in *ThR* 68, 2003).

1.1   When Moses, the servant of Yhwh, had died, Joshua, the son of Nun and servant of Moses, received orders from Yhwh to set out and cross the Jordan with the whole people and take possession of the whole land and divide it up as the heritage that Yhwh had sworn to their fathers and now wanted to give them. But he was to observe the law that Yhwh had given to Moses: 'Be bold and strong, observe the law and you will have success!' (Josh. 1.1-9; cf. Deut. 31.1ff.). Joshua immediately set to work, inspected the camp, and assured himself of the support of the two and a half tribes east of the Jordan which already had the settlement behind them (Num. 32; 34.13-15; Deut. 3.12ff.). And they crossed the Jordan and Joshua occupied the whole land, just as Yhwh had said to Moses, and divided it as a heritage to Israel after its divisions and tribes, and the land had rest from the war (Josh. 2–12; cf. 11.15, 16-23). And when Joshua was old and full of days Yhwh revealed to him that there was still much land to take possession of and to distribute, and again charged him with the distribution. Once again the whole land was distributed between all the tribes of Israel, this time by drawing lots. So Yhwh gave Israel the whole land that he had sworn to their fathers, and they took possession of it and settled in it and had rest from all their enemies round about (Josh. 12.21; cf. 21.43-45). And Joshua released the tribes east of the Jordan (Josh. 22) and twice summoned a great assembly of the people. In long speeches he warned against transgressing the law, recalled everything that had happened since the patriarchs, and pledged the people to Yhwh and his law in a covenant. Like Moses on Sinai (Exod. 24 and 34) and in Moab (Deut. 26–30), Joshua concluded the covenant and gave the people justice and law in Shechem (Josh. 23–24).

And Israel settled in Israel, observed the law, and served Yhwh as long as Joshua lived. But as soon as he and his generation had died the Israelites did evil in Yhwh's eyes and ran after other gods. There was a cycle of sin, judgment, lament and deliverance and again sin, judgment, lament and deliverance, so the people constantly fell away from Yhwh. As a result, time and again they fell into the hand of the enemy, and could be saved only by the intervention of Yhwh, who each time raised up a judge (saviour) in Israel (Judg. 2.6–3.6).

With their own collaboration, reluctant though it was, Yhwh made the judges a fixed institution and granted Israel the king they desired. Because the institution of the monarchy restricted the unlimited rule of Yhwh and his law, it was a priori under a bad sign. In an impressive farewell discourse Samuel, the kingmaker chosen by God, recalls the beginnings of the people under Moses and Aaron and their further history and summons them to observe the law: 'Only fear Yhwh and serve him in faithfulness and with your whole heart. But if you do evil, then you will immediately perish and also your king' (1 Sam. 7–12; cf. 12.12-15, 24f.).

The first king passed away, and in his place Yhwh chose for himself David and his son Solomon as kings over Judah and Israel, the one as founder of the Davidic dynasty, the other as the builder of the temple in Jerusalem (2 Sam. 7). They did much that was right, but they also did evil in Yhwh's eyes, and were admonished and punished for it (2 Sam. 11.27 and

12.1ff.; cf. 1 Kgs 15.5; 1 Kgs 11, esp. 11.9-13). And because Solomon broke the covenant and abandoned the commandments of Yhwh, Israel and Judah collapsed under his son Rehoboam.

But the chief sin was committed by Jeroboam, who sealed the division of the kingdom with two images of bulls and established his kingdom on the transgression of the First Commandment (1 Kgs 12–14, especially 12.28 = Exod. 32.4). From now on the kings and the people of Israel and Judah stood under the spell of the sin of Jeroboam and had to choose whether they did right or evil in the eyes of Yhwh, whether they wanted to observe or break the covenant and the law (1 Kgs 14.22-24; 15.3-5, etc.). As a result the northern kingdom of Israel (2 Kgs 17) and finally also the kingdom of Judah (2 Kgs 18–25) came to grief. Josiah was the last to turn to Yhwh, more than any king before him, with all his soul and with all his might, according to the whole Torah of Moses to which he committed himself in a covenant, but after him no one behaved as he did (2 Kgs 22–23, esp.23.25). Thereupon Yhwh did not cease from his anger and resolved: 'I will remove Judah also out of my sight, as I have removed Israel, and I will cast off this city which I have chosen, Jerusalem, and the house of which I said, "My name shall be there"' (2 Kgs 23.26-27).

1.2   That, by and large, is the course of the history narrated in Joshua–Kings and with some deletions retold in more recent accounts of the secular and religious history of Israel. All along the line it presupposes the law, Deuteronomy above all; however, it presupposes not only Deuteronomy but at many points (for example, in Josh. 24) the whole Pentateuch, the Torah, and in it especially the First Commandment (Exod. 20 and Deut. 5). If we remove this presupposition and take away the connecting links based on it, the whole historical construction collapses into loose, disconnected individual parts: narratives of conquest and war and mixed lists of frontiers in Joshua, narratives of individual tribal heroes and episodes from the beginnings of the kingdom in Judges, the rise and fall of the kingdom of Saul and the kingdom of David in 1–2 Samuel, annalistic notes and individual legends about kings and prophets in 1–2 Kings.

The vast majority of these are individual traditions, not of all Israel and the (broken) unity of Judah and Israel but of individual persons or groups in Israel and Judah, and they do not even have the whole history of Israel in view but only individual episodes which without the binding link of the law are far from producing an even approximate overall picture or a historical connection. The historical tradition can best be grasped in the chronological framework of 1–2 Kings and the individual brief annalistic notices on the individual kings of the two states of Israel and Judah interspersed in them. Moreover a very extensive narrative of the beginnings of the kingdom under Saul and David has been preserved in 1–2 Samuel, likewise composed of individual narratives and clusters of narratives, the story of Saul in 1 Sam. 1–15 and the court histories of David in 2 Sam. 13–20, framed by 2 Sam. 11–12 and 1 Kgs 1–2. However, these have already been redactionally interwoven and formed into a historical continuum before and independently of the historical construction under the influence of the law in 1 Sam. 16–2 Sam. 10 (cf. also 2 Sam. 21). But if we leave aside the late Israelitization and the historical construction guided by the law, not everything else in Joshua and Judges can immediately be taken as tradition and documents from the time before the state. Rather, especially the narratives about heroes in Judges and the Saul–David legend depict the conditions of the (beginning of the) monarchical period alongside the annalistic traditions of the states of Israel and Judah. The differences are not chronological but sociological. Only the material in Joshua which takes the narrative threads of the Hexateuch (Genesis/Exodus–Joshua) to an end basically deals with Israel, as already does Exod. 14.

It is the law, namely, the First Commandment, that first provides the historical connection. In the light of the law and the history of the people of God in the Hexateuch the juxtaposition of the scattered individual traditions becomes a historical sequence, and the episodes of individual persons and groups become the history of all Israel and its twelve tribes. So in Joshua–Kings we have a revision which goes beyond individual books and gives the different traditions – the conclusion of the history of the exodus of the people of Israel in Joshua, the narratives about heroes and tribes in Judges, the legends of Saul and David in 1–2 Samuel, and the extracts from the annals of the kingdoms of Israel and Judah in 1–2 Kings – a literary and historical theological connection. This revision, extending beyond individual books, speaks a quite uniform language which in many respects recalls Deuteronomy and the Deuteronomic paraenesis of the law. It has therefore long been called the 'Deuteronomistic' redaction, which means that it is not Deuteronomic and identical with Deuteronomy but is derived from it and only remotely related. There are also traces of such a 'Deuteronomistic' redaction derived from Deuteronomy in Deuteronomy itself and beyond it in the rest of the Hexateuch, especially in Exodus and Numbers.

1.3   There is unanimity over the phenomenon itself, but it is explained in different ways. Earlier scholarship reckoned with consecutive narrative threads in Genesis–Kings[1] which have been given a Deuteronomistic revision at various points. Wellhausen indicates that the source documents hardly extend beyond Numbers and that therefore Joshua is more an appendix to the Pentateuch and Judges–Kings an appendix to the Hexateuch. Noth finally discovered the 'old sources' only in the Tetrateuch (Genesis–Numbers) and in Deut. 34 and separated the books Joshua–Kings with a Deuteronomistic redaction from them; in these he discovered his Deuteronomistic history – with Deuteronomy and especially Deut. 1–3 as a beginning. For him, the redaction in Deuteronomy to Kings was the work of a single author who collected and ordered the traditions and put them in their present form. Noth explained inconsistencies in the intrinsically unitary revision which run contrary to the stereotypical language, the interpretation of history by speeches or reflections of the author (Josh. 1; 23–24; Judg. 2.6ff.; 1 Sam. 12; 2 Sam. 7; 1 Kgs 8; 2 Kgs 17.7ff.), the consistent chronology and the principles of the Deuteronomistic theology of history, either by the disparity of the earlier source material or as later expansions. He recognized as the *terminus a quo* of the Deuteronomic revision the pardoning of Jehoiachin in 2 Kgs 25, which begins in the Babylonian lists from 592 BC and can be dated quite precisely to 562 BC by the king Amel-marduk who is mentioned.[2] From his standpoint the whole depiction becomes 'as it were, a great confession of sins of the exiled nation looking back on its history'.[3]

The inconsistencies also noted by Noth are the starting point for the more recent explanations, the majority of which do not reckon with one but (again) with several Deuteronomistic revisions.[4] Different 'models' have been proposed for this: one which sees the Deuteronomistic work in blocks, for example, from a basic stem in Deuteronomy–Joshua through a pre-exilic Hezekiah or Josianic block, depending on whether one sees the editing extending up to 2 Kgs 20 or 2 Kgs 23, as far as the exilic redaction in 2 Kgs (21;) 24–25, and one which does not distinguish blocks but literary strata, for example, the annalistic basic material and alongside it a priestly, a nebistic and a levitical revision or, which roughly amounts to the same thing, the Deuteronomistic historian (DtrH = DtrG for the historical work or the basic document), the supplementers and revisers of the prophetic narratives (DtrP) and the nomists (DtrN).

Both schools, the one represented above all in the English-language and Catholic sphere, the other more in the Protestant tradition of German-language exegesis, are right in some ways and are often combined, but they must be put in the right relationship. One thing is common to all the blocks and strata proposed: the First Commandment and all that it entails for Yhwh over against the other gods, for the people of Israel over against the other peoples, and for the kings of Israel and Judah over against Yhwh's unconditional claim to rule. But that is not the case to the same degree everywhere. Whereas in Samuel–Kings the First Commandment has become the criterion for assessing the kings only at a secondary stage and has replaced another criterion, likewise derived from Deuteronomy and to that degree Deuteronomistic, namely the criterion of the unity of the kingdom and the cult, in Deuteronomy itself as in Joshua and Judges, more or less from the beginning it is the criterion of the 'Deuteronomistic' (prophetic, priestly, and other) revisions. Now that means that the beginning of the Deuteronomistic redaction does not lie in Deuteronomy but in Samuel–Kings and from here extends forwards into (Genesis–)Deuteronomy, Joshua and Judges.[5]

Furthermore we must rid ourselves of the notion of a Deuteronomistic history extending from Deuteronomy to Kings, which is presupposed in both schools; they themselves remove the ground from under this. That does not mean that we immediately have to reckon with a revision extending from Genesis or Exodus to Kings.[6] The connection first exists at the latest literary stages. Rather, we must start from the consecutive narrative threads in the Hexateuch (Genesis–Joshua), which has gradually grown into the Enneateuch (Genesis–Kings); these were found above and are interrupted by the law only in Exodus–Numbers and Deuteronomy. The reverse development which is claimed by some, the prior construction of the 'later Yahwist' in Genesis–Numbers before Deuteronomy–Kings, also stands or falls with the hypothesis of the independent Deuteronomistic history, and much else tells against it. The connection is not made by the text in Genesis–Numbers but is stamped on it secondarily at a quite late stage of the redaction. Rather, the old view of the Deuteronomistic additions to the Hexateuch is confirmed, except that the redaction went through several stages. The beginning lies in Samuel–Kings; the latest stages are largely identical with the texts in Deuteronomy–Kings, to which Noth refers for his Deuteronomists and which today scholars like to sum up under the abbreviations DtrP and DtrN (or Dtr1 and Dtr2, etc.). Noth's DtrG is DtrP + DtrN and embraces the whole Enneateuch before it was split into the two parts of the canon, the Torah and the Former Prophets.

2. Redaction and tradition in Samuel and Kings

A. Jepsen, *Die Quellen des Königsbuches*, 1953; H. Weippert, 'Die "deuteronomistischen" Beurteilungen der Könige von Israel und Juda und das Problem der Redaktion der Königsbücher', *Bib* 53, 1972, 301-39; W. Dietrich, *Prophetie und Geschichte*, FRLANT 108, 1972; id., *David, Saul and the Prophets*, BWANT 122, 1989, [2]1992; id., 'Die frühe Königszeit in Israel. 10. Jahrhundert v. Chr.', *Biblische Enzyklopädie* 3, 1997; id. and T. Naumann, *Die Samuelbücher*, EdF 287, 1995; T. Veijola, *Die ewige Dynastie*, AASF.B 193, Helsinki 1975; id., *Das Königtum in der Beurteilung der deuteronomistischen Historiographie*, AASF.B 198, Helsinki 1977; R.D. Nelson, *The Double Redaction of the Deuteronomistic History*, JSOT.S 18, 1981; I.W. Provan, *Hezekiah and the Book of Kings*, BZAW 172, 1988; S.L. McKenzie, *The Trouble with Kings*, VT.S 42, 1991.

Commentaries

K. Budde, *Die Bücher Samuel*, KHC 8, 1902; E. Würthwein, *Die Bücher der Könige*, ATD 11/1 (1977), [2]1985; 11/2, 1984; P. Kyle McCarter, *I–II Samuel*, AB, 1, 1980; II, 1984; M. Cogan, *I Kings*, AB, 2001; M. Cogan and H. Tadmor, *II Kings*, AB, 1998.

Research

T. Veijola, *ThR* 67, 403-24 (to be continued).

2.1 The history of the kingdom of Israel and Judah runs in accordance with a fixed scheme. This scheme appears in the phase of the founding of the kingdom for the first time in 1 Sam. 13.1[7] with Saul, in 2 Sam. 2.10-11; 5.4-5; 1 Kgs 2.10-12 with David, in 1 Kgs 3.1-3 and 11.41-43 with Solomon, and in 1 Kgs 14.19-20 with Jeroboam, and is fully developed only after the division of the kingdom from Rehoboam on in 1 Kgs 14.21-31 for the kings of the south and from Nadab in 15.25-32 for the kings of the north, but from here on regularly. Whereas in the earlier narrative from the beginnings of the kingdom in 1–2 Samuel it occurs only sporadically and here is secondary, in 1–2 Kings it forms the basic framework into which the narrative material has been worked. In the distribution over the whole, there is an alternation between parts in which the narrative material is predominant and the scheme has only the framework (this is especially the case in 1 Sam.–1 Kgs 14; 1 Kgs 17–2 Kgs 10 and 11; 2 Kgs 18–23), and those in which the bare scheme dominates or the narrative keeps to limits that can be surveyed (as in 1 Kgs 14.21-31; 15-16; 2 Kgs 21; 23.31ff.; 24–25). In view of the sparser implementation in the passages mentioned last, in the case of 1–2 Kings it seems likely that the bulk of the narrative material is not original but has been filled out steadily.

The scheme itself points in the same direction. The basic form appears in 2 Kgs 13.10-13 (vv. 12f. = 14.15f.) and runs like this:

In the thirty-seventh year of Joash king of Judah Jehoash the son of Jehoahaz began to reign over Israel in Samaria, and he reigned sixteen years. He also did what was evil in the sight of Yhwh, he did not depart from all the sins of Jeroboam the son of Nebat, which he made Israel to sin, but he walked in them. Now the rest of the acts of Joash [i.e. Jehoash], and all that he did, and the might with which he fought against Amaziah king of Judah, are they not written in the book of days of the kings of Israel? So Joash slept with his fathers, and Jeroboam sat upon his throne; and Joash was buried in Samaria with the kings of Israel.

Similarly, there is a brief report of a king of Judah, in 2 Kgs 15.32-38, but the other way round.

In the second year of Pekah the son of Remaliah, king of Israel, Jotham the son of Uzziah, king of Judah began to reign. He was twenty-five years old when he began to reign, and he reigned sixteen years in Jerusalem. His mother's name was Jeshua the daughter of Zadok. And he did what was right in the eyes of the Lord, according to all that his father Uzziah had done. Nevertheless the high places were not removed; the people still sacrificed and burned incense on the high places. He built the upper gate of the house for Yhwh. Now the rest of the acts of Jotham, and all that he did, are they not written in the book of days of the kings of Judah? In those days Yhwh began to send Rezin the king of Syria and Pekah the son of Remaliah against Judah. Jotham slept with his fathers, and was buried with his fathers in the city of David his father; and Ahaz his son reigned in his stead.

Fixed ingredients of the scheme are: (1) the dates of the reign, that is, the synchronism of the kings of Judah and Israel and the length of the reign, in the case of the kings of Judah also the age at accession and the name of the mother; (2) the verdict on whether the kings did right or evil in the eyes of Yhwh; (3) reference to the 'book of days' (chronicle or annals) of the kings of Israel or Judah; and (4) a note about death and burial and successor.

Element (3), the reference to the 'books of days', is of particular interest for the relationship between the scheme and the narrative. The dates of the reigns under (1) and also other information must have been taken from it. The passages quoted already mention individual outstanding events in connection with the 'book of days': 2 Kgs 13.12, the war with Amaziah of Judah; 2 Kgs 15.35, the building of the upper gate of the house of Yhwh; and in vv. 36-37, the Syro-Ephraimite attack on Judah. This kind of annals, which offer only the mere dates of reigns and in addition note a few important events and are also expanded here and there, has its closest parallel in the Babylonian chronicles[8] and will have stood at the beginning of the origin of 1–2 Kings. The brief episodes typical of it were the way in for further narrative material which inserted itself between elements (1) and (4). Everything in between fills out and extends elements (2) and (3).

In detail the scheme displays some variations, but they do not signify much. Sometimes they are occasioned by the particular fate of individual kings, as for example the absence of (3) and (4) in the case of Jehoram of Israel in 2 Kgs 3.1-3 and Ahaziah of Judah in 2 Kgs 8.25-29 on the basis of 2 Kgs 9 (added in 9.28f.), and the absence of (1) and (2) in the case of Jehu himself in 2 Kgs 9–10 (repeated in 10.28-36). The variations partially rest on later expansions, above all in the verdict on piety which – with a single exception (1 Kgs 15.3) – always has as a constant 'do what is right/evil in the eyes of Yhwh'. In substance this is a unitary redactional framework.

The variations also include the even shorter versions of the scheme in 1 Kgs 16.8-14, 15-20, 21f. and 2 Kgs 15.13-16, where the verdict on piety is completely absent (1 Kgs 16.21f.; 2 Kgs 15.13-16), has been added (1 Kgs 16.13), or is in the wrong place (1 Kgs 16.19). That cannot simply be because of the brevity of the reign, otherwise the verdict on Zechariah and Pekahiah (2 Kgs 15.8f., 23f.) would also have to be absent. So we might perhaps regard the exceptions as an indication that the source from which the Deuteronomist drew his information did not yet contain any verdict on piety at all, but that this comes from the reviser himself,[9] and in the case of the short reigns ended by usurpers was in one case put in and in another case was left out with no deeper significance. However, there is no basis here for reconstructing the original wording of the source, Jepsen's 'synchronistic chronicle'.[10] Regardless of the synchronisms in the Babylonian Chronicle which will have been behind this, the synchronization of the kingdoms of Israel and Judah is a first step in the (Deuteronomist) interpretation. Moreover the 'chronicle' in 2 Kgs 18ff. continues without synchronism, and it is impossible to see why the same chronicle should have ended in 18.1-3; furthermore the distinction between 'chronicle' and extracts from annals seems artificial, given the Near Eastern analogies. It is therefore simpler to assume that the Deuteronomist drew on annals or excerpts from annals for the two kingdoms and other sources accessible to him, or on information which he selected and presented in a uniform and synchronistic form corresponding to the annals of the ancient Near East, and supplemented them with the verdict on piety.

The distribution of the verdict on piety is systematic and betrays a tendency for the kings of Israel always to do 'evil',[11] albeit different degrees of evil, and the kings of Judah usually to do 'what is right in the eyes of Yhwh', albeit with qualifications and exceptions,[12] which is why the fate of Israel ultimately hastens upon them. The standpoint is clearly Judahite; the criterion for the assessments is the 'sin of Jeroboam', the abolition of the unity of kingdom and cult previously established by David and Solomon (1 Kgs 12–14), which makes Israel guilty per se, but evidently also affects Judah. What the 'sin of Jeroboam' has to do with Judah is said by the qualification regularly made about the kings who are assessed positively (apart from Hezekiah and Josiah): 'Only the high places did not disappear, the people still slaughtered and offered incense on the heights.' As in the north, there is a differentiation between king and people, except that in Israel the king causes the people to sin, whereas in Judah the right conduct of the kings and the actions of the people diverge. But it can also happen that the king of Judah does 'evil in Yhwh's eyes', which means that he must somehow have put the unity of the kingdom and the cult at risk either because he was related by kinship to the house of Israel (as is the case with Jehoram and Ahaziah in 2 Kgs 8.18, 27) or because he ruled in politically unstable times dominated by foreign powers, immediately after the division of the kingdom (Rehoboam and his son Abijah in 1 Kgs 14.22; 15.3), shortly before the end of Israel (Ahaz, 2 Kgs 16.2) and shortly before the end of Judah (Manasseh and his son Amon, 2 Kgs 21.2, 20; the last kings, 2 Kgs

23.32, 37; 24.9, 19). Conversely, the striving for political sovereignty to consolidate the unity of kingdom and cult in Judah is perhaps the reason why there is no qualification of the positive verdict by a note about the high places in the case of Hezekiah and Josiah (2 Kgs 18.3; 22.2). Both rebelled against the Assyrian overlordship. But for that reason we should not dispense with the notes about the high places in the case of the other kings of Judah – which beyond doubt sound lame. Without them the criterion for assessing the kings of Judah and the link which connects them with the kings of Israel would be missing. The political situation alone, which is hardly mentioned in the extracts from the annals and which does not always correspond with the theological judgment either, cannot be the common criterion.

In the text as we have it the criterion of unity of the kingdom and the cult which necessitated a differentiated verdict on the kings of Israel and Judah is overlaid with another more far-reaching criterion. As the examples show, not always, but frequently more far-reaching theological judgments are attached to the formula 'do right/evil in the eyes of Yhwh', the comparison with the fathers (David or Jeroboam and their immediate predecessors) and the note about the high places (in the case of the kings of Judah who are assessed positively): for Judah (1 Kgs 14.22-24; 15.12f.; 22.47; 2 Kgs 16.3f.; 18.4-7; 21.2-16, 21f.; 23.4-27; cf. also 1 Kgs 15.4f.; 2 Kgs 8.19), more frequently than for Israel (1 Kgs 12–14; 16.26, 31-33; 22.54; 2 Kgs 3.2; cf. also 1 Kgs 15.29f.; 16.1-4, 7, 13, 34). They add concrete cultic measures: depending on the king's piety, the introduction or the abolition of high places, altars, asheroth and mazzeboth, running after other gods, especially the worship of Baal(s), Asherah, Astarte, sun, moon and stars and other things which are contrary to or in conformity with the law. The difference is immediately clear: alongside the ideal of the unity of the kingdom and the cult there is the ideal of the purity of the cult; the First (and Second) Commandment to which Israel and Judah are equally committed replace the rivalry between Judah and Israel which – despite the Judahite standpoint – in the end will also prove disastrous for Judah. Jeroboam's bulls (1 Kgs 12), which have an affinity to the cult of Baal, offered a basis for this. The worship of Yhwh as 'Lord' (Baal) of Samaria was no longer seen just as rebellion against the unity of the kingdom and the places of worship but as apostasy to other gods, that is, rebellion against the oneness and exclusivity of Yhwh. In this way the 'sin of Jeroboam' has become sin against the one God (cf. Exod. 32–34) which – very much more than the high places – subjects the kings of Israel and Judah to one and the same verdict. Accordingly, 'doing evil in the eyes of Yhwh' means transgression of the First Commandment, and 'doing right in the eyes of Yhwh' observance of it.

Both criteria, the unity of place of worship and deity and the oneness of

Yhwh, strongly recall Deuteronomy, the first more than the second. After the insertion of the Decalogue in Exod. 20 it also dominates the Sinaitic law in Exodus–Numbers. Linguistically, however, the second is closer to Deuteronomy than the first: instead of 'any place' and 'your gates' in Deuteronomy Kings speaks of the 'high places'; the Deuteronomic 'place which Yhwh has chosen to make his name dwell there' occurs only in secondary passages in the scheme of 1–2 Kgs (1 Kgs 14.21; 2 Kgs 21.4, 7; 23.26, also 1 Kgs 8; 9.3; 11.13, 32), and conversely the formula typical of Kings 'do right/evil in the eyes of Yhwh' occurs in Deuteronomy only in secondary passages (Deut. 6.18; 12.8, 25, 28; 13.19; 21.9). That means that with the first criterion the scheme is close in substance to Ur-Deuteronomy and with the second criterion close in literary terms not only to Deuteronomy but also to the whole of the law in the Pentateuch, and therefore in the framework of the Enneateuch. Only under the sign of the First Commandment do the literary connections of Samuel–Kings to the Hexateuch and specifically to Deuteronomy begin, and Deuteronomy and lastly the whole Pentateuch are specifically designated 'the law of Moses' and cited regularly (cf. 2 Kgs 18.6; 21.8; 22.8, 10ff.; 23.1ff., 25, quotation in 14.6).

The proximity of the two criteria to Deuteronomy is justification for calling the schema in 1–2 Kings Deuteronomistic. As in Deuteronomy, the second criterion has emerged out of the first and is thus secondary.[13] Over against the basic Deuteronomic-Deuteronomistic idea, the unity of the place of worship, the original scheme in Kings presents in the language of annals and relates it to the political history of the two kingdoms of Israel and Judah, the expansions which have the First Commandment as the criterion have to do with another, second (third and fourth, etc.), Deuteronomistic level. So as not to make things too complicated I suggest designating the different levels, on the basis of P, with the abbreviations Dtr^G for the basic writing and Dtr^S for all the secondary additions – which themselves have many levels.[14]

2.2   Filling out the annalistic framework with narrative material led to a sometimes considerable inflation of the scheme. Only a very small part of the process can be derived from the basic Deuteronomistic writing (Dtr^G); for the main part it is to be attributed to the secondary Deuteronomistic revision (Dtr^S). The analysis of the framework provides the criterion for the distinction. What fits into the original stratum of the annalistic framework is original; what converges with the expansions is secondary. The architecture of the text decides whether what goes neither with the one nor the other is of either pre- or post-Deuteronomistic origin. Accordingly the narrative material can be sorted roughly as follows:

1 Kings 3–11

In the text as we have it the building of the temple and the palace stand at the centre (1 Kgs 6.1–9.9), and that is put in a double framework, an inner framework in 5.15-32 and 9.10-28 (cf. further in 10.14ff.) which deals with measures implementing the building of the temple and especially relations with Hiram of Tyre, and a second, external framework in 3.4–5.14 and 10.1-29 which depicts Solomon's wisdom and splendour. The division into two by the two related theophanies in 3.4ff. and 9.1ff. competes with this. Since Wellhausen, scholars have been fond of finding an independent tradition, 'the book of the words (things) of Solomon' (11.41) in 1 Kgs 3–11, which is said to have undergone a Deuteronomistic revision and also to have been glossed in other ways. But the very framework of this older tradition which has been put between the accession in 1 Kgs 1–2 (2.46 and 3.1-3) and the concluding note in 11.41-43 is part of the basic Deuteronomistic writing. The framework is formed by the notices about building in 6.1,[15] 37-38; 7.1, perhaps also the over-full reports with heavy glosses about further buildings in 9.15-23, and lastly the conclusion of the building measures in 9.24, 25, which is linked back to 3.1-3 and has the Jeroboam episode in 11.26(-28), 40 attached to it; this in turn prepares for the continuation of 11.41-43 in 12.2ff. The information must have been taken from annals excerpted by the Deuteronomist and was later supplemented with details from other 'sources': the temple in 6.2-36 between 6.1 and 6.37f.; the palace in 7.2-12 taking up 7.1; and, linking up with both, the vessels cast by the Tyrian craftsman Hiram of Tyre in 7.13-47 with the supplement in 7.48-51. These details already burst the framework and are hardly original, far less the rest which has accumulated around this core.

Further official or pseudo-official reports occur before the building activity in 4.1–5.8 (with 4.20–5.6 inserted into them) and after the divide in 9.25 in 9.26–10.29; no matter where they come from, they stem from the intent to project spectacular reports into the brilliant beginning under Solomon (cf. 9.26-28; 10.11, 22 with 22.49f.). The formation of the legend about Solomon's wisdom (cf. 11.41) also serves this purpose; started by Solomon's dream in 3.4-15, this clusters round the 'official' reports in 3.16-28 and 5.9-14 and inserts itself in 10.1-13 between 9.26-28 and 10.14-19; throughout it speaks the language of the secondary Deuteronomistic revision (cf. 2 Sam. 7). That is also the case with the moving of the ark, the consecration of the temple and the response to Solomon's prayer (dependent on 3.4ff.) in 8.1–9.9. These are pure additions, perhaps using older splinters of tradition (8.12f.) which have attached themselves between 6.1 and 9.10ff. to the details in 6.2–7.51 and have left their traces behind in 6.11-13. Even before 9.1-9 found its way into the text, the inner framework spun out of 2 Sam. 5.11 about king Hiram of Tyre in 1 Kgs 5.15-32 and 9.10-14 must have been put around the building of the temple and the palace.[16] 1 Kings 9.1-9 anticipates 9.10 and opens up a new section, parallel to 3.4ff. The expansion of Solomon's sins in 11.1-13 goes along with this; these in turn are presupposed in 11.29-39, and alongside Jeroboam in 11.26ff., in 11.14-22, 23-25 they bring back on the scene David's old enemies, one of whom like Jeroboam took refuge in Egypt.

1 Kings 12–14

The original continuation of the Jeroboam episode in 11.26(-28), 40 and the concluding remark in 11.41-43 appears in 12.2,[17] 20a, 25, 26-30;[18] 14.19-20. The political unity fought for under David (1 Kgs 2.46b) and the cultic unity for which the foundation was laid under Solomon (1 Kgs 6.1, 37-38; 9.25) breaks up into the two kingdoms of Israel and Judah. Alongside this aetiology of the 'sin of Jeroboam' the division of the kingdom is narrated in yet a second version, according to which the people of Israel separated from the house of David because of forced labour; here – as in 2 Sam. 5.1-5 – the view prevails that the political unity rests on an agreement: 1 Kgs 12.1, 3-19. As the second version interrupts the first and presupposes it in 12.1, 3a, 12, this is a supplement, but that is not to say anything about the origin and age of the narrative. 1 Kings 12.21-24 and the midrashic prophetic narratives in 13.1–14.18, introduced with 12.31, 32f. and reaching far forward, are further expansions, all of which presuppose the First Commandment and already recall the special material of Chronicles.

1 Kings 15–16

In the area of 14.21–16.34 the framework scheme shows certain broadenings in only a few places (1 Kgs 15.16, 17-22; 15.27-28, 32; 16.8ff., 15ff.) which belong to the basic writing, and a few expansions, especially in the verdict on piety: 14.21b (only '[in] the city, which . . .'), 22b-24, 26b-28 (after 10.16f.); 15.4-5, 6, 12-13, 15, 29-30 (after 14.10); 16.1-4, 7, 11-12 (cf. 14.7ff.), 13bβ, 19(?), 26b, 31bβγ, 32-33, 34.

1 Kings 17–2 Kings 10

The introduction of Ahab in 1 Kgs 16.29-31 is to be taken together with 22.39-40; he is followed by Jehoshaphat of Judah in 22.41-51 (without v. 47), Ahaziah of Israel in 22.52-54 (without v. 54) + 2 Kgs 1.1, 18, Joram of

Israel in 3.1-3 (without v. 2), Jehoram of Judah in 8.16-24 (without v. 19), Ahaziah of Judah in 8.25-27(, 22-29; for Joram of Israel see lastly 3.1-3, in what follows 9.14-26) and Jehu of Israel in chs 9–10 (9.14–10.17,[19] 34-46), who prepares an end for Joram of Israel and Ahaziah of Judah. Already in the basic writing there is a span from Ahab in 1 Kgs 16.29-31, the last representative of the dynasty of Omri, who not only continues the 'sin of Jeroboam', the political and cultic break with Judah, but in addition enters into an alliance by marriage with Phoenicia, to the usurper Jehu in 2 Kgs 9–10, who extinguishes the dynasty of Omri – except for Athaliah, Omri's daughter, in Judah (2 Kgs 8.26; 11) – and soon also takes vengeance on Jezebel's crime against Naboth in 1 Kgs 21.1-16 (2 Kgs 9.21b, 25). Moreover this is the only place at which the basic document diverges from the scheme and a pre-existing – Israelite – narrative is included, presumably because no other source was available for the end of Joram and the existing source also already contained the end of Ahaziah. As in 2 Kgs 15.13-16, the verdict on piety is absent and has been added (10.28f., 30f.), as in the case of the usurpers in 1 Kgs 16.8-22 (vv. 13, 19), with which there are also relations elsewhere (cf. 1 Kgs 16.1-4, 7, 11-12 with 2 Kgs 9.7-10; 10.10f., 14, 17). As in 1 Kgs 11.42 and 14.20a the information about the length of the reign in 2 Kgs 10.36 stands at the end, because the introductory formula is missing and has been replaced by the narrative.

However, in the present text the span from 1 Kgs 16 to 2 Kgs 9f. has quite a different point: the cult of Baal introduced by Ahab (1 Kgs 16.31, 32f.) is first of all fought hard against by Elijah (1 Kgs 17–22; 2 Kgs 1) and lastly exterminated from Israel by Jehu (2 Kgs 10.15f., 18-30) with the involvement of Elijah's disciple Elisha and one of his prophetic disciples (2 Kgs 9.1-13). The presupposition for this is the insertion of the prophetic legends about Elijah and Elisha into the annalistic framework of the basic Deuteronomistic writing: Elijah in 1 Kgs 17–19; 21 and the war narratives 1 Kgs 20 and 22 between 16.29-34 and 22.39-40 under Ahab of Israel; 2 Kgs 1 between 1 Kgs 22.52-54; 2 Kgs 1.1 and 2 Kgs 1.18 under Ahaziah of Israel; Elisha in 2 Kgs 3–8 between 2 Kgs 3.1-3 and 2 Kgs 8.16ff. under Joram of Israel and the kings Jehoram and Ahaziah of Judah; 9.1ff. as an introduction to Jehu in chs 9–10. 2 Kgs 2 and 13.14-25 stand outside the scheme.

The prophetic narratives have their own prehistory outside the books of Kings. The nuclei of the traditions are the narrative of Elijah the rainmaker in 1 Kgs 17.1, 5b-6; 18.1.aα, 2a + 41-46 and the small collection of miracle stories in 2 Kgs 4 + 6.1-7 with the supplement to the narrative 4.8-37 (vv. 8-17 + 18-37), which has in turn been inserted, in 8.1-6. In the framework of the books of Kings, the two miracle-workers introduced in 1 Kgs 17.1 and 2 Kgs 3.11 are assimilated to each other (1 Kgs 17.7-24 after 2 Kgs 4; 2 Kgs 3.9-20 after 1 Kgs 17f.),[20] stylized as representatives of the word of God

(1 Kgs 17.1, 2-5a, 8-9, 14, 16, 24b; 18.1; 2 Kgs 3.12; 4.44; cf. also 1 Kgs 19.9ff.; 21.17ff.; 2 Kgs 1.4, 6; 7.1f., 17-20; 8.10, 13; 9.3, 6) and put in a succession (first in 1 Kgs 19.19-21 picking up 18.46 and with 2 Kgs 3.11 in view; afterwards in 1 Kgs 19.15-18 and 21.17ff. with 2 Kgs 8.7ff.; 9.1ff. in view, quite outside the scheme in 2 Kgs 2). Whereas this more or less continues to be the case for Elisha in 2 Kgs 6.8–7.20; 8.7-15; 9.1-13 (and 13.14-25 outside the scheme), by contrast the sorry task falls upon Elijah of fighting against the house of Omri and Baal and preparing for Jehu's action: first 1 Kgs 18.17-18a, 21-39, then 18.2b, 3-16 and vv. 18b-20, 40, and last 19.1-14, 15-18; also 21.17-29 (22.38), expanding 21.1-16; 2 Kgs 1.2-8, 17; 9.7-10a and the other direct or indirect references to Elijah in 2 Kgs 9–10 (10.15f., 18ff. with 1 Kgs 18.16ff.; 2 Kgs 9.7-10a, 21b, 25-26, 36f.; 10.10f., 14bβ, 17, 32f. with 1 Kgs 14.10f.; 16.1-4, 7, 11-13; 18.13; 19.10, 15ff.; and 21.1-29). Thus the name of Elijah 'my God is Yah(weh)' has become a monotheistic programme, and Elijah has become the 'bird who sings of the morrow'.[21] In the Elijah cycle other prophets take over Elisha's task (1 Kgs 20; 22). It is impossible to decide firmly which of the two tasks, the fight against Baal or the delivery of the word of God, first accrued to the miracle workers. The word of God in the narratives of miracles and wars is a possibility without Baal, and if one removes a few passages the victory over Baal is a possibility without the word of God. But either way the conclusion of the narratives in the historical work is stamped by a tendency alien to the basic document. Despite the qualification in 2 Kgs 3.14, the word of God in the accounts of miracles and wars puts the reign of the Omrids – on which the verdict is negative – in a more favourable light, in that it works for the Israelites in the north. The fight against Baal gives the negative assessment of the Omrids a new basis, which converges with the expansions of the narrative scheme. At any rate, as soon as the two prophets intervene in the course of the narratives, both presuppose the one God and his universal sphere of activity. In 2 Kgs 1.9-16; 2 and 5 the battle over the one God seems to have long since been decided, and everything is concentrated on the man of God himself.

2 Kings 11–17

After 2 Kgs 10.34-36 the scheme of the basic document continues in 12.1-4 (without v. 3b), 20-22 with Joash of Judah; there follow Jehoahaz and Joash of Israel in 13.1-2, 8-9, and 10-13; Amaziah of Judah in 14.1-4, 18-21 (, 22); Jeroboam II of Israel in 14.23-24, 28-29; Azariah of Judah in 15.1-7; Zechariah, Shallum, Menahem, Pekahiah and Pekah of Israel in 15.8-11, 13-15, (16,) 17-22, 23-26, 27-31; Jotham of Judah in 15.32-38 (without v. 37); Ahaz of Judah in 16.1-3a, 19-20; Hoshea and the end of

Israel in 17.1-6, 21-23. Further source notes from the 'books of days' might have been worked on in 12.18-19; 13.7 (?); 14.5 (combined from 12.21f.), 7 (the basis for 2 Sam. 18.3); 14.25a; and 16.5-9. But there must also have been a narrow basis for 11.1-20 in the basic writing. Verses 1-4, 19-20[22] narrate how the king's son Joash survived the rule of Athaliah in the temple and became king, vv. 5-19 (up to 'and he took ... and all the people of the land') go into great detail, resemble the scene in chs 9f., and make the fall of Athaliah a sacred action. If we insist that the middle part around the coronation scene in v. 12 with its many glosses must be old, we must vigorously delete it and the periphery. 2 Kings 11.1 presupposes ch 9; 12.1 has been put first to make the connection; the synchronism in 12.2 includes the six years of Athaliah and thus presupposes a note to this effect. The tradition does not agree on who killed the Judahite family. 2 Kings 11.1 looks as if it is going beyond 10.12-14.

Everything else in 2 Kgs 11–17 falls out of the framework: the narrative about the improvement of the temple in 12.5-17 has a doublet in 22.3-7, 9. The dependence is manifest and lies on the side of ch. 12, not only in terms of verbal agreements,[23] but even more in connection with the occasion, the improvement of the temple, and the additional details. The twofold command by the king to the priests in 12.5-9 is the necessary occasion for the provisions for the income from the sacrifices in vv. 10ff.; without v. 10 (after 22.4) the chest in v. 11 is left hanging, v. 11 requires vv. 12f. (after 22.5f.) rather than vv. 14f. as a continuation; the qualification in vv. 14-16 again presupposes vv. 12f. and generally corresponds to 22.7 ('Only ...'). Only the neglect of the priests in vv. 7-9 and the fine distinctions in vv. 5, 17 overshoot the parallels. The inscription must have been inspired by 2 Kgs 11 (esp. vv. 17ff.) and the mention of the priest Jehoiada in 12.3; it has the purpose of justifying the positive verdict in 12.3, which in the eyes of the supplementer contradicted the source note in 12.18-19. 2 Chronicles 24 is the brilliant exegesis of this.

2 Kings 13.3-6 is a later interpretation of 13.2 in the style of the book of Judges (with a recapitulation in v. 6) and is meant to explain the losses stated in v. 7. 2 Kings 14.6 comments on the note in 14.5 spun out of 12.21f. and makes the avengers observe the law (Deut. 24.16), which on this occasion is quoted literally. 2 Kings 14.8-14, 17 is the implementation of 13.12f. = 14.15f. in combination with the note about Edom in 14.7. I would venture to doubt whether there is an old source behind the narrative. The midrash recalls the way in which Chronicles interprets the framework notes of Kings, here 2 Kgs 14.7/2 Chron. 25.11f. in 2 Chron. 25ff. Like 2 Kgs 13.3-6, 14.25b-27 is an expansion in the style of the book of Judges, meant to explain the success of Jeroboam, which does not fit into the scheme. 15.12 is a note of the fulfilment of the prophecy in 10.30 which is already secondary. 15.37 anticipates 16.5-9 and makes Yhwh responsible for the attack by the

Syro-Ephraimite coalition on Judah. 16.3b-4 supplement the framework scheme; 16.10-18 the episode 16.5-9, which comes from the 'book of days' under the sign of the first commandment and following the model of 1 Kgs 12 (cf. 2 Kgs 16.12ff.). We may leave aside the question whether the building of the altar in 2 Kgs 16.10-11, 14-16 actually happened; in any case the episode must have been attached to vv. 5-9 at a secondary stage. 2 Kings 17.7-20 generalize the 'sin of Jeroboam' of vv. 2, 21-23 and turn it into the sin of the Israelites against the God who brought them up out of Egypt. Verses 13-17 are an addition in the addition, as are vv. 19f. 17.24-41 bring the foreign peoples and their cult into play at a yet later level.

2 Kings 18–25

The starting point is again the annalistic framework scheme of the basic document with a few extracts from sources: 18.1-33(, 4aα[1]) + 20.20-21 and the episodes in 18.7b, (8,) 13-16 + 19.36-37; 20.12-13 for Hezekiah; 21.1-2a, (3a,) 17-18 for Manasseh; 21.19-20, 23-26 for Amon; 22.1-2 + 23.28-30 and the episodes in 22.4-7, 9 + 23.4a and 23.11f. for Josiah; 23.31-34(, 35) for Jehoahaz; 23.36-25.1, 5-6(, 7) for Jehoiakim; 24.8-9 and the episode 24.10-12, 15-17 for Jehoiachin; 24.18-19 and the episode 24.20b-25.7 for Zedekiah; 25.8-30 the destruction of Jerusalem (vv. 8-10, 18-21a); Gedaliah (vv. 22, 25) and the pardoning of Jehoiachin (vv. 27-30). Everything else was gradually added: in chs 18–20 the reform of the cult in 18.4-7a and the repetition of 17.1-6 in 18.9-12 and also a first legendary development of the Sennacherib episode in 18.13-16 + 19.36f. in 18.17-19.9a (for its part expanded in 18.26-36?), a second in 19.9b-35 (into which 19.20, 29-34 and vv. 21-28 have been inserted), and lastly the Isaiah legends in 20.1-19; in ch. 21 the broad development of the verdict on piety in vv. 2b, (3a,) 3b-16 and vv. 21f.; in chs 22–23 the finding of the book, the covenant and the reform on the basis of the law in 22.8, 11-20; 23.1-3; 23.4b-10, 12-20, the Passover and obedience to the law in 23.21-25, and the persistent anger in 23.26f.; in chs 24-25 some glosses in 24.2, 3-4, 13-14, 20a; 25.13-17, 21b, 23-24, 26.

If we survey all the material which has subsequently been inserted into the framework scheme of the basic document which in turn has been expanded, two constantly recurring themes can be recognized: the law and the prophets. As a rule both have to do with the cult, the prophets sometimes also with other matters, social and military. It is obvious that the remarks on the cult (1 Kgs 8.1-9.9, etc.) and the cultic integrity of the kings (1 Kgs 11.1ff., etc.) presuppose the First Commandment and are connected with the expansions of the framework scheme; consequently they belong in the secondary material of the Deuteronomistic redaction with its many levels. As far as the prophets refer to this and advocate the ideal of cultic purity (1 Kgs 11.29-39; 13-14, etc.), the same is also true of them. If we want, we can identify all these passages with DtrN or call them a 'covenant theology revision', whether or not they mention the law and the covenant with God by name.

The prophetic narratives and other legends which tell of the wisdom and wealth of Solomon (1 Kgs 3f.; 10.1ff.) or of Naboth's vineyard (1 Kgs 21.1-16), of the miracles and the political oracles of Elijah and Elisha and others (1 Kgs 17; 18.41-46; 20; 22; 2 Kgs 2–8; 13.14ff.), or of Isaiah's miracles and signs (1 Kgs 19–20), are more difficult to place. Perhaps they have an old nucleus which is pre-Deuteronomistic, but were only later incorporated into the basic Deuteronomistic writing. If we want, we can identify the prophetic narratives and the notes about fulfilment which they contain and other summary references to the 'servants of Yhwh' with DtrP, or call it 'the Word of God revision'. However, we must be clear that DtrP is not far removed from DtrN and sometimes is identical with it; it was inserted and revised either before or after the law or between one stratum of the law and the next. The sequence will presumably never be completely clarified, since this is not a unitary redaction but consists of more or less sporadic insertions and developments, though these are not arbitrary, but have been made in blocks. Not only the law which corresponds to the usual picture of the Deuteronomistic redaction, but above all the prophetic narratives, which have a completely un-Deuteronomistic flavour and are for the most part Israelite, come very close to Chronicles and the revived interest in (all) 'Israel' which is present in it.

As for the literary horizon of law and prophets in Kings, it should be noted that the reminiscences of salvation history occur in the secondary passages,[24] and both the polemic against the alien gods and the special interest in Israelite narratives combine the revision in Kings with that in Joshua–Judges. All this suggests that the secondary Deuteronomistic revision moves within the framework of the Enneateuch (Genesis–Kings). The law and covenant of Sinai (Exod. 24; 34), of Moab (Deut. 26) and of Shechem (Josh. 24) revive under Josiah in 2 Kgs 22–23, and in Samuel–Kings the prophets are what Moses, Joshua and the judges were to the people of Israel before the state (cf. 2 Kgs 14.25-27).

2.3   The Deuteronomistic framework scheme not only extends to 1–2 Kings but also includes 1–2 Samuel. The beginning of the kingdom under Saul, David and Solomon is presupposed. Because of that, and because no independent beginning can be found in 1 Kings, we must start from the assumption that 1–2 Samuel belongs to the basic document Dtr[G]. 1 Samuel 1.1 ('There was once a man … ') is the beginning of an independent narrative, and indeed the beginning of a wide narrative arch which leads through the birth of Samuel (1 Sam. 1) to the elevation of Saul to be king over Israel (1 Sam. 9–11) and from here beyond 1 Sam. 16–2 Sam. 10 to David and Solomon in 2 Sam. 11–1 Kgs 2. 1–2 Samuel were originally one book, and the cut between Samuel and Kings is also artificial. Both go back to the division into books by the Septuagint and the Vulgate – prompted in the Hebrew text by the closing chapters 1 Sam. 31; 2 Sam. 21–24 – which add up to four books of Kingdoms (1–4 Kgdms). But whereas the framework scheme in 1–2 Kgs is original, with a few episodes which broaden out here and there, and the bulk of the narrative material is secondary, in 1–2 Samuel the narrative material is original and the Deuteronomistic framework is secondary. Evidently the redactors had a narrative work about the beginnings of the kingdom in Israel and Judah which they developed in their own way around 560 BC, namely as a 'synchronistic chronicle' of the downfall of the two states, whereupon the chronicle – under the influence of the First Commandment – was in turn enriched with narrative material.

As far as the annalistic framework is concerned, the Deuteronomistic interventions in the existing narrative material are limited to a few points: 1 Sam. 13.1; 2 Sam. 2.10-11; 5.4-5 = 1 Kgs 2.10-12; 3.1-3. Probably because of the lack of sources, the revisers here worked with round figures for ages and durations of reigns which they themselves calculated or invented, and which in 1 Sam. 13.1 have not even been handed down correctly. There is similar information in 1 Sam. 4.18 about the priest Eli, who is said to have reigned as judge in Israel for forty years, but while the note between the sudden death of Eli and his daughter-in-law giving birth in terror in v. 18f. may be at an appropriate place, it has been inserted later and presupposes the (later) literary connection with the book of Judges. Moreover 1 Sam. 14.27-51; 25.43f.; 27.7; 2 Sam. 3.2-5; 5.13-16; 8.1ff. recall the annals of the books of Kings.

The Deuteronomistic redaction in 1 Sam. 7–12 seems particularly crude; here we have the installation of a first, albeit pre-Davidic king, which ran contrary to the Judahite standpoint of the redaction and therefore inevitably caused it some problems. This passage was revised time and again on the basis of the changing interests of the first and all the subsequent Deuteronomistic revisions, so that in literary terms the most varied tendencies lie on top of each other. Since Wellhausen's brilliant analysis, which was confirmed by Noth and refined by Veijola, the composition of the chapter is by and large established; it has also been widely recognized and has become a popular examination topic, so that I can be brief over it.

Two strands of tradition can be distinguished in 1 Sam. 7–12, one well-disposed towards the kingdom (9.1–10.16; 11.1-15) and one critical of it (chs 7–8; 10.17-27; 12.1-25). The former is about someone who went out to seek his father's asses and found the kingdom (1 Sam. 9.1–10.16).[25] The beginning in 9.1 resembles 1.1 ('There was once a man … '), and so the narrative may also at one time have been handed down independently in some form; the old ending is often found in 10.7, 9. However, it also fits admirably into the context. The scene of the chance encounter with the man of God, a locality and cultic high place (*bāmāh*) in the region of Zuph (9.5), and the name of the man of God who comes to meet Saul on the way, Samuel (9.14, 18ff.), which is assumed to be known, fit seamlessly with the birth story of the Zuphite Samuel in 1.1-20,[26] who came into the world in Ramah and is also at home there (1.19f.). In contrast, after the matter of the kingdom has been kept secret (10.1, 14-16), there is further need for a public proclamation of Saul as king over Israel. This takes place once in 10.17-27 by the decision through lots at Mizpah, and the second time (picking up the proving of Saul in the war against the Ammonites, 10.27b–11.11)[27] in 11.15, in Gilgal. Only one of the two versions can be original. The redactional hinge in 11.14, which makes the enthronement in Gilgal in 11.15 a 'renewal' of the kingdom, proves that v. 15 is the earlier version and 10.17-27 the later. The narrative continues in chs 13–14,[28] where with good reason there is the first Deuteronomistic note about annals (13.1) and an annal-like summary (14.47-51). Together with the previous indication in 10.8 which is inserted between 10.7 and 10.9, the expansion in 13.4b, 7b-15a already indicates the end of Saul's kingship and makes the way free for David. 1 Samuel 10.8; 13.1, 4b, 7b-15a (without vv. 13f.) represent a first stratum of revision which – in the framework of Samuel–Kings – grapples with the legitimacy of Saul's kingship. It has nothing against the kingship as such, but evidently something against Saul.

The other strand of tradition in chs 7–8; 10.17-27a; and 12.1-25 presupposes the old narrative and its (redactional) context, which has just been sketched out briefly, and gives it all a new twist. It is marked above all by the fact that in it the institution of the kingship is intrinsically viewed very critically and therefore is no longer left to chance, which is accepted gladly from God, but in all respects is put under the divine guidance. However, this strand is not a unity. The latest traces of revision can be removed most easily: 7.3-4; 8.7b-9a; 10.18-19; 12.1-25; 13.13-14. Here the kingship is rejected in principle, because Yhwh alone wants to be king over his people. The establishment of the kingship, which corresponds to the customs and usages of the peoples, is regarded as rebellion against God and is on a level with running after other gods, the transgression of the First Commandment. Behind it stands the ideal of theocracy, which has as its basis the law, Decalogue and covenant in the Hexateuch, that is, Exod. 19–24 (and 32–34), Deut. 26–30 and Josh. 23–24 (cf. 1 Sam. 12). If we omit these passages, there is still criticism of the kingship, but it is different. The wish for a king is not yet regarded as rebellion against God, but the kingship serves to some degree as an emergency solution because of the depravity of the sons of the last judge, Samuel (7.5-17; 8.1-5, 22), and the wish for a king is not good but 'evil in the eyes of Samuel' (8.6, 7a, 9b, 10-21). Yhwh gives in, the king is found and designated (9.1–10.16) and then publicly raised up from among the tribes of Israel in Mizpah, the place of assembly of 7.5f., by a procedure involving drawing lots (10.17, 20-25). Then because of internal resistance (10.26-27) the kingship is renewed (11.12-14) after the spirit of the judges has come upon Saul (11.5-8). The charisma of the time of the judges, which comes to grief on the dynasty of Samuel but is to live on in the elected kingship guided by God's spirit that is practised by the tribes of Israel (cf. 2 Sam. 5.1ff.), is characteristic of this revision. So the customary misdeeds of a king (ch. 8) indirectly take on the character of a sin against God. The explanation why Saul fails in the end, the spirit of Yhwh departs from him (1 Sam. 16.14), and the Davidic dynasty elected by God becomes established is that the spirit of Yhwh passes over to David (1 Sam. 15; 16.1-13), just like the archaizing title *nāgîd*, 'prince'.[29] Quite clearly we can trace the influence of Joshua and above all of course of Judges here, so that here too we have a revision which presupposes the combination of Samuel–Kings with the Hexateuch.

Thus at least three levels are lying on top of one another in 1 Sam. 7–12: (1) the old core and its redactional context in 1 Sam. 1–14 (1.1-20 + 9.1–10.16 + 11.1-5 + 13-14) with a first revision in 10.8; 13.1, 4b, 7b-15a (without vv. 13-14); (2) a revision in the spirit of the book of Judges in 7.5-17; 8.1-22; 10.17, 20-27; 11.5-8, 12-14; (3) a further revision in the spirit of the law in 7.3-4; 8.7b-9a; 10.18-19; 12.1-25; 13.13-14. Usually (1) – with the exception of 13.1 – is assigned to the pre-Deuteronomistic tradition (source) and (2) and (3) are assigned to the Deuteronomistic redaction, divided into DtrH and DtrN. In terms of tendency, however, (1) has more points of contact with the basic writing in Samuel–Kings (Dtr^G = DtrH), which does not object to the kingship as such but to the behaviour of the kings, especially those of the North. Above all (3) converges with the supplements to the framework of the kings (Dtr^S = DtrN), which make the First Commandment and the law the criterion for the verdict on piety; moreover explicit salvation-historical reminiscences of the history of the people appear in it (8.8; 10.18; 12.6ff.). But (2) is already on the way to this, moving between (1) and (3) and, like the book of Judges, serving to mediate between the history of the people and the tribes in the book of Judges and the history of the kingship in Samuel–Kings. I therefore no longer reckon (2) as part of the basic writing in Samuel–Kings, Dtr^G, but as secondary Deuteronomistic material, Dtr^S, except that (2) is older than (3).

First, like the basic writing, (2) presupposes the birth of Samuel in 1.1-20, still without vv. 3b, 10-12 and the story of his youth in 1.21–3.21 (cf. 7.17), and secondly the Philistine danger, which is reported by the history of the ark in 4.1–7.2. The occasion for the assembly in Mizpah (7.5ff.) is an acute danger, which can only be 4.1b-2 or an earlier episode with the ark in which the ark is irretrievably lost, thus for example, 4.1b-2 (= v. 10) + vv. 11-22. Everything else in 1 Sam. 1–7 consists of late (Priestly) expansions in the nearer or more remote sphere of the Deuteronomistic revisions (2) and (3): the sin of the sons of Eli, which explains their death in 4.11 (1.3b; 2.12-17, 22-25, 27-36); Samuel's youth in the temple of Shiloh (1.21–2.11, 18-21, 26; 3.1-21); the history of the ark (4.3-9, 10; 5.1–7.2). To this also belong the supplements in chs 13–14 which make the victory over the Philistines a war of Yhwh (14.15f., 18f., 23) and take the cursing of Saul in 14.24 as the occasion for Jonathan and the people to sin against God, and also ch. 15, which gives a long and broad theological foundation to the rejection of Saul; it competes with the resumé in 14.47-51 and other reasons for the transition to David in chs 16 and 19. All these midrashic explanations correspond to the filling out of the annalistic scheme in Kings with narrative material.

2.4   The beginning in 1 Sam. 1.1 and the end in 1 Sam. 14.46 (or 14.51) allow us to conclude that in 1 Sam. 1.1-20 + 9.1–10.16 + 11.1-15 + 13-14 (removing the additions) we have an originally independent Saul tradition which has grown redactionally; it emerged from the core in 1 Sam. 9–10 and other formerly independent traditions and was then incorporated into the Deuteronomistic basic writing more or less unchanged, being merely adjusted somewhat in 10.8; 13.1, 4b, 7b-15a. By analogy to this, scholars also reckon that in 1 Sam. 16–1 Kgs 2 there are formerly independent pre-Deuteronomistic traditions which were brought into the present narrative context either before the Deuteronomist or by the Deuteronomist himself. A distinction is made between the 'history of David's rise to the throne' in 1 Sam. 16–2 Sam. 5(; 7 or 8) and a 'succession narrative' in 2 Sam. 6 (or 7 or 9)–1 Kgs 2, and also a 'history of the ark' in 1 Sam. 4–6; 2 Sam. 6(; and 1 Kgs 8). The crux of these assumptions is that the postulated narrative works lack either a beginning or an end or both, and are interwoven in a variety of ways, not just at the level of the Deuteronomistic redaction but in the narrative substance. The 'history of David's rise' is the natural continuation of the Saul tradition; with the dual kingship over Hebron and Jerusalem (in 2 Sam. 2–5) it prepares for the 'succession narrative' and with the dual kingship over Judah and Israel (in 2 Sam. 2.1-4 and 5.1-5) for the later division of the kingdom. The 'history of the ark' presupposes the connection between the 'history of David's rise' and the 'succession narrative', and has an even wider horizon. The impression forces itself upon us that these are not independent narrative works at all but part of a greater whole.

Only parts of the 'succession narrative', the nucleus of which, 2 Sam. 11–1 Kgs 2, is composed of individual narratives, have an independence comparable to the Saul tradition in 1 Sam. 1–14. These are the narratives about Amnon and Absalom in 2 Sam. 13–14, which together with the narratives of the revolts of Absalom and Sheba in chs 15–19 and 20 form a little Absalom cycle, and the Solomon narratives in 2 Sam. 11–12 and 1 Kgs 1–2, which are about the birth of Solomon, the palace revolt of Adonijah and the enthronement of Solomon as David's successor. They are put round the Absalom cycle in 2 Sam. 13–20 as a framework. 2 Samuel 21–24, which are inserted between the Absalom episodes and the end of the succession narrative, are generally held to be appendices which presuppose the linking of the traditions about Saul and David and which in 2 Sam. 23–24 prepare for David's end.

The little collection of Jerusalem court stories in 2 Sam. 11–1 Kgs 2 is by no means free of narrative and literary links to the preceding tradition about Saul and David in 1 Sam. 1–2 Sam. 10, especially 2 Sam. 2–9. However, on closer inspection these links prove to be secondary. The narrative about Amnon's shameful act and Absalom's (self-interested) revenge in 2 Sam. 13–14 prove to be least influenced by the context. The persons involved are introduced separately; the course of the narrative has perhaps grown up gradually (13.1-22; 13.23–14.23, 33; 14.24-32), but is rounded off and has merely undergone two expansions, in 14.2-22 (cf. 2 Sam. 12; 1 Sam. 25.24ff.; with 14.17, 20 cf. 19.28) and 14.25-26, 28 (v. 28b = v. 24b; but cf. 18.18), which seem to presuppose the prehistory in literary terms but not in the action. The Solomon cycle in 2 Sam. 11–12 and 1 Kgs 1–2 is very much more strongly interwoven into the prehistory. But there is much to suggest that the links arise from a secondary revision. In 2 Sam. 11–12 they go back to Nathan's speech announcing punishment, the death of the first child and the birth of the second in 11.27b–12.24bα[30] and the additions in 12.24bβ, 25, in 1 Kgs 1–2 the additions (which themselves have many layers) 1.(1-4,) 20b, 35-37, 46-48; 2.1-12, 15aβ, bβ, 24, 26b-33.[31]

The narratives of the revolts of Absalom and Sheba in 2 Sam. 15–19 and 20 are most strongly woven into the context; they hardly ever seem to have led a life of their own, but continue the Absalom narrative in 2 Sam. 13–14. I see the main difficulty of these narratives in their presupposition that David was king over Israel and Judah, which could hardly have been said before there were two states, and that he operates in the region of the Benjaminite sons of Saul (Mahanaim), which clearly requires the literary connection with the prehistory in 2 Sam. 2–9. However, as is shown by the indication in 18.6, which is usually neglected or explained away by exegetes, this does not seem to be original. The battle against Absalom does not take place in Transjordan but in Ephraim, that is, west of the Jordan (cf. also 18.23). The gate of the city where according to 18.4 and 19.9 David stands and receives the people is therefore not in Mahanaim (thus according to 17.24); it is the same gate as that at which according to 15.1-6, 13 Absalom steals the hearts of the Israelites going to Jerusalem. 19.6 seems to know nothing (yet) of the appropriation of the concubines in Jerusalem (12.11f.; 15.16; 16.21-23). Now that means that the whole account of the flight from 15.14 in chs 15–17 and 19.9b, 10ff. must have been added later.[32] The narrative originally comprised only 15.1-6, 13; 18.1–19.9a, and has been handed down largely intact.[33] Here, too, the Israelites and their opposition to Judah and Jerusalem under Davidic rule play a role (15.2, 13; 18.7, 16, 17b), but the precise relationship and the extent of Davidic rule still remains very uncertain. In this narrative David need not be Saul's successor, and 'the Israelites' appear merely as an indefinable and uncontrollable potential danger of which Absalom skilfully makes use. The opposition is sharpened in the appendix 2 Sam. 20.1–22,[34] which duplicates the revolt of Absalom and accordingly puts the battle slogan 'To your tents, Israel', also quoted in 1 Kgs 12.16, at the beginning. The fact that it is a Benjaminite who tries to rebel already suggests the prehistory of the Davidic kingdom in 1–2 Samuel. The prehistory, namely the kingship of the sons of Saul in Mahanaim (2 Sam. 2.8f.; 4.4) and the kingship of David over Israel (5.3; 8.15), is completely presupposed, but only in the account of the flight in chs 15–17 and 19 and in the Benjaminite episodes 2 Sam. 9; 16.1-14 (with a resumption of 15.37 in 16.15-19); 17.27-29 and 19.17-41, which are taken up by the additions in 1 Kgs 2.5-9, 36ff. (v. 44), and also when a basic stratum and a supplementary stratum are distinguished in 2 Sam. 9.

If we remove the passages which in some way take note of the prehistory, a collection of Jerusalem court stories remains in 2 Sam. 11–1 Kgs 2 which centres on the question which of David's sons will enter into his heritage. If we want, we can find here something like an earlier 'succession narrative', but not of the extent usually assumed by scholars and with the qualification that it is composed of individual episodes (Solomon–Adonijah in 2 Sam. 11–12 and 1 Kgs 1–2, Amnon–Absalom in 2 Sam. 13–14, Absalom and the Israelites in 2 Sam. 15.1-6, 13 + 18.1–19.9a; 20). I cannot recognize in this collection the tendency to criticize the king which it is often thought to contain; it describes the kingdom as it is (cf. 2 Kgs 9–10). Only in a later stage of the tradition and in accordance with our moral sensibility shaped by it is the Bathsheba episode regarded as a transgression (1 Sam. 12) and does Solomon's brutal action against his rivals in the royal family need to be justified by the testament of David in 1 Kgs 2.5-9. Rather, both, like the Absalom cycle in 2 Sam. 13–20, are interested only in the turbulence in the royal family, a good story and all in all the legitimation of the Davidic dynasty. Solomon is in fact a son of David and not, say, of the Hittite Uriah, who therefore with good reason has to sleep outside the house (2 Sam. 11.10, 13). He has rightly won through against the self-nominated successors. The divine promise in 2 Sam. 7 is unknown to this narrative.

2.5   The earlier Saul tradition in 1 Sam. 1–14 and the collection of Jerusalem court stories in 2 Sam. 11–1 Kgs 2 originally had nothing to do with each other. Everything in between, the so-called history of David's rise in 1 Sam. 16–2 Sam. 8, serves as a connecting link to bring Saul and David together and to make a common beginning out of the beginnings of the two kingdoms. Different interests are evidently in play here: on the one hand David is to be stylized as Saul's legitimate successor, perhaps to tie Israel to Judah. On the other hand the common beginning introduces a continuous history of the kingdom in Israel and Judah-Jerusalem and suggests a unity which never was but had to have been, so that as already in 2 Sam. 15–20 it can collapse again in 1 Kgs 12–14 after Solomon and can issue in the 'synchronistic chronicle' of the two kingdoms in 1–2 Kgs. Because of the different tendencies, several hands must have been at work in the secondary combination of Saul and David; this is also already suggested by the overloaded text in 1 Sam. 16–2 Sam. 10. My conjecture is that: (1) there was a pre-Deuteronomistic bridge between 1 Sam. 1–14 and 2 Sam. 11–1 Kgs 2, which related the house of Saul (Israel) to the house of David (Judah and Jerusalem); (2) a revision within the framework of the Deuteronomistic basic writing which has taken over the narrative connection of 1 Sam. 1–1 Kgs 2 more or less unchanged and incorporated it into the synoptic framework, the history of the kingdom of Israel and Judah in Samuel–Kings; and (3) a wealth of supplements, expansions and accumulations of narrative material, before and after the linking of Samuel–Kings with the narrative of the Hexateuch through the Deuteronomistic revision in Joshua and Judges. The result of this was that the two kingdoms came ever closer together for the beginning and issued in the history of the people of Israel, which is not about Judah and Israel, but only about the one people of the twelve tribes. I shall now attempt a rough distinction between the original narrative thread and the haggadic accretions.

The hinge verse which links the old Saul tradition with its continuation is 1 Sam. 14.52, which fits admirably both to v. 46 and to v. 51: 'There was hard fighting against the Philistines all the days of Saul; and when Saul saw any strong man, or any valiant man, he attached him to himself.' That is the starting point for the introduction of David into the history of Saul and the first encounter between Saul and David: it is narrated in three versions: 1 Sam. 16.1-13; 16.14-23 and 17.1-18.5. The first version, the anointing of David by Samuel in 1 Sam. 16.1-13, which declares David to be Saul's successor, is felt in chs 9–10 and already presupposes the rejection of Saul in ch. 15. Both are later than the preparation for the succession in 10.8; 13.7-15 and likewise later than the two following versions of the encounter between Saul and David. Only one of these can be original, and as a rule priority is given to 16.14-23. In 16.14ff,[35] David arrives at Saul's court as a lyre player to free him from his evil thoughts. The strange motif occurs yet again in

18.10f. and 19.9f., and is the motive for David's flight from Saul: Saul goes raving mad and wants to kill David on the spot. The link with 14.52 is also given: David is already an experienced and able warrior (16.18), who incidentally can also play the lyre. In 17.1ff. David is still a boy, is discovered as a warlike hero and thus comes to Saul's court. That also fits well with 14.52, where David is properly introduced, as if Saul and the reader did not yet know him. But despite the fine beginning, the narrative, which may once have been handed down independently, proves to be secondary at least in the literary context. In 17.15 it presupposes knowledge of the first version, and the continuation in 18.17ff., where David gets a daughter of Saul as his wife, bears no relation at all to the promise in 17.25. Furthermore the intimate friendship between David and Saul's son Jonathan begins in 18.1-4; time and again it plays a role in what follows, but it is always a later addition. In short, 17.1–18.5 followed 16.14-23 first and (15;) 16.1-13 last. The Greek version of the text (G) has solved the problem of the three versions in its own way and again offers a different shorter version in chs 17f.

From 18.6 onwards, two reasons are also given for the hostility between David and Saul. The first, 18.6-9, sees the reason in David's military success and the threat that he could seize the kingdom for himself. The remarks in 18.13-15, 29f. are similar. According to the second, 18.10f. and 19.9f. give Saul's uncaused attacks of mania as the reason for the enmity. Again it is not easy to decide which has the priority;[36] any decision is already prejudiced by the verdict on 16.14ff. and 17: the military and political rivalry in 18.6-9 is based on the victory against the Philistines in ch. 17; the psychologically conditioned murder attempt in 18.10f. and 19.9f. refers back to 16.14-23. Moreover the course of the narrative is disturbed in 18.6–19.10. Although the enmity already exists after 18.6ff., in vv. 17ff. Saul promises David his daughter Merab, and afterwards in vv. 20ff. gives him his daughter Michal as wife, this time, however, with the idea, which is not at all easy to follow, that the women may be a snare for David and bring him into the power of the Philistines. But in any case David had to fight the Philistines; Saul did not need to give him his daughter as wife for him to do this, and the relationship by marriage is more appropriate for easing his way towards the kingship. In literary terms the ulterior motive is doubtless secondary, so that Saul's gesture in 18.17a, 18-20(, 22-27) which, while arbitrary, is meant in a friendly way, stands in blatant contradiction to the political rivalry in 18.6-16. Accordingly it looks as if priority has to be given to the motif of spontaneous attacks of rage, and the political rivalry has been added later. The original narrative thread which begins in 16.14-23 continues in 18.10f. or 19.9f. The only question is whether Saul agrees to the marriage of his daughter Michal to David before or after his attack of rage. I think that it is more plausible if he first gives David Michal as his wife

(18.17a, 18-19, 22-27) and then once again an evil spirit falls upon him (19.9f., read only 'evil spirit' or 'spirit of God' as in 18.10), which sparks off further events, Saul's intent to kill David and David's flight. Everything in between (17.1–18.5, 6-9, 10-11, 12-16, 28-30) has been inserted. Here the manic attack is put after 18.10f. to give it a political motive, and supplemented in 18.12, 13-15, 16 along the lines of 18.5, 6-9.[37] We can also see that this reconstruction is approximately right from the fact that after 16.14-23; 18.17-27 and 19.9f., in 19.11ff. Michal helps David to flee. By contrast, Jonathan's help in 19.1-8 (with the resumption of 18.30 in 19.8) and ch. 20, which is dependent on it, is secondary.

This marks out David's further way. From now on he is fleeing from Saul: 19.11f. (like v. 10: 'And he fled and escaped') + chs 21–27. This complex, too, seems overloaded and has grown up over a long period, as can be seen roughly from the many resumptions of 19.11f. in 19.13-18aα[1] ('And David fled and escaped'), 19.18–20.1 ('And he came to Samuel to Ramah ... And David fled from the abode in Ramah'); 20.2–21.1 ('And he came and spoke to Jonathan ... And he arose and went'), up to the original connecting point in 21.2 ('And David came to Nob'), by excursuses like 24.1-23 (to the 'fortresses' in 22.4 and between 23.19-28 and 25.2ff. in Maon) or by the doublets in chs 23.19–24.23 and 26.1-25. We find the basic framework of the narrative, which has been filled out by a number of episodes, in connection with 19.11-12, in 21.2-7 ('And David came to Nob to Ahimelech the priest'); 22.1-4 ('And David went from there and escaped to the cave of Adullam'); 23.14f., 19-28 (in the wilderness of Ziph, in the steppes of Maon, and starting from there 25.2ff. and the excursus in chs 24–26); 27.1ff. ('I will escape into the land of the Philistines'). The narrative comes to a kind of conclusion in chs 27–31. David changes sides, goes over to the Philistines (27.1-4, 12; v. 3 presupposes 25.42f.), and is given the city of Ziklag, from where he undertakes plundering forays (vv. 5-7, 8-11). David is to take part in a war of the Philistines against Israel as the bodyguard of Achish of Gath (28.1f.); Saul dies in this war (31.1ff.: vv. 9b-10a is an addition). However, 29.1-11 reverses David's involvement and makes him return to Ziklag. Like 2 Sam. 1, chs 28 and 30 are additions and are intended to give further reasons for the end of Saul and the rise of David: in 28.3-25 the spirit of the dead Samuel confirms the rejection of Saul in ch. 15; the battle with the Amalekites in ch. 30 is the positive counterpart to this and is presupposed in 2 Sam. 1.1-16, which is in turn picked up by the song in vv. 17-27; the distribution of the booty in 1 Sam. 30.26ff. prepares for the kingship over Judah in 2 Sam. 2.11ff.

After the death of Saul in 1 Sam. 31, the main narrative continues in 2 Sam. 2.8f. Abner the son of Ner and Saul's general makes Ishbosheth (Ishbaal), Saul's son, king in Mahanaim over the regions of Israel, an appropriate opportunity for the Deuteronomist to attach his annalistic note about the two kingdoms, the kingship over Israel and the house of Judah (2.10f.). Then there is a trial of strength at the pool of Gibeon between Ishbosheth's (Ishbaal's) people and the people of David, which David's people decide for themselves. Abner escapes and returns to Mahanaim, Joab and his people go to Hebron (2.12-32). After this Abner enters into negotiations with David over the ownership of the land; he wants to unite with him in a treaty and bring Israel over to David's side (3.12-13, 21).[38] But before anything has been achieved he is killed by Joab, the son of Zeruiah and David's general (3.22-27), in revenge for the murder of Joab's brother Asahel (2.18ff.).[39] Then Ishbosheth (Ishbaal), too, is killed by two of his (*sic*!) generals (4.1, 2f., 6-8aα^1, 12).[40] David makes a treaty with the elders of Israel and they anoint him king over Israel (5.3), again an appropriate occasion for the first Deuteronomist to add an annalistic note (5.4f.) and an occasion for later hands to introduce the ideal of the elected monarchy (5.1f. with 3.17f.).

The development of the Saul tradition in 1 Sam. 1–14 could once have ended with this, with or without the added summary in ch. 8, which resembles 14.47-51. But a decisive element is still lacking, namely, the anointing of David as king over Judah in Hebron in 2 Sam. 2.1-4a.[41] This is not only presupposed throughout 2 Sam. 2–4 but together with the capture of Jerusalem in 5.6aα, 9 (linking to 5.3) and the children from Hebron and Jerusalem in 3.2-5 (linking to 2.32) and 5.13-16 (linking to 5.9) also serves to attach the Jerusalem court stories in 2 Sam. 11–1 Kgs 2 to the Saul–David tradition in 1 Sam. 1–2 Sam. 5(; 8). The anointing in 2 Sam. 2.1-4a interrupts the connection between 1 Sam. 31 and 2 Sam. 2.8f. and is very remarkably introduced by the enquiry of the oracle in 2 Sam. 2.1f., which takes place abruptly. Here of course we immediately think of the beginning of the book of Judges in Judg. 1.1f. and conjecture a late insertion. In contrast, David is named king in 3.21, 23f., and above all in 5.3 (not to mention the additions 3.1, 6-11, 17f., 28ff.) and Hebron as the place of the action of 2.12; 3.12ff. is better understood with the prehistory in 2.1-4a than without it, since according to 1 Sam. 28.1f.; 29.1ff. David is still with the Philistines in Ziklag. However, we can regard only 2 Sam. 2.1aα^1 ('And it happened after that'), 3-4a as original. The gap is further bridged by the war reports in chs 8 and 10 ('And it happened after that', as in 2.1; 13.1; 15.1) and ch. 9 and the Benjaminite passages in chs 16–19 (21); 1 Kgs 2, which continue the threads of 2 Sam. 2–4. The inquiry of the oracle and the holy war against the Philistines in 5.17-25 (cf. 1 Sam. 14.15ff., 37), the ark narrative in ch. 6 (cf. 1 Sam. 4–6 and 1 Kgs 8.1ff.) and Nathan's promise in 2 Samuel, which relates to Solomon and the building of the temple in 1 Kgs 1–11, fall right outside the sequence. All these additions, like many of the apologetic additions in 2 Sam. 2–5 and the late passages in 1 Sam. (for example, 16.1-13), make Saul's rival and successor the elect of Yhwh and beatify David. They are on the way towards the picture of David in Chronicles.

2.6   If we may assume a first, pre-Deuteronomistic composition in 1 Sam. 1–2 Sam. 5 or at the same time 1 Sam. 1–1 Kgs 2, which brings Saul and David together through the link in 1 Sam. 16–2 Sam. 5.(8-10) and makes Solomon follow in 2 Sam. 11–1 Kgs 2, its purpose is simply to declare David and Solomon legitimate successors to Saul. Historically there is a degree of probability that the freebooter David – in a quarrel with the ruling stratum of the city states of Philistia – once took over the contemporaneous kingdom of Saul, which was very limited in area and controlled it for a while. But hardly anything of this can now be traced in the narrative. David's plundering forays are directed exclusively against the enemies of Israel and Judah. Saul and the rebellious Israelites are always generously spared, and the sons of Saul have themselves to blame for their cruel fate in 2 Sam. 21 and 1 Kgs 2.36ff. (with the identification in 2 Sam. 2.8f., 44). The true story seems to lie far back in the narrative: in it, in a comparable way to the figures in the book of Judges, Saul has become a cipher for the house of Israel, David a cipher for the house of Judah, and the Philistines, as in the Samson narratives in Judg. 13–16, are ciphers of the enemies of Israel and Judah at the time of the beginning of the monarchy. It is not that these persons are invented. Their historicity is already evident from the fact that they pose so many problems for historical and literary reconstruction. But they have become symbolic figures for the time of the foundation of the kingdom. The states of Israel and Judah are related by means of the founder figures. If the Israelite Saul tradition in 1 Sam. 1–15 is meant to give a foundation for the kingship in the state of Israel, the transfer of the Israelite kingship to David, the founder of the Judahite dynasty, and Solomon his successor means no less than the levelling down of Israel as a separate state and its attachment to the kingship in Judah and Jerusalem. Here the narrative reverses the historical conditions. It is not David who drives Saul out of the kingship, but Saul hunts David. It is not David who pursues the Israelites, but the Israelites make common cause with the usurpers in the house of David. Saul falls victim to the Philistines, from whom David frees Israel, and the revolt of Israel stands and falls with the palace revolt in Jerusalem. So it comes about that the men of Israel voluntarily go over to David and make him king over Israel (2 Sam. 5.3) and finally, as soon as the turbulence within Judah has been settled, Solomon too receives the kingship 'over Israel' (1 Kgs 1.34; also 1.39, 45; 2.46b).

The only situation in which this view of things seems plausible is the time after the downfall of Israel around 720 BC, when Israel faced the choice of giving itself up or surviving in the state of Judah. The original composition of the Saul–David tradition argues for a link. We know virtually nothing about the actual circumstances in Palestine in the period before the state and the early monarchical period, and even the narratives in Judges and Samuel do not make us any wiser. In the era when there were two states, Israel and Judah, which to some degree are tangible historical entities, there was no occasion for such canvassing, rather the opposite, and this was even less likely after the end of the state of Judah. That leaves the era between the times, that is, the period of the pre-exilic monarchy of Judah between 720 and 597 BC, in which the basic legend of the foundation of the Israelite monarchy and the small collection of Jerusalem court stories could become a foundation legend for the twofold kingdom of David and Solomon over Israel and Judah. Historical experiences of the rivalry between the two states from the time before 720 BC, like the Syro-Ephraimite war, reflected in the rivalry between the house of Saul and the house of David in 1–2 Samuel, especially 2 Sam. 2–5, are to be overcome in this way, and the claim of Judah to Israel's former territories is to be legitimated.

It is not easy to say where the narrative material comes from. Whereas we can well imagine a tradition which has developed and is at home in Israel or Judah during the monarchy for the basic material in 1 Sam. 1–14 and 2 Sam. 11–1 Kgs 2, the origin of the material for 1 Sam. 15–2 Sam. 10 remains to some degree enigmatic. Some features, like the knowledge of Saul, his psyche, his family, his death and the fate of his descendants, must come from Israelite tradition, though it is not possible to construct an independent source out of this. Other material, like the dominant motif of David's flight from Saul and the itinerary in the wilderness, may draw on reminiscences of David's times as a freebooter, which perhaps once brought him into contact with Saul's people, whether on the side of the Philistines, or on his own initiative. However, it is impossible to locate the reminiscences historically in any way, unless one thinks that they are all made up. The latter is even more the case for the rich elaborations of the earlier narratives in 1 Sam. 1–14 and 2 Sam. 11–1 Kgs 2: the story of Samuel's youth in 1 Sam. 1–3; the history of the ark in 1 Sam. 4–6 (and 2 Sam. 6; 7.2; 1 Kgs 8.1ff.); the account of the flight in 2 Sam. 15–19, which recalls David's flight before Saul; and the Benjaminite passages in 2 Sam. 9–21 (and 1 Kgs 2) inserted into it, which presuppose the history of the succession to Saul's throne in 2 Sam. 2–5. All this may have points of contact in the tradition, but as things are now, like the Israelite traditions and Judahite legends in 1 Sam. 15–2 Sam. 10 it owes itself to the refined narrative art and many-layered tendency of the later interpretation of history which shifts the history into the fate of individuals. Perhaps it is also due to a delight in story-telling before and after the exile.

Some time between the first pre-Deuteronomistic composition in 1 Sam. 1–1 Kgs 2, which put Saul, David and Solomon in a succession, and the further haggadic elaboration of this composition, the first Deuteronomistic revision took place. This developed the prehistory of the kingdom in the 'synchronistic chronicle' of the two kingdoms of Israel and Judah. In it the break in the unity of the kingdom prefigured in 2 Sam. 15–20 becomes a break in cultic unity. The duality of the kingdoms of Israel already presupposed in 1 Sam. 1–1 Kgs 2 but concealed by the personal union of David and Solomon breaks open; this corresponds more to historical reality than the attempt to unite the kingdoms under David and Solomon. On the basis of the idea of unity given to him by the tradition and which he himself shared, the Deuteronomist could understand this break only as the violent 'division of the kingdom' after the model of 2 Sam. 15–20. In addition to that it was the effect of a grave sin, the 'sin of Jeroboam', which in the end also drew Judah and Jerusalem into the abyss. Before and after this first Deuteronomistic revision the narrative material in Samuel–Kings still continued to grow powerfully, making the connections between the formerly independent traditions increasingly close.

As in 1–2 Kgs, so too in 1–2 Samuel the Deuteronomistic revision moves more and more towards the First Commandment and the law (cf. 1 Sam. 7–12; 13.13-14; 1 Kgs 2.3f.). Signs of this are the texts in which Yhwh is made responsible for everything, especially for the change from the office of judge to the kingship, the appointment of the first king as *nāgîd*, 'prince', over Israel (1 Sam. 7f.; 9.15-17, etc.) and the election of David and the promise of the eternal dynasty (1 Sam. 13.14; 15; 16.1-13, etc.; 2 Sam. 7). Yhwh and not the kings wages wars, holy men like Samuel and prophets like Nathan and the hosts of the 'servants of Yhwh' take over the mediating role between Yhwh and people, and the relationship between Yhwh and his people generally becomes more important than the state of the kingdom, until Yhwh finally enters into competition with the kingdom.[42] The law, above all the First Commandment, has a direct or indirect effect here. It results in the radical condemnation of the earthly kingdom which was known neither by the old narrative in 1 Sam. 1–14 and 2 Sam. 11–1 Kgs 2, however vividly they portray the monarchy, nor by the first Deuteronomistic revision in Samuel–Kings. The claim of Yhwh to be the sole king over Israel brings the monarchy in Israel and Judah as such into disrepute, but also puts the relationship between Yhwh and the people on a new basis. With the law as criterion the opportunity opens up both for the people and for the Davidic kings to find Yhwh beyond the lost political institutions and to bring the relationship between Yhwh and the people into play independently of this.

2.7   Summary: the earliest tradition in the books of Samuel–Kings is made up of the Israelite narrative of the origin of the kingdom of Saul in 1 Sam. 1–14 (1.1-20 + 9.1–10.16 + 11.1-5 + 13-14) and the Judahite court narratives in 2 Sam. 11–1 Kgs 2 (2 Sam. 11.1-27; 12.24b + 13-14 + 15.1-6, 13; 18.1-19.9a; 20.1-22 + 1 Kgs 1–2). Both collections are to some degree

Table B.II.1

Sources	Dtr^G	Supplements (Dtr^S)
Saul		
1 Samuel⌐		
1.1-20		1.3b, 10-12
		1.21–7.2; 7.3-4
		7.5-17
		8.1-5, 22; 8.6-7a, 9b, 10-21; 8.7b-9a
9.1–10.16 ⌐		9.2αβb, 9, 11-17, 20-24a
	10.8	10.1, 5-6, 10αβ-13
		10.17, 20-27; 10.18-19
11.1-15		11.5-8, 12-14
		12.1-25
13–14 ⌐	13.1, 4b, 7b-12, 15a	13.3b, 5bβ, 7a, 13-14, 19-22
		14.3, 6f., 8-10, 11b, 12b, 14b-16, 18f.,
		21, 23b
	(14.47-51)	14.24-45
	14.52	15
		16.1-13
	16.14-23	
		17.1–18.16
	18.17-27	18.17b, 21, 28-30
	19.9-12	19.1-8, 13-20.42
	21–27	
	28.1-2	28.2-25
	29	
		30
	31	
2 Samuel		1
2.1–5.16	2.10-11	2.1-2, 4b-7
	(3.2-5)	3.1, 6-11, 14-20, 28-39
		4.4-5, 8aβ-11
	5.4-5	5.1-2, 6-8, 10-12
	(5.13-16)	5.17-25
		6–7
	(8–10)	8–10
David and⌐		
Solomon		
11–14		11.27b; 12.1-24bα[1]
		14.2-22, 25-27
15.1-6, 13		15.7-12, 14–17.29
18.1–19.9a ⌐		19.9b-44
20	(20.23-26)	20.3-5, 8-13
		21–24

1 Kings 1–2		
	2.10-12	1.2-4, 20b, 34b-37, 46-68
		2.1-12, 24, 26b-33, 36-46a
1 Kings		
Annals	3.1-3; (4.1-19; 5.7-8)	3–11
Narrative	6.1, 7, 37-38; 7.1;	
material	9.(15-23,) 24-25 (9.26-	
	28; 10.14-29); 11.26,	
	(27-28,) 40-43	
	12.2, 20a, 25-30a	12.1, 3-19, 20b-24, 26b, 27aβb,
		28b-29, 30b-33
		13.1–14.18
	14.19–16.31	14.21bα², 22b-24, 26b-28
		15.4, 12-13, 15, 29-30
		16.1-4, 7, 11-12, 13bβ, 26b
		16.31bβ–22.38
	22.39-53	22.47, 54
2 Kings		
	1.1, 18	1.2-17; 2.1-25
	3.1-2a, 3	3.2b, 4-8.15
	8.16-27	8.19
	(8.28f.), 9.14–10.17	9.1-13, 21bβ, 22bβ, 25-26, 28-29,
		36-37
		10.10-11, 14bβ-16, 17aβ-33
	10.34-36	
	11.1-4, 19-20	11
	12.1-3a, 4, 18-22	12.3b, 5-17
	13.1-2, 7-13	13.3-6, 14-25
	14.1–16.20	14.6, 8-17, 25b-27
		15.12, 37
		16.3b-4, 10-18
	17.1-6, 21-23	17.7-20, 24-41
	18.1-3, (4aα¹,) 7b, 8,	18.4-7a, 9-12, 17-19, 35
	13–16	
	19.36-37	
	20.12-13, 20-21	20.1-11, 14-19
	21.1-2a, 17-20, 23-26	21.2b, 3-16, 21-22
	22.1-2, 3-7, 9	22.8, 10-20
	23.4a, 1, 12aα¹, 28-36	23.1-3, 4b-10, 12-27
	24–25	24.2-4, 13-14, 20a
		25.11-17, 21b, 23-24, 26

the bridgeheads of a first composition in 1 Sam.–1 Kgs 2, which makes David and Solomon, the kings of Judah, the successors to Saul in the kingship over Israel through the interlude in 1 Sam. 16–2 Sam. 6 (1 Sam. 14.52; 16.14-23 + 18.17-27 + 19.9f., 11f. + 21-31 + 2 Sam. 2–5 [8–10]) and thus unites the formerly independent kingdoms of Israel and Judah. The succession is explained by the downfall of Israel, which lives on in Judah. In the framework of the tradition the two kingdoms come increasingly close together, until the people of Israel is the primary entity which embraces both the house of Israel (later the tribes of Israel) and the house (later the tribe) of Judah. The Deuteronomistic revision builds up the way to this. After the downfall of Judah it continues the first composition of the united kingdoms in 1 Sam. 1–1 Kgs 2 in the annalistic scheme of 1–2 Kgs, which makes the scattered information of the 'books of days' of the kings of Israel and Judah into a 'synchronistic chronicle'. Thus in Samuel–Kings there arises a history of the kingship in Israel and Judah which had a common origin and was maliciously divided by the 'sin of Jeroboam' and driven to destruction. The criterion is the idea of the centralization of the cult in Deut. 12. A variety of Deuteronomistic, Priestly, legendary, etc. elaborations attach themselves to the basic stratum of the Deuteronomistic revision in Samuel–Kings (if one likes, DtrH); for the most part they presuppose the First Commandment or the whole law and assimilate the history of the kingship to the history of the people dominated by the law in the Hexateuch. The connecting link is the Deuteronomistic revision in Joshua and Judges.

3. Redaction and tradition in Joshua and Judges

L. Schwienhorst, *Die Eroberung Jerichos*, SBS 122, 1986; K. Bieberstein, *Josua – Jordan – Jericho: Geschichte und Theologie der Landnahmeerzählungen Jos 1–6*, OBO 143, 1959; W. Richter, *Traditionsgeschichtliche Untersuchungen zum Richterbuch*, BBB 18 (1963), [2]1966; id., *Die Bearbeitungen des 'Retterbuches' in der deuteronomischen Epoche*, BBB 21, 1964; U. Becker, *Richterzeit und Königtum*, BZAW 192, 1990; V. Fritz, 'Die Entstehung Israels im 12. und 11. Jahrhundert v. Chr.', *Biblische Enzyklopädie* 2, 1996; Y. Amit, *The Book of Judges: The Art of Editing* (Hebrew 1991), BIS 38, 1999.

Commentaries

M. Noth, *Das Buch Josua*, HAT I/7, [3]1971; R.G. Boling and G.E. Wright, *Joshua*, AB, 1982; V. Fritz, *Das Buch Josua*, HAT I/7, 1994; R.D. Nelson,

Joshua, AB, 1997; K. Budde, *Das Buch Richter*, KHC 7, 1897; R.G. Boling, *Judges*, AB, 1975; M. Görg, NEB 1993.

Research

E. Noort, *Das Buch Josua: Forschungsgeschichte und Problemfelder*, EdF 292, 1998; R. Bartelmus, 'Forschung am Richterbuch seit Martin Noth', *ThR* 56, 1991, 221-59; T. Veijola, *ThR* 67, 391-402.

3.1   As in Samuel–Kings, so also in Joshua and Judges the redaction can be detached from the tradition relatively easily. The main passages are: Josh. 1; 11.16-23 and 12.1-8; 13.1-7; 21.43-45 and 22; 23–24; the scheme of judges in Judg. 2.6–3.6 and its implementation in 3.7-11 (Othniel); 3.12-15 + 3.30 (Ehud); 3.31 (Shamgar); 4.1-3 + 4.23-24 and 5.31b (Deborah and Barak); 6.1-6 + 8.28 (8.29ff. + 9) (Gideon and Abimelech); 10.1-5 (Tola and Jair); 10.6-18 + 12.7 (Jephthah); 12.8-15 (Ibzan, Elon and Abdon); 13.1 + 15.20 and 16.31 (Samson).

In both books the redactional passages dominate the structure. Joshua 1 introduces the narrative of the settlement in Josh. 2–12, 11.16ff. concludes it together with Josh 12. Joshua 13.1-7 introduces the distribution of the land to the tribes in Josh. 13–21; 21.43-45 and ch. 22 conclude it. Joshua's two farewell speeches in Josh. 23–24 round off the whole. The redactional passages contain theological commentaries and above all speeches which put the settlement and the distribution of the land under Joshua in the right light. Everything is ordained by Yhwh and takes place in accordance with his command and the law of Moses; the conquest embraces the whole land, all Israel is involved in it, the whole land is distributed to all the tribes on both sides of the Jordan, and all the tribes of Israel are once again committed to the law by the aged Joshua, so that Yhwh also drives out the rest of the people in the land and the periphery and Israel keeps the land. In terms of the material this view of things corresponds to the tribal geography in Josh. 13–22. The narrative about the settlement in Josh. 2–12 has not remained uninfluenced by it, but nevertheless clearly indicates that the radius here was originally very much smaller. After the crossing of the Jordan (Josh. 2–5) the conquest really extends only to the two ruined hills of Ai and Jericho (Josh. 6–8); there follow reactions and attacks of other cities which collaborate against the Israelites (Josh. 9–12). Accordingly in the book of Joshua we can distinguish three levels: (1) an early narrative about the settlement in Josh. 2–12; (2) the tribal geography in Josh. 13–22; (3) the redaction which brings both under the same roof.

In the Book of Judges we are 'given the right standpoint'[43] by the prelude in Judg. 2.6–3.6: after the death of Joshua the Israelites do evil in the eyes of

Yhwh and as a result are delivered by Yhwh into the hands of their enemies. But Yhwh raises up judges and saves the Israelites from their distress. As long as the judges are in office, rest prevails, but after their death everything goes wrong again. Apart from the Calebbite Othniel, it is always regions and places in the (Israelite) north that are involved in the implementation of the scheme (Benjamin, Ephraim, Napthali and Zebulun, Gilead and Dan, in Judg. 5 the ten tribes of the north), and not the region of Judah (but cf. Judg. 1 and 17–21); the enemies are the surrounding peoples of the Aramaeans, Moabites, Philistines, Canaanites, Midianities, Ammonites and finally the Philistines again. Shamgar in 3.31 and Abimelech in Judg. 9 stand outside the scheme, as do the lists of the cities which are conquered and not conquered in Judg. 1.1–2.5 and the narratives about tribal history in Judg. 17–21. These have their own formula: 'In those days there was no king in Israel; everyone did what was right in his eyes' (17.6; 18.1; 19.1; 21.25). As in Josh. 2–12, so too in Judges the narratives given a framework by the redaction have a profile of their own. Ehud in Judg. 3, Deborah and Barak in Judg. 4–5, Gibeon–Jerubbaal in Judg. 6–8, Abimelech in Judg. 9, Jephthah in Judg. 10–12 and Samson in Judg. 13–16 are figures who, with the exception of the anti-hero Abimelech, have only been made judges of Israel and saviours secondarily as a result of the distress it has brought upon itself. The redaction puts them in a succession with a consecutive chronology and explains the distress by the sin of the Israelites. It is the framework scheme which first brings together what are timeless legends and thus completely unconnected episodes into a single epoch in the history of Israel, the epoch of the 'judges' of Israel, which precedes the epoch of the kings of Israel and Judah. Consequently the epoch of the judges is not a historical fact but a redactional construction.

3.2   The theological commentaries and speeches in Joshua recall the texts in 1 Sam. 12; 1 Kgs 8.1–9.9; 2 Kgs 17 and 2 Kgs 22–23. These are related in content, and like them refer back to the covenant and law in Exodus–Deuteronomy; the formulas in the scheme in Judges recall the scheme for the kings in Samuel–Kings. It is therefore all too understandable that the same revision is seen at work everywhere and is identified with the Deuteronomistic redaction. But the identification is correct only with qualifications.

The redaction in Joshua picks up Deut 31.1ff. and 34.1-6 narratively in Josh. 1.1ff. and presupposes the prehistory of the exodus from Egypt and the wandering in the wilderness as far as the land of Moab from Exodus–Deuteronomy. That distinguishes it from the first annalistic redaction in Samuel–Kings (Dtr^G = DtrH), but connects it with the secondary Deuteronomistic revisions (Dtr^S = DtrP and DtrN or the like), which in both places refer to the patriarchs, the exodus and the time of the judges.

Moreover the theological commentaries and speeches of Josh. 1 and 11–12, Josh. 13 and 21–22 and Josh. 23–24 implicitly or explicitly have the whole law and especially the First Commandment as the criterion. That also connects them with Dtr^S in Samuel–Kings. The contour line runs from the Sinai covenant in Exod. 19–24 and 32–34 through the Moab covenant in Deut. 26–28 to the Shechem covenant in Josh. 24 and from here to the discovery of the covenant document and a renewal of the covenant under Josiah in 2 Kgs 22–23. That means that the redaction in Joshua is not identical with the original Deuteronomistic redaction in Samuel–Kings, but presupposes it and above all the secondary Deuteronomistic strata, and forms a literary connection with the latter.

The annalistic scheme in the book of Judges is very similar. Judges 1 and 2.6ff. each in their way pick up the redactional pieces in Joshua; the scheme of judges prepares for the transition from the time of the judges to the time of the monarchy in 1 Sam. 7–8; 10.17-27 (casting lots as in Josh. 13–21); 12 (especially vv. 9-13), which puts the earlier version of the origin of the kingdom in 1 Sam. 9–14 in a new context. The Deuteronomistic basic writing in Samuel–Kings presupposes only the earlier version; the narrative and theological links with the time of the judges which go beyond this are dependent on it, but secondary.

In addition there are the differences in the redactional scheme itself. The scheme of judges already differs from the scheme of the kings in Samuel–Kings in the way in which it is made. In contrast to Samuel, where the scheme has necessarily been introduced into an existing context, in both Judges and Kings it constitutes the literary context. But in contrast to Kings, where the scheme represents the basic framework for the later filling out with narrative material, in Judges it is not viable without the narrative included in it. Judges 2.6–3.6 is not an era of its own but the theological programme for the whole period of the judges; the chronology begins only from 3.7ff. on.

A further difference consists in the chronology, in which scholars since Noth have been fond of finding a unifying link. In Judges the round numbers which we know from David and Solomon prevail, and give the impression of being artificial; the odd numbers are as authentic or fictitious as the two years of Saul in 1 Sam. 13.1. However we count and correct the numbers from Samson in Judg. 13–16 and 1 Sam. 4.18; 7.2; 13.1; 2 Sam. 2.10f.; 5.4f. up to the key date of 480 years in 1 Kgs 6.1,[44] the sum never adds up without some exceptions. All that is clear is that an attempt is being made to achieve a chronology which extends from the exodus, taking in the forty years of wandering in the wilderness, to the building of the temple, and thus spans the literary context of Exodus–Kings. But it is also clear that the chronology in Samuel–Kings, with or without the secondary synchronization in 1 Kgs 6.1, stands by itself, whereas in Judges it is calculated with a view to the 480 years of 1 Kgs 6.1. Consequently, while the chronology is dependent on Samuel–Kings, it does not lie on the same level.

Finally, the schemes of judges and kings are also different in their theological aims. 'Doing evil in the sight of Yhwh' does not originally mean the same thing in both contexts and is sometimes also dealt with quite differently. In Judges the whole people, as distinct from the 'judges', does evil in the eyes of Yhwh; in Kings the kings do evil in the eyes of Yhwh, and also lead the people to sin, unless as on some occasions in Judah the kings do 'right' and only the people sacrifice on the high places. It is the secondary Deuteronomistic expansions, for example, in 2 Kgs 17.7ff., which as in Judges make the whole people sin. In Judges the sin of the people consists quite generally in falling away from Yhwh: more specifically, as far as this is said (Judg. 2.7, 10, etc.), in transgressing the First Commandment and the whole law. From the beginning the scheme of judges also moves on the level of the secondary Deuteronomistic redaction in Samuel–Kings (1 Sam. 12.1ff., etc.). The idea of the centralization of the cult, which is significant for Samuel–Kings, does not occur in Judges. The punishment for sin immediately follows in Judges, but each time is again averted by the people 'crying' to Yhwh, being heard by him and being saved for the next twenty, forty or eighty years. This scheme, imitating the ritual of lament and petition, links the time of the judges with the experiences of Israel at the exodus (in Exod. 3 and 14; cf. 1 Sam. 12.8ff.) and is more reminiscent of the Chronistic version of the history of the kings in 1–2 Chronicles than of the Deuteronomistic version in Samuel–Kings. There the 'sin of Jeroboam' is punished only at the end with the definitive rejection of Israel and finally with the rejection of Judah. It is the late-Deuteronomistic expansions in Samuel–Kings, for example, 1 Kgs 8, which here too first open up the possibility of repentance and salvation from distress. Observing the law is the presupposition for this.

It can be objected against this that the idea of the unity of the kingdom and the cult and everything else that distinguishes Samuel–Kings from Joshua and Judges play no role because there is as yet no kingdom and no one place of worship (Jerusalem) chosen by Yhwh. But the remarkable thing is that in Joshua and Judges the people does not rush as quickly as possible to the chosen place of worship, as would be expected after Deut. 12–26, there to observe the commandments and the covenant with or without the king, to bring the gifts of the land before Yhwh and rejoice. Yhwh waits hundreds of years before he inaugurates the kingship, chooses David and promises him that Solomon, the builder of the temple, will be his successor. If things went in accordance with Deut. 12 and the first Deuteronomist in Samuel–Kings, Samuel–Kings would have had to follow immediately after the death of Moses in Deut. 34 and the settlement through Joshua in Josh. 1–12. Instead of this, first of all there is the constitution of the twelve tribes in the land, once immediately and without a gap in the distribution of the land in Josh. 13–22, and following that once again in the battle of the judges against the surrounding peoples, with whom later the kings of Israel and Judah have to cope once again. The artificial digression about the tribes and the judges is subsequently given a historical foundation in Judg. 1 and Judg. 17–21, passages which stand outside the Deuteronomistic scheme, and the modern accounts of the history of Israel do the same with them. In fact there is a theological reason for the diversion: the goal is not the centralization of the cult, the unity of deity, cult and kingdom (Deut. 6.4-5 and 12.13ff.), but the demand of the oneness and exclusivity of Yhwh, the First Commandment, and the counterpart to the one God is not primarily the united kingdom but the unity of the people of Israel. The unity of the people is also the reason why Judah is absent from the framework of the scheme of judges in Judg. 3.7–16.31; it belongs to Israel only from the time of David. What is presupposed is a concept of 'Israel' that is not calculated on either the one great kingdom comprising the two states of Israel and Judah or the kingdom of the twelve tribes, but means the people of the Israelites as this appears from the exodus from Egypt to the settlement in Exodus–Judges. Moreover that is an argument which suggests that the Enneateuch constituted through Judges initially comprised only the books of Exodus–Kings. The presupposition for the later states of Israel and Judah also forming a unity as a people before the foundation of the states is the preface provided by Genesis with the genealogical link between Israel and Judah in the patriarchal narratives (Gen. 29.35) and the system of the twelve tribes. In one way or another it is always the whole people, not the united or divided kingdom of David, which stands over against the one and only God. Yhwh is the God of Israel and Israel is the people of Yhwh. That is the slogan which in Joshua and Judges governs the Deuteronomistic redaction orientated on the law in Exodus–Deuteronomy from the beginning, but in Samuel–Kings only from the second, third and all further phases of literary development.

So the comparison can be summed up as follows. The Deuteronomistic redaction in Joshua and above all in Judges is later than the Deuteronomistic basic writing in Samuel–Kings (Dtr^G), and like the many late-Deuteronomistic expansions in Samuel–Kings (Dtr^S) serves to combine in both literary and theological terms the history of the people of Israel in the Hexateuch (Genesis or Exodus–Deuteronomy), which is already dominated by the law, with the Deuteronomistic history of the kingdom in the two synchronized states of Israel and Judah (Samuel–Kings). The Deuteronomistic redaction in Joshua and Judges is the connecting link which brings the formerly separate narrative works, which were perhaps already read in historical order, the history of the people in (Genesis;)

Exodus–Joshua and the history of the kingdom in Samuel–Kings, into the salvation-historical context of the Enneateuch.

3.3   The Deuteronomistic redaction in Joshua and Judges is complex in itself. In accord with the commissioning of Joshua by Moses in Deut. 31.1f., 7f., it first limits itself to two perspectives: the occupation and distribution of the land, which after Moses' death in Josh. 1.1-2, 5-6 are ordained by Yhwh himself and are carried out in 11.16-23. The main interest of the redaction focuses on the 'rest' ($\check{s}qt$) before the war, which is achieved with the occupation of the whole land under Joshua: 'And Joshua occupied the whole land, and the land had rest from the war' (11.16aα^1, 23b). After the narrative of the settlement in Josh. 2–11, which joins on to Deut. 34.5f. seamlessly in 2.1 or 3.1, this is the starting point for the era of the judges which follows. In it the 'rest' is lost again because of the sin of the Israelites, and constantly has to be fought for again (Judg. 3.11, 30; 5.31; 8.28). The second task, given in Deut. 31.7f.; Josh. 1.5f., of distributing the land to Israel ($n\underline{h}l$, hiphil), follows a subordinate aim. Its accomplishment is communicated in 11.23a, and it was either attached directly to 11.16aα^1 with v. 23aα – without the gloss on 12.7f. and chs 13ff. 'to the tribes according to their divisions' – or already presupposes the insertions in vv. 16-22 – for example, vv. 16f. or vv. 16-19 after chs 9–11 and with a view to 12.1a, 9ff. also chs 13ff.? – and the recapitulation of 11.(15,) 16aα^1 in v. 23aβ: 'And Joshua occupied all this land according to all that Yhwh had said to Moses, and Joshua gave it to Israel as a heritage.' The few verses in Josh. 1 (vv. 1f., 5f.) and 11 (vv. 16-23) together form the basic stratum of the Deuteronomistic redaction in Joshua, but presumably are not all on the same level. As the redaction already had the transition from Deuteronomy to Joshua before it, initially the hinge 11.16aα^1, 23b, which opens up the earlier narrative of the settlement to the continuation in Judges, was sufficient for this. By contrast, Deut. 31.1f., 7f. and the commissioning by Yhwh dependent on it in Josh. 1.1f., 5f. (cf. Deut. 31.2b) seem to be a later formation. It introduces a further break (with Josh. 1.1, cf. Judg. 1.1; 2 Sam. 1.1; 13.1) in the earlier transition from Deuteronomy to Joshua in Deut. (26.16 +) 34.1a, 5f. + Josh. 2.1 – perhaps already in respect of insertions in Deut. 26–30 – and here in a special way emphasizes the initiative of Yhwh and the identity of the commissioning by Moses and Yhwh.

Abundant details have attached themselves to the basic stratum of the Deuteronomistic redaction in Josh. 1.1f., 5f.; 11.16-23. Joshua 1.3-4 adds a description of the territory (cf. Deut. 34.1b-4). Joshua 1.7, 8-9 links the promise of support in vv. 5f. with an admonition to study the law (cf. Deut. 31.3-6, 9-10). Joshua 1.10-18 involves the two and a half tribes east of the Jordan who have already completed their settlement (cf. Num. 32; 34.13-15;

Deut. 3.18-20; and Josh. 12.1-8; 13.8ff.). Further descriptions of territory which supplement the territory of the kings fought against previously and listed in Josh. 12.1a, 9-24 are also added in 11.16-22 and 12.1b-8. And although according to Josh. 11–12 the whole land has already been occupied and divided, 13.1-7 begins once again with the enumeration of territories on the periphery which have not been conquered and the charge to Joshua to distribute the whole land by lot to the nine and a half tribes west of the Jordan as a heritage. This then happens in Josh. 13–21[45] and is completed with the summary in 21.43-45 and the release of the two and a half tribes east of the Jordan in Josh. 22. Joshua 13–22 is composed of various lists of places and territories which are forced into the concept of the twelve tribes and is certainly not a unity, though in the original stratum – however defined[46] – it already represents an alien body which holds up the programme of the narrative in the book of Judges indicated in 11.23b. The priests, the tent and the procedure with lots show a Priestly influence throughout; the procedure with lots can be kept out of the basic material only by resorting to the Septuagint. We recognize by the summary of the distribution of the land (*nḥl*, hiphil) in 21.43-45, which duplicates 11.16-23, that the whole passage is an addition; it puts special emphasis on the taking possession of the land (*yrš*)[47] and uses the root *nwḥ* (usually in the hiphil) rather than *šqṭ* for the 'rest'.[48] That it is an addition is also evident from the resumption of 13.1a in 23.1b ('and Joshua was old and full of days'). Everything in between, that is, 13.1b-23.1a, is an insertion; 13.1a = 23.2b, the introduction to the farewell discourse in Josh. 23–24, is original. But the farewell speech itself is also an addition and is not a unity. In part it already presupposes the expansions in Josh. 1; 11–12; and 13–22, for example, the question of the other people in 23.3ff., the fulfilment of the promise in 21.45 in 23.14ff., the tribes and the occupation of the land in 24.1ff., and the law as a whole as in 1.7ff. The mutual relationship of the two additions, Josh. 13–22 and Josh. 23–24, is decided by the analysis of chs 23–24; this in turn is connected with the literary relationship between them and the continuation in Judg. 1–3.

3.4   Before we come to that, we shall first take a look at the layout of the Deuteronomistic scheme in the book of Judges. The simple scheme occurs in Judg. 3.12–15.30 and has the following elements:[49] (1) the formula about sinning, 'And the Israelites did (continued to do) evil in the eyes of Yhwh', v. 12; (2) the Israelites are delivered into the hand of the enemy for so many years, vv. 12-14; (3) they cry to Yhwh (this is followed by their deliverance in narrative form), v. 15; (4) the formula about subjugation and rest, v. 30; (5) the formula about dying, here repeated in 4.1b. The basic scheme is the same everywhere, but the formulations display a number of variations in detail: in 3.8 and 10.7 the 'wrath of Yhwh' is added to (2), the deliverance into the hands of the enemy is usually expressed with the formula 'sell into the hand of' (3.8; 4.2; 10.7) but also 'give into the hand of' (6.1; 13.1) or 'strengthen over Israel' (3.12); on (3), only in 3.9, 15 is the raising up of the saviour expressly noted (cf. also 10.1, 3; 13.5), and in 3.10; 6.34; 11.29; 13.25; 14.6; 15.14 the gift of the spirit to the saviour; in the case of Samson the crying which precedes this is absent after 13.1; in 3.10 and 4.4 the formula about the judge is added to (4), here without a date, but in 12.7 and 15.20; 16.31 with a date in place of the missing time of rest, as is customary in the list of the so-called minor judges in 10.1-5; 12.8-15 (cf. also 9.22). Three variants on (5) are offered by 3.11; 4.1b; and 8.28; in the case of Deborah and Barak in Judg. 4–5 the note about dying is absent and in 8.32; 12.7; and 16.30f. we have a note about a judge dying and being buried, as in the case of the list of the minor judges in 10.1-5 and 12.8-15. Again things look different in the prelude in 2.11-19, where not only do the formulations differ considerably, but a number of elements are missing: apart from the dates – which of course are given only in individual instances – and the notes about dying and being buried, the crying to Yhwh and the formulae about subjugation and rest.

On the basis of the variations it has been inferred that the book of Judges grew in several stages, starting from a pre-Deuteronomistic 'book of saviours' in Judg. 3–9 which had first a Deuteronomic and last a Deuteronomistic redaction.[50] The correct insight here is that the composition is clearly divided into two by the variations of the scheme: in Judg. 3.7–8.28 and Judg. 10–16. In the first part the 'saving' (*yš*, hiphil) and the 'rest' (*šqt*) dominate, and in the second the 'judging' (*špt*), which here means ruling or reigning, and the 'spirit of Yhwh' (*rūªḥ yhwh*). The intermediate link is the kingdom of Abimelech in Shechem in Judg. 9, which is presupposed in the list of minor judges in 10.1-5, as is the 'judging' of the chieftain Jephthah over Gilead in 12.7, 8-15. The first part provided a certain basis for the activity of judging (cf. 4.4f., but here explicitly in the meaning 'pronounce justice'); the other overlaps are based on secondary assimilation or identification of saviours and judges: in 2.11-19; 3.10; 6.34 the saviour is a judge endowed with the spirit; in 10.1; 13.5 the judge is at the same time the saviour. The two parts may have arisen in succession, the passages Judg. (6.25-32; 7.1; 8.29-35 +) 9 and 10.1-5; 12.8-15 having been inserted subsequently. Alternatively, just the harmonization of 'saviour' and 'judge' may have been undertaken subsequently. But that does not produce a pre-Deuteronomistic 'book of Judges'. The formula about sinning, 'And the Israelites did evil in Yhwh's eyes', which is used throughout and constitutes and links the two parts, is taken from the Deuteronomistic scheme about the kings and like the redactional version of the narratives about saviours and judges in Judg. 3–8 and 9–16 from the beginning has the function of constructing a transition from the history of the people in

Genesis–Joshua to the history of the kingship in Samuel–Kings. If the 'saving' in the first part, Judg. 3–8, recalls more the prehistory (especially Exod. 3 and 14), the 'ruling' and 'judging' in the second part, Judg. 9–16, which in 9.22 and 10.1-5; 12.7, 8-15 takes on an annalistic colouring, recalls more the time of the monarchy in Samuel–Kings. But both the 'saving' and the 'judging', like the gift of the spirit to the judges, prepares for the transition from the time of the saviours or judges to the monarchy – which for its part has a corresponding introduction in 1 Sam. 4 and 7–8; 10.17-27 and 12.[51] This preparation takes place not in one but in several stages.

The filling out of the formula about sinning is clearer than the gradual harmonization of the 'saviours' and 'judges' who are said to have preceded the kings of Israel and Judah; this suggests a unitary criterion for measuring evil and justice in the history of the people and the monarchy. The bare formula 'And the Israelites did evil in the eyes of Yhwh' is original; this brings together the 'Israelites' as the subject of the history of the people from (Genesis;) Exodus–Joshua with the censure of the kings of Israel and sometimes also of Judah from Samuel–Kings (Judg. 3.12; 4.1; 6.1; 13.1, correspondingly also 3.7; 10.6). What 'evil in the eyes of Yhwh' means is not said, but follows from the context for which the formula is made. The criterion is generalized when transferred to the people. The demand for unity of kingdom and cult made in Deut. 12 and Ur-Deuteronomy and scorned by the kings in Samuel–Kings, according to Deut. 6.4 based on the unity of Yhwh, has turned into the general claim of the one Yhwh to the one people, which manifests itself in the demand for obedience to the law, regardless of what the law requires. This claim is announced positively for the first time in the additions to Deut. 12.13-18 in vv. 19-28 (vv. 25, 28 and also 13.19; 21.9 and 6.18). The situation which occurs in Judges where this claim is scorned is foreseen in Exod. 15.26, likewise without further specification of the content of the commandments (cf. further Num. 32.13, and with a further explanation Deut. 4.25; 9.18; 17.2; 31.29). Accordingly, 'doing evil in Yhwh's eyes' means scorning or transgressing the whole law revealed in Exodus–Deuteronomy, on the fulfilment of which the relationship between Yhwh and Israel depends. Yhwh is Israel's God and Israel is Yhwh's people, but Israel fulfils Yhwh's will. The substance of the law and covenant in Exod. 19–24 (32–34) and Deut. 5–30 and the First Commandment, which puts the relationship between Yhwh and Israel on the basis of the law and declares it to be exclusive, has long been presupposed here. But this connection is initially not made explicit in the bare formula of the book of Judges. The renewal of the covenant in Josh. 23–24 first clarifies what is in the making with the generalization of the scheme of the kings in the book of Judges. As in Josh. 23–24 and the scheme of the kings, in the scheme of the judges, too, the secondary, detailed remarks about the sins of Israel, serving strange gods and mingling with the peoples of the land, attach themselves to this: Judg. 2.1–3.6; 3.7; 10.6, 10-16 (only here does the 'wrath of Yhwh' also appear, 2.14, 20; 3.8; 10.7!).

Finally, the appendices describing tribal history in Judg. 1 and Judg. 17–18; 19–21 attach themselves around the narratives about the judges in Judg. 2–16 as though there were no Deuteronomistic scheme of judges or era of the judges. The framework passages continue the narrative of the settlement of the tribes in Numbers, Deut. 1–3, Josh. 1 and Josh. 13–22, and add detail to the only partially successful conquest of the Canaanite cities and the conflicts within Israel in the course of the occupation of the land; here, in contrast to Judg. 3–16, Judah and the opposition to the north Israelite tribes play a not inconsiderable role. And whereas the scheme of judges suggests a continuity and similarity of sin from the entry into the land onwards, which only through the long-suffering nature of Yhwh and his ceaseless care of Israel lasted until the downfall of Israel and Judah, the formula which holds together the appendices in Judg. 17–21 (17.6; 18.1; 19.1; 21.25; cf. Deut. 12.8 for the time before the entry into the land) draws a distinction between a time when everyone did what was right in his eyes and the time of the kings, in which an improvement seems to be promised. If Judg. 3–16 were not there, one could think that the appendices in Judg. 1 and 17–21 were the natural continuation of the narrative of the settlement in Numbers/Deut. 1–3 and Joshua and attribute them either to one of the old narrative strands of the Pentateuch or to the first (Judahite) redactor of the Deuteronomistic work (DtrH) who is 'friendly to the monarchy'. But the continuation is anything but natural, and in a quite artificial way reckons the whole period of the judges, when Israel had long established itself in the land, as part of the time of the settlement. If we leave out the preliminary traditio-historical stages in Judg. 17f., Judg. 1 and 17–21 consist purely of filling-out passages and particularly in Judg. 19–21, as in Josh. 13–22, indicate Priestly influence. Language and content alone prove the passages to be post-Deuteronomistic; they are very reminiscent of the Chronistic view of the period before the monarchy (cf. 2 Chron. 15.1-7). Like the 'historicizing' framework passages in Deut. 1–3, Josh. 1 and 13–22, the appendices contribute towards integrating the book of Judges into the salvation history and at the same time making it independent. The beginnings of narratives ('There was once a man') in Judg. 17.1 and 19.1, which correspond to 13.2 on the one hand and 1 Sam. 1.1; 9.1 on the other, are significant. The beginning in Judg. 1 and the division of eras by the formulae in Judg. 17–21 have the significance of neutralizing the remarkable interim between the law for living in the land in Exodus–Deuteronomy and the rise of the institutional framework for observing the law under the kings – of Judah – in Samuel–Kings, which has come into being with the time of the judges – introduced by the first Deuteronomistic redaction in Judges and reordering it (cf. 1 Kgs 3.2f.). The purity and unity of the cult according to Deut. 12

presuppose the temple in Jerusalem, and it is no coincidence that Deut. 12.9f speaks of the 'rest' (*nwḥ*) which is achieved not in Judges (*šqṭ*), but first under David and Solomon in 2 Sam. 7.1, 11; 1 Kgs 5.18; 8.56. Therefore the time of the judges is not added to the era of the monarchy but to the ongoing era of the settlement before the monarchy. Thus Joshua and Judges each deal in their own way, in accordance with the precepts of the Mosaic law in the Pentateuch, with the settlement of the tribes under Joshua and after Joshua's death: Samuel–Kings also deal with it in their own way, in the context with David and the monarchy. Here the Chronistic division into eras in the tribal history (1 Chron. 1–9) and the history of the monarchy is heralded (1 Chron. 10ff.).

Given all this, in both Joshua and Judges we must keep separate a Deuteronomistic basic stratum (Josh. 11.16aα[1], 23b or Josh. 1.1f., 5f.; 11.16-23; the simple schema of the judges in Judg. 3.7–16.31) and a series of supplementary Deuteronomistic and post-Deuteronomistic strata of expansion (some of them influenced by the Priestly Writing), which have in common not only a redactional interest in a balance between the history of the people and the history of the monarchy but also the fact that they bring both under the sign of the law, Yhwh's exclusive claim on his people. However, they differ in the way in which they articulate this claim. In the process it becomes evident that the general claim becomes more and more concrete and is filled out with cultic, genealogical and political-geographical definitions. Here the polemic against strange gods, the system of the twelve tribes, the lists of peoples, regions and localities, wherever they come from, and the theme of the conquest of the whole land which is still to come, have their place.

3.5   This development can be examined in exemplary fashion by the relevant redaction-historical shift in Josh. 23–24; Judg. 1–3.[52] The situation is as follows: the conclusion of the book of Joshua in Josh. 24.28-31 is repeated almost word for word in Judg. 2.6-10, and Josh. 24.28/Judg. 2.6; Josh. 24.29f./Judg. 2.8f; Josh. 24.31/Judg. 2.7(, 10) resemble one another. Judges 1.1–2.5 pushes itself in between, and on the external peripheries Josh. 23–24 and Judg. 2.(7, 10,) 11–3.6 display close relations. Usually an earlier connection between Josh. 21.43-45 and Judg. 2.8–10, 11ff. is reckoned with which has been gradually filled out by the successive insertion of Josh. 23–24 and Judg. 1.1–3.6, for example, first through Josh. 23/Judg. 2.6-10 and subsequently through Josh. 24/Judg. 1.1–2.5. Noth[53] already recognized the secondary character of both Josh. 13–21(; 22) and 21.43-45 over against 11.16-23 and therefore reckoned with a continuation of Josh. 11–12 in Josh. 23/Judg. 2.6ff., into which first Josh. 24.1-28 and Judg. 2.1-5 (according to Blum only 2.1-5) and lastly Josh. 24.29-31, 32, 33 and Judg. 1 (according to Blum the whole of Josh. 24 and Judg. 1) have been inserted. If we combine the one with the other and take the differentiation in the Deuteronomistic redaction made above into account, we very soon see that the earliest connecting link is in Josh. 11.16aα[1], 23b (+ 12.1a, 9-24) and Judg. 2.8f. + 3.7ff (simple scheme), which after the 'rest' (šqṭ) fought for under Joshua leads through the death of Joshua to the onset of the evil and the 'rest' fought for by the saviours and judges in the original scheme of the judges.

Everything else, Josh. 13–21 (22), Josh. 23, Josh. 24, Judg. 1, Judg. 2.1-5 and the overlapping text in Josh. 24.28-31 and Judg. 2.6, 7, 10 are secondary insertions, but they pose the question of the relative chronology. The relationship between Josh. 13–21 (22) and Josh. 23–24 is decided by the relationship of 13.1a to 23.1b. The introduction 'And Joshua was old and full of days' has its original context in the farewell discourse in Josh. 23–24; by contrast, the framework of the tribal geography in Josh. 13.1–23.1a (with the connecting link in 23.1a to 21.43-45 and the recapitulation of 13.1a in 23.1b) proves to be secondary. Consequently, first the farewell discourse in Josh. 23–24 has been attached to Josh. 11–12 with 13.1a = 23.1b, and then the tribal geography in Josh. 13.1-23.1a has been inserted.

For the transition from Josh. 23–24 to Judg. 1–2, we do best to begin from the textual overlap in Josh. 24.28-31/Judg. 2.6-10. It confirms the widespread assumption that the conquest of cities built up in terms of tribal history in Judg. 1 and the passage Judg. 2.1-5, which is rather lost in its context, have been inserted between an early connection between Josh. 23–24 and Judg. 2.6-10 (2.11–3.6), centring on the 'service' of Yhwh. The demarcation from the book of Judges in Josh. 24.29-31, 32, 33, which concludes the book of Joshua and puts Judg. 2.7-9 before Judg. 1.1, is also connected with the insertion of Judg. 1. This marks the beginning of the book of Judges, as Judg. 17–21 mark the end. The reverse relationship is excluded, since Judg. 2.7-9 can hardly be the resumption of Josh. 24.29-31 after the insertion of Judg. 1.1. The overlap in Josh. 24.28 = Judg. 2.6 (cf. Josh. 13.1a = 23.1b) forms the literary intersection for the insertion of Josh. 24.29-33/Judg. 1.1–2.5.

Within the connection between Josh. 23.1–24.28 and Judg. 2.6–3.6 we must once again distinguish between texts about the service of Yhwh, contrasting Yhwh and the other gods, and those which connect this theme with the question of the other peoples (in the land or on the periphery) and the aspect of the complete conquest of the land (yrš). In Judg. 2.6–3.6 the decision is not difficult to make: 2.7, 10 and the programme 2.11-19 belong to the first category and 2.20–3.6 (and 2.1-5.6) to the second.

In Josh. 23–24 things are rather more complicated. Here the themes overlap, and thus views are divided as to which of the two speeches is the earlier and which the later. Noth's hesitant judgment is symptomatic of the uncertainty: sometimes he regards the one and sometimes the other as original. Most recently scholars have inclined towards the priority of Josh. 23, but this does not fit with the stratification in Judg. 2.6–3.6, where the question of true worship (Josh. 24) comes first and the question of the peoples (Josh. 23) second. The solution presumably lies in the stratification of Josh. 23–24. The natural beginning of Joshua's farewell speech in connection with Josh. 11–12 is in 23.1b-2: 'And Joshua was old and well advanced in years, and Joshua summoned all Israel, etc. and said to them, "I am now old and well advanced in years".' In 23.3 there follows a recollection of what Yhwh has done with all 'these', namely, the kings and people conquered in Josh. 2–12, before the eyes of Israel and how he fought for Israel. From Josh. 23.4 on the strongly edited[54] text diverges, and up to the end of the first discourse in 23.16 discusses the theme of the 'other peoples' and the conquest of the land which is still to come. There is a concluding admonition in 23.14-16 which quotes 21.43-45. The second farewell discourse begins in 24.1, this time with the summoning of all the tribes of Israel to Shechem. This is the place where Abimelech will rule as king (Judg. 9); where Rehoboam will be made king of all Israel (1 Kgs 12.1), though it is suppressed by Jeroboam I; and to which the choice for the one and only God will be moved, to some degree as a counterpoint to the foundation of the northern Israelite monarchy (cf. 1 Sam. 10.17-27). The word-for-word agreements in 24.1 with 23.2 and the surpluses which take account of the tribes of Josh. 13–22 and put these as it were before God indicate that this is a redactional hinge which in literary terms is dependent on 23.1; after the divergence in 23.4-16, likewise connected with Josh. 13–21, it makes Josh. 23–24 into two speeches. Originally the summoning of Israel presumably took place in the camp in Gilgal (cf. Josh. 4.19b, lastly 10.43 and still Judg. 2.1). Through Josh. 24.1 this becomes the assembly at Shechem. The new introduction in 24.2-13 takes the place of Josh. 23.3; again it is a historical retrospect, but a much broader one, which finally gets to the point in 24.14, introduced by 'and now'. If we leave out of account the excursus in 23.4-16 and the new introduction to which it gives rise in 24.1-13, the subsequent section in 24.14-28, with the removal of a few additions,[55] fits seamlessly on to the opening of the speech and the short reminiscence of the acts of Yhwh in 23.1b-2, 3:

'You have seen all that Yhwh your God has done to all these nations for your sake, for it is Yhwh your God who has fought for you. Now therefore fear Yhwh and serve him in sincerity and in faithfulness ... And if you be unwilling to serve Yhwh, choose this day whom you will serve. As for me and my house, we will serve Yhwh.' Then the people answered, 'Far be it from us that we should forsake Yhwh, to serve other gods. We also will serve Yhwh, for he is our God.' And Joshua said to the people, 'You are witnesses against yourselves that you have chosen Yhwh, to serve him.' And they said, 'We are witnesses.'

Joshua 24.25-27 take up the secondary thread of 24.1 again, and again end with the witnesses. Thus the choice of God in Gilgal becomes the making of the covenant at Shechem. The dismissal of the people in 24.28 fits v. 22 as well as it does v. 27. So the basic text in Josh. 23–24 proves to be Josh. 23.1b-3; 24.14a, 15-16, 18b, 22, 28. It continues in Judg. 2.7-10.

The analysis of the compositional knot in Josh. 23–Judg. 3 confirms the differentiation in the Deuteronomistic redaction made above. The first redaction in Joshua and Judges (Josh. 11.16aα[1], 23b + Judg. 2.8; 3.7ff.) combining (Genesis) Exodus–Joshua with Samuel–Kings is followed by a renewed commitment to the First Commandment (basic text in Josh. 23–24 and Judg. 2.7, 10). Previously this is implicit in the literary context (cf. Deut. 31.1f., 7f.; Josh. 1.1f., 5f.), and from now on is explicitly the criterion for 'doing evil in the eyes of Yhwh' in the Judges scheme and the Kings scheme. The universal claim of Yhwh to exclusive worship becomes the starting point for the cultic explications of the First Commandment in Judg. 2.1-10 and the scheme of judges and kings itself (cf. also Josh. 24.14b, 19-21, 23f.), the expansion of the legal paraenesis (Josh. 1.7-9; cf. 23.6), the tribal geography (Josh. 1.10ff.; 13.1–23.1a) and the question of the peoples in connection with the conquest of the whole land (Josh. 1.3f.; 11.16-23; 12.1-8; 23.4-16; 24.15, 17-18a; Judg. 2.1-5 with the resumption of Josh. 24.28 in Judg. 2.6; Judg. 2.20–3.6). Lastly the limits of the book in Josh. 24.1-13, 25-27, 29-33 and Judg. 1 shift between Josh. 23.1–24.28 and Judg. 2.1–6.7ff.

Table B.II.2

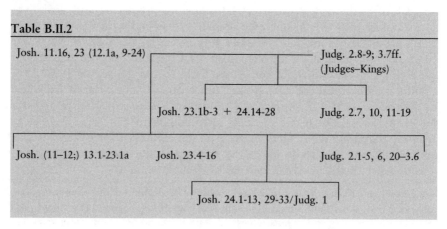

3.6   If we remove the various strata of redaction, in Josh. 2–12 and Judg. 3–16 we come up against the material of which Joshua and Judges are made. This, too, has not remained intact from the redaction, but still is sufficiently clearly distinct from it.

In the book of Joshua we have a more or less consecutive narrative thread, the theme of which is the settlement of the Israelites. It is based on an originally independent Joshua tradition in Josh. 6 and 8 which has its home in the region of Jericho and Ai and which through the addition of the crossing of the Jordan in Josh. 2–4 becomes the narrative of the settlement. The original stratum begins in Josh. 2.1 and narrates something like the following: from Shittim in Transjordan Joshua sent spies into Jericho, which lay opposite. The king of Jericho had them pursued, but they found refuge and support in the house of the prostitute Rahab, returned safely and gave their report (2.1-7, 15f., 22f.). The next morning Joshua arose and led the people from Shittim[56] over the Jordan, which on this occasion ceased its flow. They set up camp in Gilgal, on the edge of Jericho (Josh. 3.1, 14a, 16; 4.19b). Jericho was closed to them, but Yhwh told them what to do and gave the city into their hand. Early in the morning Joshua arose and they circled the city. Blowing the horns, they uttered the war cry, the walls collapsed and they captured the city (6.1-3, 5, 12a, 14, 20b).[57] After Jericho came Ai. Yhwh gave the orders, Joshua set out in the morning with the whole people and camped in front of Ai. When the king of Ai saw that, the men of the city went out early in the morning, and joined battle with Israel without suspecting that a rearguard posted by Joshua was waiting for them. This seized the city and set fire to it (Josh. 8.1-2a, 10a, 11a, 14, 19).[58] The Israelites dealt with all the other kings whose names and cities are listed under the heading 'and these are the kings of the land whom the Israelites smote' in 12.1a, 9-24 in the same way as they did with the kings of Jericho and Ai.

The rest of what can be read in Josh. 2–12 is the result of various revisions which spin out the original narrative thread and interpret it theologically. Some of this may be pre-Deuteronomistic, above all the narratives of the wars against the kings of the south and the north in Josh. 10–11 which in some way are based on old reminiscences of the sun and moon standing still at Gibeon in 10.12f., the waters of Merom in 11.5, 7 and the stones in front of the cave at Makkedah in 10.16-27, as Josh. 6 and 8 form a pair and report devastating destructions of cities in the style of the additions to Josh. 6 and 8. They have Josh. 6 and 8 as their model and add the wars against the cities and kings mentioned in Josh. 12.9-24. We can recognize that they are additions from the fact that unlike Josh. 6 and 8, they do not really report the conquest of the land but defensive wars, and the list of kings in Josh. 10–11 is different from that in 12.9-24. The additions are presupposed in the version of 11.16-23 (vv. 18-20), expanded by the distribution of the land.

However, most is the work of Deuteronomistic and post-Deuteronomistic revisions in Josh. 2–12, sometimes with a strong Priestly stamp: the broad elaboration of the crossing of the Jordan in Josh. 2–4 which makes the simple crossing into a cultic procession; the episodes in Gilgal (the second circumcision, 'rolling away' the shame of Egypt and Passover by replacing the manna with the produce of the land), and the theophany before Jericho in Josh. 5 which makes Joshua a second Moses; the numerous supplements in Josh. 6 and 8 to the cultic origin of the wars and the ban, together with an exemplary story about dealing with the booty under the ban in Josh. 7; the covenant with the Gibeonites in Josh. 9 (10.1b, 4; 11.19) which interrupts the connection between 10.1a, 3ff. and Josh. 6 and 8 and puts the scene of the battle (10.5, 10, 12) in a special relationship with Israel; the implementation of the ban in 10.28-43 and 11.10-15 in accordance with Josh. 6 and 8, and not least the passages Josh. 1; 11.16-23; and 12.1-8 which have already been discussed.

The pre-Deuteronomistic narrative thread in Joshua cannot have existed by itself but is dependent on the literary context: not necessarily, however, that of the whole Enneateuch or the Deuteronomistic history postulated by Noth, but the prehistory from the exodus to the gateway to the land. As we have already seen, the primary narrative and literary connecting point for Josh. 2.1; 3.1 is the arrival of Israel in Shittim in Num. 25.1a and the death of Moses in Deut. 34.5f. (without additions). The Deuteronomistic redaction already presupposes in Josh. 1.1f., 5f., the insertion of the Deuteronomistic law and in Deut. 3.1f., 7f. the premonition of Moses which concludes the legal treaty.

3.7   In the book of Judges, in contrast to Joshua, after removing the redactional framework in which the first example of a saviour or judge, the Calebbite Othniel in 3.7-11, is also to be included,[59] we do not encounter a consecutive narrative thread but a variety of individual traditions which are well rounded, and also related. They narrate memorable events connected with individual heroes from different regions of Israel as follows:

1. Ehud, the son of Gera, a Benjaminite (3.15), who kills Eglon, king of Moab, in a curious way (3.16-26).
2. Barak, the son of Abinoam, from Kedesh in Naphtali, who is summoned by the prophetess Deborah, the wife of Lappidoth, from the hill-country of Ephraim,[60] against a certain Sisera from Harosheth-ha-goiim. From his post on Mount Tabor he forced Sisera to flee by the brook Kishon and Sisera was killed, not by Barak but curiously by a woman, Jael, the wife of Heber the Kenite (4.4a, 5a, 6a, 7, 10a, 12, 13, 14b, 15b, 17aβγ, 18-22).[61] The event is handed down twice, once as prose in Judg. 4, and the other time in poetic form in Judg. 5. Since Wellhausen the priority of the song of Deborah in Judg. 5 has been regarded as settled. However, there are also pointers in the other direction. Thus the joint departure by Deborah and Barak, of which 4.12

still seems to know nothing and which has been added in 4.8f., 10b, 14a, is already presupposed in Judg. 5 The significance of Deborah, which increases in Judg. 4, reaches its high point in Judg. 5.7, 12. In 5.19f. the link between Sisera and Jabin of Hazor from Josh. 11 seems to be presupposed; Jabin becomes king of Canaan in 4.2, 7, 17b, 23f. The Israelitization of the narrative, which is beyond doubt secondary in Judg. 4, is taken yet one stage further in Judg. 5. Israel is the 'people of Yhwh' and is divided into ten tribes of the north – the southern tribes of Judah, Simeon and Levi are completely left out from Judg. 3–16, and Manasseh's sons Machir and Gilead appear in place of the two part-tribes of Manasseh. This considerably extends the radius of the version of Judg. 4, according to which only Naphtalites and Zebulonites are involved. I cannot see any reason for a later reduction of the tribes in Judg. 4.

3. Gideon, the son of Joash, from Ophrah in Abiezer, to whom the angel of Yhwh appeared. Thereupon he set up an altar of Yhwh in his home; with the slogan 'for Yhwh and Gideon' he went into battle against the Midianites and conquered them in a curious way, taking blood vengeance on two Midianite kings, Zebah and Zalmunna (6.11a, 19, 21, 24; 7.1b = 8b, 13-14, 15a, 16-21, 22b; 8.4, 10-12, 18-21bα). The individual episodes seem already to have been put together in a little narrative cycle before being included in the book of Judges. In addition, as everywhere else, there was an Israelitization and further theological interpretation of the earlier material within the framework of the book of Judges and the Deuteronomistic scheme of judges in 6.1-6 and 8.28: 6.7-10, 11b-18, 20, 22-23, 33-35, 36-40; 7.2-8a, 9-11, 12, 14a (only 'man of Israel'), 15b, 22a; 7.23–8.3; 8.5-9, 13-17; 8.21bβ-27. But the zeal of Gideon for Yhwh and against Baal in 6.25-32, which was kindled by the building of the altar in 6.11-24 and the battle cry 'for Yhwh and for Gideon' in 7.18, 20 and prompted the name Jerubbaal in 9.1f. can hardly have been sparked off outside the Deuteronomistic book of Judges. The identification of Gideon from Judg. 6–8 and Jerubbaal from Judg. 9 through 6.25-32; 7.1; 8.29-32, further supplemented in vv. 33-35, is either responsible for the insertion of ch. 9 and with it the linking of the 'judges' in chs 10–16 (especially 10.1-5; 12.7, 8-15) to the 'saviours' in Judg. 3–8, or it presupposes that Judg. 9–16 once followed the last 'rest' formula in 8.28 without any connection. In substance the bare confrontation between Yhwh and Baal moves between the first Deuteronomistic revision in Judges, which dovetailed (Genesis;)

Exodus–Joshua and Samuel–Kings together, and the Deuteronomistic supplements to the framework scheme in Judges and
Kings, which elaborate the First Commandment. It presupposes
Josh. 24.14-28; Judg. 2.7, 10 and has points of contact with the
divine judgment on Carmel in 1 Kgs 18 and the complete
removal of Baal under Jehu in 2 Kgs 10.18-28. In other words,
Dtr^G in Samuel–Kings was followed first by the redactional
connection with (Genesis;) Exodus–Joshua through the Deuteronomistic revision in Joshua and Judges (Josh. 11.16aα^1, 23b;
Judg. 2.8f.; 3.7–8.28; and 9.1–16.31), then by the renewed
inculcation of the First Commandment and the battle against
Baal (Josh. 23.1b-3; 24.14-28 + Judg. 2.7, 10; Judg. 6–9 through
6.25-32; 7.1; 8.29-32; 1 Kgs 18; 2 Kgs 10), and finally by the
explanation of the First Commandment as polemic against the
cult in the additions to the scheme about the judges and kings
and at many other points (Judg. 8.33-55; 9.4, 46, etc.).

4. Abimelech the son of Jerubbaal, a tragic hero; people told of his
rise, his defeat of the revolt by Gaal and the shameful end of his
kingship of Shechem, again curiously brought about by a woman
(9.1-3, 6, 26-41, 50-54). Everything else, the narrative and literary
connections with Judg. 6–8 in 9.4-5, 22-25, 42-49, 55-56 and the
corresponding use of what is called Jotham's fable in 9.8-15 in
9.7, 16-21, 57, which makes Abimelech a cruel usurper in Israel,
presupposes incorporation into the book of Judges, the
identification of Gideon with Jerubbaal in 6.25-32; 7.1; 8.29-32,
33-35, and consequently also the battle against Baal, and has
points of contact with the Deuteronomistic criticism of the king
in Judg. 8.22-27; 1 Sam. 8 and 12.

5. Jephthah the Gileadite, the son of a harlot, who nevertheless
becomes the chief of Gilead. Because he was of illegitimate origin
he returned to the land of Tob and built up a troop of
mercenaries, and when the elders of Gilead thereupon wanted to
recruit him as (army) leader in the fight against the Ammonites
he could dictate his conditions (11.1a, 3, 5b, 6-8, 11a). The old
narrative has been given a framework in 10.6-10, 17f.; 11.29, 33b;
12.7 by the Deuteronomistic redaction and likewise expanded in
11.1-11 and then successively extended in 10.10-18 (especially vv.
11-16); 11.12-28; 11.30-33a, 34-40; 12.1-6. The additions make
use of a widespread theme in 11.30f., 34-40; in 12.5f. an older
local tradition may have found its way in, but otherwise we have
literary constructions which fill out the scheme of judges with
polemic against the cult along the lines of the First Commandment and in the style of Josh. 24.1-13 recall the prehistory of the

settlement in the Hexateuch in Exodus–Deuteronomy, especially Num. 20–24 and Deut. 1–3.

6. Samson, a muscle-man, who looked round among the daughters of the land and made his choice among the Philistines, but his womanizing proved his downfall. The core of the tradition is contained in Judg. 14.1–15.8.[62] Presumably before being included in the book of Judges this was expanded by the aetiology of the place Ramath-lehi in Judah in 15.9-19,[63] the continuation of the stories about women in 16.1-30,[64] and the birth legend in 13.2-24.[65] This gives Samson a home among the Manoahites of Zorah, who are here included in the clan of the Danites. The formerly independent narrative cycle with a style like that of Judg. 9–12 (8.29-32; 10.1-5; 12.7, 8-15) has been integrated into the scheme of judges by 13.1; 15.20 and 16.31 (both the bestowing of the spirit in 13.5, 25; 14.6, 19; 15.14 and other supplements). In the framework of the Deuteronomistic scheme 'the shadow of Saul may be recognized' in Samson.[66]

7. It is quite uncertain whether and in what form the lists of the so-called minor judges in Judg. 10.1-5 and 12.8-15 go back to a pre-Deuteronomistic tradition. 10.1 presupposes Judg. 9 and with the infinitive 'to save ...' the narratives in Judg. 3–8; the whole list presupposes the Israelitization of the old material with its limitation to particular localities. The collection of names, numbers and places can no more and no less be invented than the information in the lists of Chronicles. The lists may have provided the model for the deviations from the scheme in Judg. 8.29-32; 9.22; 12.7; 15.30; 16.31 and the supplementation of the 'judge' in 3.10 and 2.11-19, but could just as well have been derived, like 3.31, from the 'saviour' scheme in Judg. 3–8 and inserted subsequently in order to fill out the 480 years from 1 Kgs 6.1.

As I have said, the individual narratives and smaller narrative cycles in Judges do not form a consecutive narrative thread and basically do not deal with Israel either, but were first put into a historical continuum in the framework of the Israelite salvation history by the Deuteronomistic redaction. However, they breathe the same spirit and may once have been in a loose collection. All of them have particular local points of contact, usually places in Ephraim or Benjamin. They deal with individual heroes of their region, and narrate remarkable events, warlike incidents which were of particular importance to the place or clan concerned, and strange deaths, often brought about by women. They all have an archaic religious stamp, and wide stretches of them seem very 'profane'; alternatively, they have marked miraculous features, and in both respects distinguish themselves from the theological system of the Deuteronomistic revision, according to which nothing happens without the calculable action of Yhwh. And they all take place at the transition from the tribal to the monarchical form of organization, whether by reflecting this transition, or by reflecting the conditions of rule during the monarchy at a level below the nation, that is, against the background of individual places and clans up to the tribal level under the monarchy.

The traditions in Judges closely resemble the patriarchal narratives of Genesis, which offer the same kind of material in the garb of family history, with the difference that the patriarchal narratives construct a genealogical or at least a contractual bridge to the surrounding clans and peoples of the Ammonites, Moabites, Edomites, Aramaeans and Philistines, whereas the traditions in Judges start from hostile relations. As a rule this is attributed to different phases of the history of Israel, with scholarly historiography succumbing to the suggestion of the biblical account and putting the time of the patriarchs before the era of the Judges. In fact the relationship must be reversed. The still-unconnected traditions are about more or less the same locally restricted living conditions, which are perceived and interpreted simply from different social levels and different perspectives. The patriarchal stories, and especially the Jacob–Laban narrative in Gen. 29–31 or Isaac in Gen. 26, move on the level of semi-nomadic clans and the population of the land. The narratives about judges move at the level of regional sub-kingdoms and tribal chieftaincies. The pre-Deuteronomistic sources in Samuel describe the same conditions at the level of the nascent monarchy. All the traditions are conceivable in the framework of the pre-exilic monarchy of Israel (and Judah). In the works of literature they are forced into a historical context and a pan-Israelite concept of history: first the patriarchal narratives of Genesis by the 'Yahwistic' redaction, which reshapes the hostility of the world of small states in Syria–Palestine into an affinity under the uniting roof of the one God Yhwh; alongside them the traditions of the two kingdoms in the foundation legend of the Davidic-Solomonic kingship over Israel and Judah in 1 Sam. 1–1 Kgs 2, both after 720 BC; and finally the narratives in Judges through the Deuteronomistic redaction, which combines the pre-Deuteronomistic history of the people in the Hexateuch (Genesis or Exodus–Joshua) with the Deuteronomistic basic document in Samuel–Kings from the period after 587 BC.[67]

3.8.   Summary. The two independent Joshua legends in Josh. 6 and 8 and the narrative of the settlement in Josh. 2–12[68] based on them are the earliest tradition in the book of Joshua; this already deals with Israel in its basic literary form and relates the end of the exodus story in the Pentateuch (Exodus–Numbers), the absence of which is often felt. The settlement under

Joshua fits smoothly on to Num. 25.1a/Deut. 34.5f. With this connection we come upon a pre-Deuteronomic and consequently also pre-Deuteronomistic Hexateuch. The earliest traditions in the book of Judges are the individual narratives about heroes in Judg. 3–16, which in Judg. 6–8 and 13–16 have already grown into little narrative cycles and have become assimilated to one another, and perhaps have been handed down in a loose association. The sequence is not compelling either chronologically or in subject-matter.

The Deuteronomistic redaction is responsible for bringing the traditions together. It put the individual traditions from Judg. 3–16 in their present order and overlaid on it the simple judges scheme, differentiated in Judg. 3.7–8.28 and (8.29-32;) 9.1–16.31 by the concluding formulae. The scheme is modelled on the Deuteronomistic scheme of kings in 1–2 Kings and is prepared for in Josh. 11.16aα^1, 23b. It proves to be secondary both over against the pre-Deuteronomistic Hexateuch (along with Deuteronomy) and the Deuteronomistic basic document in Samuel–Kings (Dtr^G), and thus represents a first stage of the secondary Deuteronomistic revision; its purpose is to bind together the Hexateuch (in the extent of Exodus–Joshua) and Dtr^G (in Samuel–Kings), the history of the people and the history of the monarchy, the will of the one God and the failure of the one kingdom. The literary hinge is the death of Joshua in Judg. 2.8f., which marks the transition from Josh. 2–12 to Judg. 3.7–16.31; 1 Sam. 1.1ff. can attach itself directly to Judg. (8.28 and) 16.13. The time of the judges serves as a bridge over which the sin responsible for the judgments of 720 and 587 BC can be loaded on the people of Israel, the people of Yhwh, and not just on the kings of Israel and in part of Judah. On the basis of the successful redactional operation, perhaps this stage even deserves its own abbreviation. Basing oneself on the 'block model', one could call the first redaction in Samuel–Kings Dtr 1 and the first redaction in Joshua–Judges Dtr 2. However, to clarify the difference in the basic document in Samuel–Kings and characterize the redactional process as such, basing myself on the abbreviations for the 'sources' in the Pentateuch I propose the abbreviation Dtr^R ('R' for the Judges [German *Richter*] redaction).

The basic document in Samuel–Kings (Dtr^G) and the first connection (Dtr^R) are followed by a wealth of further Deuteronomistic and post-Deuteronomistic expansions (including Priestly expansions), which make the mesh of the Enneateuch (Genesis–Kings) ever tighter (Dtr^S) by adding the commissioning of Joshua by Moses and Yhwh (Deut. 31.1f., 7f.; Josh. 1.1f., 5f.; 11.16-23), the choice for Yhwh and against Baal (Josh. 23–24 + Judg. 2.7, 10; and 6.25ff.), the polemic against the cult (Judg. 2.11-19, etc.), the criticism of the king (Judg. 8.22ff.; and 9), the priests and the ark (Josh. 3–4), the circumcision, Passover and a theophany (Josh. 5), the holy war and the ban (Josh. 6–11), the tribal organization (Josh. 1.10ff.; 13-22; Judg.

Table B.II.3

Sources	Dtr^R	Supplements (Dtr^S)
Hexateuch		
Deut. 34.5-6		31-34 (31.1f., 7f., etc.)
Joshua		1–11 (1.1f., 5f., etc.)
2.1-7, 15-16, 22-23		
3.1, 14a, 16; 4.19b		
6.1-3aα, 5, 12a, 14aα^1, 20b		
8.1-2a, 10a, 11a, 14, 19		
(10-11)		
12.1a, 9-24	11.16aα^1,23b	11.16aα^2-23a
		12.1b-8
		13.1-23.1a
	23.1b-3	23.4-16
		24.1-13
	24.14-28	24.14b, 17-18a, 19-21, 23-24
		24.25-27, 29-33
Narratives about heroes		
Judges		1
		2.1–5.6
	2.7	
2.8-9		
	2.10, 11-19	2.20–3.6
	3.7-14	3.7aβb
3.15, 16-26	3.15, 27-30	
	3.31	
	4.1-3	
4.4-22		4.4b, 5b, 6b, 8-9, 10b-11, 14a, 15a, 16-17aαb
	4.23-24; 5.31b	5.1-31a
	6.1-6	6.7-10
6.11-24	6.25-32; 7.1a	6.11b, 18, 20, 23, 33-40
7.(1b,) 8b-22		7.1b-8a, 9-12, 15b, 22a, 23–8.3
8.4-21		8.5-9, 13-17, 21bβ-27
	8.28	
	8.29-32	8.33-35
9.1-54		9.4-5, 7-25, 42-49, 55-57
	10.1-5	
	10.6-10, 17-18	10.6, 8bβ, 9, 10b-16, 17b
11.1-11a	11.11b, 29, 33b(, 30–40)	11.1b-2, 4, 5a, 9-10, 12-28
	12.7, 8-15	12.1-6
13.2-24	13.1, 25	13.3-5, 8-23, 24b-25
14.1-15, 8, 9-19	15.20	14.4, 6, 19; 15.3, 14
16.1-30	16.31	16.17, 20, 23b-24, 28
		17–21
Dtr^G		
1 Sam. 1–2 Kgs 25		

5, etc.), the law and the peoples and their territories (Josh. 1.3f., 7-9; 11.16-22; 12.1-8; 13.1-6; 23f.; Judg. 2.1-6; 2.20–3.6) and much else. Among the latest are the literary reminiscences of the preceding salvation history including Genesis, which mark out the limits of the books in Josh. 24 (vv. 1-13, 29-31) and Judg. 10.10ff.; 11.12-28 and the appendices on tribal history in Judg. 1 and 17–21. Thus the books of Joshua and Judges stand by themselves. Both, each in its own way, deal with the settlement of the tribes. In the context of the Former Prophets or read by themselves, these, like the history of the monarchy in Samuel–Kings, become the example for the law in the Pentateuch, the Torah.

4. Result

The Deuteronomistic redaction in Joshua–Kings and its subsequent revisions are based on the following sources: the independent Joshua tradition in Josh. 6 and 8, the narratives about heroes in the book of Judges, the old Saul tradition in 1 Sam. 1–14 and the Jerusalem court histories in 2 Sam. 11–1 Kgs 2, all from the period before 720 BC, that is, from the period of the Israelite monarchy. The old narrative of the conquest in Josh. 2–12, the conclusion of the history of the people in the Hexateuch, and the combined Saul–David–Solomon tradition in 1 Sam. 1.1–1 Kgs 2, the foundation legend of the Davidic kingship over Israel and Judah, both from the time between 720 and 587 BC, that is, from the period of the Judahite monarchy, had already progressed further. The 'books of days' of the kings of Israel and Judah which found their way into the annalistic scheme of kings likewise come from the period of the monarchy.

Once the law had established itself in the Hexateuch, around 560 BC the Deuteronomistic redaction began. It grew up in blocks over a lengthy period and has many layers. The beginning is formed by the basic writing in 1 Sam. 1– 2 Kgs 25 (Dtr^G = DtrH), a first block which brings the history of the Israelite-Judahite kingship from Saul to Zedekiah into the synchronistic framework scheme under the theological influence – taken from Deuteronomy – of the unity of the kingdom and the cult.

We find the next stage in Joshua and Judges, a second block which in the basic material (Dtr^R) through Josh. 11.16aα[1], 23b (later Deut. 31.1f., 7f.; Josh. 1.1f., 5f.; 11.16-23); Judg. 2.8f., and the simple scheme of saviours or judges in Judg. 3.7–16.31 combines the history of the people in the Hexateuch with the history of the monarchy in Samuel–Kings. A literary complex comes into being which extends from Exodus and in late passages also from Genesis to 2 Kgs 25, and thus comprises the whole so-called 'Enneateuch'. To this, extensive elaborations which are not only Deuteronomistic but also post-Deuteronomistic attach themselves; these equally are distributed over the books from Joshua to Kings, and under the influence of the First Commandment both expand the framework scheme with additions which are polemic against the cult and also develop and increase the narrative material (Dtr^S = DtrP, DtrN, etc.).

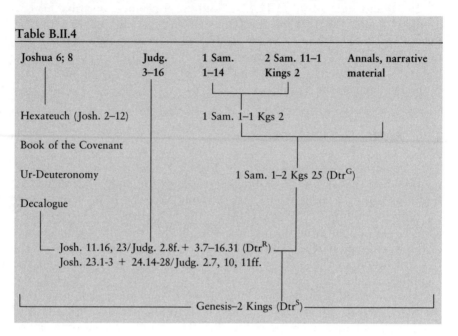

Table B.II.4

Joshua 6; 8	Judg. 3–16	1 Sam. 1–14	2 Sam. 11–1 Kings 2	Annals, narrative material

Hexateuch (Josh. 2–12)   1 Sam. 1–1 Kgs 2

Book of the Covenant

Ur-Deuteronomy   1 Sam. 1–2 Kgs 25 (Dtr^G)

Decalogue

Josh. 11.16, 23/Judg. 2.8f. + 3.7–16.31 (Dtr^R)
Josh. 23.1-3 + 24.14-28/Judg. 2.7, 10, 11ff.

Genesis–2 Kings (Dtr^S)

Notes

1   Thus still or again G. Hölscher, *Geschichtsschreibung in Israel*, 1952. What continues to be right about this view is the way in which it preserves the narrative connection, which now extends from Genesis to Kings.

2   Cf. Noth, *ÜSt*, 12 [ET, 27], and *TGI*^{3}, 78f.

3   Wellhausen, *Proleg.*, 278.

4   Stimuli were provided by H.W. Wolff, 'Das Kerygma des deuteronomistischen Geschichtswerkes' (1961), in id., *Gesammelte Studien zum Alten Testament*, TB 22, 1964, 308-24; R. Smend, 'Das Gesetz und die Völker' (1971), in id., *Die Mitte des Alten Testaments*, Gesammelte Studien 1, BEvTh 99, 1986, 124-37; F.M. Cross, 'The Themes of the Book of Kings and the Structure of the Deuteronomistic History', in id., *Canaanite Myth and Hebrew Epic*, Cambridge, MA 1973, 274-89. All of them are reprinted (and translated into English), in G.N. Knoppers and S.G. McConville (eds), *Reconsidering Israel and Judah*.

5   To this degree I agree with E. Würthwein, 'Erwägungen zum sogenannten Deuteronomistischen Geschichtswerk', BZAW 227, 1994, 1-11. Cf. also K. Budde, 'Geschichte der althebräischen Litteratur', in *Die Litteraturen des Ostens in Einzeldarstellungen* 7, 1906, 115-35, esp. 127ff.

6   Thus evidently K. Schmid, *Erzväter und Exodus*, WMANT 81, 1999, 162-5, against the usual separation of the Tetrateuch and the Deuteronomistic history, ibid., 18-39; others, ibid., 34 nn. 197, 198. However, the pre-redactional units of tradition which are indicated in ibid., 163, again correspond to the dividing line that has been rejected.

7   His age on accession has fallen out; the 'two years' duration of his reign could be a copyist's error or are intended to defame Saul's kingship. The note is missing from G.

8   A.K. Grayson, *Assyrian and Babylonian Chronicles*, TCS 5, Toronto 1975.

9   That is by no means a matter of course. As we are shown by the Chronicle of Nabonidus, where the king is judged on whether or not the New Year Festival takes place, the verdict on piety is occasionally an element of the genre. Cf. Grayson, *Chronicles* (n. 61), 104ff.

10   Jepsen, *Die Quellen des Königsbuches*, 30ff.

11   1 Kgs 12.30; and 13.33-34; 15.26, 34; 16.13, 19, 25-26, 30-33; 22.53-54; 2 Kgs 3.2-3; 10.28-31; 13.2, 11; 14.24; 15.9, 18, 24, 28; 17.2, 7ff.

12   Positively (with or without reservations): 1 Kgs 3.2-3; 15.11-15; 22.43-44, 47; 2 Kgs 12.3-4; 14.3-4; 15.3-4, 34-35; 18.3-7; 22.2 + 23.4-27. Negatively: 1 Kgs 14.22-24; 15.3-5; 2 Kgs 8.18-19, 27; 16.2-4; 21.2-16, 20-22; 23.32, 37; 24.9, 19.

13   For the original stratum cf. Würthwein, ATD 11/2, 505-15. However, the beginning is not in 1 Kgs 4 but in 1–2 Sam.

14   Dtr^G roughly corresponds to what others call DtrH but is limited to Samuel–Kings. In extent and theological tendency Dtr^S corresponds to Noth's DtrG = DtrP + DtrN in the framework of Genesis–Kings. Cf. O. Kaiser, *Grundriss der Einleitung in die kanonischen und deuterokanonischen Schriften des Alten Testaments* 1, 1992, 85.

15   Only: 'And it happened in the fourth year, in the month Ziv, that he built the house for Yhwh.'

16   That the name Hiram is identical with that of the man skilled in artistic matters in 1 Kgs 7.13ff. is remarkable, as is the lack of any designation of Hiram's origin in the reports 9.26-28 and 10.11, 22, which are usually regarded as being older.

17   In 1 Kgs 12.2b read 'And Jeroboam returned from Egypt'.

18   Removing the glosses in 1 Kgs 12.26b, 27aβb, 28b, 30b and the additions in vv. 31, 32f. (13.1ff.).

19   The narrative ends with the arrival in Samaria in 10.12, 17aα. In the basic document the participation of Ahaziah of Judah is presupposed in 8.28f. (cf. 9.14b-15a); 9.16, 21, 23, 27; 10.4, 12-14. That is the only explanation of the lack of a concluding note, which has been added in 9.28f. at an inappropriate place. Further additions are the references to Naboth in 2 Kgs 9.21bβ, 25-26, the polemic against the cult in 9.22bβ, the references to Elijah with additions in 9.36f.; 10.10, 11, 14bβ, 17 (cf. 9.7-10a), the destruction of the worshippers of Baal in 10.15f., 18-29, with additions in vv. 30f., 32f.

20   Only the rainmaker who can overcome the drought by magical action is evident (cf. 2 Kgs 3.14, 17 with 1 Kgs 17.1; 18.41ff.) and not yet the clash with the prophets of Baal in 1 Kgs 18.2-40, to which the addition 2 Kgs 3.13 alludes. 2 Kgs 3.18f. could also be an addition; it attributes vv. 24f. to the word of God in Elisha's mouth, but contradicts the outcome of the narrative. The beginning of the scene in vv. 7ff. is somewhat reminiscent of 1 Kgs 22.

21   J. Wellhausen, 'Israelitisch-jüdische Religion', in J. Wellhausen, *Grundrisse zum Alten Testament* (ed. R. Smend), TB 27, 1965, 90.

22   Note the resumption of 2 Kgs 11.4 in vv. 17f., 19. 'And they led down the king . . .' in v. 19 attaches directly to v. 4.

23   Cf. H. Spieckermann, *Juda unter Assur in der Sargonidenzeit*, FRLANT 129, 1982, 179ff.

24   Above all the mention of the exodus (1 Kgs 6.1; 8.9, 16, 21, 51, 53; 9.9; 12.28; 2 Kgs 17.7, 36; 21.15; Horeb/Sinai in 1 Kgs 19) and the – twelve – tribes of Israel (1 Kgs 8.16; 11.13, 29ff.; 12.20b, 21; 14.21; 2 Kgs 17.18; 21.7), rarely the patriarchs (1 Kgs 18.31, 36; 2 Kgs 13.23; 17.34).

25   1 Sam. 9.1, 2aα, 3-8, 10, (11-14,) 18-19, 24b-27; 10.(1,) 2-4, 7, 9, 10aα, 14-16 are original. The additions are 9.2aβb (cf. 10.23), the gloss 9.9, and some if not all of the section in vv. 11-14 (vv. 12aα², 13aβγ, 14b), the anticipations in 9.15-17, 20-21, the corresponding elaboration of the meal scene in 9.22-24a, the definition 'to be ruler over his heritage' in 10.1b (even more in the double translation of G in assimilation to 9.16; cf. then 13.13-14), the rage as a sign in 10.5f., 10aβ-13 (cf. 19.18-24) and the reference forward to 13.7b-15a in 10.8.

26   Still without the sons of Eli in 1 Sam. 1.3b and the oath in vv. 10-12. Chapters 9f. and 7.17 presuppose that Samuel grew up with his parents in Ramah, in the land of Zuph. His youth in the temple of Shiloh in 1.21–3.21 is therefore secondary. Nor are 4.1–7.14 (and 8.1-22) presupposed in 9.1-10.16: the danger first threatens from the Ammonites (ch. 11) and only then from the Philistines (chs 13f.), who prove Saul's undoing and assist in the rise of David.

27   In 10.27b corrected in accordance with G, in 11.1-11 without vv. 5, 6-8 and vv. 12-14. The plural in v. 9 follows on from v. 4. Should the singular read by G, etc., be original, v. 5 is the original connecting point. Verses 12f. take up 10.27 again, v. 14 balances 11.15 with 10.24f. and anticipates the arrival of Samuel in Gilgal announced in 10.8 but narrated only in 13.7ff.

28   At the centre stands the well-rounded tradition in 14.1-14, which narrates how Jonathan, the son of Saul, and his armour-bearer from Gibeah attack a post of the Philistines between Michmash and Geba: for example, vv. 1, (2, 4-5,) 11a, 12a, 13 (, 14a). Through 13.2 and the framework spun out of 14.1-14 in 13.3-5 (originally perhaps only 13.3aα, 5abα) and 14.17, 20, 23a, it became an occurrence in Saul's war with the Philistines attached to the coronation in Gilgal in 11.15. The flight of the Israelites in 13.6; 14.22 explains the difference in the strength of the troops and motivates the change of place from 13.2 to 14.2. Geba is an intermediate stage in 13.15b-16 (cf. 13.3; 14.5); the advance of the Philistines in 13.5 continues with the disengagement of three Philistine armies in 13.17-18, to some degree a recapitulation of 13.2-5 after the flight in 13.6 (and the insertion in vv. 7b-15a). The advance of the Philistine post in 13.23 leads on to the ancient narrative in 14.1ff. The Samuel episode announced in 10.8, localized in Gilgal in 13.7b-15a, has been inserted before or after the change of place in 13.6, 15b-18 between 13.2-5 and (13.23) 14.1ff. The people dismissed in 13.2b have been recalled for this in 13.4b and it ends with the departure of Samuel for Gibeah. Further additions are the formulae and requisites of the holy war inspired by 14.20, 23a (cf. Exod. 14.24f., 30a) in 13.5aβ; 14.3, 6-7, 10aββ, 12b, 14b, 15f., 18f., 23b (with 9.16 according to Exod. 3.7, 9), the Hebrew glosses in 1 Sam. 13.3b, 7a, 19-22; 14.11b, 21 (cf. 4.6, 9; 29.3) and Saul's curse and its consequences in 14.24-45.

29   1 Sam. 9.16; 10.1 of Saul; 1 Sam. 13.14; 25.30; 2 Sam. 5.2; 6.21; 7.8; 1 Kgs 1.35; 14.7; 16.2 of David, elsewhere only once again of Hezekiah, 2 Kgs 20.5.

30   'And she bore a son' is a recapitulation of 2 Sam. 11.27a. 2 Sam. 11.27b, 'And the thing that David had done was evil in the sight of Yhwh' attests the origin of the insertion.

31   The basis remains 1 Kgs 1.(1,) 5-19, 20a, 21-34, 38-45, 49-53; 2.13-23, 25, 26a, 34-35, 46b. Also 2.36-43, 46a, in so far as it is about the Shimei of 1 Kgs 1.8 who was

formerly a supporter and meanwhile has become an enemy, and not the Benjaminite of 2 Sam. 16.5ff.; 19.16ff. (thus 1 Kgs 2.8f., 44); cf. Dietrich, *Königszeit*, 255. In 1.34 the 'over Israel' or 'king over Israel' has to be deleted (cf. 2.38, 45).

32 The flight narrative comprises 2 Sam. 15.14-23, 30-37; 16.20–17.26; 19.9b-15, 16, 41bβ; the Benjaminite episodes 2 Sam. 9; 16.1-14(, 15, 16-19 = 15.32-37); 17.27-29; 19.17-41 have been prefixed and inserted into this; further additions are the Ammonite war in 2 Sam. 10 (cf. 1 Sam. 11; 12.12; 2 Sam. 8.3ff.), the Ahithophel glosses in 15.12, 31; 16.21-23; 20.3 (cf. 12.11f.), and presumably also the counsel of Hushai in 17.5-14, 15b, 23 (15.14f. relates to the betrayal in 17.15a, 16ff.), the priests and the ark in 15.24-29 (vv. 35f. and 17.15ff. do not presuppose the whole scene), and the quarrelling around the king in 19.42-44 (cf. 1 Kgs 11.31).

33 E. Würthwein, 'Die Erzählung von der Thronnachfolge Davids – theologische oder politische Geschichtsschreibung?', *ThSt* 115, 1974, 44f. excludes 2 Sam. 18.2b-4a, 10-14; Veijola, *Dynastie*, 53 n. 40, suspects 18.28b.

34 Without 2 Sam. 20.3 (with 15.16; 16.21-23) and the Amasa episode, 20.4f., 8-13 (with 17.25; 19.14).

35 From 1 Sam. 16.14b and without the lame 'of Yhwh', cf. v. 23.

36 O. Kaiser, 'David und Jonathan. Tradition, Redaktion und Geschichte in 1 Sam. 16–20: Ein Versuch', *EThL* 66, 1990, 281-96: 285f., wants to find both already in the original stratum and reads them out of 18.5 + 19.8 + 18.6-9 + 19.9f. together, but this is only to transpose texts. An alternative to the reconstruction undertaken here which is well worth considering has now been offered by E. Aurelius, 'Wie David ursprünglich zu Saul kam (1 Sam 17)', in C. Bultmann et al. (eds), *Vergegenwärtigung des Alten Testaments (Festschrift R. Smend)*, 2003, 44-68.

37 Note the regular conclusions in 1 Sam. 18.5 after 17.1–18.4; 18.16 after 18.6-15; 18.(28-)30 after 18.17-27.

38 2 Sam. 3.14-16 have been added in retrospect to 5.1f. on the basis of 1 Sam. 25.44 and with a view to 2 Sam. 6.3, 17-20. 2 Sam. 3.1, 6-11 explain the readiness to negotiate – probably likewise by way of an addition – by Abner falling out with Ishbosheth (Ishbaal) in the war between the house of Saul and the house of David and as in 3.17-20 adopting Yhwh's decision.

39 2 Sam. 3.28-39 are apologetic additions.

40 2 Sam. 4.4f. go to 2 Sam. 9; vv. 8aβ-11 presuppose 2 Sam. 1.

41 2 Sam. 2.4b-7 is an apologetic addition on the basis of 1 Sam. 31.11-13.

42 See Veijola, *Dynastie*, esp. 127-42. The Deuteronomistic strata (DtrH, DtrP, DtrN) discovered here indicate a by no means low level of common themes and features and common language; the picture of David in Veijola's DtrH hardly differs from that of his DtrN. The reason for that is that all the strata are later than the first Deuteronomistic redaction in Samuel–Kings.

43 Wellhausen, *Proleg.*, 228.

44 Cf. ibid., 229f.; id., *Comp.*, 211-13; Noth, *ÜSt*, 18-27 [ET, 34-44]; more recently Fritz, *Entstehung*, 39, 63-5.

45 Chapter 13 the two and a half tribes east of the Jordan; ch. 14, another introduction and Caleb; chs 15–19 the nine and a half tribes west of the Jordan (15–17 Judah, Ephraim and Manasseh, chs 18–19 a new introduction and the other seven tribes concluding in 19.49-51); ch. 20 the cities of refuge; ch. 21 the levitical cities (cf. 13.14, 33).

46 Cf. A.G. Auld, *Joshua, Moses and the Land*, Edinburgh 1980 (²1982); E. Cortese, *Josua 13–21*, OBO 94, 1990; Fritz, HAT I/7 *ad loc.*

47 Cf. Josh. 1.11, 15; 12.1, 6f.; 13.1, etc., here as also in Deuteronomy always in late passages.

48 Thus still Josh. 1.13, 15; 22.4; 23.1a; and Deut. 3.20; 12.9f.; 25.19, evidently with an eye to the building of the temple, cf. 2 Sam. 7.1, 11; 1 Kgs 5.18; 8.56.

49 Cf. the table in Becker, *Richterzeit und Königtum*, 83.

50 Cf. already Wellhausen, *Comp.*, 214f., and at length Richter, *Bearbeitungen*.

51 The 'saving' in 1 Sam. 4.3; 7.8 (the 'humble' in 7.13 as in the formula of subjugation in Judg. 3.30; 4.23; 8.28; 11.33; cf. also 2 Sam. 8.1; 2 Kgs 22.19!); 9.16; 10.27; 11.3; 14.6, 23, 39, etc., especially 2 Kgs 13.5; the 'judging' in 1 Sam. 4.18; 7.6, 15-17; 8.1-2, 5, 6, 20 (cf. 12.9-13); 2 Sam. 15.4 and 2 Kgs 23.22 (!); the bestowing of the spirit in 1 Sam. 10.6, 10; 11.6; 16.13; 19.20, 23, supplied in the source 16.14-23; 18.10 = 19.9.

52 Cf. E. Blum, 'Der kompositionelle Knoten am Übergang von Josua zu Richter: Ein Entflechtungsvorschlag', in M. Vervenne and J. Lust (eds), *Deuteronomy and Deuteronomistic Literature*, BEThL 133, 1997, 181-212; K. Latvus, *God, Anger and Ideology*, JSOT.S 279, 1998, 28-41, 85f.

53 Noth, *ÜSt*, 8, 45-7 [ET, 22, 41-3].

54 Cf. Latvus, *God, Anger and Ideology* (n. 105), 31-5.

55 Cf. C. Levin, *Die Verheissung des neuen Bundes*, FRLANT 137, 1985, 114-15.

56 The double indication of place in Josh. 2.1 and 3.1 is perhaps to be explained by the major insertion of Deuteronomy, which interrupts the earlier connection between Num. 25.1a; Deut. 34.5f.; and Josh. 2.1; 3.1.

57 In Josh. 3.3, 14, originally only '"And you shall go round the city" ... And they went round the city'.

58 In Josh. 8.1-2 originally only 'And Yhwh said to Joshua: Behold, I have given the king of Ai and his people and his city and his land into your hand. And you shall deal with Ai and its king as you have dealt with Jericho and its king.' Cf. 6.2. The outstretched hand which after the ambush in 8.18 gives the sign to set out is clearly an addition in v. 19.

59 I cannot give a reason why the choice fell in particular on the Calebbite Othniel, son of Kenash (cf. Josh. 15.17; Judg. 1.13), except perhaps that Judah was to be kept away from the sin of the Israelites at any price. There is also no basis in the sources for the saviour Shamgar son of Anath in Judg. 3.31 (cf. 5.6), with whom the total number of the judges, major and minor together and counting Deborah and Barak only as one, amounts to twelve.

60 The identity of the name with Rebecca's nurse in Gen. 35.8 has led to the judge of Israel in Judg. 4.5a also sitting under a tree, the palm tree between Ramah and Bethel in the hill country of Ephraim. Cf. Wellhausen, *Comp.*, 216f., who still refers the 'oak of Tabor' of 1 Sam. 10.3 to the 'Deborah tree' in the text that has been handed down.

61 In Judg. 4.6f. Deborah speaks for herself; the question in 6b which makes Yhwh the one who gives the command is secondary, as is the apposition 'Jabin's general' or simply the name 'Jabin' in v. 7 (with vv. 17b, 23f. after Josh. 11), which confuses the syntax, and the agreement to set out together, in vv. 8f., 10b, which – albeit indirectly – anticipates the point and leads back to Yhwh (thus with vv. 14a, 15a). Verse 16 can be recognized as an addition by the recapitulation of v. 15 b in 17aα; v. 11 gives Jael, the wife of Heber the Kenite, a place in the Israelite salvation history.

62 Without Judg. 14.4; 15.3 and the formula 'and the spirit of Yhwh came upon him' in 14.6, 19.

63 Originally perhaps only Judg. 15.9, 14a, 15-17. The episode is supplemented with a further aetiology in 15.10-13, 14b (without the formula 'and the spirit of Yhwh came upon him') and the conflict of Judah with the Philistines, in 15.18f. (originally the invocation of Yhwh in v. 18). The (Deuteronomistic) formula 'and the spirit of Yhwh came upon him' in 14.6, 19; 15.14 might have been spun out of v. 19a (cf. 1

Sam. 30.12) in combination with the invocation of Yhwh in v. 18; cf. Judg. 3.10; 6.34; 11.29; 1 Sam. 10.6, 10; 11.6; 16.13, the departure of the 'spirit of Yhwh' in Judg. 16.20b (only Yhwh); 1 Sam. 16.14a(; 1 Sam. 18.10); 19.9 differ and the evil 'spirit' in Judg. 9.23; 1 Sam. 16.14f., 23.

64 Without Judg. 16.17aβ, 20bγ, 23b-24, 28.

65 Originally perhaps only 13.2, 6-7, 24a. In 13.3-5 the man of God is made the 'angel of Yhwh' and in view of 16.17f. the 'Nazirite' is made someone whose hair may not be cut (cf. 16.17aβ and Num. 6, where the continence of the mother has also become one of the virtues of the Nazirite). Judg. 13.8-23 add the request of the parents (cf. 1 Sam. 1) and assimilate the encounter with the 'angel of Yhwh' to the opening of the story of Gideon in Judg. 6. Judg. 13.24b-25 add Yhwh's blessing and 'spirit' and make the clan of the Danites (v. 2) the camp of the tribe of Dan.

66 Wellhausen, *Comp.*, 227.

67 The great similarities between Judg. 6.11-24 and 13 (and 1 Sam. 1) and the building of altars and birth legends in Genesis rest either on a pre-Deuteronomistic revision or on post-Deuteronomic assimilations in the framework of the Enneateuch. The pre-Deuteronomistic revision presupposes that the narratives about the judges have been handed down in very close proximity, perhaps as a kind of appendix to the patriarchal history or to the Hexateuch. This in turn would explain how the material fell into the hands of the Deuteronomistic redaction. Moreover the parallels to the patriarchal stories in the Moses narrative Exod. 2–4 fall under the same category as Judg. 6 and 13. More on that below.

68 More precisely: Josh. 2.1-7, 15f., 22f.; 3.1, 14a, 16; 4.19b; 6.1-3aα, 5, 12, 14aα[1], 20b; 8.1-2a, 10a, 11a, 13, 19; 12.1a, 9-24.

III. The Enneateuch

1. The 'Deuteronomistic history' in the light of the Hexateuch

In the light of the 'Deuteronomistic history' postulated by Noth and extending from Deut. 1 to 2 Kgs 25, the Hexateuch hypothesis, the assumption of a literary complex extending from Gen. 1 to Josh. 24, which had previously been regarded as valid, seemed to him to be an 'error of scholarship'.[1] He was quite right in disputing the desperate and almost absurd quest for the source documents in Joshua but also in Judges, Samuel and Kings. But the alternative, the unitary Deuteronomistic redaction active from Deut. 1 to 2 Kgs 25, has not been confirmed by scholars since Noth. The unitary nature of the Deuteronomistic work has (again) been put in question from various sides by the rediscovery of either its growth in blocks, its literary stratification, or both. But with the unity, the existence of the 'Deuteronomistic history' is also lost, except that scholars have evidently not noticed or do not want to notice this. Insight into the gradual growth of the Deuteronomistic redaction in (Deuteronomy;) Joshua–Kings removes the basis from Noth's hypothesis. Almost everything on which the hypothesis is based – the beginning in Deut. 1–3, the connecting speeches and theological interpretative texts in Josh. 23–24; Judg. 2–3; 1 Sam. 12; 2 Sam. 7; 1 Kgs 8; 2 Kgs 17, etc. – consists of late and very late formations which break up the framework of Deut. 1–2 Kgs 25. These either, like the last version of Chronicles, presuppose the literary complex of the Enneateuch (Genesis–Kings) or serve to separate the books so that they can be read by themselves and at the same time in a salvation-historical context.

Moreover the hypothesis of the 'Deuteronomistic history' is a very costly one. It robs the Tetrateuch, the narrative work about the exodus from Egypt with the promised land as its destination, of its natural end. The hypothesis necessitates the additional assumption that the end of the Tetrateuch (Pentateuch) was lost when the 'Deuteronomistic history' was worked together. That is not only unsatisfactory but also quite improbable, given that there is an old narrative of the settlement in Joshua which continues the narrative of Genesis–Numbers seamlessly. The narrative thread is slight and concealed by later literary connections, but it is there. The place at which Israel arrives after the exodus from Egypt and the wandering through the wilderness is the place from which Joshua sends out the spies and Israel crosses the Jordan: Num. 25.1a–Josh. 2.1; 3.1. In between, initially there is only the death of Moses in Deut. 34.5f., which attaches itself to Num. 25.1a, as previously the death of Miriam attaches itself to the arrival in Kadesh in Num. 20.1. If this combination seems to be too bold and the gap between the links in the text too great, it should be remembered that everything between the links, the law on Sinai between Exod. 15 and Num. 20 and the law in the wilderness and in the land of Moab between Num. 25.1a and Deut. 34, is secondary. Even Noth[2] thinks that there was an account of the death of Moses in the 'old sources', but finds in Deut. 34 only the end of the Priestly Writing in connection with Num. 27, because he needs Deut. 34.5f. for his Deuteronomist, who has doubtless intervened in v. 5 (from 'the servant of Yhwh' on, cf. Josh. 1.1f.) but cannot positively be demonstrated as such in the notice of Moses' death. And if we have the choice between a hypothetical death notice and one handed down in the text, I would prefer the one that has been handed down, even if it is incompatible with another hypothesis. The same goes for the note of the itinerary in Num. 25.1a, which seems rather lost in the text; Noth conjectures that it is a late addition,[3] but it is the indispensable presupposition for everything that takes place in Num. 25–Josh. 2 between the last camping place in Transjordan and the departure into the land. There is no more need of a special introduction for Joshua, who is taken from Josh. 6 (and 8) and suddenly appears in 2.1, than there is of the introduction of Miriam in Exod. 15.20f. Only we may not expect that Joshua was originally what the later revisions have made of him.

The literary link between Num. 25.1a + Deut. 34.5f. + Josh. 2.1; 3.1 brings the old Hexateuch hypothesis back into play. And in the light of the Hexateuch the postulate of a 'Deuteronomistic history' extending from Deut. 1 to 2 Kgs 25 proves to be an 'error of scholarship'. However, Noth's hypothesis is justified in so far as Deuteronomy increasingly gains an independent place in the framework of the Hexateuch, which grows into the Enneateuch. It becomes the embodiment of the Mosaic law and, vicariously for the whole law in the Pentateuch, the basis for the further history in the books of Joshua, Judges, Samuel and Kings, which for their part become independent. In the late programmatic texts claimed by Noth for his 'Deuteronomistic history' they often refer back to Deuteronomy, but not just to it. And only under the sign of the law does Moses become the predecessor and Joshua the successor. However, this development does not belong at the beginning but at the end of the origin of the Enneateuch; it prepares for the division into the two parts of the canon, the Torah and the Former Prophets.

2. From the Hexateuch to the Enneateuch

The presupposition for the development from the Hexateuch to the Enneateuch was the implanting of the law in the earlier Hexateuch. It began with the insertion of the pre-exilic Book of the Covenant – stylized as a speech of God and supplemented with the address in the second person singular – into the Sinai pericope between Exod. 19.2-3a and 24.18b (20.1 or 20.22a + Exod. 20.24-23.19) and the insertion or writing-in of Ur-Deuteronomy, a copy of the Book of the Covenant under the influence of the centralization of the cult, presumably from the early exilic period, between the arrival of Israel in Shittim in Num. 25.1a and the death of Moses in Deut. 34.5 as a public proclamation of the law (Moses' farewell speech) with a view to the imminent settlement (Deut. $5.1a\alpha^1$; 6.4-5 + 12-21 + 26.1f., 11, 16; 34.1a).

This was the version of the law on which the basic Deuteronomistic writing in Samuel–Kings (Dtr^G) is based. It made use of the earlier foundation legend of the kingship of David and Solomon over Israel and Judah in 1 Sam. 1–1 Kgs 2 from the time after 720 BC and developed it about 560 BC under the influence of the chief Deuteronomistic commandment round the history of the two synchronized kingdoms of Israel and Judah up to the downfall of Judah in 587 BC. The basic Deuteronomistic writings in Samuel–Kings combine the ideal of the unity of the kingdom taken from the source in 1 Sam. 1–1 Kgs 2 with the idea of the one Yhwh (Deut. 6.4) and the one place of worship (Deut. 12.13-18) from the Deuteronomic law. One Yhwh, one place of worship, one monarchy – that is the theological slogan according to which the basic Deuteronomistic writing writes history in Samuel–Kings. But at first only the substance of the Deuteronomistic law is received. No literary connection can (as yet) be recognized.

In Exod. 20 the Yhwh of the 'Hear, Israel' of Deut. 6.4 becomes the one and only God alongside the other gods of the Decalogue which, in accordance with the framework in Deut. 6.4-5 and 26.16, is prefaced to the revelation of the Book of the Covenant and in Exod. 24 is confirmed by a covenant relating to the whole law in Exod. 20–23. The prefacing of the Decalogue was preceded by the addition of the theophany in Exod. 19, so that the Decalogue of Exod. 20.2-17 was inserted either with 20.22a between 19.10-20/20.1 and 20.24ff. or with 20.1 between 19.10-19 and 20.18, 21, 22a, 24ff. It became the starting point for the varied developments in Exod. 19–24 and 32–34 and in Deut. 5–11 and 26–30, the majority of which move within the framework of the Enneateuch.

The First Commandment and the covenant between Yhwh and his people Israel in Exod. 19–24; 32–34; and Deut. 5–30 were the presupposition for the secondary Deuteronomistic redaction in Joshua and Judges, linking together the Hexateuch, which had meanwhile come to be dominated by the law, the history of the covenant of Yhwh and Israel which begins in Exodus with the leading up out of Egypt (Exod. 20.2), and the history of the monarchy 1 Samuel–Kings (Dtr[G]). On the basis of the 'evil in Yhwh's eyes', the sin of Jeroboam (1 Kgs 12), this leads into Yhwh's judgment of 720 and 587 BC (Dtr[R]). To make the transition, the redactors used a series of old narratives about heroes from the pre-exilic period which had previously been handed down individually or in a loose collection, and from this constructed a separate period of the history of Israel, the age of the 'judges'. This links the history of the people under the leadership of the charismatic personalities of Moses and Joshua in the Hexateuch (Exodus–Joshua) to the history of the kings of Israel–Judah in Samuel–Kings. The literary connection is brought about by the 'rest' formula in Josh. 11.16aα[1], 23b (later Deut. 31.1f., 7f.; Josh. 1.1f., 5f.; 11.16-23), which points to the time of the judges; the note about Joshua's death in Judg. 2.8f.; and the (simple) judges scheme in Judg. 3.7–8.28 and 8(.29-32); 9.1–16.31, developed from the scheme of the kings in Samuel–Kings. The theological censure 'do evil in Yhwh's eyes' passes over from the kings to the whole people of Israel and from now on – at first implicitly, and with the insertion of the choice by God in Josh. 23.1b-3; 24.14-28 + Judg. 2.7, 10 – also explicitly means transgressing the First Commandment. The First Commandment does away with the distinction between the history of the people and the history of the monarchy, and in this way the monarchy, too, gradually falls into disrepute (Judg. 1 and 1 Sam. 7f.).

Both the First Commandment and the reservations about the kingship form the starting point for extensive Deuteronomistic and post-Deuteronomistic supplements in Joshua–Kings (Dtr[S]), which survey the whole Enneateuch including Genesis. They correspond with the developments in Exod. 19–24; Exod. 32–34; and Deut (4;) 5–34, and at other points in the Tetrateuch which, like the golden calf in Exod. 32–34 (after 1 Kgs 12), were added after the books were put together, both before and after they were combined with P. We owe to these expansions the picture of Israel in the books as we have them, for which the tribes, the priests and prophets and not least the special status of Israel in salvation history and its segregation from the other peoples of the land and the surrounding lands, in short, the ideal of theocracy, is characteristic. Thus the revision of the books Joshua–Kings already comes very close to the Chronistic historiography.

The Priestly Writing went its own way in the Persian period, soon after or at roughly the same time as the formation of the Ennateuch. It extended the older Hexateuch not backwards but, as we shall see immediately, forwards into the patriarchal history and subsequently was integrated into the Enneateuch or the Pentateuch which was splitting off from it. It originally extended from Gen. 1 to Exod. 40 (P[G]). It was filled out in Exod.

25–40 and expanded by the laws in Leviticus, above all the Holiness Code in Lev. 17–26 (27), a novella of Deuteronomy. In P the covenant with Abraham (Gen. 17) takes the place of the Sinai covenant (Exod. 19–24; 32–34), the Moab covenant (Deuteronomy) and the choice of God at Gilgal (Josh. 23f.), which in Josh. 24.1, 25 became the Shechem covenant.

The literary inclusion of P in the first part of the Enneateuch brought with it a wealth of further writing, above all in the sphere of the wilderness wandering in Numbers and the separation of the books (R^P). The development has points of contact with some of the late or post-Deuteronomistic strata in Joshua–Kings (Dtr^S), which, as in the case, say, of the distribution of the land by lot in Josh. 13–21 or the narrative in Judg. 19–21, presuppose the Priestly Writing. Numbers 27.12ff. marks off a demarcation from the book of Deuteronomy, which is becoming independent, and this resulted in the elaborations in Num. 27–36 on the one hand and Deut. 1–3 on the other. At the same time it introduces a narrative arch as far as the death of Moses in Deut. 34. With the repetition of the scene of Num. 27.12ff. in Deut. 32.48-52 and all the other traditions in Deut. 31–34, this separates the Pentateuch from the Former Prophets.

3.   The Torah and the Former Prophets

The last step was the division of the Enneateuch into the two parts of the canon, the Torah and the Former Prophets. It already began with the composition of the Priestly Writing and its incorporation into the Enneateuch. It was the Priestly Writing that first reduced the Pentateuch, which had become the Enneateuch, to the Tetrateuch. The literary combination with the non-Priestly primal history and patriarchal history in Genesis and the story of the exodus in Exodus–Numbers isolated Deuteronomy, which became the embodiment of the law in Joshua–Kings; corresponding additions in Deut. 31–34 isolated the Pentateuch, which came to be dominated by the Priestly writing and was supplemented in its spirit. Thus it came about that the redaction in the Pentateuch has more of a Priestly stamp and the redaction in (Deuteronomy;) Joshua–Kings more of a Deuteronomistic stamp.

At the same time, there were reciprocal assimilations, that is, additions with the tone of the late-Deuteronomists in Genesis to Numbers, and Priestly expansions in Joshua–Kings, and above all literary cross-references in Genesis–Deuteronomy (for example, Gen. 15; Exod. 17.8ff.; 23.20ff.; 32–34; Num. 10–36) to Joshua–Kings or in Josh. 5; Judg. 11.12-28; 1 Sam. 12, etc. to the history of the Pentateuch. In many cases it is hard to tell whether the assimilations serve to provide a link or take account of the separation of the books. The supplements on the peripheries in Num. 27–36; Deut. 1–3;

31–34; Josh. 1 and 24 (vv. 1-13, 29-33); Judg. 1 and 17–21; 1 Sam. (1;) 2–3 and 2 Sam. 21–24 play their part in separating the books from each other and at the same time preserving the connections within the framework of the salvation history.

The literary entities of the Tetrateuch (Genesis–Numbers) and the 'Deuteronomistic history' (Deuteronomy–Kings) which are often accepted in research thus prove to be late stages on the way from the Enneateuch to the two parts of the canon, the Torah and the Former Prophets. The way in which the books become independent goes with the formation of the canon. Apart from the history of the text, which fluctuated for still longer, this is the last stage in the coming into being of the narrative books Genesis–Kings; it is also presupposed by the final form of Chronicles, which recapitulates the history from Adam to Zedekiah. Further testimony to this process within the Bible is the framing of the books Joshua–Kings and Isaiah–Malachi, the Former and Latter Prophets, by the literary bracket of Josh. 1.7f./Mal. 3.22-24 (cf. Ps. 1). It marks a clear break between the Torah of Moses, the Pentateuch, as the authoritative original stratum, and the subsequent writings which relate to it. The Septuagint, the Samaritan Pentateuch and the hymn to the fathers in Sir. 44–49 (46.1) presuppose the separation for the third and early second century BC, and the textual witnesses from the Dead Sea presuppose it from around the middle of the second century BC. The prologue to the Greek translation of Sirach (c.132 BC), the epistle 4QMMT from Qumran (4Q397, fr. 14-21 line 10) and the New Testament (Luke 24.44) finally call the three parts of the later canon by name.

Notes

1   Noth, *ÜSt*, 180ff.
2   Ibid., 212f.; *Pentateuch*, 160, 170f.
3   In *ÜSt*, 117, Num. 25.1-5 is still counted among the 'ancient sources'; in *Pentateuch*, 32 n. 125, Num. 25.1a is – consistently – excluded, in *Numbers*, 196f. it is again assigned to J. For the original connection between Num. 25.1a and Josh. 2.1 cf. already Wellhausen, *Comp.*, 111, 117 (JE). By contrast, the late episode Num. 25.1b-5, further elaborated in Num. 25.6ff., which echoes the problem of mixing with the peoples before the distribution of the land in the east and in the west (cf. Exod. 23.20ff.; Deut. 7; Josh. 23f.; Judg. 2.1-5; 3.5f.), is secondary.

C. The Myth of Israel

I. The Priestly Writing

1. The state of Pentateuchal criticism

T. Nöldeke, *Untersuchungen zur Kritik des Alten Testaments*, 1869; Wellhausen, *Composition*, 1-134; id., *Prolegomena*, 297-367; H. Holzinger, *Einleitung in den Hexateuch*, 1893; R. Smend, *Die Erzählung des Hexateuch auf ihre Quellen untersucht*, 1912; P. Volz and W. Rudolph, *Der Elohist als Erzähler: Ein Irrweg der Pentateuchkritik? An der Genesis erläutert*, BZAW 63, 1933; W. Rudolph, '*Der Elohist*' *vom Exodus bis Josua*, BZAW 68, 1938; M. Noth, *A History of Pentateuchal Tradition*; id., *Überlieferungsgeschichtliche Studien*, 180-217; G. Hölscher, *Geschichts-schreibung in Israel: Untersuchungen zum Jahvisten und Elohisten*, 1952; S. Mowinckel, *Tetrateuch – Pentateuch – Hexateuch*, BZAW 90, 1964; S. Tengström, *Die Hexateucherzählung*, CB.OT 7, 1976; R. Rendtorff, *Das überlieferungsgeschichtliche Problem des Pentateuch*, BZAW 147, 1976; E. Blum, *Die Komposition der Vätergeschichte*, WMANT 57, 1984; id., *Studien zur Komposition der Vätergeschichte*, WMANT 57, 1984; id., *Studien zur Komposition des Pentateuch*, BZAW 189, 1988; C. Levin, *Der Jahwist*, FRLANT 157, 1993; J. van Seters, *Prologue to History: The Yahwist as Historian in Genesis*, Louisville, Ky 1992; id., *The Life of Moses: The Yahwist as Historian in Exodus–Numbers*, Louisville, Ky 1994; A. Rofé, *Introduction to the Composition of the Pentateuch*, The Biblical Seminar 58, 1999; J. Blenkinsopp, *The Pentateuch: Introduction to the First Five Books of the Bible*, ARBL, 2000.

Commentaries

H. Gunkel, *Genesis*, HK I/1, [3]1910; E.A. Speiser, *Genesis*, AB, 1964; G.von Rad, *Genesis*, OTL, [2]1972; M. Noth, *Exodus*, OTL, 1962; *Numbers*, OTL, 1968; C. Westermann, *Genesis* (3 vols), 1983–87; W.H. Schmidt, *Exodus*, BK I/1, 1988; I/2, 1995ff.; W.H. Propp, *Exodus*, AB, 1999; J. Milgrom, *Leviticus*, AB, I, 1991; II, 2000; B.A. Levine, *Numbers*, AB, I, 1993; II, 2000.

Research I (Pentateuch)

C. Houtman, *Der Pentateuch: Die Geschichte seiner Erforschung neben einer Auswertung*, Contributions to Biblical Exegesis and Theology 9, Kampen 1994; A. de Pury and T. Römer, 'Le Pentateuque en question: Position du problème et brève histoire de la recherche', in A. de Pury, *Le Pentateuque en question*, MoBi 19 (1989), ²1991, 9-80; E. Otto, 'Kritik der Pentateuchkomposition', *ThR* 60, 1995, 163-91; id., 'Einleitungen in den Pentateuch', *ThR* 62, 1996, 332-41; id., 'Forschungen zum nachpriester-schriftlichen Pentateuch', *ThR* 67, 2002, 125-55; E. Nicolson, *The Pentateuch in the Twentieth Century: The Legacy of Julius Wellhausen*, 1998.

Research II (individual books)

C. Westermann, *Genesis 1–11*, EdF 7, 1972 (⁴1989); id., *Genesis 23–50*, EdF 48, 1975; W.H. Schmidt, *Exodus, Sinai und Mose*, EdF 191, 1983; H. Schmid, *Die Gestalt des Mose*, EdF 237, 1986.

The Pentateuch has a long and complicated history behind it, which biblical critics have laboured for around 250 years to clarify. In the course of the previous accounts we have already got to know some of the various ingredients of which it is composed: Deuteronomy, the Priestly law in Exod. 25 to Num. 36 and the non-Priestly Sinai pericope in Exod. 19–24 and 32–34. If we remove the law, we come upon the narrative of the Hexateuch, which comprises the following texts: the primal history in Gen. 1–11; the patriarchal history in Gen. 12–50; and the narrative of the exodus from Egypt in Exod. 1–15, which continues with the wandering through the wilderness up to the death of Moses in Exod. 15–18 (19–40) + Num. 20.1–25.1 + Deut. 34.5f., and reaches its goal with the settlement under Joshua in Josh. 2–12. There is largely agreement over excluding the law. That is no longer the case in the analysis of the narrative parts, and the model for sources which has been valid for a long time has become shaky. It will therefore be useful to make ourselves clear about the various options before approaching the text.

Modern Pentateuchal criticism started from the change of designations of God, *ʾᵉlōhīm* (God) or *yhwh* (the divine name 'Yahweh'), in Gen. 1–3. The difference became the basic criterion for literary analysis, initially in Gen. 1–3, soon throughout Genesis, and finally throughout the Tetrateuch and beyond, with the exception of Deuteronomy. Three hypotheses were developed one after the other to explain this phenomenon: the documentary hypothesis, the fragment hypothesis and the supplementary hypothesis.

According to the documentary hypothesis, the Pentateuch or Tetrateuch, Hexateuch, etc., is made up of two or three sources and a series of side traditions. In this context 'source' means a more or less independent writing. Among the two or three sources, parallel versions are to be understood, which all contain approximately the same narrative, but in different words. The documentary hypothesis found and finds its strongest support in Genesis.

According to the fragment hypothesis there are no written sources running through the Pentateuch, but smaller and larger pieces of tradition without any original connection; these 'fragments' have been put together one after another. The thesis is essentially based on the evidence which is less favourable to the documentary hypothesis in Exodus–Deuteronomy (and Joshua–Kings).

Finally, the supplementary hypothesis reckons with both, that is, with a consecutive source as a literary basis which has gradually been filled out by fragments, separate pieces of tradition or literary elaborations.

The so-called new documentary hypothesis, for which Wellhausen provided the conclusive proof, gained general recognition. Unlike the earlier documentary hypothesis, which reckoned with two source writings, it distinguished three, one characterized by the divine name Yhwh (J = Yahwist)[1] and two characterized by the divine designation Elohim (E = Elohist and P = Priestly Writing).[2] If the earlier and initially also the more recent documentary hypothesis saw P as the earliest writing and J as a later supplement, Wellhausen put the literary elements in the correct theological order: J is followed by E and both are followed by the pre-Priestly 'Jehovistic' historical work JE, made up of J and E; then comes D, after that P modelled on JE, and finally the combination of JE + D + P by the Pentateuch redactor R. At the level of the redactor the earlier documentary hypothesis and the supplementary hypothesis came into their own again in their original sense: R uses P as the basis for incorporating JE and D. However, Wellhausen reckoned with a variety of expansions at every literary level and several editions of the same writing, so that with him 'the so-called supplementary hypothesis in fact finds its application' alongside the documentary hypothesis in explaining the origin of the various writings, 'in a different sense from that originally intended'.[3] Accordingly the three parallel source writings did not arise independently of one another or all at once, but are dependent on one another in literary terms and grew up by the constant revision of a literary core before, during and after the time when writings were brought together.

The fact that there were many strata in the three source writings which had been observed for a long time was soon explained in turn by means of the documentary hypothesis. The observation that Wellhausen had thrown out[4] about the various editions J^1, J^2, J^3 and E^1, E^2, E^3 was taken literally, and the same of course also went for D and P; there was a concern to identify more and more new sources. Otto Eissfeldt[5] called a moderate variant of this procedure 'the newest documentary hypothesis'. He used its results in his 1922 Hexateuch synopsis. By contrast, the supplementary hypothesis redefined by Wellhausen found virtually no further application.

Instead of this, interest turned to the oral prehistory of the three sources or the sources themselves, which had meanwhile multiplied ad lib. The so-called form-critical or tradition-critical questioning which aimed to do this was not really meant to replace literary-critical analysis but to complement it. However, in the course of time the literary-critical indications were increasingly explained in terms of tradition history, that is, from the prehistory of the text. The climax and conclusion of this development was Noth's 1948 *A History of Pentateuchal Tradition*. Noth returned to the more recent documentary hypothesis and yet again marked out the three parallel versions J, E and P verse by verse; he postulated a common 'foundation', G, for them.[6] Following Hermann Gunkel[7] and G. von Rad,[8] he then went behind the text and the postulated foundation, differentiated the individual themes of the Pentateuch, and described each of their tradition histories and the way in which they were gradually combined into the wider narrative context of the Tetrateuch. In his view the source writings did not originate in the text but prior to that, that is, in the hypothetical coming into being of the hypothetical 'foundation' G, from which the two earlier sources J and E (and P?)[9] branched off independently of each other. The custom of pursuing the sources only in the Tetrateuch and no longer into the Hexateuch or further, which was usual up to then, goes back to Noth. He put the 'Deuteronomistic history' in their place.

More recent criticism of the source hypothesis has already been addressed in the introduction. The main objections are: (1) the literary unravelling or, what amounts to the same thing, the diffuse and always complicated traditio-historical differentiation of the text into a variety of source writings or pre-literary traditions; and (2) the dissection of the narrative threads of the Hexateuch (the patriarchs, exodus, wandering in the wilderness, settlement) in the Tetrateuch and Deuteronomistic history. Both operations create more problems than they solve. If we omit both of them, the situation becomes very much simpler. We can take the Priestly text in Genesis–Numbers as the starting point; its extent has been established since Nöldeke's 'Investigations' and is still more or less undisputed. The non-Priestly text in Joshua needs to be distinguished from it as follows: like P it contains a primal history in Gen. 1–11, a patriarchal history in Gen. 12–50 and a narrative of the exodus from Egypt under Moses up to the settlement under Joshua in Exod. 1–24; Num. 20.1–25.1; Deut. 34.5f. and Josh. 2–12 (classical JE).[10] The non-Priestly narrative is substantially earlier than Deuteronomy and P, but in execution is often later. As in Joshua–Kings, the supplementary hypothesis rather than the source hypothesis is more likely for the non-Priestly text of Genesis, Exod. 1–24 and Num. 20–24. Thus the problem of the analysis is reduced to a distinction between the Priestly and the non-Priestly text along the lines of the source hypothesis (P and JE) and in the two between the basic document and the supplement along the lines of the supplementary hypothesis; here we have to reckon with two kinds of expansions, those which move only within the horizon of one or another strata of the text (P^S and JE^S), and those which have behind them the combination of the non-Priestly and Priestly texts (classical R). In accordance with the state of Pentateuchal criticism I shall begin with the Priestly Writing.

2.   Survey

K. Elliger, 'Sinn und Ursprung der priesterlichen Geschichtserzählung', *ZThK* 49, 1952, 121-43; N. Lohfink, 'Die Priesterschrift und die Geschichte', *VT.S* 29, 1978, 189-225 = id., *Studien zum Pentateuch*, SBAB 4, 1988, 213-53; E. Zenger, *Gottes Bogen in den Wolken: Untersuchungen zu Komposition und Theologie der priesterschriftliche Urgeschichte*, SBS 112, 1993; L. Schmidt, *Studien zur Priesterschrift*, BZAW 124, 1993; T. Pola, *Die ursprüngliche Priesterschrift*, WMANT 70, 1995.

Research

E. Otto, 'Forschungen zur Priesterschrift', *ThR* 62, 1997, 1-50.

The beginning of the Priestly Writing lies in Gen. 1.1–2.4a. I have already discussed the end above (under B.1, 2). Accordingly the original Priestly Writing, P^G, extends from Gen. 1 to Exod. 40. All the laws in Leviticus belong to secondary layers of expansion (P^S), the Priestly texts on the wandering in the wilderness in Numbers to an even later stage at which the Priestly Writing is an element of the Enneateuch and the later Pentateuch (R^P). In what follows I shall therefore limit myself to an analysis of P in Gen. 1–Exod. 40, removing the supplements in Exod. 30–31 and the account of the implementation of the commands in Exod. 35–40 which have already been excised; P^G is to be found only in Exod. 25–29 and 40.16f., 34f.

The so-called toledot formula is a clear characteristic of P. It occurs for the first time as a signature to Gen. 1.1–2.4a in 2.4a and afterwards as a heading in 5.1; 6.9; 10.1; 11.10, 27; 25.12, 19; 36.1, 9; and 37.2 (in the secondary material once in Num. 3.1). 'Toledot' is derived from the root *yld*, 'bear, beget', and means something like 'genealogy'. That fits admirably with the many genealogies reported under this heading (Gen. 5; 11; 36), but also with the way in which the history of Israel is 'narrated' in P. The Priestly Writing is more report than narrative and to some degree deals with 'procreations of God': the genealogy of the covenant with humankind and with Israel from the creation of the world in Gen. 1 to the establishment of the cult on Sinai in Exod. 25–40. 'Toledot of NN' then means: descendants and/or history of the descendants of NN, not, say, history of NN, since the history of an ancestor's descendants is always described under his name.

The formula is distributed with some degree of regularity over the creation stories and the patriarchal stories; from Terah the father of Abraham, notices about deaths conclude the sections, and the history of the people of Israel is subsumed from Exod. 1 under the toledot of Jacob = Israel.

Table C.I.1

1. Toledot of heaven and earth	Gen. 1.1–2.4a
2. Toledot of Adam	Gen. 5
3. Toledot of Noah	Gen. 6–9
4. Toledot of the sons of Noah	Gen. 10
5. Toledot of Shem	Gen. 11.10-26
6. Toledot of Terah	Gen. 11.27–25.1; notices of death 11.32; 23; 25.7-11
7. Toledot of Ishmael	Gen. 25.12-17; notice of death 25.17
8. Toledot of Isaac	Gen. 25.19–35.29, notice of death 35.29
9. Toledot of Esau	Gen. 36, two formulae vv. 1, 9. Conclusions in vv. 8, 19, 43
10. Toledot of Jacob	Gen. 37.2–Exod. 40. Notice of death Gen. 49.33; 50.13

Within the individual sections, long programmatic texts alternate with usually very monosyllabic connecting links, which are sometimes more extended, as seen in Table C.I.2.[11]

Looked at as a whole, the outline gives the impression of being a well-arranged unity. As well as the toledot scheme the monotonous language, the ongoing genealogy, the chronology[12] and the theological system see to that. The blessing for humankind (Gen. 1) is matched by the blessing for Abram/ Abraham and his descendants (Gen. 17), from whom the people of Israel emerges (Gen. 28.3f.; 35.9-13; 48.3f.; Exod. 1.7). The covenant with Noah and his descendants (Gen. 9) is matched by the covenant with Abraham and his descendants (Gen. 17), of whom Yhwh is mindful in Exod. 2.24; 6.2-7; it is primarily focused on Yhwh being God for Israel in the cult of Sinai (Exod. 25.8; 29.45f.). The corresponding differentiation in the name of God,

Table C.I.2

1.	The creation	Gen. 1.1–2.4a
2.	Genealogy from Adam to Noah	Gen. 5
3.	The flood, the covenant with Noah	Gen. 6–9
4.	Genealogy of the sons of Noah	Gen. 10.1-7, 20, 22f., 31f.
5.	Genealogy from Shem to Terah	Gen. 11.10-26
6.	Genealogy from Terah to Abraham	Gen. 11.27-32
	Itinerary of Abraham	Gen. 12.4b-5; 13.6, 11b-12; 19.29
	Genealogy: birth of Ishmael	Gen. 16.1a, 3, 15f.
	The covenant with Abraham	Gen. 17.1-27
	Genealogy: birth of Isaac, death of Sarah and Abraham	Gen. 21.1b-5; 23.1-20; 25.7-11a
7.	Genealogy of Ishmael	Gen. 25.12-17
8.	Genealogy of Isaac	Gen. 25.19-20…26b; 26.34f.
	Itinerary of Jacob	Gen. 27.46–28.9; 31.18; 33.18a; 35.6
	Promise to Jacob-Israel in Beth-el	Gen. 35.9-13a, 15
	Genealogy of Jacob	Gen. 35.22b-29
9.	Genealogy of Esau	Gen. 36
10.	Itinerary of Joseph and journey of Jacob to Egypt	Gen. 37.1f.; 41.46a; 46.6, 7, 8-27; 47.27b, 28; 48.3-6; 49.1a, 29-33; 50.12f.
	Israel in Egypt	Exod. 1.1-7, 13-14; 2.23-25
	Call of Moses, revelation of the name of Yhwh	Exod. 6.2–7.7
	Genealogy to Moses and Aaron	Exod. 6.14-30
	Plagues and Passover	Exod. 7–12
	Itinerary of the exodus	Exod. 12.40f. and 12.42, 43-51
	Miracle by the sea	Exod. 14
	Itinerary of the wilderness wandering	Exod. 15.22, 27; 16.1
	Manna	Exod. 16
	Itinerary of the wilderness wandering	Exod. 17.1; 19.1f.
	Foundation of the cult on Sinai, the glory of Yhwh	Exod. 24.15b-18; 25–40

who appears to the patriarchs under the name El-Shaddai and first introduces himself with his name Yhwh to Moses for the people of Israel (Exod. 6.2f.), is carried out consistently in the Priestly stratum. All this makes it clear that this is a planned complex which extends from the creation of the world through the patriarchs and Moses to Sinai and groups the individual stages (toledot) around the two covenants, the covenant with humankind and the covenant with Abraham, even if the proportions of the main passages and the link passages and their distribution over the ten toledot are not always right. Not least because of this, scholars usually differentiate the text once again into original stratum (sources), basic writing (P^G) and secondary expansions (P^S) of the Priestly Writing in Gen. 1–Exod. 40.

The original stratum doubtless includes the non-Priestly text in Genesis and Exodus: although it is not difficult to detach this from P, in a way not dissimilar to the relationship between Chronicles and Genesis–Kings, P seems to presuppose it, down to specific formulations. The blessing for the world and for Israel by Abraham recalls the non-Priestly promise to Abraham in Gen. 12.1-3 which stands over against the curse on humankind in Gen. 2–3 – only a little mitigated in 8.21f. after the flood in Gen. 6–8. The covenant with Noah for humankind and the covenant with Abraham for Israel anticipate the covenant with Moses and Israel on Sinai and in the land of Moab (Exod. 19–24; 32–34; Deut. 26.17-29; 29.12). The revelation of the name of Yhwh recalling the covenant with the patriarchs in Exod. 6.2-8 is a theological variant on Exod. 3–4. All these and many other points of contact, and the fact that the precise demarcation and isolation of the Priestly thread causes difficulties at some points, have sparked off a dispute among scholars as to whether the Priestly Writing was originally independent, as most assume, or was composed a priori for the context, that is, whether it is 'source' or redaction.

In short, in principle the identification and literary demarcation of the Priestly text in Gen. 1–Exod. 40 is completely undisputed. What remain open are: (1) details in the demarcation from the non-Priestly text; (2) the literary differentiation of P itself (into original stratum, basic writing and supplements); (3) the literary independence of P.

3. The covenant with Noah

3.1   The Priestly Writing begins with the creation of heaven and earth in Gen. 1.1–2.4a. Some scholars also add 2.4b, but this is a redactional bracket between 1.1–2.4a and 2.5ff. The report is framed by a double heading and ending in 1.1/2.4a and 1.2/2.1-3 and enumerates the individual works of creation in accordance with a fixed scheme. The divine word is followed by the divine action, introduced by a formula of accomplishment:[13] 'And God said' – 'And it was so' – 'And God did'. As a rule every work of creation is completed with the so-called formula of approval, 'And God saw that it was good',[14] and after one or more works the days of creation are numbered consecutively: 'And it was evening and it was morning, a first, second, third day', etc. until the seventh day, on which God rests from his work.[15]

The scheme displays some irregularities and also some deviations in the text of the Greek translation, the Septuagint. Thus the formulae do not always agree in the accounts of word and action; works and days are not congruent; the formula system is not complete; and individual formulae are put in different places. The differences suggest that the report is not all of a piece. Scholars have wanted to find two independent accounts of creation in it, a word account and an act account, which have been worked together later. But that is just not possible. The word needs the action which follows; the accomplishment formula is not enough for that, but relates word and action. Only the action makes sense without the word, and thus as a basis we must reckon at all events with an older list of seven or eight works which develop out of the initial chaos either automatically or through the action of the creator, before the word and everything else are expanded in Gen. 1.

It is hardly possible now to say what the list looked like in detail. Reconstruction depends on how much we trust the Septuagint, which in many passages offers a smoother, not to say smoothed out, text, and in 1.9 the account of the action which is lacking in the Massoretic text; and on the criterion we use to distinguish tradition and reaction. If we remove all the Priestly interpretative elements, we do not get a consecutive text, so it seems advisable to forego a precise demarcation of the original basis. It is also difficult to say whether the Priestly interpretative elements have been expanded all at once or gradually. As Odil Hannes Steck has demonstrated in a critical discussion with Werner H.Schmidt,[16] there is a system to most of the irregularities. However, that does not exclude the possibility that the pre-Priestly list was first adorned with the divine word, the formula of accomplishment and approval, within the framework of the basic document P^G, whereas by contrast the numbering of the days and sabbath were done by a secondary revision (P^S). The basis for the assumption is offered not so much by the divergence of works and days as by the double conclusion in 2.1, 2a, from which we can once again distinguish the hallowing and blessing of the seventh day in vv. 2b-3. The decision depends not least on the controversial question of how much 'law' we want to allow the basic writing of P.[17] Outside the framework doubt has also been cast on the instructions about food in 1.29-30, which are connected with the reason for the flood, the 'violence' between living beings in 6.11-13, and the new regulation in 9.1-17, which takes account of this.

3.2   The toledot of heaven and earth (Gen. 2.4a) are followed by the toledot of Adam in Gen. 5.1a, 3ff. The connection is interrupted by the insertion of Gen. 2–4; 5.1b-2 then restores the original link and adds the mention of human beings. At one point presumably the text in v. 3aβ was also disturbed and altered following 1.26. The possibility of a deliberate resumption in the style of 5.21/6.9f. or 11.26, 27 is ruled out because the repetition presupposes not only 1.27f. and 2.4a but already 2.4b and the namings in 2.19ff.; 3.20 and makes a new statement. Originally the change of the designation of genre, 'the human being' (without an article in 1.26, with an article in 1.27), to the proper name which is intrinsically determined in 5.1, 3a was self-evident. The filling-out has sometimes been seen as an indication of an older toledot book which served P as a model. But that is erroneous, since Gen. 5 is constructed from Gen. 4.

Like the creation in Gen. 1, the genealogy of Adam, from Adam to Noah, ten generations in all, always runs according to the same scheme: (1) age and firstborn; (2) age and further descendants; (3) summary of age and death. The two lines of Cainites (from Cain to Lamech) and Sethites (Seth and Enoch as a substitute for Abel) in Gen. 4.1, 17-24, 25-26 become an ongoing line in Gen. 5: Sethites and Cainites to Lamech. The chain makes use of the identical meanings of Adam and Enosh, both of which mean 'human being', and is achieved by a simple transposition. Noah and the flood are attached to Lamech (5.28-31, 32; 6.9f.).

The scheme has been expanded in two passages: in the seventh generation with Enoch in 5.21-23, 24, and at the end in the tenth generation with Noah and his sons in 5.32, with a continuation in 6.9f./9.28f. Noah's first fathering in 5.32 is repeated in 6.9f.; the tenth generation is to some degree broadened out first in the toledot of Noah of Gen. 6–9. Both passages take account of the introduction of particular traditions, the somewhat intangible but evidently well-stamped Enoch tradition, and the flood tradition, which is broadly attested in the ancient Near East. Nevertheless 5.32 gives rise to doubts, not because of the resumption in 6.9f. (cf. 11.26, 27), but because of the chronological inconsistency with 7.6 and 11.10 – Shem must have been 101 'two years after the flood' or, calculated from the end, even 102 – and the tenth generation, which overshoots by comparison with the 9 + 1 generations in 11.10-26, 27ff. The verse may have been inserted in order to prefix the fathering of the sons of Noah with the resolve to destroy the earth in 6.1-8 or 6.5-8. However, as the chronological discrepancy only arises as a result of 11.10, and the dating after the flood is no longer in place here – in contrast to 9.28f.[18] – it would also be conceivable for only 11.10b to be an addition which takes up the original thread of 9.28f. (and 10.1) interrupted by 10.1–11.9. I do not see any basis for a firm decision; perhaps both are glosses.

At one point, in 5.28f. in the framework of the Lamech note, the scheme has been disrupted. Instead of 'and he became the father of Noah' we read '28 he became the father of a son, 29 and called his name Noah, saying, "Out of the ground which Yhwh has cursed this one shall bring us relief [Septuagint: create rest] from our work and from the toil of our hands."' This is an etymological interpretation of the name 'Noah' (*nḥm*, 'comfort'; *nwḥ*, 'rest'), referring back to 3.16f. and looking forward to 6.6 and 8.21f. (9.18-27). It is generally reckoned that here we have a splinter of tradition from the pre-Priestly text, but it will not join up either with 4.25-26 or with 4.17-24. Perhaps this is a post-Priestly addition which presupposes P and the combination with the non-Priestly text. The divergent birth notice with the express mention of Noah (5.28, 29a) is original. The explanation of the divergence is that in P Noah replaces the descendants of Lamech in the basic material in 4.19-22, and with him there is a new beginning, namely, the flood.

3.3   The account of the flood is framed in 6.9f. and 9.28f. with a toledot formula in the style of Gen. 5. Like the account of the creation in Gen. 1, in its way it too is no more than a broad elaboration of the genealogical scheme. The Priestly ingredients produce a consecutive, coherent textual connection:

(a) the announcement of the flood, 6.9-22;
(b) the flood, 7.6–8.14 (7.6, 7-9, 11, 13-16a, 18-21, 24; 8.1-2a, 3b-5, 13a, 14);
(c) the end of the flood, 8.15-19 + 9.1-17, 28f.

The complex is characterized by the two great speeches of God at the beginning and the end (cf. Gen. 1; 17; 35.9ff. and Exod. 25ff.), and internally by the precise correspondence between the coming and the going of the flood. This has its axis in 8.1, where God thinks of Noah. In addition there is the pedantic chronology, in which at least three systems overlap: (1) the dating from the 600th year of Noah through 1.X.600 up to 1.I.601 in 7.6; 8.5 and 8.13; (2) the dating from 17.II.600 through 17.VII.600 to 27.II.601 in 7.11; 8.4; 8.14; (3) the calculation by days in 7.24; 8.3b, as in 7.4, 10, 12, 17; 8.6-12, the chronology of the non-Priestly text. The first two systems each run through a full year: once, if we take 1.I.600 as the starting point, a lunar year with 354 days, the other time a solar year with 354 + 11 days. In the case of the third system the numbers are less important than the symmetry: for 150 days the waters rise; after (another) 150 days they recede again; and the other details of days show the same picture: 7–40–150/150–40–7 (two or three times).

Presumably, however, none of the three chronological systems belongs to the basic writing of P. The simplest way of explaining them is to leave aside the usual source division and start from the final text. That applies above all to the second system, which can be derived without any problems from the two others. The 17.II in 7.11a is calculated by assuming that a month has 30 days, from the 7 + 40 days announced in 7.4; the 17.VII in 8.4a from the 150 days of 7.24 and 8.3, which if we count them only once, produce precisely five months; and the 27.II.601 in 8.14a from the rounding up to a solar year (17.II + 11 days). Certainly the sum does not add up completely, as the 40 days of 7.4 stand in 7.12 after the date in 7.XI, and it is not clear whether the 150 days of 7.24 and 8.3 count once or twice. However, that does not alter the possibility that a third party was inspired by the figures and made his own calculations. I do not know whether he was aware that the intervals between the individual dates in 7.6, 11 (47 days); 8.4, 5 (73 days); and 8.13, 14 (57 days), taken together, add up to 177 days, that is, half a lunar year of 354 days. The removal of the dates in 7.11a; 8.4a, 14 leaves no gaps. In 7.11b, 13, the 'On this day' originally refers to the moment after the interval of 7 days in 7.4, 10. In 8.4a we need only take out the date to get a smooth text ('And the ark ... settled on Mount Ararat'). Genesis 8.14 presupposes 8.6f. and with 8.6-12, 13 interrupts the original link of 8.15f. to 8.4.

The two other systems of dating, too, can hardly have come into being independently of each other, but it is harder to discover the direction of the dependence. The dates in (7.6;) 8.5, 13a do not exclude the information about days – if we count the 150 days in 7.24 and 8.3 only once – but cannot be harmonized with them. At any rate the twice 150 days in 7.24; 8.3 and the 54 days of 8.6, 10, 12 could have led a supplementer to calculate the flood as a lunar year from 1.I.600 to 1.I.601. The placing of the dates does not seem to take account of the non-Priestly text in 8.6-12, 13b. The Priestly account of the flood would not lose anything if we removed 8.5, 13a from it.

There remains the counting by days, probably the earliest system of dating; however, not only in 7.24 and 8.3b but also in 7.4, 10, 12, 17; 8.6-12 this is post-Priestly. After 7.18-20 and 8.1-3a, for the umpteenth time the 150 days in 7.24 and 8.3b report the rising and subsiding of the waters which already in 7.19, 20b and 8.2-3a is due to the further work on 7.18 and 8.1. The doublet in 7.7-9 and 7.13-16a is also connected with the chronology. Usually vv. 11, 13-16a are regarded as original, vv. 7-9 as secondary, but the opposite relationship has also been proposed. In fact it can be explained by the insertion of the numbering of days of 7.10, 12, which in turn attracted to itself 7.11, 13 and 8.2-3a on the one hand and the assimilation to 7.1-5 in 7.8f. on the other. Genesis 7.13 is a resumption of 7.7: vv. 14-16a join up seamlessly with vv. 6-7.

In Gen. 6–9 not only the chronology but also often parts of the speech of God in 9.1-17 are denied to the basic writing. Dubious features are the exclusion of eating blood in 9.4-6 (with the resumption of v. 1 in v. 7), which is meant to tame the 'violent act' in 6.13, or the regulation about food as a whole in 9.1-7 (with 1.29-30), and the repeated promise in 9.16-17 or the sign of the covenant as a whole in 9.12-17 (cf. 17.9-14). With the detailed descriptions, the covenant announced in 6.18 and concluded in 9.8-11 is referred back to Gen. 1 without relating just to the flood; in any case, together with Gen. 1 it points forward to the making of the covenant in Gen. 17.

If we take the basic writing and possible supplements within the Priestly Writing (P^G and P^S) together, the following text results: 6.9-22;

7.6-7, 14-16a, 18-21; 8.1, 4a (without the date), b, 15–19; 9.1-17, 28f. The passages 7.8f., 11b, 13; 8.2a and the dates in 7.24/8.3b; 7.11a; 8.4a (only the date), 5, 13, 14 are supplements which presuppose the non-Priestly text in Gen. 6–8 (R^P).

3.4   After the creation in Gen. 1, the genealogy of Adam in Gen. 5 and the flood in 6–9, the table of nations in Gen. 10 and the Semite genealogy in 11.10-26 are assigned to the Priestly primal history. That is quite obvious for the genealogy of the Semites in Gen. 11: it has the toledot formula as a heading (v. 10), follows the same scheme as Gen. 5, and lists nine generations, the last of which, the generation of Terah, from which Abraham emerges, gets its own heading (11.26, 27, cf. 5.32/6.9f.; 9.28f.). After the death of Terah (11.32), Abraham and his sons stand in tenth place in the genealogy, corresponding to Noah and his sons in Gen. 5.32 and 6-9. And as in the toledot of Terah from 11.27, only one of the three sons mentioned by name, Abraham, becomes the chief figure; thus the Semite genealogy in 11.10-26 could also have followed immediately after the toledot of Noah in 6.9f./9.28f.

In relation to this, the table of nations in Gen. 10, the toledot of the 'sons of Noah', seems to be an alien body. Certainly it is introduced and ended in the Priestly style (10.1, 32), but this unusual framework itself seems strange – also by comparison with Gen. 1. Genesis 10 also follows a fixed scheme: 'The sons of NN are ... '/'These are the sons of NN ...' The sons of Japheth (10.2-5), Ham (10.6-7, 20) and Shem (10.22-24, 31) are listed in order according to this pattern. But the scheme is a different one from the Priestly scheme in Gen. 5 and 11.10-26. Moreover the order of the sons of Noah is different from that in 5.32; 6.9(; 9.18; 10.1), and with 10.22-24, 32 a doublet arises with the following genealogy of Shem in 11.10ff. It emerges from this that there is a separate tradition in the scheme of Gen. 10; this has been supplemented in 10.8-19, 21, 25-30, which has been incorporated secondarily into the context by 10.1, 32. The only question is whether the inclusion took place between 9.28f. and 11.10-26 in the framework of the Priestly Writing, or comes from a later redactor who imitated the Priestly style and also the headings and endings in Gen. 10.2-31, and sought to take up 9.19. The sum of ten toledot, five for the primal history and five for the patriarchal history (including the exodus), which cannot lack Gen. 10, though that can also be secondary, suggests P. Even without Gen. 10 the Priestly Writing would be built up no less systematically according to the scheme 2 + 2 + 1 + 2 + 2 toledot (creation and Adam, flood and Shem, Terah/Abraham, Ishmael and Isaac, Esau and Jacob). In cases of doubt the indications against belonging to P have priority. Where the post-Priestly redaction has taken the table of nations from depends on the analysis of the non-Priestly text and the ordering of the glosses in 10.8-19, 21, 25-30.

4. The covenant with Abraham

4.1   If we remove Gen. 10, four toledot follow one another in the primal history: (1) the creation (Gen. 1.1–2.4a); (2) from Adam to Lamech or Noah (Gen. 5); (3) Noah and the flood (Gen. 6–9); (4) from Shem to Terah (Gen. 11.10-26). The toledot of Terah occupy a kind of interim position between the primal history and the patriarchal history, which extend from 11.27 to the death of Abraham in 25.7-11. Four further toledot attach themselves in turn to this: (1) Ishmael (25.12-17); (2) Isaac (Gen. 25.19 to 35.27-29); (3) Esau (Gen. 36); (4) Jacob (Gen. 37.2 to Exod. 40). As in the primal history, programmatic leading texts alternate with genealogical, biographical and geographical transitional passages. The programmatic leading texts occur only with the three main lines, Abraham, Isaac and Jacob; in the case of the subsidiary lines, Ishmael and Isaac, P limits itself to biographical data (notices about births and deaths) and itineraries.

4.2   The transition from the toledot of Shem to the toledot of Terah is unproblematical. Genesis 11.27 repeats 11.26 and lists the three sons of Terah: Abram (from Gen. 17 Abraham), Nahor and Haran. Terah's journey attaches itself seamlessly to this, from Ur-kasdim in the direction of Canaan, initially to ḥārān, where Terah dies (11.31-32). It is a little surprising that Terah takes only Abram and his grandson Lot, the son of Haran and nephew of Abraham, and Sarai (from Gen. 17 Sara), Abram's wife, with him on the journey, but this is explained by the progress of the narrative in 12.5 and 13.6, 11f. and by the fact that P knows the pre-Priestly Abraham narrative, especially Gen. 12–13 and 18–19, and selects from it. A later hand adds the reason and further details of the family history in 11.28-30. Moreover P may have chosen the name Haran for the brother of Abraham and father of Lot on the basis of the north-Syrian city of ḥārān (cf. Gen. 27.43; 28.10; 29.4). Serug, Peleg, Nahor and Terah in 11.10-26 are also all cities in the neighbourhood of ḥārān.

After the death of Terah, Abram, his wife Sarai, and Lot set off from ḥārān for the land of Canaan (12.4b-5). On their arrival there Abram and Lot separate (13.6, 11b, 12abα, the same motif in 36.7f.; 37.1). It has become customary to add to this the note about the downfall of Sodom and the preservation of Lot in 19.29 (the designation Elohim for God and the phrase 'God thought'), but it is superfluous in P. It has been added in Gen. 19 instead of v. 26 as a connecting link between vv. 27f.and 30ff. Rather, the birth of Ishmael, the promise to Abraham and the birth of Isaac in Gen. 16; 17; and 21.1-5, and then the death and burial of Sarah and Abraham in Gen. 23 or 25.7-11a, follow the separation and settlement in the land of Canaan (13.6, 11f.).

The text seems to have been preserved complete; however, perhaps it has been glossed at some points. The detail of age in 12.4b perhaps presupposes the non-Priestly v. 4a, but cf. also 16.16; 21.5; 25.20; 26.34; 41.46. Genesis 13.6b duplicates v. 6a, taking account of v. 5. In ch. 13, v. 12bα takes up v. 11a and leads on to the note about Sodom in 13.12bβ, 13 (chs 18–19). The dating in 16.3 picks up the old connection in 13.12a after 13.12b-18 (and chs 14–15). Quite often the command to circumcise and the actual circumcision, the sign of the covenant, in 17.9-14, 23-27; 21.4 are seen as additions. However, the new beginning in 17.15-21 is essential. It makes it clear that the covenant with Abram/Abraham runs only through the main line, Sarai/Sara and her son Isaac (cf. Exod. 6). The broad narrative about the purchase of the cave of Machpelah as a family tomb, to which allusion is made on various later occasions (25.9-10; 49.29-32; 50.13), is quite unusual. The narrative clearly diverges from the normal course of the Priestly Writing and must be an addition. It arises out of the need for a partial fulfilment of the promise of increase in Exod. 1. Originally the fulfilment of the promise of increase and land is tacitly presupposed or regarded as an eternally valid hope depending on the decisive promise that Yhwh is God, which takes form in the cult of Sinai.

The two birth narratives in Gen. 16 and 21 cause considerable difficulties, as does Gen. 25.19-26. The births of Ishmael, Isaac and Jacob and Esau are each reported only once. But according to the source hypothesis all the sources must have related them, so it is assumed that one version or another was lost when the sources were worked together. Genesis 16.1a, 3, 15f. and 21.1b-5 are usually assigned to P, and by contrast 25.21-26a to J. Accordingly, only fragments are left for J (and E) in Gen. 16 and 21 and for P in Gen. 25. Since this is a universal theme, and nothing typical of P is to be found in Gen. 16 and 21 except for the datings in 16.3, 16 and 21.5, we can also reverse the relationship and reckon everywhere with a complete report by JE and fragments of P.[19] The simplest explanation of the evidence is then that P is not an independent writing at all, but a stratum of the revision.[20] But neither argument holds. If we maintain the distinction between at least two independent narrative works, P and 'JE', which cannot be avoided elsewhere, but do not want to operate with the inconvenient assumption of losses of text, two possibilities offer themselves. (a) We are content for P with the brief, resultative formulations in 16.1a, 3, 16 and 21.1b, 5; 25.19f., 26b (cf. 12.4b), and assume that both names have dropped out in 25.26b ('Isaac was sixty years old when *they* were born'), being replaced with the *nota accusativi* with a retrospective suffix. (b) The birth stories in 16.1a, 3, 15f. and 21.1b, 2f., 5, which are constructed in the same way, and the similar version in 25.19f., 24-26 (without the etymologies in vv. 25f.) all come from P and were supplemented following the Priestly Writing, whereas the pre-Priestly text narrated only one birth very briefly (21.1a, 6f.) and did not yet contain the two others, which are not even presupposed in Gen. 18f. and 26ff.[21] The latter explanation is by no means improbable, since the genealogical link is carried through consistently only in P, and Ishmael and Esau play a supporting role as genealogical sidelines (cf. Gen. 17.15ff. and 25.12-17; 26.34f., 27.46–28.9; 36.1ff.). The opposition between Ishmael/Isaac and Esau/Jacob takes the place of the opposition between Abraham and Lot in Gen. 12–13 and 18–19, which is completely blanketed out or only hinted at in P; in the pre-Priestly text the Ishmael chapter Gen. 16 and Gen. 14–15 are inserted into this in a disruptive way. P can also have arrived at the Ishmaelites without a parallel in the basic material, perhaps on the basis of the genealogy of the sons of Keturah in 25.1ff.

After the birth of Ishmael in Gen. 16, the basic promise to Abraham in Gen. 17 and the birth of Isaac in 21.1-5, the toledot of Terah, who has already died, end with the death of Abraham in 25.7-8, supplemented by the burial of Sarah and Abraham in the cave of Machpelah in Gen. 23 and 25.9-10, together with the transition to the toledot of Isaac in 25.11a.

4.3   The death of Abraham is followed by the toledot of Ishmael in 25.12-17 and the toledot of Isaac from 25.19. In accordance with the genre, these begin with the birth of Jacob and Esau (25.19f., 26b or 25.19b, 24-26) and immediately turn to the marriage of the sons, which the main lines and the sidelines separate from one another: the ones are recipients of blessing and covenant, the others recipients only of the blessing (26.34f. and 27.46–28.9). There may be some additions in 27.46–28.9, for example, 28.6-7 (cf. v. 1) and the kinship of Esau with Ishmael in 28.8-9, which competes with 36.3.

After that the Priestly thread loses itself somewhat, but not much need have stood between the departures of Jacob in 28.5(, 7, 9) and the return in 31.18; 33.18 and 35.6. In P the births of the children of Jacob cannot already have appeared in Gen. 29–30 – despite the Priestly-sounding formulation in 30.22 – but can only have come after the promise of blessing in 35.9ff. A protasis is missing in 31.18 (cf. 12.5), and finally 33.18 and 35.6 either attach directly to 28.5(-9) or are interim stages after 31.18. Only one of the three notices about the return is needed, but the theophany in 35.9 could have also followed directly after 27.46–28.9. The result of the journey is recorded in 35.22b-26 in connection with the promise of blessing on the way back in 35.9-13.[22] In 35.27-29 Jacob arrives home and the toledot of Isaac end with this homecoming. Esau has married into the Canaanites and Ishmaelites and thus excluded himself from the covenant (cf. 17.20f.). By contrast Jacob has married into the family and fathered the twelve tribes of Israel. The next generation to which the covenant with Abraham passes has been born, and so Isaac can die and be buried.

4.4   The toledot of the sideline of Esau in Gen. 36 are again limited to genealogy and itinerary. Genesis 36.1-8 is original, as is 37.1, the counterpart of 36.8 (cf. 13.6, 11f.). 36.3 competes with 28.9; and in 36.9-43 further notes about Edom have gradually accumulated.

The toledot of Jacob begin in 37.2 and continue in the Joseph narrative and in Exod. 1–40. Jacob is Israel (Gen. 35.10) and father of the twelve tribes (Gen. 35.22b-36). His way from Canaan to Egypt is reported only very briefly, as is customary in P: when Joseph was seventeen years old he and his brothers were watching the sheep. And Joseph reported 'their evil calumniations' (37.2 without 2aβ) to his father, perhaps the same kind of rumours about the land of Canaan which the spies later disseminate and for which they are severely punished (cf. Num. 13.32; 14.36f.). 'They', namely, Jacob and his sons, thereupon left the land of Canaan and moved to Egypt, were fruitful and increased there (Gen. 46.6-7, supplemented with the list of descendants in vv. 8-27; 47.27). When Jacob had died (Gen. 47.28; 49.33b, supplemented with the burial in the cave of Machpelah in 49.1a, 29-33a; 50.12-13),[23] the sons of Israel were enslaved in Egypt (Exod. 1.13-14).

There are additions only between the death and burial of Jacob in Gen. 47–50 and the further fate of the sons of Israel in Exod. 1.13f.: yet another listing of the sons of Israel in Exod. 1.1-5 after Gen. 35.22b-26; 46.26-27; the stay of Joseph in Egypt in Exod. 1.5b after Gen. 50.22; the death of Joseph in Exod. 1–6 = Gen. 50.26 (here, however, in an addition with 50.22 being taken up in v. 26); and the further increase in Exod. 1.7 (after Gen. 47.27 and in view of Exod. 1.9). The additions presuppose the link with the non-Priestly text and are connected with the separation of the book (cf. the transition from Josh. 24/Judg. 2.6ff.). The transition in P: P^G Gen. 49.33b (50.22) or P^S 49.1a, 29-33 + 50.12-13(, 22)/Exod. 1.13-14; after the working together of P and 'JE': Gen. 50.14-22/Exod. 1.6-7, 8ff.; after the separation of the books, Gen. 50.22, 23-26/Exod. 1.1-5, 6ff.

The Israelite cry for help along with the remembrance of Yhwh in Exod. 2.23aβ-25 and the call of Moses in 6.2-8, which replaces the revelation scene of the non-Priestly text in Exod. 3–4, attach themselves seamlessly to Exod. 1.13-14. The revelation of the name of Yhwh makes sense only in the framework of an independent Priestly Writing. I do not miss the introduction of Moses which scholars often call for; instead of this Yhwh presents himself to Moses – who is known to the reader and whose significance is somewhat reduced. The link of 6.4, 5 to 2.23-25 supports the original connection.

The call of Moses and announcement of the Exodus in 6.2-8 is continued in Exod. 6.9–11.10 with the plague narrative and in 12.1-28 and 12.42-51 with the instructions on the Passover, in 12.40-41 with the departure from Egypt, and in 14.1-29 with the miracle by the sea. Quite apart from the need to distinguish between P and the non-Priestly text in Exod. 6–11 and 14, the

Priestly text also gives the impression of being overloaded and heavily concentrated. More than elsewhere this therefore suggests a differentiation into P^G, P^S and R^P. The main thread (P^G) runs from the call of Moses in Exod. 6.2-8 through the note about the departure in 12.40f. to the miracle at the sea in 14.1-29.[24] The instructions for the Passover, including the announcement of the killing of the firstborn, which have found a place in 12.1-28 between 11.10 and 12. (29ff.,)[25] 40f., and in 12.42-51 between 12.40f. and 14.1ff. (with the recapitulation of 12.41 in 12.51, and therefore presumably before the insertion of 13.1-22) are additions.

There remain the plagues in 6.9–11.10. The opening scene 6.9-12 + 7.1-7, which prepares for the journey to Pharaoh and introduces Aaron, is supplemented in 6.13-30 by the genealogy which runs up to Moses and Aaron. The addition can be recognized by the anticipation of 7.1ff. in 6.13 and in the recapitulation of 6.9-12 in 6.26-30. The journey to Pharaoh begins with 7.8. A first demonstration miracle in 7.8-13 is followed by four plagues, all of which are constructed on the same model: (1) command: 'Yhwh said to Moses, Say to Aaron …'; (2) implementation: 'And they (Moses and/or Aaron) did likewise …'; (3) rivalry: 'And the Egyptian magicians did likewise', lastly 'could not do likewise'; (4) departure: 'And the heart of Pharaoh became hard (*ḥzq*, qal with the heart of Pharaoh, hiphil with Yhwh as subject), and he did not listen to them, as Yhwh had foretold to Moses.' The scheme begins like this or in a similar way in 7.19-22 (I. water into blood); 8.1-3, 11 (II. frogs); 8.12-15 (III. flies) and 9.8-12 (IV. boils). The last plague deviates somewhat; here Moses is actively involved and Yhwh hardens the heart. We must assume a disruption of the scheme in 8.11, where instead of the hardening (*ḥzq*), as in the non-Priestly plague the heart is made stubborn (*kbd*). The conclusion is formed by a retrospect on all the plagues in 11.10. This originally followed 9.12 immediately; with the reference to the exodus of the Israelites it leads towards 12.40f.

The Priestly plagues are assigned to the basic writing. What is surprising, though evidently it does not disturb any scholars, is the breadth of the narrative, to which only the programmatic leading texts of P and Gen. 23 are comparable. But the plagues are not among the leading theological texts. On the contrary, as in the non-Priestly text between Exod. 1–4 and 12–14 (see below), in P too they hold up the action. Because the Israelites do not listen to Moses, he is sent to Pharaoh, and when he protests, he is given Aaron to stand as a spokesman beside him. That only happens because Yhwh wants to harden Pharaoh's heart (*leb* + *qšh* hiphil!) in order to do his signs and wonders and to lead Israel up out of Egypt so that Egypt recognizes 'that I am Yhwh'. The first aim is thus not to lead Israel up out of Egypt but to demonstrate the power of Yhwh before and in Egypt. The motif, which also occurs in Exod. 14, takes the glory from the miracle by the sea, regardless of whether the glorification of Yhwh through the Egyptians here is original or not. And as soon as the plagues are over, Aaron disappears from the scene again and only appears once more where he belongs, in the cult on Sinai. All this nurtures the suspicion that the 'signs and wonders' (7.3; 11.10) are secondary (P^S). If we remove them, the announcement of 6.6[26] refers only to the exodus in 12.40f. and the miracle at the sea in Exod. 14.

It is hard to say whether any plagues at all are presupposed in the non-Priestly text, and if so, which. It is remarkable that in 7.14-25 and 7.26–8.11 P and the non-Priestly text are worked together and combined into one plague (cf. especially 8.11), whereas 8.12-15 (flies) are simply duplicated in 8.16-28 (mosquitoes) and 9.8-12 (boils) in 9.1-7 (pestilence), just as three further plagues attach themselves in 9.13–10.27, and in 11–13 the killing of the firstborn. On the basis of the architecture of the text one can easily come to think that all the non-Priestly plagues are post-Priestly.

4.5   The next stage after the exodus from Egypt in Exod. 1–14 P is Sinai: 'In the third month after the exodus of the Israelites from the land of Egypt, on that same day they arrived in the wilderness of Sinai' (19.1).

And the glory of Yhwh descended on Mount Sinai, and the cloud covered him for six days and on the seventh day he (Yhwh) called to Moses from the midst of the cloud ... And Moses went into the midst of the cloud and climbed the mountain. And Yhwh spoke to Moses ... (24.16-18a; 25.1ff.)

There follows the establishment of the cult, in which Yhwh's promise of Gen. 17 and Exod. 6.7 to be Israel's God, the covenant with Abraham, is confirmed: Exod. 25.1–29.46 + 40.16f., 34 (especially 25.8; 29.45f.; 40.34). Thus just as the creation ends in the covenant with Noah after the crisis of the flood, so the covenant with Abraham finds its goal after the crisis of the exodus in the Sinai cult

The itinerary in Exod. 16.1; 17.1, on which 19.2a is in turn dependent, and the narrative about the manna in Exod. 16, show Priestly influence. It is therefore assumed that 15.22aα, 27; 16.1; and parts of chs 16; 17.1abα; and 19.2a (before 19.1) stood in the Priestly Writing between 14.29 and 19.1. But this assumption reckons with a non-Priestly text: 15.22aα is the necessary presupposition for the non-Priestly note about the wandering in 15.22aβb and the episode of bitter water in Mara, 15.23-25a; the oasis of Elim in 15.27 is the counterpart to this and is attached to P only because it is used for 16.1. But that means that the itinerary in 16.1 and 17.1 which seems to be Priestly is in truth post-Priestly. It also explains the apparently senseless positioning of 19.2a after 19.1, which can only be removed if need be by a transposition. It goes back to the pre-Priestly itinerary which leads from 15.27 (Elim) through 16.1aα ('And they set out from Elim') to 19.2a ('And they arrived in the wilderness of Sinai'). Subsequently the itinerary of the Priestly Writing dated by the exodus (19.1 between 16.1aα and 19.2a) and on this occasion, or rather later, also the deviation from Elim into the wilderness of Sin in 16.1, which is formulated in Priestly style, an artificial intermediate stage on the way between Elim and Sinai with a derived date in the second month, and from the wilderness of Sin to Rephidim ('camping place') in 17.1; 19.2aα[1], have been inserted into this itinerary. The same must also hold for the narrative about the manna and the narrative material in Exod. 17–18. The only passage that I think can already have been inserted in the pre-Priestly text between 16.1aα and 19.2a is the literary core of Exod. 16, the discovery of the manna in 16.(4a,) 13b-15, 21, 31,[27] that is, on the way from Elim into the wilderness. This has been done in order to supplement the motif of providing water with the motif of providing food. The motif of murmuring (16.2f., 6-13a, 32-36) taken from 15.24 and the sabbath (16.4b-5, 16-20, 22-30) presuppose the Priestly Writing; the duplication and heightening of the murmuring and the miracle of the water in 17.1-7, along with the battle with Amalek in 17.8-16, presuppose the itinerary formulated in the style of the Priestly Writing in 17.1; and the midrashic appendix in Exod. 18 anticipates the arrival at the mountain of God (18.5).

5.   Result

With a few exceptions, the elements of the Priestly stratum in Gen. 1–Exod. 40 form a consecutive, complete narrative thread. Much suggests that this is an independent writing and not a stratum of the redaction. There is both the literary context and also the well-arranged, systematic construction, and not least the cumbersome nature of the programmatic leading texts in P, which can only be smoothed out in a makeshift way alongside the non-Priestly doublets: Gen. 1 alongside Gen. 2–3; Gen. 5 alongside Gen. 4; Gen. 6–9 and 11.10ff. alongside the non-Priestly parts in Gen. 6–9 and 10–11; Gen. 17 alongside Gen. 12; Exod. 6 alongside Exod. 3–4; the Priestly plagues in and alongside the non-Priestly plagues in Exod. 7–9; the miracle by the sea in Exod. 14; the Sinai pericope in Exod. 19.1 + 24.16-18a + 25-29 + 40 alongside Exod. 19–24 and 32–34. All this indicates that this an independent writing and not a stratum of the redaction. And even in the case of the few exceptions, the births in Gen. 16; 21 and 25 and the gap between Jacob's departure for Paddan-Aram in 27.46–28.9 and his return in Gen. 31.18; 33.18; 35.6, 9ff., which look most like a stratum of revision, one can manage without assuming the loss of text.

The alternative 'source or redaction?' is difficult to resolve with a relief description which wants to find in P both a revision stratum which is internally consistent and a systematic construction. But the alternative is made less stark by the fact that P knows the non-Priestly text of the patriarchal history and the exodus narrative including the Sinai pericope, uses it as the basis for its own disposition, and also presupposes the knowledge in its readers. P is related to its basic material as Chronicles is to Samuel–Kings.

There are no other basic materials or sources which have found their way into P. Because of the characteristic language and thought world of P, the search for them is understandable, but in vain. Here and there, for example, in Gen. 1 and Gen. 6–9, we have merely additional tradition of which P took note in the new version of his basic material. By contrast, at many points indications of later work within the Priestly Writing have arisen which suggest a differentiation between P^G and P^S in Genesis–Exodus as well. In addition there are texts which have the flavour of P but presuppose the link between P and the non-Priestly textual material (R^P); here the boundaries between P^S and R^S are fluid.

As for the dating and context of P^G in literary and theological history, since Wellhausen, scholars have been agreed on an exilic/post-exilic date. P presupposes a non-Priestly primal history and patriarchal narrative and a non-Priestly exodus narrative which are brought together into a coherent connection; whether this is done in accordance with the original stratum or for the first time remains to be seen. Moreover P presupposes Deuteronomy and the First Commandment. The single place of worship and the one and unique God are regarded as demonstrated and take on a new theological focus. The Sinai and Moab covenants are replaced with the Noah covenant with the world and the Abraham covenant with Israel, which, as well as the traditional promises of blessing (Gen. 12) and land (Gen. 12.7 or Exodus–Joshua) that also apply to humankind in the Noah covenant and the subsidiary lines of Abraham, concentrates on the promise made only to Abraham, Isaac and Jacob/Israel that Yhwh will be God and on the relationship between Yhwh and Israel (cf. Deut. 26.17-19), binding this promise to the cult established on Sinai. For this reason the basic writing of P abbreviates the narrative of the Hexateuch and deletes the way from Sinai into the land. In contrast, the establishment of the covenant is moved far back into the patriarchal period, and the covenant with humankind is put before the covenant with Israel. The nearness of this concept to Second Isaiah needs to be noted in the dating. All this points to a time close to the Second Temple, the foundation legend of which is contained in P; this has the character of both confirmation and, like Zech. 1–6 and Ezek. 40–48, a programme. The programme certainly does not belong to the initial hopes in the exilic period, but like the universal concept of the Priestly creation story presupposes the Persian period and the constitution of the province of Judah within the safer limits of the Persian empires which is taking shape. I therefore think it very probable that P^G should be put in the time around 500 BC (in Jerusalem).

Notes

1. Formerly 'Jehovist', in accordance with the reading of the tetragrammaton then current. Wellhausen gave the designation new content and understood by it the combination of the Yahwist and Elohist (the consonants of Yhwh with the vowels of Elohim).
2. Formerly (earlier) Elohist or basic writing (*Grundschrift*, thus still Nöldeke); in Wellhausen Q for *quatuor* = *liber quatuor foederum*, 'Book of Four Covenants' or 'Priestly Codex' for the Book of the Four Covenants supplemented with the law.
3. *Comp.*, 315; cf. ibid., 207.
4. Ibid., 207.
5. Eissfeldt, *The Old Testament: An Introduction*, Oxford 1965, 169.
6. Noth, *Pentateuch*, 17-19, 28-32, 35-36 and 38-41.
7. Gunkel, *Genesis*, HK I/1, [3]1910.
8. Von Rad, 'The Form-Critical Problem of the Hexateuch' (1938), in *The Problem of the Hexateuch and Other Essays*, Edinburgh 1966, 1-78.
9. Cf. Noth, *Pentateuch*, 11 n. 23, according to which P is said to have knowledge of the traditions but not the literary versions of J and E.
10. In some respects identical with the (late) Yahwist in van Seters, the D composition in Blum, $J^s + R^s$ in Levin; for the settlement see Mowinckel.
11. The following information is provisionally given after Noth, *Pentateuch*, 17f.
12. The figures in Gen. 5.1ff.; 11.10ff.; 21.5; 25.26; 47.28; and Exod. 12.40f.; 40.17 are a key factor. Alongside this there is a multiplicity of subordinate or secondary datings.
13. Gen. 1.7, 9, 11, 15, 24, 30, in the Septuagint v. 6 instead of v. 7 and additionally v. 20.
14. Gen. 1.4, 10, 12, 18, 21, 25, 31, in the Septuagint also v. 8.
15. Gen. 1.5, 8, 13, 19, 23, 31; 2.2-3.
16. W.H. Schmidt, *Die Schöpfungsgeschichte der Priesterschrift*, WMANT 17, 1964, [3]1973; O.H. Steck, *Der Schöpfungsbericht der Priesterschrift*, FRLANT 115, 1975, [2]1981.
17. For the theme see M. Köckert, 'Leben in Gottes Gegenwart: Zum Verständnis des Gesetzes in der priesterschriftlichen Literatur', *JBTh* 4, 1989, 29-61.
18. Strictly speaking, Gen. 9.28f. does not correspond with 7.6 either, depending on whether one counts from the beginning or from the end.
19. Thus Levin, *Jahwist*, 150, 172, 200.
20. Thus Blum, *Komposition*, 66f., 279f., 315f., 432ff. Levin's analysis is the strongest argument for Blum.
21. In 27.1 Esau is introduced as the elder son, and in 27.5ff. Jacob is introduced separately as the son of Rebecca and brother of Esau.
22. Without the 'again' in v. 9, which refers back to Gen. 28 and is to be attributed to R. Verses 35.14f., which Noth distributes between E and P, both presuppose 35.9-13.
23. Gen. 48.3-7, which is usually assigned to P, presuppose the non-Priestly text in v. 5 (41.50-52) and v. 7 (35.16-19).
24. Verses 1-4, 8-9 (either vv. 8a, 9b, or just v. 9, the rest expanded), 15-18 (in v. 15 with 'what are you crying to me'), 21aα^1b ('And Moses stretched out his hand over the sea ... and the water divided'), 22-23, 26, 27, 28aα^1 ('And Moses stretched out his

hand over the sea'), 28, 29. The features of the demonstrative miracle (vv. 3-4, 8, 17-18) have presumably been added; they have points of contact with the plagues in Exod. 6.9–11.10. Moreover vv. 23-29 are doubtful, as the announcement of 14.16 is fulfilled in 14.21, 22 and 14.29 is a recapitulation of v. 22.

25 The announcement of 12.1-28 goes into thin air without any account of its being carried out – which is non-Priestly.

26 Perhaps still without the 'great judgments', which could refer to the killing of the firstborn in 12.12. Perhaps the 'outstretched arm' is also secondary. In the tradition it is associated with the Exodus; in 7.5 it is the outstretched hand, but in the plagues and in Exod. 14 only Aaron or Moses stretch out their hands.

27 For analysis see the clarifications of Levin, *Jahwist*, 352-5.

II. The Non-Priestly Narrative

1. Survey

Literature as for I.1 above.

1.1   After removing the Priestly Writing, the legal parts in Exod. 19–24; 32–34 and Deuteronomy, we come upon the non-Priestly narrative of the Hexateuch. The beginning is formed by the history of humankind, which, hardly having been created, comes under the curse of Yhwh and is dispersed over the earth (Gen. 2–11). From the dispersal of humankind Yhwh selects a clan, Abraham, leads it into the promised land and lays his blessing on it (Gen. 12.1ff.). Lot, the father of Ammon and Moab, comes from the same clan (Gen. 12–13; 18–19). Ishmael (Gen. 16; and 21) and Isaac (Gen. 21) and some Arab tribes, the sons of Keturah (Gen. 25.1-6), emerge from Abraham; Esau-Edom and Jacob-Israel (Gen. 25–33), the father of Judah (Gen. 29.35), emerge from Isaac. The Aramaeans Nahor, Bethuel and Laban are also related to Abraham. The wives of Isaac (Gen. 24) and Jacob-Israel (Gen. 29–30) come from them. Only with the Philistine Abimelech of Gerar is the relationship not one of kin but an alliance by treaty. Thus after his return from Aramaean ḥārān, Jacob-Israel lives in the promised land under the blessing of Yhwh, surrounded by his more or less close relations. Here Rachel gives him a last son, Benjamin, and is carried to the grave (Gen. 35). Joseph, the beloved son of Jacob-Israel, is sold by his brothers into Egypt, where he survives, to the happy surprise of his father (Gen. 37–45). Jacob-Israel goes after him and dies in Egypt (Gen. 45–50). Yhwh leads the people of Israel out from there under the leadership of Moses, a man of levitical descent (Exod. 1–14). After a victorious battle against the pursuing Egyptians and the song of Miriam (Exod. 15.20f.), the people go through the wilderness and make a stop in Kadesh, where Miriam dies (Exod. 15.22a; Num. 20.1aβb). Israel goes past Edom and through the middle of the territory of the Amorites into Transjordan, to Moab, and camps in Shittim opposite Jericho. There Moses dies (Num. 25.1a + Deut. 34.5f.). From Shittim the people cross the Jordan under the leadership of Joshua the son of Nun, occupy Jericho and Ai and possess the whole land (Josh. 2–12).

1.2   Reduced to the basic framework of the action, what has just been described presents itself in the text as a quite complicated web of individual narratives and collections of narratives which have very different literary and theological stamps. It is here that the most difficult problem of Pentateuchal or Hexateuchal analysis lies. On the presupposition of the source theory, the whole mass of text must be distributed between several parallel narrative works: the Yahwist (J), the Elohist (E) and the Jehovist (JE), which combines the written two sources – that is, if we do not reckon with yet other editions or written sources. The procedure for demarcating the variety of written sources and editions – which have been preserved only in fragments – is that of subtraction. As we have been able to see so far, this process is intrinsically not the worst, but one must know something about at least one of two or more entities to be able to subtract. However, in the case of J, E and JE we do not know that, since all three are hypothetical entities, which moreover in the case of J and E are more or less fragmentary. Still, they are fragmentary only because it is thought necessary to distribute the JE material which remains between the two hypothetical sources after taking away the clearly identifiable P stratum. So in this case we have a vicious circle.

In more recent research this dilemma is coped with in two ways. Some regard the whole non-Priestly text (classical JE) as more or less a unity; here basically it does not matter whether one sees it principally as the (late) 'Yahwist' or a pre-Priestly D composition with a Deuteronomic-Deuteronomistic stamp, or recognizes the 'final redactor' (R) in each and everything. Others reduce the text to a minimum in which they find a(n early) Yahwist, a proto-Yahwist or the sources of the Yahwist and the Yahwistic redaction, but distribute the bulk of the text between pre- and post-Priestly, final-redactional and post-final-redactional elaborations. Both variants presuppose the preliminary view of source division, and work with observations on texts which are considered after the process of subtracting J or E or JE. Moreover the classical analyses from Wellhausen to Noth offer abundant food for both assumptions, for the 'kerygma of the Yahwist' which can be rediscovered in the texts, taken up into a lexicon of the Yahwist (and his supplementer, that is, the Jehovist), and used as a positive criterion or literary identification of the Yahwist, and likewise for the kerygma of a late-Yahwistic, Deuteronomistic or final redactional (formerly Jehovistic) redaction, which in any case is thought to be sufficient in the sphere of Exodus–Numbers.

As so often, the solution lies in reconciling the extremes. There is only one way of escaping the circle of the source hypothesis: it has to be abandoned. But that in no way means that the whole of Pentateuchal research so far has to be thrown overboard and the non-Priestly text has to be taken simply as it has been transmitted. On the contrary, all the observations and literary-historical differentiations which have been made under the influence of the source hypothesis continue to be right. But they must not be forced into the strait-jacket of the source hypothesis, which is useful for explaining the literary composition of the Priestly and non-Priestly text, but fails in the non-Priestly text. As is confirmed by many more recent works, whether these adopt a literary-critical and redaction-historical approach or a composition-historical approach, a combination of modified fragmentary and supplementary hypotheses is of much more use than a mechanical division of sources.[1] As in the books of Joshua–Kings with a Deuteronomistic revision, the composition is made up of individual elements of the tradition. These are the 'main themes of the tradition', the 'filling out of the framework given thematically with narrative material' and the 'growing together of the themes and individual traditions' investigated by Noth and explained in terms of tradition history. However, we have only to translate the process into literary categories, and change the order, and we come upon more or less firmly sketched, self-contained original stratum which has found its way into a basic document and there has been combined redactionally into a literary and narrative complex, then successively expanded and developed. In this process we have to reckon with pre- and post-Priestly and pre- and post-Deuteronomistic supplements and developments.

The composition of the individual parts which did not originally stand in any context is based on a redactional plan. Whether this plan a priori foresaw the whole narrative of the Tetrateuch (Genesis–Numbers) or Hexateuch (Genesis–Joshua), or developed out of small units cannot simply be presupposed by the criterion of P and the finished Pentateuch, but must be examined independently of the prior views of the source hypothesis. We can learn from the history of research that the earlier assumption of the Hexateuch was abandoned because Wellhausen and finally Noth already found the sources – with certainty really only P, and by forcing them into a system also JE – simply and solely in Genesis–Numbers. If we drop the 'JE game', the possibility (again) arises of taking note of the narrative complexes and the factors in the text which scholars have often observed but have neglected in favour of the source hypothesis, the striking break between Genesis and Exodus, and the Hexateuchal narrative thread from the exodus from Egypt to the settlement (Exodus–Joshua). Likewise we are free to take the criteria for distinguishing tradition, basic writing and elaboration from the texts themselves and their compositional architecture. If in many cases this leads to an agreement with the demarcation of the text by source division that is no bad thing; on the contrary, it represents a fine confirmation. The abandonment of the source hypothesis by no means makes literary criticism superfluous, but literary criticism does not necessary lead to the source hypothesis.

2.   The primal history

2.1   The non-Priestly primal history is composed of the following ingredients: (1) the creation and fall of the human being (Gen. 2–3); (2) Cain and Abel and the cultural development of humankind (Gen. 4); (3) the Flood (Gen. 6–8); (4) Noah, the vintner (Gen. 9.18-27); (5) the table of nations (Gen. 10); (6) the tower of Babel (Gen. 11.1-9).

A well-arranged layout has been discovered in this. In it various narratives about the sin and punishment of the human being are put in a ring around a core, the account of the flood. Thus before and after the flood Gen. 2–3 and 11.1-9; Gen. 4 and 10; Gen. 6.1-4; and 9.18-27 correspond. It is hard to say what the circular layout means. A brake is put on the much quoted avalanche of sin[2] by the flood and it is difficult to understand how after Yhwh's intervention and the promise in 8.21f. the sin can continue to take its course as if nothing had happened. That is one of the reasons why recently scholars have made the primal history end with Yhwh's theological statement about himself in 8.20-22, and in Gen. 9–11 want to find only P and post-Priestly additions.

Wellhausen's observation[3] that there are passages in the primal history which know nothing of the flood leads in another direction. Wellhausen reckons that these are Gen. 2–3; 4.16-24; and 11.1-9. But the same is also true of 4.1-15; 6.1-4; and 9.20-27. This phenomenon cannot be explained by the independent prehistory of the material alone, since the narratives are all related to one another. However, in the flood story the position is that especially the constitutive frameworks in 6.5-8; and 8.20-22 know about the other narrative, but these do not know about the flood.

In addition, there is the strange situation that the narratives in Gen. 2–4; 9.20-27 and 11.1-9 have been preserved complete, but the flood in 5.29 and 6–8 and according to the usual source division also the table of nations in Gen. 10 (vv. 8-19, 21, 25-30) only fragmentarily. To explain the situation by a combination of the two source writings does not explain why one procedure was adopted in one case and another in another. To mention an opposite example: in Exod. 14 both versions have been worked together completely.

The theological interpretation of the flood story in the two framework pieces 6.5-8 and 8.20-22 is also substantially different from the tendency of the narratives which frame them. The usual interpretation of the whole primal history as an almost Pauline-sounding doctrinal passage about the anthropological constitution of human beings generally is based on the framework passages round the flood. The narratives also have their anthropology; not, however, that of the Pauline doctrine of sin but of a humankind which is differentiated into various groups of tribes and peoples, of the kind that one also finds in the patriarchal history.

All this indicates that it is not the continuation of 8.20-22 in Gen. 9.18–11.9 but the flood in Gen. 6–8 which represents an alien body in the framework of the non-Priestly primal history. Here as in the Priestly Writing it is bound up with Noah and his sons. Thus in the non-Priestly text the other traditions of Noah and his sons in 9.20-27 and Gen. 10 compete. Noah can be original in only one of these traditions. Presumably he became the hero of the flood on the basis of Gen. 9–10,[4] both in P and also in the fragments in Gen. 6–8, which fall outside the context of the non-Priestly primal history. Consequently we must distinguish two versions of the primal history, one which did not yet contain the flood (Gen. 2–4 + 9–22), and one in which it was added later, either before or after the Priestly version, in which the flood plays a key role.

2.2   A remarkable ambivalence runs through the first section of the primal history, Gen. 2–4. On the one hand it narrates, not without pride, the creation of the human being, his procreation and his cultural progress; on the other the upward development of the human being is disrupted by an increasing alienation from God, for which human sin is responsible. This brings with it the curse of Yhwh and the expulsion of human beings eastwards from the garden in Eden. As has long been known, the ambivalence lies in the use of earlier material. Whereas the earlier material discovered the initial divine ordering of things and human cultural process in the toil of everyday life, the revision made the toil of life the theme and derived it from the connection between sin and punishment and the will of Yhwh.

In Gen. 2–3 the distinction between tradition and redaction follows from a quite simple observation. The well-composed narrative consists of two narrative threads: the creation story in Gen. 2 with an end in 3.20f., and the paradise story in Gen. 3 with the precondition in Gen. 2.9, 16f. Of these only the creation story can have existed by itself; the paradise story is dependent on it and not viable without it. Consequently in the creation story (2.5, 7a,[5] 8, 19a, 20a, 21-22 + 3.20f.[6]) we have a basic stratum, and in the paradise story (2.9abβ, 16-17,[7] 25; 3.6-13a, 16, 17-19a) a first revision. The basic stratum and the revision stratum were subsequently glossed abundantly.

The original creation story deals with the foundations of life: Adam ('ādām) is made from the ground ("ᵃdāmāh) and is there to till it; Eva (ḥawwāh), the mother of all that lives (ḥay), is made in order to ensure the procreation of the human being as distinct from the animals. The revision puts the existing tradition in a new context and makes the foundations of human life disastrous for men and women. The curse affects both the ground and giving birth. Both are to cause human beings toil; birth becomes a torment and work on the field forced labour – not, as in the ancient Near

Eastern tradition, for the service of the gods, but something caused by the God Yhwh. The curse also affects the close relationship between man and woman (3.16b, 17a) which results from the creation (2.21f.) and is really intended in 2.18, 20b, 23f. (subsequently). In particular it becomes a bane for the woman, as the ground does for the man. Death waits at the end, and the human being returns to the ground. The occasion for the curse is the divine prohibition against eating the fruits of the tree of the knowledge of good and evil. Without knowing it, the first couple transgress the prohibition, lose their childlike naivety and achieve awareness. Thus what causes human beings to know what furthers life and what is a hindrance to them is put in an unfavourable light and is dependent on Yhwh's care and blessing. Later theologians have connected this state with human hybris and as a result have banished the human being from paradise and refused him eternal life.[8] In so doing they are reacting to the good order of Gen. 1 (1, 26f., 31) and blaming human beings for the divine judgment of the flood in Gen. 6–9. That presupposes the combination of the basic writing and the revision in Gen. 2–3 with the Priestly Writing. Genesis 2.4b is the redactional hinge which dovetails Gen. 1 with Gen. 2–3.[9]

The same textual stratigraphy – a basic stratum, a first revision and additions – also occurs in the following chapter, Gen. 4. The basic stratum consists of the cultural historical genealogy of the Cainites in 4.1abα, 17-22, and continues the creation story of Gen. 2.5–3.21: Adam, the farmer, and Eve, the mother of all things living (all human beings), produce Cain, and the rest of humankind proceeds from him, those who live in cities and tents and all the itinerant professions. The genealogy is not viable in itself, but together with the creation story in 2.5–3.21 forms a closed narrative complex, a kind of anthropogony. Cain's murder of his brother Abel, whose name 'breath') is his fate, has been inserted in 4.1-16 (more precisely vv. 1bβ, 2-5, 8-12, 16). Like the paradise narrative in Gen. 3, the narrative is not independent, and in other respects too it recalls the revision stratum in Gen. 2–3. Genesis 4.2 takes the cultivation of the ground from Gen. 2–3 and the rearing of cattle from 4.20, constructs an artificial opposition between them, and thus anticipates the differentiation of forms of life in 4.17ff. The action is quickly told: the conviction of the perpetrator and the pronouncing of the curse resemble Yhwh's dialogue with Adam and Eve in 3.9-13a and the cursing in 3.16-19. However, the curse goes very much wider: after the ground in Gen. 3, now the person himself is cursed and driven out from the cultivated soil to the land of Nod, east of Eden (2.8), where Adam, Eve and Cain have been living hitherto.[10] The fratricide and the cursing of Cain draw after them the development of the genealogy in 4.25f. Seth ('substitute') and Enosh ('man') are born as a substitute for Abel, and with them the history of humankind makes a new beginning. The beginning of the worship of Yhwh coincides with them. 4.1-16, 25f. thus proves to be a revision of the basic document in 4.1, 17-22, which puts the cultural development of the Cainites in a bad light. Like the basic stratum, the revision in Gen. 2–4 also lies on the same level. And just as in Gen. 2–3, in Gen. 4 a series of additions is made (4.6-7, 13-15, 23-24) which interpret the event theologically and, as the expression 'bear the blame' (cf. for example, Lev. 5.1; 7.18; 17.16, etc.) or the protecting sign (cf. Exod. 12.13) show, presuppose the Priestly Writing.

Thus three literary levels can be distinguished in Gen. 2–4.

1. The original anthropogony, which narrates the origin and cultural progress of Cainite humanity: 2.5, 7a, 8, 19a, 20a, 21-22; 3.20f.; 4.1abα, 17-22.
2. A revision stratum which brings the curse upon humankind and makes survival dependent on relationship to Yhwh: 2.9abβ, 16-17, (18, 20b, 23f.,) 25; 3.6-13a, 16-19a; 4.1bβ, 2-5, 8-12, 16, 25-26. On the basis of its interest in Yhwh and the worship of Yhwh (4.25f.) it can be called the 'Yahwistic' revision or the 'Yahwist' (J).
3. Mixed expansions to the basic Yahwistic stratum (J^G), which lie partly before (J^S), but for the most part after the origin and incorporation of the Priestly Writing (P + J = R^{PJ}).

2.3   The natural continuation of the anthropogony of Gen. 2–4 lies in Gen. 9–11. Humankind comes into being in the east (2.8; 4.16), and 'from the East' it sets out westwards (11.2). If we rid ourselves of prior exegetical judgments and reduce the text to its basic material, the hinge that holds the two parts together can be found in 6.1, 4aβb: after the new beginning of humankind and the beginning of the Yhwh cult in 4.25f., humankind begins to increase on the soil, and daughters are born to it who give birth to the heroes of prehistoric times, 'men of name'. Terminologically the passage refers back to 4.26 and points beyond the flood to Noah and his sons in Gen. 9–11, especially to Shem (*šem*, 'name'), the ancestor of the Hebrews, and the God of Shem ('God of the name') in 9.26f., to the role of the 'name' in 11.4 (and 12.1-3), the hero Nimrod in 10.8f., and the further 'beginnings' in 9.20; 10.8; and 11.6. The close connections suggest that the multiplication became the occasion for the flood only at a second stage, as in the Mesopotamian tradition (thus also P in Gen. 5 + 6.9ff.). The additions in 6.2, 3-4a which make the multiplication a transition provide an additional motive.

Noah and his sons emerge from the multiplication or, if we do not want to follow the interpretation of Gen. 6.1-4 proposed, from the new beginning of humankind in 4.25f. In contrast to Gen. 5 (P), no continuous genealogical thread is spun from Enosh (4.26) to Noah in 6.5–9.18; 9.19, 20ff. The note in 5.29b (from 'in speaking') which is always used in connection with this,

and which besides is separated by 6.1-4 from its closest point of reference in
6.5-8, is an addition to P: a mere reference to the Priestly Writing is not
sufficient argument that the non-Priestly text must also have contained a
similar genealogy. Here as also in other passages of the pre-Priestly
'Yahwistic' narrative the redactional seams can still be seen very much more
clearly than in the Priestly Writing, which, as we can see specifically from
the genealogy constructed from Gen. 4, is fond of smoothing over difficult
transitions.

Three passages come under consideration for the literary link to 4.25f. or
6.1, 4aβb: 9.18, 19, 20. Of these, 9.18 presupposes the flood and is a
transition to vv. 20-27. Verse 19 is a new beginning and points forward to
the table of nations in Gen. 10 structured by the three sons of Noah. Verses
20-27 have been inserted between v. 19 and the table of nations in 10.2ff. As
the table of nations in Gen. 10 is normally attributed to the Priestly Writing,
we would have to see 9.19 as a post-Priestly addition between v. 18 and vv.
20-27. But the addition would be quite superfluous and out of place.
Rather, on the basis of the architecture of the text the relationship has to be
reversed. It is not 9.19 but (6.5-)9, 18 and 9.20-27 that seem to have been
inserted. Moreover the assignation of Gen. 10 to P already proved
problematic for intrinsic reasons. If we leave out the secondary framework
formulae in 10.1, 32, which pick up 9.19 after 9.20-27 and 9.28f., there is
nothing against assigning 9.19^{11} + 10.2-31 to the non-Priestly text.[12] Here
the table of nations forms the original continuation of the anthropogony in
Gen. 2–4 and represents the earliest Noah tradition, on which the account
of the flood and Noah the vintner depend. For only in the table of nations in
Gen. 10 is the fact that Noah has three sons determinative; it plays no role
at all in Gen. 6–8 and in 9.20-27 disturbs the dualism intended.

As in Gen. 2–4, so too in Gen. 9.19 + 10.2-31 it is possible to distinguish
a basic stratum, a first revision and supplements. The basic stratum consists
of the scheme of the three sons of Noah to which 9.19 is the heading: 10.2-5
(the sons of Japhet); 10.6-7, 20 (the sons of Ham); 10.22-23, 31 (the sons of
Shem). This is an independent source, to some degree a subsidiary tradition
to the anthropogony in Gen. 2–4 but originally having no kind of literary
connection with the basic material of Gen. 2–4.

The connection is first made by the supplements in 10.8-19, 21, 24-30,
which are completely independent and therefore do not belong to any
source, and the development of Gen. 10 in 11.1-9. The expansions are not
all on the same level. The first revision embraces some material in ch. 10,
for example, 10.8f., 21, 24f. and the basic material of 11.1-9 (vv. 2-5, 6a,
8a);[13] the rest is the result of later expansions. The original stratum in 11.1-
9 takes up the motif of 'dispersion' in 9.19 and explains the ordering of the
geography of the table of nations implied in the names of 10.2-31. It is not
at all surprising that 11.1-9 stands after Gen. 10. In the eyes of the reviser

the 'dispersion' announced in Gen. 10 has not yet taken place. The names merely indicate the direction in which the dispersion narrated in Gen. 11 is moving. At the same time, in this way the ancient tradition is given a new interpretation. Yhwh, who gives the heroes their fame (10.8f.) and does not allow humankind to make a 'name' for itself (11.4), is responsible for the dispersal of humankind. Like the anthropogony in Gen. 2–4, here the geography is overshadowed by the theological judgment. As the revision also has linguistic points of contact with the revision in Gen. 2–4 and continues the narrative thread of 2.8; 4.16 in 11.2, it is reasonable to suppose that this is one and the same 'Yahwistic' revision (J^G) which developed and combined the two independent traditions in Gen. 2–4 and 9.19 + Gen. 10. The revision, which puts the history of the cultural development of humankind under the curse and Yhwh's power, continues in 12.1-3, 7, where one person from the human world dispersed over the earth by Yhwh is given the blessing, a great name and a new dwelling-place among the clans of the cultivated ground. Thus the goal of the first revision in Gen. 2–4 and 9.19 + 10-11 is the key text which has always been regarded as the programme of the 'Yahwist'.

The post-Yahwistic expansions in Gen. 9–11 embrace the additions in 10–19, 26–30 (further peoples) and 11.1, 6, 7, 8b-9 (confusion of languages and aetiology of the name Babel), and the passage 9.20-27, which has inserted itself between 9.19 and the table of nations in Gen. 10.[14] Whether the supplements came into the text before (J^S) or after the incorporation of the Priestly writing (R^{PJ}) into the text cannot easily be decided. 11.6b recalls the 'post-Priestly' motive of the hybris of the human being in Gen. 3, and despite the evident points of context with texts of the Yahwistic redaction, I do not think it improbable that 9.20-27, too, is of post-Priestly origin. The land of Canaan and the contrast between Canaan (Hamites) and Israel (Semites) play virtually no role in the non-Priestly writing, but play a central role in the thought of the Priestly Writing, which defines the Abraham covenant by the genealogy (cf. Gen. 17), and elsewhere in late-Deuteronomistic thought. Moreover, only in the Priestly Writing is Abraham also explicitly a descendent of Shem (11.10-26). Furthermore, the motif of the curse, which is taken from Gen. 2–4 and looks like a resumption after the incorporation of the flood, has quite a different function. The blessing of Noah in 9.26f. anticipates the focus of the curses in Gen. 2–4, the blessing of Yhwh in 12.1-3.

2.4   The non-Yahwistic expansions also include the non-Priestly account of the flood in Gen. 6–9,[15] which has inserted itself between Gen. 2–4 + 6.1, 4aβb and 9.19 + 10–11. It is not, as one often reads, complete, but has been preserved only in fragments. There is no announcement of the flood, no command to build the ark and no account of how Noah and his family enter the ark and go out of it again (cf. 9.18 after 8.20-21). The shutting up of the ark (7.16b) occurs after the coming of the rain and flood in 7.10, 12. The formulations resemble those of the Priestly Writing, often word for word. The explanation of this depends on whether one wants to discover in the non-Priestly fragments at any price an independent narrative thread cannibalized by R according to criteria which are not easy to see, or, as in comparable cases,[16] one takes them all as what they are: supplementary passages to presupposed basic material, here the Priestly account of the flood (R^{PJ}).[17]

The supplementary hypothesis proves itself admirably where the non-Priestly text is apparently complete, in the prologue and epilogue to the flood in 6.5-8 and 8.20-22, according to the source hypothesis an independent doublet to the Priestly framework in 6.9-13; and 9.1-17. If we look more closely, it becomes clear that this is by no means a doublet; rather, the formulations are dependent on the Priestly framework. Genesis 6.5-8 and 8.21f. interpret the event exclusively in a statement which Yhwh himself makes. If the announcement to Noah in 6.13ff., 9.1ff. did not also follow, Noah would know nothing of all this and could not be saved. The non-Priestly pieces of framework are theological reflections in the sense of the word; they explain the flood in terms of the wickedness inherent in the human being (from Gen. 2–4 and 6.1-4) and derive the resolve and removal of the event in P from reflections in God's heart about the human heart.[18]

The other pieces of text which are assigned to a separate source only for the love of theory can be read in a very much less forced way as supplements. There is nothing at all in them to indicate 'the Yahwist'. Genesis 7.1-5 follows the notice about the carrying out of Yhwh's intention in 6.22 and adds details to the commands which have already been given and carried out in 6.13-22. With regard to the sacrifice in 8.20, the animals are differentiated into clean and unclean and their number is increased. Instead of a pair of each animal Noah is to take one pair of each of the unclean animals and seven pairs of the clean animals with him, an interpretation of 6.19f. Noah has time for this, since he is given a reprieve of seven days. After that it will rain for forty days and forty nights. The counting by days converges with 7.24 and 8.3b (P); the aim is simply to make the 'windows of heaven' (P) in 7.11b, 12 and 8.2a, b specific. Genesis 7.1b recalls 6.9; 7.5 is a resumption of 6.22.

On the basis of the new modalities the original report of the causing of the flood in 7.7, 14-16a is duplicated by the insertion of 7.8-12, 13, 16b, 17a and thus assimilated to 7.1-5. The mixture of 'Yahwistic' and Priestly language in these verses has always been striking, and this is a very simple explanation, as it is for the position of 7.16, since, as the supplementer understands it, the process of entering the ark is completed only in 7.16. The duplication of the whole process is connected with the introduction of the numbering of the days in 7.4, 10, 12, 17. Genesis 7.7-12 report everything in order; vv. 13(-16a), 16b, 17 once again state that everything takes place within the correct framework, indicated by Yhwh in 7.4 and scrupulously observed in 7.7-12.

Genesis 7.22f. inserts itself into the chain of glosses of 7.17-24; v. 17b depends on 17a and as a presupposition for v. 18 first has the ark raised from the earth. Verse 19 heightens v. 18 and adds the mountains (cf. 8.4f.), v. 20 the measurements and v. 24 the days. In the same style, 7.22f. supplement the announcement of destruction in v. 21 and in terminology take up Gen. 2–3; however, they also use Priestly terminology (for example, 7.15). According to the Massoretic vocalization in v. 23 God is the subject, and the exception of Noah and those 'who are with him' is once again stated specifically.

In 8.6f., 8-12, twice the experiment with a bird is added: first the raven, the third bird after the dove and swallow in the eleventh tablet of the Gilgamesh epic,[19] and after it three times the dove; both are appropriately inserted between the settling of the ark in 8.4 and the command to get out in 8.15ff. P does not give the experiment, but would certainly not have omitted it had it already had the non-Priestly text. In general, it is striking that the Priestly account of the flood is closer to the earlier versions of the Mesopotamian tradition, the Sumerian tablet of the flood and the Atrahasis epic, whereas the non-Priestly parts of the text add details from the version of the Gilgamesh epic: the counting of the days, the closing of the ark, the rain, the experiment with the birds, the sacrifice. That is hardly fortuitous, especially when we reflect that the serpent, the 'being like God' associated with it and the motif of 'eternal life' in Gen. 3, all in post-Priestly additions, recall the epic of Gilgamesh and especially the eleventh tablet. After their deliverance, Utnapishtim, the hero of the flood, and his wives will 'be like us gods' and live in Paradise, 'in the distance at the mouth of the rivers'; the serpent steals from Gilgamesh the herb of eternal life. The late additions in particular often draw on old tradition.

The sacrifice in 8.20 also comes from this tradition; the redaction of Yhwh in 8.21f. is related to 9.1-17 as 6.5-8 is related to 6.9-13. Genesis 9.28f. once followed 9.1-17 in P. With 9.18a (+ 'those who went out of the ark'), 19, the flood is given a conclusion of its own which refers back to 5.32 and 6.9f., and thus also integrates the non-Priestly text of 6.1-8. At the same time it is a transition to the conclusion of the toledot of Noah in 9.28f. 9.18b prepares in 9.18-19 for the insertion of 9.20-27. The table of nations in 10.2-31, isolated from 9.19, is instead given a new framework in 10.1, 32, following the Priestly toledot formula.

All the non-Priestly additions in Gen. 6–9 are not only post-Yahwistic but also post-Priestly, that is, they presuppose the combination of Priestly and pre-Priestly, 'Yahwistic' primal history; moreover they were not all introduced all at once but gradually.

2.5 Summary. Two related but independent traditions about the beginnings of humankind are the basis of the primal history: the Cainite anthropogony in Gen. 2.5–4.22 and the Noachite table of nations in Gen. 9.(18a,) 19 + 10.2-31. They have been combined by a first revision and interpreted throughout in such a way that the development of human culture depends on Yhwh and comes under Yhwh's curse because of mistakes made by human beings. We can call this revision the 'Yahwistic' revision and identify it with the traditional Yahwist (J). The Yahwistic primal history in Gen. 2.5–4.26 + 6.1, 4aβb + 9 (18a,) 19 + 10.2-31 + 11.2-8a was the basis for the Priestly primal history (P). In Gen. 1 this imitated in its own way the creation narrative of Gen. 2–3, in Gen. 5 the Cainite genealogy of Gen. 4, in Gen. 11.10ff. the table of nations in Gen. 10, and in Gen. 11.27ff. the wandering of humankind from Gen. 11.1-9/12.1ff. From the transition relating to clan history and geography in J, P, stimulated by the genealogical threat in the patriarchs in J, also constructed an ongoing genealogy from Adam to Abraham. Noah and his sons, especially Shem, who was attached to the reversed genealogy of Sethites and Cainites and made the hero of the flood added by P, became the connecting link. Both versions were initially handed down independently (J^G and P^G) and glossed here and there (J^S and P^S); finally they were worked into each other and then abundantly supplemented and interpreted theologically (P + J = R^{PJ}).

Table C.II.1

Sources	Basic writing (J^G)	Additions (J^S and R^{PJ})
Genesis Anthropogony		
2–4	2.9aβ, 16-17, (18, 20b, 23f.) 25	2.4b, 6, 7b, 9bα, 10-15, 19b
	3.6-13a, 16-19a	3.1-5, 13b-15, 19b, 22-24
	4.1bβ, 2-5, 8-12, 16, 25-26	4.6-7, 13-15, 23-24
	6.1, 4aβb	6.2-4aα
		6.5–8.22
Table of nations		
9.(18a,) 19	9.18, 20-27	
10.2-31	10.8-9, 21, 24-25	10.1, 10-19, 26-30
	11.2-5, 6a, 8a	11.1, 6b, 8b-9, 28-30
	12.1ff.	

3.   Abraham, Isaac and Jacob

3.1   The non-Priestly patriarchal narrative comprises two very different sets of narratives, the patriarchal narratives in Gen. 12–35 and the Joseph story in Gen. 37–50. The first set of narratives deals with Abraham and Lot and their children in Gen. 12–25, especially with Isaac and his sons in Gen. 26–27 and with Jacob and Esau and Jacob and Laban in Gen. 28–35. Right away, a number of passages can be removed which hold up the course of the narrative and are usually assigned to another stratum of texts. These are the late midrash in Gen. 14 which brings Abraham together with Melchizedek the priest-king of Jerusalem, and the development in Gen. (33.18-20;) 34 which presupposes the commandment about circumcision in Gen. 17 (P) and by means of this follows through the relationship between the non-Israelite Shechemites and Jacob-Israel at various levels.

We can also cut out the special traditions in Gen. 15 and 20–22 (with the exception of 21.1-8 and 22.20-24), which are generally attributed to the Elohist. These passages are by no means sufficient to postulate the existence of an independent source E. Rather, as in Gen. 14 and 34, we have midrash-like additions. Like Gen. 14 and 17, Gen. 15 interrupts the connection of Gen. 12–13 (16) and 18–19 and belongs to a group of promises which are dependent on Gen. 12.1-3, 7 and 28.13-15, but are all later.[20] We can recognize the difference from the fact that the later group is often no longer concerned solely with the content but for the most part with the endangering of the promise to Abraham and the other patriarchs, and the conditions attached to it. The promise has become problematical; it is connected with the behaviour of Abraham and is extended in time. It comes to be enjoyed no longer by the patriarchs themselves but by their children and grandchildren, namely, the generation of the exodus (Gen. 15; 46.3f.; 50.24; Exod. 3.7f.) and, so far as the multiplication and care of Yhwh is concerned, as in Gen. 17 also the Ishmaelite sideline (16.10; 21.12f., 17f.).

Genesis 20–22 interrupt the narrative flow running up to Isaac in 18–19 + 21.1-8 + 22.20-24 + 24-26. Genesis 20 and 21.22-34 are an interpretation of Gen. 26 (and 12.10ff.) which transfers the encounter with Abimelech from Isaac to Abraham and in the course of this modifies it morally and theologically. Genesis 21.9-21 is a development of Gen. 16–17 which removes the fate of Hagar's son Ishmael, who in Gen. 17.18-21 is explicitly declared to be a sideline, from the whim of Sarah and puts it in God's caring hand. Finally, Gen. 22.1-19 is an elaboration of Abraham's obedience and faith (cf. Gen. 15), as a result of which for the umpteenth time he gets a promise. All the passages are post- rather than pre-Priestly and fit well into the context in which they now stand: the covenant related to the land in Gen. 15 mediates between Gen. 12–13 (blessing for Abraham) and 16–21 (blessing for all the descendants of Abraham, covenant for

Isaac); Gen. 20–22 resume the preceding Abraham story mirror-fashion: Gen. 20 is the positive counter-example to the sin of Sodom in Gen. 18f. (18.17ff.); 21.8-21 take up Gen. 16–17 in literary terms, but in content go back to Gen. 15; Gen. 21.22-34 correspond to the separation from Lot in Gen. 13; Gen. 22.1-19 put the promise and the beginning of Abraham's 'settlement' in a new light with the establishment of a cult in Gen. 12.

So the passages need not come from another context, but could have been composed for their present context. It is remarkable, but not surprising, that the midrash is attached above all to Abraham. Less had been handed down about Abraham and Isaac than about Jacob, so that here there was a need for further elaboration. And with Abraham – very much in line with Gen. 17 – the foundations have been laid for all that follows; in it everything that applies to Isaac and Jacob-Israel, in short to Judaism of all times, was already to be present. In this way the descendants of Abraham become the descendants of the godfearing and pious man of Gen. 15 and Gen. 20–22 and because of him get the promise. Here is the root of the late-Israelite Abraham theology in which Abraham has become 'our father', first of all the father of the pious, then of the proselytes, and finally the father of believers.[21]

3.2   If we remove the late passages, what remain are: (1) Gen. 11.28-30/ 12.1-3, the transition from the primal history to the patriarchal history; (2) Gen. 12–13 and 18–19, Abraham and Lot, with Gen. 16, Hagar and Ishmael, in between; (3) Gen. 21.1-8 and 25.1-6, Isaac and the sons of Keturah, and between them in 22.20-24 the kinsfolk of Abraham; Gen. 24, the getting of a bride for Isaac and attached to it in 25.21-34 the birth of the twins Jacob and Esau and the sale of the rights of the firstborn; (4) Gen. 26, Isaac and Rebecca with Abimelech of Gerar; (5) Gen. 27–33 and 35, Jacob and Esau, and in this Jacob and Laban, Gen. 29–31 (up to and including 32.2a).

In this order we can see the outlines of the tradition history of the patriarchal narratives. As Gen. 26 in particular shows, at the beginning stand independent traditions about individual patriarchs, which were dovetailed at a secondary stage and linked to one another both genealogically and geographically. Thus round the core of Gen (25;) 27–35 were placed the Jacob–Laban story in Gen. 29–31 and the fraternal conflict between Jacob and Esau in Gen. (25;) 27–28 and Gen. 32–33, in which again the local aetiologies of Beth-el in Gen. 28(and 35) and Penuel in Gen. 32 stand out as separate traditions. In Gen. 26 Isaac and Rebecca are without children; in Gen. 25 and 27ff. they are the parents of Jacob and Esau. Lot is firmly associated with the local aetiology of Sodom in Gen. 19; in Gen. 12–13 he is the kinsman of Abraham; through Gen. 18; 21.1-8, 11, 29f.; 22.20-24 and 24 Abraham and Sarah become the parents of Isaac and kinsfolk of Isaac's wife Rebecca.

If we are to be able to find our bearings to some degree in the complicated tradition history and to understand the composition, we need a positive criterion by which tradition and redaction can be separated. We do not need to search long for it; it was found a long time ago in the redactional hinge of Gen. 12.1-3 at the transition from the primal history to the patriarchal history.[22] The promise to Abraham, in which the concept of blessing dominates, forms a counterpart to the curse of the primal history, especially Gen. 2–4, and spans an arch with the Jacob narrative in Gen. 27–28, especially 28.13-15. It is worth beginning with the transition in 11.28-30 and 12.1-3.

As we saw, 11.1-9, originally vv. 2-5, 6a, 8a, is the last pre-Priestly text in the Yahwistic primal history. To this vv. 28-30 are usually attached; they are taken from the Priestly tradition in 11.27, 31-32 and assigned to the Yahwist or Jehovist. However, this assignation can hardly be correct. Verse 28 mixes non-Priestly ('land of his kinsfolk' as 12.1-3) and Priestly formulations (Ur-kasdim, Haran as a person alongside the place *ḥārān*) and is orientated on the model of v. 32; it thus presupposes the combination of non-Priestly text and Priestly Writing. Verses 29f. certainly point to non-Priestly passages, v. 29 to 22.20-24 and 24.30 to ch. 16 and chs 18–21, but these are in turn partly suspect of being additional verses, especially the genealogies in 22.20-24 and ch. 24. According to these genealogies, as in P, Bethuel, one of the eight sons of Nahor, the brother of Abraham and Haran, is the father of Laban and Rebecca; according to 29.5, 10, Nahor, who lives in the city of *ḥārān*, is the father of Laban and Rebecca. And above all there is no literary link between 11.28 and 11.1-9, which is usually reconstructed on the model of P (11.19-26, 27), although here quite different relationships prevail.[23] Thus 11.28-30 looks more like an addition to P in 11.27-32. The addition explains why Haran and Nahor do not go with Abraham and Lot. The one has already died; the other marries his daughter and settles in the city which gave its name to his father-in-law. The transitional passage is attributed to the pre-Priestly text only because J and JE are thought of as being like P and, as in the case of Noah (5.29), it is thought that the pre-Priestly text must, like P, have contained an ongoing genealogy from Adam to Abraham. But in neither case is this convincing. Genesis 12.1-3 originally attached itself directly to 11.1-8a: from humankind dispersed over the earth under the curse Yhwh selects one man and puts the blessing on him. Lot and Sarah are introduced only when they are needed, Lot in 12.4a or 13.5, Sarah in 16.1 or 18.9.

There is a contrast with the Yahwistic primal history in two respects. First, the wandering of humankind, which is first driven eastwards and then sets out westwards from the east, reaches its goal for Abraham and his descendants and kinsfolk not just in one of the regions mentioned in Gen. 10, but specifically in a land assigned by Yhwh (12.1-7). Secondly, after the 'one people' of humankind has been dispersed (11.8a), Abraham in particular will become a 'great nation'. Like the 'heroes of prehistory', among them above all Shem, Abraham and his seed receive what is refused the whole of humankind (11.4), a 'great name' (12.2). Only the later Israel can be meant by this 'great nation' and 'great name'. Both the saving goods promised by Yhwh, the land and the great nation, single out Abraham, above all the clans of the cultivated land, the clans of the Noachite table of nations in Gen. 10, and especially the surrounding clans of the surrounding cultivated land of Syria–Palestine (12.3). For and in Abraham and his seed the curse on humankind turns into blessing. Work on the land is and remains toil, the land is cursed and so is Cain, but Abraham is shown a land in which he may hope for a rich yield. Birth is and remains difficult, but Abraham is promised a future as a nation with a resounding name that gives hope for rich descendants. All the clans of the cultivated land are well advised not to make him an enemy but to get a blessing for themselves through him, for Yhwh blesses the one who blesses him, and will curse the one who curses him.

The blessing and the two respects in which Gen. 12.1-3 does not do away with the primal history but turns it to good also dominate the continuation of the patriarchal narrative. I have already referred to the two literary pillars of a bridge, the resumption of 12.1-3, 7 in 28.13-15. These are the earliest promises in Genesis, on which all the others depend, and they function as redactional brackets. They therefore represent the earliest stratum of composition which links the primal history and the patriarchal history through the element of the promise. In them the many blessings experienced by Abraham and along with him Lot (13.2, 3; 24.35), Isaac with Abimelech (26.12-16, 22, 28-29), and Jacob from his father Isaac (27.27-29) and with Laban (30.27, 29-30; 32.5-6), especially the blessing of Isaac in 27.29b, are derived from Yhwh.

In addition these passages formulate the programme for the genealogical and geographical conception which holds the patriarchal narratives together. Abraham and Lot, Ishmael and Isaac, Moab and Ammon, Jacob and Esau, Jacob and Laban are all related to one another in some way. The goal of the genealogical branches is the birth of the sons of Israel, including Judah, in Gen. 29f. and the renaming of Jacob in Israel in Gen. 32. Judah and Israel stand for the two states which are here genealogically united in the midst of the rest of the world of the small states of Syria–Palestine, which is likewise organized genealogically. The promise that Abraham, whose descendant is the father of Judah and bears the name Israel, will become a people is fulfilled with the birth of Judah in 29.35 and the renaming of Jacob in 32.28.

Geographically the patriarchs are linked by the itinerary attached to 12.1-3. Abraham, coming from the east, the land of Shinar (11.1-9), travels straight across the promised land and first arrives at Shechem (12.6), then further south in the hill-country between Bethel and Ai (12.8); from there he goes further south and then – after the insertion of 12.10–13.1 – back to the place between Bethel and Ai (13.3f.). The last stage of the separation from Lot in 13.2, 5-13 is the terebinth of Mamre, a city near Hebron (13.18), where Yhwh appears to him in 18.1. There or – according to 20.1 – further south, Isaac is born (21.1-8); in Gen. 26 Isaac goes to Abimelech in Gerar and from here moves to Beersheba (26.23). From Beersheba in 28.10 Jacob goes to Laban in *ḥārān*, where he stays until 30.25; in Gen. 31–35 he returns from there to the promised land via a number of intermediate stages (Gilead, Mahanaim, Penuel, Succoth, Shechem, Bethel, Ephrathah-Bethlehem, Migdal-eder), taking almost the same route as his grandfather Abraham. In 31.3 Yhwh gives the command to set out with the words of 12.1-3. The land 'of your fathers and your kinsfolk' is now no longer the east, from where Abraham comes, but the promised land, to which Jacob is to return. The wandering of the patriarchs through the land, which also includes the establishment of cults (12.8 = 13.3f.; 13.18; 26.25; 28.16-19) and the return of Jacob-Israel is a kind of 'settlement'. With it the promise of land in 12.1-3, 7 is fulfilled.

How far the blessings and the genealogical and geographical arrangements come from the author of 12.1-3 himself or how far they pre-existed him must be examined case by case. Nevertheless, it is clear that these perspectives are brought together in the two promises 12.1-3, 7 and 28.13-15, and make up the redactional scheme by which the patriarchal narratives have been composed. The references back to the primal history and the exposed position of the deity Yhwh who bestows the blessing and guards over the genealogical and geographical branchings connect this redactional concept with the Yahwistic revision of the primal history and are on the same level. Here we have a revision which is responsible for the collection and first editing of the first individual traditions and therefore for the basic document of the primal history and patriarchal history in Gen. 2–35. Classically this revision is called the 'Yahwist' (J), and there is nothing against keeping this designation, at least in Genesis.

Not only the Yahwizing but also the nationalization of the earlier material is characteristic of J. The accursed history of humankind, which is finally divided and dispersed in clans, languages, lands and nations, continues in the history of the small states of Syria–Palestine on the cultivated land of Palestine, rich in blessing. The (one) national God Yhwh is worshipped at various altars in the land in accordance with the law of the altar in Exod. 20.24, and gives the blessing wholly in the fashion of family and local religion. The commandment calling for centralization in Deut. 12 does not yet seem to be known. Nor does the first commandment need it. Only Yhwh is mentioned as deity because of his exceptional status as the national God; as such he is common to Israel and Judah, and is an appropriate foundation for the brotherhood of the two monarchies, which are independent and usually at enmity with one another.

The remarkable combination of the world of states, especially the two states Israel and Judah, with the no less remarkable mixture of the levels of pre-exilic national, local and family religion under the sign of the one national God, are by no means as much a matter of course as they are usually taken to be. There must have been a special occasion for the redactional concept of the Yahwist, and it is conceivable only under certain conditions. It is most easily explained from the case of Samaria around 720 BC and the situation between the times, between 720 and 587 BC, in which there was no kingdom, but one people Israel alongside and in the kingdom of Judah. Thus the Yahwistic primal history and patriarchal history can be read as the foundation legend of the states of Israel and Judah in a non-state garb and as legitimation for the worship of the national God Yhwh, which had perished in Israel but lived on in Judah, and certainly continued to be practised in the territories of Israel in the form of pre-exilic local and family religion. In this way the Yahwistic primal history and patriarchal history is saying what Samuel–Kings is expressing with the union of the kingdoms, the house of Saul and the house of David, in David's empire. In their way the primal history and the patriarchal history are not the prehistory to the exodus-settlement narrative in Exodus–Joshua but a parallel to it. I do not know what Gen. 12.1-3 and the Yahwistic primal history and patriarchal history stamped by it have to do with the exile, life in the Diaspora and the universalism of Deutero-Isaiah, as is often claimed today. Isaiah 40–48 certainly presuppose the patriarchal history, but for another reason go quite different ways and meet up more with P than with J. In this case, too, the custom of reading J through the spectacles of P again has exerted an influence – successfully planned, as we can see, by P and R.

3.3   The redactional perspectives of Gen. 12.1-3 require and make possible a distinction between tradition and redaction in the patriarchal narrative. This can be carried through most simply in the Jacob tradition, which extends from Gen. 25 to Gen. 35 and is composed of three strands of tradition: (1) Jacob and Laban in Gen. 29–31; (2) Jacob and Esau in Gen. 25–28 and 32–33; (3) Jacob and Bethel in Gen. 28 and 35, Jacob and Israel in Gen. 32. The three strands are linked by the motif of the dispute between the two brothers Jacob and Esau over the right of the firstborn (Gen. 25 and 27), which prompts Jacob's flight to Laban in ḥārān, the return and the reconciliation. It should be noted that the motive is not yet the commandment of endogamy, as in P (27.46; 28.1ff.) and in the case of Isaac in Gen. 24; the marriage to Laban's daughter in Gen. 29–31 becomes the reason for the journey only at a secondary stage. Of course the link is secondary and the question is which of the three strands of tradition is original. The decision is not difficult to make. The only tradition which has a beginning and an end, does not presuppose anything else, and thus can once have existed independently, is the narrative about Jacob and Laban in Gen. 29–31. Neither the link with Esau nor the encounters with God in Bethel and by the Jabbok are independent; they are thus expansions. The Jacob tradition, moreover, is so complex that apart from the Yahwistic revision (J^G) we must reckon both with a pre-Yahwistic original and also with post-Yahwistic (J^S) and post-Priestly supplements (R^{PJ}). I shall go through the transitional stages briefly in order.

'And Laban had two daughters, the name of the older was Leah and the name of the younger Rachel ... And Jacob loved Rachel.' That is the beginning of the story in Gen. 29.16-18, which merely requires one to know who Jacob and perhaps also who Laban was. Everything else follows from the beginning: the twice seven years that Jacob serves Laban for the two wives (29.16-30),[24] the birth of the children (29.31–30.24),[25] the separation from Laban and the pursuit (30.25–31.31),[26] and finally the reconciliation with Laban in the treaty of Gilead (31.43–32.2a).[27] The narrative is not fixed in time or place; only crossing the river in 31.21 suggests Mesopotamia, and at the end Gilead is mentioned as the scene of the concluding of the treaty; thus we have an early tribal narrative from northern Transjordan. There is no mention as yet of *ḥārān* in Mesopotamia. The narrative is very similar to the still independent Isaac tradition in Gen. 26, and the separation of Abraham and Lot in Gen. 12–13 is dependent on both.

The Yahwistic revision of the basic narrative can be recognized above all in the introduction to the births in 29.31, the secondary etymologies in 29.32f. (Reuben and Simeon alongside Levi), the addition of the birth of Judah in 29.35, the reference forward to the birth of Benjamin (Gen. 35) in 30.24b, the blessing of Jacob in 30.27, 29-30, 43, the command to set out in 31.3, and the expansion of the local aetiology of Gilead in 31.49. Jacob is blessed by Yhwh; the children (Reuben, Simeon and Levi, Joseph) become tribes, regions and nations. Judah becomes the son of Jacob, who shortly afterwards is called Israel. All the other births in Gen. 29–30 which everyone will feel not to be a unity and which are therefore usually divided between the different sources, are post-Yahwistic (and post-Priestly) supplements in order to arrive at twelve tribes for Israel; the daughter Dinah has been added to Gen. 34 in retrospect. The justification of Jacob in 31.1, 5b-13, 15-16, 18, 24-25, 29-30a, 32-42 and the episode of the theft of the teraphim woven in at 31.19b, 30b, 32-35, the elaboration of the covenant in 31.45, 47, 50-54, and lesser additions in the core which has been given a Yahwistic revision for 29.16-35; 30.14, 23-24, 25-43; 31.2-31, 43-49; 32.1-2a, are likewise post-Yahwistic, sometimes post-Priestly, expansions (cf. 31.18).

Like Jacob and Laban, Isaac and Esau also have an independent prehistory. There is more or less a consensus over Isaac and Rebecca in Gen. 26. This is a small narrative collection which has itself grown successively; in the original stratum it as yet knows nothing of its present context, the genealogical links with Abraham, the Aramaean parents of Rebecca and kinsfolk of Abraham, and the sons of Jacob and Isaac. Its content is as follows: Isaac went to Gerar to Abimelech, the king of the Philistines, and in order to protect himself from possible attacks pretended that his wife was his sister. But the trick was discovered. Abimelech saw Isaac (*yiṣḥāq*) 'making love' (*meṣaḥeq*) with his wife and accused him. However, contrary to Isaac's fears, he and his wife were not killed, but declared untouchable on pain of death (vv. 1aαb, 7-9, 11). And Isaac went on and settled in the valley of Gerar, since he thought himself under the protection of the king (v. 17). There was a dispute there with the shepherds of Gerar over drink for the animals. They dug well after well until there was no longer a dispute. Therefore the places are called Esek ('quarrel'), Sitnah ('dispute') and Rehoboth ('broad land') (vv. 19-22bα). And Isaac went on to Beersheba (v. 23), where in keeping with the name of the place ('well of oaths') Abimelech and Isaac united by treaty in an oath and parted in peace (vv. 23, 26-31).[28]

The independent Isaac tradition is akin to the Jacob tradition and like it is timeless, but it comes from quite another region, southern Judah, where not the Aramaeans but the Philistines were the neighbours. Originally Isaac and Jacob had nothing to do with each other. And before they became father and son, Esau, the eponymous ancestor of a group which likewise had its home in the south, seems to have been adopted by the tradents of the Isaac tradition. For the blessing of Gen. 27.28 originally applied not only in the dim and deceived eyes of the dying Isaac, but also in fact to Esau, Isaac's elder son: 27.1-4, 5b, 18a, 24-27bα, 28. Genesis 27.1 attaches itself seamlessly to 26.31 and adds a further Isaac episode after vv. 1, 7-9, 11, vv. 17, 19-22 and vv. (23,) 26-31: Isaac is the father of Esau and gives him the paternal blessing. Like Jacob's marrying into the family of Laban and the union by treaty, but independently of that, the development of Gen. 26 in Gen. 27 reflects links in the tribal history at the time of the pre-exilic monarchy.

Next the two formerly independent traditions, the Isaac–Esau narrative in Gen. 26–27 and the Jacob–Laban narrative, were combined. That happened by Esau and Jacob being declared brothers – not yet necessarily twins as in Gen. 25. The younger brother, Jacob, surreptitiously obtains the blessing in place of the older, Esau, through the mediation of Rebecca. At this stage of the tradition, in Gen. 27 the intrigues of Rebecca (27.5a, 6-10[,11-13], 14[-16], 17, 18b, [21-23]), the discovery of the intrigue (27.30-33, the replacement blessing in vv. 34, 39-40?), Esau's planned murder (27.41), and the advice to flee (27.42-45) were added. Verse 43 advises flight to *ḥārān*, to Laban, who is taken from Gen. 29–31, made the brother of Rebecca, and localized for the first time in a Mesopotamian city with a basis in 31.21. Here the closer kinship relationships are of interest only because the question is that of an appropriate place to which to flee. The obligation to endogamy which arises incidentally does not as yet play any basic role (Gen. 22.20-24; 24.3f., 37f. and P in 27.46; 28.1ff.). Genesis 28.10 or 29.1 fits on seamlessly to 27.44-45. One of the two notes, presumably 28.10, is original; the other supplements 28.11-22 in the course of the insertion of the Bethel scene. 28.10 is in turn the hinge for the attachment to the older Jacob–Laban narrative in Gen. 29–31 (from v. 16). Thus the Isaac tradition in Gen. 26–27 about the intrigue in Gen. 27 and the flight of 27.43-45; 28.10 becomes the prehistory of the Jacob–Laban narrative in Gen. 29.16–32.2a, and this in turn has become the intermediate stage on Jacob's flight to his brother Esau. Correspondingly, at the other end the separation from Laban became Jacob's return journey in Gen. 32–33, on which there is a reconciliation with Esau. The narrative thread picks up the old end of the Jacob–Laban narrative in 32.2a and makes Jacob reach the place Mahanaim ('double camp', 32.2b-3), from where he sends messengers to Esau (32.4-22)[29] prior to meeting him and coming to an agreement with him (33.1-15).[30] The narrative ends in a similar way to the parting of Jacob and Laban in 32.1-2a: Esau returns to Seir and Jacob goes on to Succoth in Transjordan and settles there (33.16f.). The narrative cycle of the combined Isaac/Esau and Jacob/Laban narrative could once have ended here. Presumably the move of Jacob from Succoth to central Palestine somewhere between Luz/Bethel (cf. 28.11-19) and Ephrat(ah)/Bethlehem and the death and burial of Deborah and the burial of Rachel attached themselves to this, though the presupposition for that is that 35.6 does not belong to P but to the pre-Priestly text: 35.1, 6-8, 16-20.

Finally, the insertion of the theophanies in 28.11-22 and 32.23-33, which already presuppose Jacob's flight and return journey and therefore the complex of Gen. 26–35, is later than the union of the two independent traditions. Genesis 28.11-12 can be recognized as an insertion by the resumption of 28.10 in 29.1. As 28.11 does not specifically mention the subject (Jacob), the insertion develops the prior text and is formulated for the context, even if perhaps an earlier anonymous tradition stands in the background. The basic text, the aetiology of the cult of Bethel in 28.11-12, 17-19, spans an arch from the beginning to the end of the flight in 35.1, 6-8, 16-20. The appearance of God on Jacob's return journey in 32.23-33, inserted into the encounter with Jacob between his spending the night in 32.14a or 32.22 and lifting up his eyes in 33.1, is to some degree a counterpart of this. The episode is sparked off by the assonance between the name Jacob and the name of the river, Jabbok, and therefore makes

Jacob 'strive' (*'ābaq*, niphal) with God.[31] Originally the tradition – again perhaps at first anonymous, and related to Jacob at a secondary stage – focused on the gaining of the blessing (32.25-27, 30b) and in connection with Jacob on the aetiology of the place Penuel (32.31, 32, like 28.11-12, 17-19; 32.2b-3).

In view of the genealogical and geographical combinations and the theme of the blessing, the question naturally arises whether the composition in Gen. 26–35 is the work of the Yahwist or belongs in the pre-Yahwistic history of the tradition. The fact that in the original stratum the composition does not yet seem to know the Abraham narrative and, as in Gen. 29–31, has undergone Yahwistic supplements in Gen. 26–28 and 32–33 + 35 which take note of both the context of Gen. 26–35 and the prefacing of the Abraham narrative, supports the second possibility and tells against the first. Consequently we must reckon with a pre-Yahwistic composition of the Isaac/Esau and Jacob/Laban tradition in Gen. 26–35, which must have stimulated the Yahwist (J^G) to his subsequent revision. Apart from the additions in Gen. 29.16–32.2a (especially 29.31-33, 35; 30.24b, 27, 29-30, 43; 31.3, 49) which have already been mentioned, these include the Yahwistic question of Gen. 3.13; 4.10 in 26.10a; the blessings in 26.12-14, 16, 28a, 29b; the aetiology and building of the altar in 26.22b, 25; the aetiology of Beersheba in 26.32f., which is dependent on 26.25; the success and blessing in 27.20, 27bβ, 29 (perhaps also the substitute blessing in 27.34, 39-40); the promise in 28.13-15, 16, which corresponds to 12.1-3, 7; the still very vague genealogical link of Laban as 'brother' (here 'kinsman', cf. 29.4, 12) of Rebecca through the common ancestor and 'brother', that is, kinsman of Jacob, Nahor, in 29.2-15; the renaming of Jacob as Israel in 32.28-30a corresponding to the addition of Judah in 29.35; and presumably also some other elements in the overloaded text of Gen. 32–33, though no specific formulations can be identified in it, merely a series of later explications of the basic scene. At the latest after the Yahwistic revision, Esau, whether explicitly[32] or not, is a sign of the nationalizing of the material in terms of Edom-Seir. The Yahwistic revision of the patriarchal history ends with the note about the settling of 'Israel' in the land, beyond Migdal-eder, in 35.21; granted, this is not a very spectacular ending, but it does shed some light on the time of origin: 'Israel' is no longer living on in the political frontiers of the pre-exilic monarchy but in no-man's land between Israel and Judah, alongside and under the monarchy of Judah, the 'son of Israel'. Moreover, as in Gen. 29–31, we again come upon a series of post-Yahwistic and post-Priestly supplements (J^S and R^{PJ}).[33]

Last of all, the birth story of Jacob and Esau in Gen. 25 was put before the formerly independent composition in Gen. 26–35, at the earliest by the Yahwistic revision. Genesis 25.21ff. presupposes the marriage of Isaac and Rebecca in Gen. 24 and mediates between the preceding Abraham–Isaac narrative in Gen. 12.1–25.6 and the composition in Gen. 26–35, in which the sons of Isaac are initially not even in view – Isaac could not have given his wife to be his sister in ch. 26 had she already given birth – and are only introduced when their turn comes (ch. 27). Even the insertion of Abraham as the father of Isaac does not need the birth story in Gen. 25. After 21.1-8 and 25.5f. it is clear even without the birth story that Isaac is the son of Abraham and Jacob the son of Isaac. The genealogical bridge serving the notion of endogamy – which is predominant in the Priestly Writing – in 22.20-24; 24 and 25.31-34, according to which not Nahor (thus 29.5) but Bethuel is the father of Rebecca and Laban, and the kinship relations indicated in 29.2-15 run in a clear genealogical succession (cf. 25.20; 28.2, 5 P), can therefore also be post-Yahwistic or even post-Priestly. The decision depends not least on the literary analysis of 25.19-26, on which in turn the reference forward to Gen. 27 in 25.27f. and the anticipation of Gen. 27 in 25.29-34 which attempts to balance out 27.35f. are dependent. If we go by the traditional source distinction, 25.21-26a (or also even vv. 21, 24-26a) continues chs 24 and 25.5,[34] and is an independent special formulation in the framework of J (J^G or J^P). If on the basis of the similar cases in Gen. 16 and 21.1-8 we assign not only 25.19-20, 26b but also vv. 24-26a (without the etymologies) to P, in vv. 21-23 we have independent post-Priestly additions (R^{PJ}). Either way, that Jacob and Esau are twins seems secondary by comparison with the pre-Yahwistic composition in Gen. 26–35, nor does it play a role in the Yahwistic and post-Yahwistic revision of these chapters.

3.4   In contrast to Isaac and Jacob, Abraham has no specially broad basis in the tradition. Only chs 12–13 + 16 + 18–19 + 21.1-8 + 24 + 25.1-6 come under consideration. The core of the composition is the narrative about Lot and Sodom in Gen. 19. It is the only passage that can be isolated as an independent tradition and originally knows nothing of Abraham. At the centre stands an aetiology of place, primarily for the desert landscape by the Dead Sea (19.1-16, 26),[35] which has a double culmination: the rescue of Lot (v. 16) and Lot's wife being turned into a pillar of salt (v. 26). Secondarily it is an aetiology for the place Zoar (19.17-23).[36] To this is attached the etymological aetiology of the states of Moab ('from the father') and Ammon (Ben-ammi, 'son of my kinsman') in 19.30-38, who emerge from the incest with Lot's two daughters – made unavoidable after 19.26. The episode serves to nationalize the earlier material and comes either from the pre-Yahwistic tradition or from the Yahwistic reviser himself. Later Yahwistic insertions are absent. The additions in 19.1-6, 17-23, 26 and vv. 24-25, 27-29 are to be attributed to the Yahwist and the post-Yahwistic enlarger.

The narrative about Abraham and Sarah in Gen. 12–13 and 18 attached itself to the independent tradition about Lot in Gen. 19; in the course of this Abraham and Sarah became Isaac's parents: 21.1-8. In substance the text arises from the beginning in 12.1-3 and the orientation on Lot in Gen. 19 and Isaac in Gen. 26ff. After the command to set out into the land destined by Yhwh, Abraham goes wandering with Lot in and through the land which Yhwh has shown him (12.4a, 6a, 7-9).[37] There both are richly blessed (13.2, 5), and the dispute sparked off among the shepherds (13.7a, 8-11a), which leads Lot with reference to Gen. 19 to Sodom (13.12bβ, 13) and Abraham to the terebinths of Mamre (13.18), attaches itself to this. Genesis 18.1 ('And Yhwh appeared to him by the terebinths of Mamre and he sat . . .', cf. 26.2) immediately takes up 13.18 and is dependent on the previous naming of Abraham as subject of the action. The scene, the visit of the three men, has been spun out of Gen. 19 and has as its content the announcement of the birth of Isaac (18.1-16a).[38] As in 19.17-23 there is an alternation between the plural (for the 'three men') and the singular (for Yhwh). But unlike 19.17-23, the change in number cannot be resolved by literary criticism, as in the later addition 18.16b-22a. If we take out the speeches of Yhwh in vv. 10, 13f. and with them the whole course of the narrative in vv. 9-15, the scene lacks content; conversely the speech in v. 10 is dependent on the plural in v. 9. Verse 14 speaks of Yhwh in the third person. The mixture is already produced deliberately at the beginning: in 18.1a Yhwh appears to Abraham by the terebinths of Mamre (13.18), in 18.2 Abraham sees the 'three men'. From there on the narrative moves consistently on two levels, apart from the exception in 18.3b which can easily be deleted: Abraham and Sarah have to do only with the 'three men'; the reader is told that this is Yhwh, who appears in the three men and announces the birth of the child. In the following birth narrative, which is dependent on ch. 19 (and the note about the itinerary in 20.1 = 12.9?), presumably only 21.1a, 6-8 are original. After 18.9-15 it is clear what is meant by the formula of accomplishment in 21.1a and the allusions in 21.6f.: the 'laughter' ($s^e\underline{h}oq$) that God has prepared for Sarah is Isaac ($yi\underline{sh}\bar{a}q$). The Isaac narrative in Gen. 26ff. could once have followed on directly from here.

It is hard to say whether Abraham and Sarah also have a pre-Yahwistic foundation like Lot in Gen. 19 and Jacob in Gen. 26–35. An independent Abraham tradition can be ruled out. The scene in Gen. 18 is dependent on Gen. 12–13 and 19, the dispute of the shepherds in Gen. 13 on Gen. 12 and 26, and the itinerary of Abraham in Gen. 12 on 12.1-3. The narrative seems to be based on no more than the tradition of the names; in substance it has been composed for the wider complex of the patriarchal history. The only question which arises is therefore whether the larger complex is possibly pre-Yahwistic. Indications of this might be either that the Abraham of 12.6-9 is initially only made the father of Isaac in 21.2f., 6-8 and later – through 12.4a and the resumption of 12.9 in 20.1 – is connected in chs 13 and 18–19 with Lot, and afterwards in ch. 16 with Ishmael, or that in 13.7-18 and chs 18–19 he is initially connected only with Lot, and through 18.9-15 in 21.1-8 is made the father of Isaac. But neither possibility offers a pre-Yahwistic beginning. Abraham's itinerary in 12.6-9, whether with or without Lot in 12.4a, presupposes the command to set out in 12.1-3, and the dispute of the shepherds and the division of the whole land in 13.7-18 presuppose not only Gen. 26 but also the prehistory in 12.4; 13.2, 5. Thus the question of a pre-Yahwistic Abrahamic tradition may be left aside.

By contrast, we must ask whether Ishmael in Gen. 16 and the wooing of a bride for Isaac in 22.20-24 and ch. 24 are an original element of the Yahwistic composition or have been inserted subsequently. Like Gen. 14–15 and 17, Ishmael has inserted himself between Abraham and Lot in Gen. 12–13 and 18–19. P presupposes him in Gen. 17 and 25.12-17; the non-Priestly text speaks of him only in the late midrash 21.9-21. He can well be absent from the pre-Priestly composition. Moreover we can no more be sure to what sources the birth notices in Gen. 16 belong than we can in the case of 21.1-8 and 25.21-26, so that we should not build anything much on those. If we assign all the births to the pre-Yahwistic source and the Yahwistic revision, there is no equivalent in P; if we distribute them between J (21.1a, 6f.) and P and reckon with post-Priestly expansions (21.1b-5; 16; 25.19-26), we can manage with the existing text. The wooing of a bride for Isaac in 22.20-24 and ch. 24 has inserted itself between the birth of Isaac and his attaining manhood in 21.1-8 and the Isaac episodes in Gen. 26 by means of the resumption of 21.8 in 25.5, like Gen. 21.9–22.19; 23 and everything else in ch. 25. The genealogical succession in 22.20-24, on which ch. 24 rests, goes with the Priestly Writing in 28.1-7 and the post-Priestly addition in 11.28-30, but not with the Yahwistic revision in 29.2-14. Like Gen. 23, Gen. 24 drops out of the framework simply because of the length and narrative mode, and this is not changed by any literary criticism, however fundamental. The model for the narrative is the marriage of Jacob in Gen. 29–31, discovered in the kinship between Rebecca and Laban which has been produced in the meanwhile, but more closely than the original wanted. The command to engage in endogamy and the demarcation against the Canaanites are not a theme of the pre-Yahwistic composition or the Yahwistic revision in Gen. 26–35, but they are a dominant motif in the later Priestly Writing. So there is much to suggest that in Gen. 16; 22.20-24; 24.1-67; 25.1-6 and 25.21-34 we have post-Yahwistic (J^S), if not post-Priestly (R^{PJ}), supplementary passages. Whether or not they rest on an earlier special tradition, as in the case of the Abraham midrash in Gen. 14–15 and 20–22, is an open question.

3.5   Summary. The basis of the patriarchal history is the – pre-Yahwistic – composition in Gen. 26–35, which is composed of two formerly independent narrative cycles, the Isaac–Esau narrative in Gen. 26–27 and the Jacob–Laban narrative in Gen. 29–31. The narrative cycles were combined by means of the motif of the surreptitious obtaining of the blessing in Gen. 27–28, which turns Jacob's stay with Laban into the intermediate stage on his flight from Esau and the separation from Laban (32.1-21a) in Gen. 32–33 + 35 into Jacob's return and peaceful parting from Esau, and makes all those involved kinsfolk. The Abraham–Lot narrative cycle in Gen. 12–13 and 18–19 + 21.1a, 6-8 was inserted in front of the composition in Gen. 26–35; this emerged from the formerly independent Lot tradition in Gen. 19 and explains Abraham and Sarah as the parents of Isaac. The way in which Abraham is put first is dependent all along the line on the redactional hinge in 12.1-3, which links the primal history and the patriarchal history, and in this converges with the Yahwistic revision in Gen. 26–35. Abraham and Sarah have been developed as contrast figures to Lot and his wife. Whereas Lot loses his homeland in Sodom and his wife, and only through incest achieves male descendants, the states of Moab and Ammon east of the Jordan, Abraham and Sarah are promised and given land and descendants by Yhwh. Their sudden appearance is explained by the prehistory of humankind in Gen. 2–11, which stands under the curse of Yhwh and is dispersed over the earth. The figures of Abraham and Sarah, who are at most known by name, are chosen to create a transition from the history of humankind to the history of the people of Israel in Gen. 26–35. The Yahwistic primal history and patriarchal history in Gen. 2–35 (J^G) which come into being in this way are subsequently expanded many times, and above all powerfully filled out in the sphere of the Abraham narrative (Gen. 14; 15; 16; 20–22; 24; 25), but also in Gen. 26–35 (chs 34, etc.). As in Gen. 1–11, the additions are partly pre-Priestly (J^S), but the majority are of post-Priestly origin (P + J = R^{PJ}).

The original material of the Yahwistic revision, the anthropogony in Gen. 2–4, the Noachite table of nations in Gen. 10, the Lot tradition in Gen. 19 and the composition in Gen. 26–35, which in turn has grown out of different individual traditions, clearly belongs in the pre-exilic period and reflects the living conditions of individual groups of bands of groups in the north and in the south at a sociological level below the monarchy. By contrast the basic document, the Yahwistic primal history and patriarchal history (J^G), offers a foundation legend of Israel and Judah. The two monarchies appear in a non-stately garb, united under the roof of the one national God Yhwh, and made brothers in the genealogical system of the tradition of tribes and families. 'Israel' is not yet the 'all Israel' of the later Deuteronomistic and Chronistic tradition, but the son of Abraham and Isaac and the father of Judah. The remarkable mode of description reflects the relations between 720 and 587 BC, in which 'Israel' survives in the environment of the monarchies of Judah and the other surrounding states, which are all Assyrian provinces and vassal states.

Table C.II.2

Sources	Basic writing (J^G)	Additions (before and after P)
Genesis		
	2.4b-11.8	
Abraham	12.1-4a, 6a, 7-9	12.6b, 10–13.1
	13.2, 5, 7a, 8-11,	13.3-4, 7b, 14-7
	12bβ, 13, 18	
		14-16
Lot	18.1-3a, 4-16a	18.3b, 16b-33
19.1-38	19.9aα²β, 13b, 14aβ,	19.15aβb, 16aβ, 27-29
	18b-19, 20b-22a, 24-25	
	21.1a, 6-8	21.9-22, 24
		24
Isaac–Esau		25.1-6, 18, 21-34
26.1-31 ⎤	26.10a, 12-14, 16,	26.1aβ, 2-6, 10b, 15, 18, 24
	22bβ, 25, 28aα, 29b,	
	32-33	
27.1-4, 5b, 18a, 24-28		
27.5-45	27.20, 27bβ, 29, 34,	27.35-38
	39-40	
28.10, 11–19	28.13-16	28.20-22
29.1		
Jacob–Laban	29.2-15, 31, 32b,	
29.16-34 ⎤	33α²β, 35	29.24, 29
	30.24b, 27, 29-30, 43	
30.14-42	31.3, 49	30.1-13, 15-22
31.2-48		31.1, 5b-13, 15-16, 19b, 24-25,
		29-30, 32-42, 45, 47, 50-54
32.1-2a ⎦	32.28-30a	
32.2b-32		32.10-13, 23-24, 33
33.1-17		33.1b-3, 5-7, 19-20
	35.21	34
35.1, 6-8, 16-20		35.2-5, 14-15, 22a

4. Joseph

4.1   In a broader sense the Joseph story in Gen. 37–50 also belongs to the patriarchal history of Genesis: at the same time it spans an arch to the exodus narrative which follows and serves as a transition to the stay of Israel in Egypt. That is by no means a matter of course. For with a very few exceptions, for example, Gen. 15 or the indications in 12.10–13.1, the primal history and patriarchal history in Gen. 2–35 contain no kind of references forward to the exodus. On the contrary, with the birth of Judah and Benjamin, the renaming of Jacob as Israel and the return of Jacob-Israel to the land of his fathers, Israel is established in the land, and the promise of Gen. 12.1-3 is fundamentally fulfilled. The pre-Priestly, Yahwistic primal and patriarchal history extending to Gen. 35 does not look for a continuation. That only changes with the Joseph story, and there too to begin with only hesitantly.

One has a suspicion that the strange intermediary position of the Joseph story has something to do with its literary composition. To see through it we must first detach ourselves from the traditional explanation of the division of sources which even Wellhausen practised in the Joseph story, though only for the sake of the hypothesis; as it will prove, with moderate success. Apart from a few Priestly parts of the text (37.2; 46.6-7, 8-27; 47.27, 28; 49.1a, 29-33; 50.12-13) the documentary theory is not applicable to the Joseph story.

So for some years more and more scholars have come to regard the Joseph story as an entity *sui generis*. Here three larger insertions are undisputed: the narrative about Judah and Tamar in Gen. 38, which interrupts the connection between Gen. 37 and 39; the blessing of the sons of Joseph born in Egypt (cf. 41.50-52); Manasseh and Ephraim in Gen. 48; and the tribal sayings in Gen. 49, which interrupt the connection between 47.29-31 and 50.1. Otherwise the text is regarded as more or less a unity. However, it is impossible for the Joseph story, which is a literary unity, to have stood by itself. Most scholars ignore the fact that the present text has links both with the patriarchal history and the exodus narrative but, since this is the case, Noth[39] already put forward the thesis that, while the Joseph story is a separate piece, it must really have been composed for the transition. It has rightly been objected to this that it is really far too long and rambling to serve such a purpose and conversely that the links are far too loose.

Thus a view is beginning to get established in more recent scholarship which combines the two earlier explanations, the division into different sources and the unitary hypothesis. Scholars reckon with an originally independent basic narrative which was put into the context of the patriarchal history and the history of the exodus at a secondary stage, and in the course of this was expanded in literary terms and assimilated. Here the old literary-critical observations relating to a division into sources again come into play, but now along the lines of the supplementary hypothesis. Thus it has always been striking – to give just one, albeit not completely untypical, example – that in the exposition of the narrative in Gen. 37 Joseph is on the one hand sold to the Ishmaelites and Judah pleads for him, and on the other hand is taken out of the cistern by the Midianites and carried off, and Reuben is the one who pleads for him. The change of the name Jacob or Israel and the designation of God as Elohim or Yhwh (in Gen. 39) are often connected with this. There is no agreement on the literary tendency: some regard the Midianite–Reuben–Jacob line as original, and others – in my view rightly – the Ishmaelite–Judah–Israel(–Jacob) line; in each case the other line is thought to have been added. Whatever decision one arrives at, the example teaches that the explanation is wrong on one point. The persons acting are the same as those who also occur in the Yahwistic patriarchal history in Gen. 12–35; furthermore they appear – almost throughout – in a constellation which occurs elsewhere only in the (Yahwistic) patriarchal history (Gen. 29–30; 32): Jacob is Israel; Joseph is the first, favourite son of the preferred Rachel; Reuben, Simeon and Judah are the sons of Leah, who has been displaced but is the first to give birth; Benjamin is the youngest son of Rachel and the special pledge in the Joseph story. Levi and the other mothers and children added in Gen. 29–30 do not (yet) occur in the Joseph story.[40]

However, that means that the Joseph story, which was dependent on the exposition in Gen. 37, was never independent, but from the start belongs in the context of the patriarchal history. Noth's thesis proves to be right, except that the narrative is not a unity but has grown up and perhaps has been supplemented, hence the few discrepancies – which are claimed for an original independence – for example, the contradiction between 37.10 and the death of Rachel in 35.18-20. And we must make yet another qualification to Noth's thesis: the narrative did not come into being as a bridge between the patriarchs and the exodus but primarily as a continuation and further conclusion of the patriarchal history; it is used only secondarily as a bridge pillar, as in the Priestly Writing.

4.2   After the birth of Benjamin, the death of Rachel and the settlement beyond Migdal-eder in 35.16-21, with the beginning in 37.3 the non-Priestly Joseph narrative turns to the further fate of Israel. Israel, the new name given to Jacob in Gen. 32, loved Joseph, the firstborn of his beloved wife Rachel of Gen. 29, more than Joseph's (four) brothers, whose birth is related in Gen. 29–30 and 35. Everything that follows develops from this: the hatred of the brothers (37.3-4a), which subsequently is further heightened by and grounded in the dream in 37.5-8;[41] the plan to kill Joseph (37.12-18 and vv. 19-20, 23-24; cf. Gen. 4); the objection of Judah, who is born in 29.35 (37.25-27); the sale to the Ishmaelites and Joseph's journey to Egypt, which is noted twice: in 37.28[42] and – after the insertion of 37.31-35 (and ch. 38) – in the recapitulation in 39.1a. Joseph's career at the Egyptian court, in which, secretly supported by Yhwh or God (39.2-6, 21-23; also 40.8; 41.16, 25, 32, 38f.), he is outstanding both morally (Gen. 39) and in matters of prophecy (Gen. 40–41), begins in 39.1b; he rises to become second man in Egypt after the king, which fulfils the dream in Gen. 37.5-8. The distinctive part of the Joseph story, which cannot be derived, and draws on typical folk-tale motifs, lies in Gen. 39–41[43] and comes to a climax in 41.54: in the seven lean years there is famine all over the world; only in Egypt is there bread. In the background is the motive of the exaltation of the lowly. The material in Gen. 39–41 may be older, but the narrative does not work without the introduction in terms of family history in Gen. 37, and the arch opened up by it is not yet at an end in Gen. 41.

The end of the narrative, which picks up the thread of Gen. 37, introduces 42.1 or 42.5: as all over the world (41.54, 56, 57), so too in Canaan famine prevails, and like all the world Jacob sends his sons, 'the sons of Israel', to Egypt to buy grain (cf. Gen. 26 and 12.10ff.). There follow in Gen. 42–44 the two journeys of Joseph's brothers to Egypt; these are related in a very long-drawn-out way and are constantly extended by a number of complications which are inserted later. They are concerned above all with the fate of the younger son of the beloved Rachel from Gen. 35.17f., Benjamin, who, once Joseph had gone, became the favourite child of his father Jacob-Israel (44.20). In the background stands the question of the fate of Judah and the fact that the territory of Benjamin belongs to Judah after the downfall of Israel. Reuben and Simeon also come into view here as subsidiary figures.

As so often, the story ends in two climaxes. A first climax is reached in ch. 45 (vv. 1-4, 14-15, 25-27): Joseph makes himself known to his brothers and sends them home to tell their father that he is alive, which again revives Jacob-Israel (45.25-27, cf. also 42.38; 43.7, 27f.; 44.22, 27ff.). With this the narrative thread spun in Gen. 37 comes to a good and sufficient conclusion. Joseph, Israel's son, is alive, but he is alive in Egypt.

The second climax likewise begins in Gen. 45, but two further chapters, Gen. 46–47, are needed for it to be reached in Gen. 50: Joseph invites his father Jacob-Israel to move to Egypt (45.9-13, 16-42); Jacob-Israel wants to see his son once more before he dies (45.28). Thereupon Israel goes to Egypt, where Jacob dies. From there he is brought back to the land of his fathers to be buried, as a pledge for the impending liberation of Israel from Egypt in Exod. 1ff. The famous, theologically significant closing scene in 50.15-21 spans an arch back to 37.4: whereas the brothers did not say a peaceful word to Joseph at the beginning, at the end Joseph speaks comforting and good words to his brothers. His brothers had evil in mind, but God had good in mind, namely to keep 'a great people' alive. Here the conclusion of the Joseph story at the same time refers back to the climax of ch. 45, especially 45.5-8, but interprets it in a far more wide-ranging and deep way in terms of the salvation history, building a bridge from Gen. 12.1-3 to Exod. 1.9. Only with the revision of Gen. 45 and the appendix in chs 46–50 does the Joseph story become the transition from the patriarchs to the exodus.

As is shown by the literary intersection in ch. 45 and the closing chapter, 50, the Joseph story has been revised several times. There is a tendency to build up the tribal and national history more and more strongly after the climax of Joseph's career in ch. 41. The Reuben–Midian additions in ch. 37, the addition of the sons of Joseph and their blessing in 41.50-52 and ch. 48, the Benjamin passages in chs 42–45, the tribal sayings in ch. 49, and also the addition of the Judah–Tamar narrative in Gen. 38, which centres on the law of levirate marriage, serve this purpose. The way in which the story is increasingly shaped into a national history, to the point of accumulating Joseph's brothers to become the twelve tribes of Israel in Gen. 37.9; 42.3, 13, 32 and ch. 49, binds it increasingly into the literary context of the Hexateuch and the Enneateuch.

4.3   In the tone and the broad manner of the narrative, with many repetitions in its early discourses, not all of which can be cut out as secondary additions, the Joseph story is very reminiscent of the narrative about wooing a bride for Isaac in Gen. 24, the development within the Priestly Writing in Gen. 23, or the Abraham midrash in Gen. 20–22. With these it also shares an interest in the individual, the secret entanglements guided by God, and the moral virtues. Basically the Joseph story is a Joseph midrash which is attached to the elder son of the beloved Rachel of Gen. 29f. and belongs to the same stage as the other expansions of the patriarchal history. Even if most of the characteristics mentioned are based on later revision and the appendix in Gen. 46–50, the basic stratum itself in Gen. 37–45 is not wholly free from them and is clearly distinct from the originals and the Yahwistic revisions in Gen. 2–35. The Yahwistic revision does not continue in the Joseph story; rather, the Joseph story continues the Yahwistic primal history and patriarchal history in Gen. 2–36. In the original stratum of Gen. 37–45 the Joseph story is a post-Yahwistic appendage (J^S).

We must seek the occasion for the development of the story in the special features which are peculiar to the Joseph narrative, namely in Joseph's stay in Egypt (Gen. 39–41), motivated in Gen. 37 and artificially combined with the patriarchal history that precedes it. Scholars have made various proposals, extending from an explanation in terms of the national history of the tenth to eighth centuries to a Diaspora novella of the sixth or fifth century BC.[44] All of them are right in some respects. Both the national history and the Diaspora situation play a role. Just as Abraham became the father of the faith, so Joseph becomes more and more the paradigm of the kingdom and people of Israel which is lost and has fallen into the hands of its enemies. At any rate the fall of the northern kingdom of Israel is presupposed and, if we add the additional caravan of Jacob and all his sons, also that of the southern kingdom of Judah. In concrete terms we will have to think here of the Egyptian Diaspora, which existed at the latest post-587 BC after the failed restoration under Gedaliah, but presumably previously to that. The Jeremiah narratives tell of it, and it is well known to us from the papyri from the island of Elephantine on the Nile, which date from the Persian period. The basic stratum of Gen. 37–45 derives from a situation in which Israel and Judah are living in the land, but the better part of Israel, the oldest son of beloved Rachel, who is Israel's favourite, has been sold by his own brothers into Egypt. That suggests rivalry. The Israelites in the Diaspora feel written off by the 'sons of Israel', the Israelites in the mother country, and Benjamin is caught between the two. Only Judah (later Reuben) attempts to prevent the worst. Just as later in parts of the book of Jeremiah (for example, Jer. 24 and 29) and in Ezra–Nehemiah the Babylonians make themselves heard, so in the Joseph story the Egyptian Diaspora makes itself heard and clearly indicates that there are also Israelites outside Judah and the other territories in the land inhabited by Israelites: Joseph in Egypt is not dead, as is said in the Jeremiah narratives, but alive. In a way, here we already have the later duality of Alexandrian and Babylonian Judaism in the making.

The Egypt theme in the Joseph story also perhaps stems from a sideways look at the exodus tradition, which celebrates the liberation from slavery in Egypt as a primal datum of the foundation (election) of Israel. However, this was initially a polemic against the exodus creed. In a way which differs from the exodus story, the original Joseph story makes it clear that Israel survived even in Egypt and gained great respect. A connection is obvious. Legends about the origin of Israel which were formerly contradictory were assimilated to one another in a way which made one the prehistory of the other. The move of Jacob-Israel, including Judah and all the other brothers, to Egypt in Gen. 46–50 serves this end. However, the material and the literary elaboration of the Yahwistic primal and patriarchal history, including the Joseph narrative, did not originally intend this combination. The *terminus ad quem* for the Joseph narrative is the Priestly Writing, which in 46.6-7 relates the later journey of Jacob to Egypt and thus seems to presuppose a connection – however loose – between the patriarchs and the exodus.

5. Moses, Miriam and Joshua

5.1. A new king ruled over Egypt who knew nothing of Joseph. The Israelites were too numerous and too powerful for him, so he used them as forced labour in building Pithom and Ramses and, since they kept multiplying, commanded first the midwives and finally, when even that was no use, his people to kill the male descendants of the Hebrews (Exod. 1).

With the new king over Egypt a new time dawns for the 'sons of Israel' who came to Egypt with Jacob. This time immediately follows the time of the patriarchs. However, the continuation is not as direct as all that. Exodus 1.1-7 first recapitulates the move of the Israelites to Egypt, the death of Joseph and his generation and the multiplication of the Israelites in Egypt, which had already been spoken of at length in Gen. 45–50 (46.6-27; 47.27; 50.22-26). The duplication is connected with the separation of the books, and as in Deut. 34/Josh. 1; Josh. 24/Judg. 1–2 or 2 Chron. 36/Ezra 1 is meant to indicate the literary and narrative connection beyond the limits of the books. It presupposes the Priestly Writing and its combination with the non-Priestly text. If we cut out the recapitulation and the Priestly thread in Exod. 1.13-14, the beginning of the exodus narrative lies in Exod. 1.8-12, on which in turn the episode of the midwives in vv. 15-22 depends.

Attempts have recently been made to explain this text, usually distributed between J and E, say the Yahwist and the Elohist or the Yahwist and expansions, as non-Priestly, with the argument that Exod. 1.8-12 compellingly presupposes the Priestly verse in 1.7. Apart from the fact that 1.7 (with *waya'as^{e}mū*, 'and everywhere they became strong', and the unusual accumulation of statements about multiplying) in turn must be post-Priestly, this argument does not work, because the references to the size and strength of the people can stand without a previous note about multiplication, as Num. 22.3f., 6 shows (cf. also Gen. 26.16). But that does not mean that Exod. 1.8-12, 15-22 is therefore pre-Priestly or even Yahwistic. The supposed indications of this are more than sparse. Thus 1.8-12 does not necessarily presuppose 1.7, but at least in vv. 10b, 12 (with *rbh*, qal, 'multiply') the Priestly motif of increase on which 1.7 is also dependent. The motif of forced labour in v. 11, which gives a historical touch to the exodus creed, is also above all firmly anchored in the Priestly Writing as the reason for the exodus from Egypt (1.13-14; 6.6f.), whereas the forced labour in 2.11 is merely part of the background and otherwise appears in additions (3.7b, 9b; 5.3–6.1). Accordingly, the beginning in 1.8-12 must be reduced to 1.8-10a, to which the episode with the midwives in 1.15-22 is seamlessly attached.

But even then not all the problems are resolved. Exodus 1.8 (cf. Judg. 2.10) presupposes the death of Joseph. This occurs only in late additions, in Gen. 50.23-26 and Exod. 1.1-7; the selection of 1.6 or Gen. 50.26aα is arbitrary and is by no means suggested by the text. The connection between Exod. 1.9(, 20) and Gen. 12.1-3 which is often claimed exists at most in terms of subject-matter. The formulation does not point to Gen. 12, but shows points of contact with Gen. 18.18 and 50.14-21 (cf. also Num. 14.12; 22.3, 6), and thus with post-Yahwistic passages. The motif of the greatness and strength of Israel – presumably taken from Num. 22.3, 6 – which prompts the command to kill them in 1.15ff. – plays no further role in the course of the non-Priestly exodus narrative. However much one reduces the text, which has been heavily glossed, the twofold commandment to kill in 1.15-22 provides a secondary reason, not very well constructed, for the subsequent narrative about the exposure of Moses in 2.1-10. The narrative has most to do with this in 2.2b-3a, but here too only in a completely indirect way, and originally not at all. The original reason for the exposure of the child lies in the dubious marriage of a man from the house of Levi with the 'daughter of Levi' (a female levite?), and is immediately evident from its basis in tradition, the legend of Sargon.[45] Moses, the man with the Egyptian name, is indeed a Hebrew of prominent birth, but his origin remains obscure. He discovers it to some degree first in the dispute between Hebrews and Egyptians (2.11ff.). From the beginning Exod. 2.1 is an independent tradition.

According to all this, 1.8-10a, 15-22, like the post-Yahwistic appendage to the Joseph story in Gen. 45–50 which the opening of the book of Exodus presupposes in Exod. 1, proves to be a redactional hinge linking the patriarchal history with the narrative of Moses and the exodus which begins in Exod. 2. The link is a very thin thread, specifically only 1.8-9, which prompts the attack by the king of Egypt in 1.10a, 15-22 spun out of Exod. 2. There is nothing to support the assignation of this thin thread to J apart from the obsession of the documentary hypothesis, with finding at least a second ongoing narrative thread alongside P. However, the non-Priestly combination of the patriarchs and the exodus through Gen. 45–50 and Exod. 1.8-10a, 15-22 is neither Yahwistic nor Elohistic nor part of a source at all, but secondary by comparison with both the Yahwistic primal history and the patriarchal history in Gen. 2–35 + 37–45 and the Moses–exodus narrative which begins in Exod. 2. It is hard to say whether the redactional hinge in Exod. 1 is pre-Priestly or post-Priestly.[46] However, as the Priestly Writing knows the settlement of Jacob-Israel from Egypt in Gen. 45–50 which focuses on the exodus, that is not important.

For the continuation of the analysis, that means that from Exod. 2.1 we can no longer reckon just with the Yahwistic revision which is responsible for the connection of the primal history and the patriarchal history in Genesis; here there is a new development. What is new is a tradition of Israel extending from the exodus from Egypt under Moses (Exodus–Numbers) to the entry into the promised land under Joshua (Joshua). I call this tradition the exodus narrative after its main content, and to distinguish it from the Yahwistic revision of the primal history and patriarchal history (J) I use the classical siglum 'E' (for exodus narrative). That has the advantage that one can also go on speaking of J and E and JE, except that this does not mean parallel threads of sources which contain approximately the same narrative twice, but, as we shall see, two independent rival myths in the Hexateuch, the primal history and the patriarchal history in Genesis

(J) and the exodus narrative in Exodus–Joshua (E), which have subsequently been linked together as two eras of the one salvation history, initially before (JE) and finally in and with P (P + JE = R^PJE).

5.2 'Now a man from the house of Levi went and took to wife a daughter of Levi, and the woman conceived and bore a son.' This was Moses, whom his mother exposed and whom the Pharaoh's daughter took out of the Nile. In this way Moses comes to the court of the Pharaoh and gets his Egyptian name, and thus begins the exodus narrative in Exod. 2.1-10.[47] The interlude in 2.11-14,[48] in which Moses – consciously or unconsciously – takes vengeance for one of his Hebrew brothers on an Egyptian, for the first time brings him together with his like and leads him to flee to Midian (2.15). By this he prefigures the destiny of his people (cf. 14.5). Here, of course by a well (cf. Gen. 24 and 29), he meets the seven daughters of the priest of Midian, who take him for an Egyptian. He gets one of them, Zipporah, as his wife and has a son by her, Gershom, the child of 'abroad' (Exod. 2.15-22). That is the starting point for everything else. In the wilderness, where Moses is tending his father-in-law's sheep,[49] Yhwh appears to him (3.1-6)[50] and announces that he will liberate his people from the misery of Egypt (3.7-8, 21-22).[51] Moses goes to his father-in-law, bids him farewell, and returns to Egypt (4.18, 20a).[52]

We read the consequences of the announcement of 3.7-8, 21-22 in Exod. 12–15. The Israelites plunder the Egyptians with Yhwh's help, as Yhwh orders in 3.21f. and as Moses has meanwhile told them to do (12.35-36). After that they set out, from Ramses to Succoth (12.37-38), and from Succoth to Etam on the edge of the wilderness, accompanied by Yhwh in a pillar of cloud and fire (13.20-22).[53] It is here that there is an encounter with the Egyptian king who, as in the case of Moses in 2.15, had heard of the flight and immediately set off after the Israelites. The Israelites see the Egyptians coming and are very frightened. In accordance with the promise of Yhwh in 3.7f., Moses says to them, 'Do not fear'. And Yhwh saves them from the hand of the Egyptians (Exod. 14).[54] The prophetess Miriam appears out of the blue, takes her drum in her hand and sings a hymn appropriate to the miracle by the sea: 'Sing to Yhwh, for he has triumphed gloriously, the horse and its rider he has thrown into the sea' (15.20-21).[55]

After the victory over the Egyptians, the journey through the wilderness begins, or rather, the wandering in the wilderness continues. Exodus 15.22a ('Then Moses led Israel onward ... and they went into the wilderness of Shur')[56] again takes up the thread of 13.20, but the notices about wandering cannot simply be brought together over and above the miracle by the sea. On the contrary, if we remove the law in the Pentateuch and everything connected with it, the immediate connection with 15.22a comes in Num. 20.1aβb, and presupposes the appearance of Miriam. Having arrived in the wilderness of Shur, the people settles in Kadesh (cf. Gen. 20.1), and there Miriam dies. In the meantime further stages and incidents have been attached, but only very few of them continue the old narrative thread. A thirsty stage of three days' journey is inserted between Shur and Kadesh, which takes the people to Marah (15.22-25a), and from there to the oasis of Elim with its abundance of water (15.27).[57] From Elim the way leads into the wilderness of Sinai (16.1aα; 19.2a: 'And they set off from Elim and came into the wilderness of Sinai and they camped in the wilderness'), where Moses spends forty days and forty nights with God on the mountain (19.2b, 3a; 24.18b) and where Kadesh now also lies (Num. 20.1aβb).[58]

From Kadesh, in Num. 20.1aβb Israel goes into the fields of Moab opposite Jericho (Num. 22.1), where the people settle in Shittim (Num. 25.1a). Lesser episodes have also been interposed here in order to fill out the journey: the request to Edom for permission to pass through, which is rejected and necessitates a detour (Num. 20.14-21, originally vv. 14a, 17-18, 21), and the negotiations with Sihon the king of the Amorites, which spark off a war (Num. 21.21-24a). They are later expanded by a number of reports about Heshbon and the double, Og of Bashan, who is added from Deut. 3.1-7 (21.24b-35). Here we have two variants of the same narrative, which hardly came into being independently of one another. If we regard 20.14-21 as primary, both 22.1 and also 21.21ff. can be attached to this without a problem. If we regard 21.21-24a as the earlier text, we must add the itinerary in 20.22a; 21.10f., which leads Israel from Kadesh into Transjordan before it has to go round Edom. The Balaam tradition in Num. 22–24 has been inserted between the arrival in the fields of Moab (Num. 22.1) and the settlement in Shittim (Num. 25.1a).

In Shittim in the fields of Moab, opposite Jericho, Moses dies and is buried (Deut. 34.5f.), and from Shittim Joshua sends out the spies (Josh. 2.1-7, 15f., 22f.), crosses the Jordan with the people (3.1, 14a, 16; 4.19b) and occupies Jericho and Ai and subsequently further cities of the land (6.1-3aα, 5, 12a, 14aα[1], 20b; 8.1-2a, 10a, 11a, 14, 19; 12.1a, 9-24). What began with the birth of Moses in Egypt in Exod. 2.1 and the announcement of Yhwh in Exod. 3.7f. comes to a conclusion in Josh. 2.1-12.

5.3   This is the framework of the exodus narrative in the oldest complex that we can arrive at. Already in the basic literary material it is about Israel and Yhwh, and offers a self-contained and rounded legend of the origin of Israel. In contrast to the primal history and the patriarchal history in Genesis, but in a way comparable with the Abraham tradition, a division between tradition and redaction will not really be successful. Certainly the whole can be dissected into different 'themes' – Moses, the miracle at the sea, the wilderness itinerary, Joshua and the settlement – but everything is in some way linked. It therefore makes no difference whether in the exodus narrative we reckon with diffuse oral tradition which can no longer be grasped precisely, and also with a more or less unitary written composition, or cut up the literary complex and for the sake of the ongoing threads of sources, or, in principle, forcibly divide the fragments into written (pre-Yahwistic) sources and (Yahwistic) redaction.

Only at two points can formerly independent traditions still be recognized. The first is in Exod. 12–15, in so far as we can leave aside Moses and the exodus from Egypt. This is easiest in the case of the song of Miriam in Exod. 15.20f., which, taken by itself (v. 21b), has nothing at all to do with the exodus; it is merely about the victory of Yhwh over some horses and riders whom he has at one point thrown 'into the sea', to some degree reversing the classic notion of the fighter against chaos who compels the sea (cf. also 15.6-12). The victory of Yhwh over the Egyptians in Exod. 12–14 can be understood in a similar way. If we reduce the text to the bare essentials, it is about an Israelite caravan which is on its way back from Egypt (12.37; 13.20), is suddenly attacked by Egyptians and saved in a miraculous way by Yhwh (14.10bα, 19b, 20aαb, 24, 25b, 30a). Moses (only vv. 13f.) and the sea (only vv. 21, 27, 30b) are not needed here,[59] since in 12.35f., 38 and 13.21f. the one presupposes the link with Exod. 2–4, the other the combination with Exod. 15.21b. It has always been striking that the miracle at the sea in Exod. 14–15 seems like an insertion into the itinerary of 12.37; 13.20, which continues in 15.22ff. In fact it is not an insertion; the itinerary and the Moses story of Israel in Egypt which it presupposes are formed around the miracle at the sea in Exod. 14–15 in order to make Yhwh's victory over the enemies of the Israelites a stage on the way of the people of Israel in the exodus from Egypt.

The other tradition which displays a certain independence is the occupation of Jericho by Joshua in Josh. 6, which had a double in Josh. 8 with the conquest of Ai. Without the framework narrative in Josh. 2–4, which binds the event into the exodus narrative and has been assimilated in the course of the origin of the text, the tradition deals with two ruined hills around which a Joshua legend has grown. Originally it had nothing to do with the 'settlement', but more with the claim of 'Israelites'[60] or the crowd (*hā'ām*) around Joshua and the territory around Jericho and Ai in the region of Benjamin that was most frequently a matter of dispute between Israel and Judah. Like Miriam, Joshua, too, became the protagonist in the legend of the origin of Israel, which only at a later stage described the exodus from Egypt and the subsequent settlement.

A similar assumption has also been made in connection with Moses, for whom scholars are fond of postulating a special tradition in Exod. 2.11-22, 23aα + 4.20a, which can still be detached in individual scenes or in the basic text (2.1-15, up to 'and settled in the land of Midian') and expansions (2.15–22ab, 'and he sat by a well': 2.23aα + 4.20a), on the basis of the alternating terminology ('Pharaoh' in 2.5, 15, 'king of Egypt' in 2.23) and the seam in 2.15 (the double 'and he sat down'). However, this is a fragment, and no one can say where it comes from or what it is meant to be. What is called the infancy story of Moses uses well-known material: the legend of Sargon in Exod. 2.1-10 and a historical reminiscence of conditions in the Bronze Age cities in 2.11-12; and the remembrance of the existence of semi-nomads (Shasu nomads) and other marginal elements, the so-called Hapiru (Hebrews), who sometimes hired themselves out as mercenaries or workers in Egypt or elsewhere in the lands of the Fertile Crescent. Both motifs have an ancillary function: the Sargon material suggests that the little Hebrew boy with the strange name who has been exposed will become a great man; the reminiscence of the Hapiru/Hebrews provides the motive for flight. Since the story is about the fate of the Hebrews and not the fate of the Midianites, its goal is not reached either in Exod. 2.15 or in 2.22, far less in 4.20. What is lacking is the resolution of the expectations which have been aroused, an account of how things developed with Moses and the Egyptians in Egypt, that is, precisely what one reads in Exod. 3–4 and in the following exodus narrative with the 'flight' of Israel in Exod. 12–15 (14.5 corresponding to 2.15). Hence it is reasonable to conclude that the figure of Moses has been portrayed a priori for the exodus narrative as we find it in the text. If we look more closely, the apparent insertion in Exod. 3–4 in truth proves to be a seamless continuation of Exod. 2.1-22. With the expression 'king of Egypt', 2.23aα presupposes Exod. 1.8, 15, etc. (also 14.5), and is a redactional bracket which combines the non-Priestly text in 2.1-22 with the Priestly continuation in 2.23aβ-25. The appearance of Yhwh and the announcement of the exodus in 3.1-6, 7f., 21f. is attached to 2.22 or 2.15 through 2.23-25. The story of Moses' marriage in 2.15 (from 'and he sat down by a well') up to 2.22 in fact seems to be a secondary expansion of the story of his flight in 2.15. This perhaps explains the confusion in the name of Moses' father-in-law in 2.18 and 3.1 and the difference in the number of children in the relationship between 2.15-22 and 4.20a, though this is not important. Exodus 4.20a again attaches seamlessly over the addition in 4.19 to (3.1-6, 7f., 21f. +) 4.18.[61]

It is the same with the independent character of the wilderness itinerary from Exod. 15. If 12.37 and 13.20 possibly belong to the older tradition, 12.35f. presupposes the instructions in 3.21f., 13.21f. the miraculous appearance in 14.24, and the whole itinerary between Exod. 15.21 and Josh. 6.1 in Exod. 15.22a (15.22b-25a, 27; 16.1aα; 19.2, 3 + 24.18b) + Num. 20.1aβb; Num. 25.1a + Deut. 34.5f.; Josh. 2.1; 3.1 the connection between Exod. 14–15 and Josh 6 + 8 in the framework of the exodus narrative.

Of course, even so questions remain open. Where does Moses comes from? What is the significance of his Egyptian name and his Midianite origin or kinship? Why has he in particular been chosen as the hero of the exodus narrative? Somewhere or other one keeps coming up against a point that can no longer be derived or explained. Speculation about the history of the tradition or literary-critical reduction does not help, but merely shifts the problem to another level. However, that does not mean that Moses has so to speak dropped down from heaven. Some tradition, presumably a reminiscence of Shasu and Hapiru experiences and a Midianite origin, will already have been associated with him before his role as leader at the exodus. So he must have been a quite unspectacular figure. Perhaps he was chosen precisely because of that. With him and the Hebrews in Egypt, Israel, the people of Yhwh (3.7), emerges into the land to some degree out of nothing, out of the misery of Egypt and from outside. It is also meant to be noted that Israel does not enter and occupy the land from the south (through Judah), but from the east, into Benjamin. Both these features give Israel an identity which is not explained by the – God-given – kingship in Israel or by some common feature with Judah, but is based solely on the saving act of Yhwh. Therefore, too, Yhwh's counterpart is not the monarchy but 'my people' (Exod. 3.7). The people of Israel is granted an existence beyond the natural living conditions in Israel and Judah. This 'primal confession of Israel'[62] does not come from the time before the state, in which 'the people Israel' did not yet exist, nor is it a suitable basis for the legitimation of the Israelite kingship, for which in any case there are the independent traditions: the victory over the Egyptians in Exod. 12.37 + 13.20 + 14, the song of Miriam in Exod. 15.20-21, and the Joshua tradition in Josh. 6 and 8. The exodus creed presupposes the downfall of the monarchy, that is, the date 720 BC, and formulates an alternative theology of history. Israel did not perish, but Israel is the people of God, and Yhwh, the former national God, is the God of the people Israel. The foundation datum of the relationship is not the monarchy, which has perished in the meantime, but the liberation from Egypt; its presupposition is not the independent possession of the land but the divine gift of the land in the settlement. In its own way the exodus tradition, like the primal history and the patriarchal history of Genesis, shows a way out of the disaster of 720 BC, with the difference that the former has 'Israel' incorporated into the great family of small states in Syria–Palestine which remained alive and make it live on in Judah and Benjamin (Gen. 29.35; 35.18), and later also in the Egyptian Joseph (Gen. 37–45), while the latter emphasizes the uniqueness and independence, indeed the strangeness, of 'Israel' in the context of the world of the states of Syria–Palestine.

5.4   The basic framework of the exodus narrative was subsequently filled out in different ways. The story of Moses' marriage in Exod. 2.15-22, which give the wife and children of 4.20a a name, and the episodes dispersed throughout the wilderness itinerary between Exod. 15.22a and Num. 20.1

(Exod. 15.22b-25a, 27 + 16.1aα; 19.2, the ascent of Moses to God in 19.3 + 24.18b), between Num. 20.1 and 22.1 (Edom and Sihon, 20.14-21; 21.21-24a), and between Num. 22.1 and 25.1a (Balaam in Num. 22–24), are early expansions. It is hardly a chance resulting from the genre that most of these insertions, namely the scene in Exod. 2.15-22 (cf. Gen. 24 and 29), the encounter with God in Exod. 19.3; 24.18b (cf. also Exod. 3.1-6; and also Gen. 28–32), the sending of messengers to Edom in Num. 20.14ff. (cf. Gen. 32), and the blessings of Balaam in Num. 22–24, especially Num. 22.6; 24.9 (cf. Gen. 12.1-3), display points of contact with the Yahwistic primal history and patriarchal history. That is not a sign of an ongoing source or a unitary redaction. The formulations and interests are too different. Moreover the parallels in the primal history and patriarchal history are part of the Yahwistic basic document (J^G), whereas in the exodus narrative they presuppose the basic writing (E^G) in the exodus narrative and have been added to it. In the case of the Balaam tradition, the addition has its own basis in a source. Not only the redactional transition in Num. 22.2-4a but also the old beginning in 22.4b-6, which reflects the hostility between Israel and Moab at the time of the early monarchy, clearly indicate in v. 6 that the insertion moves within the literary horizon of the exodus narrative.[63] Here we have texts which, while they do not produce the combination of J and E (JE), at least prepare for it and are concerned for an approximation. Like the patriarchs, Moses, the son of Levi (cf. Gen. 29.34), is said to have been married and to have had children. God is said to have appeared to Moses, as he did to the patriarchs, and like the patriarchs, Moses, too, is said to have come in contact with the brother states east of the Jordan (Edom and Moab, Amorites = Ammon?). Just as perhaps in Gen. 37–45 and quite certainly in 12.10ff. the Egypt theme owes a sidelong glance at the exodus narrative, so the first additions in the exodus narrative owe a sidelong glance at the primal history and the patriarchal history. It is the later additions (Gen. 45–50/Exod. 1 or Exod. 3.6, etc.; here Num. 25.14b-16 after Deut. 26.5ff.) that first make the exodus and the military settlement under Joshua a second act of the salvation history following the first peaceful settlement of the patriarchs and the emigration of Jacob-Israel to Egypt which has been put in between. The 'settlement models' of a peaceful infiltration followed by the military expansion of the Israelite tribes in the land are not based on historical facts but on this momentous step in the composition of the narrative books of the Old Testament.

The plagues, which have pushed themselves in 4.20b–12.34 between the old point of attachment in 4.18, 20a and 12.35-37, are a further insertion into the basic framework of the exodus narrative. The non-Priestly plague cycle is composed of the following elements: (1) the announcement in the framework of the revelation scene of Exod. 3–4 in 3.9-12, 16-20; 4.1-17; (2) the appearance of Moses and Aaron before Pharaoh in 4.20b–6.1, and in it the announcement of the killing of the firstborn in 4.21-23 and the encounter of Moses and Aaron in 4.27-31; (3) the series of plagues in 7.14–9.7; (4) the intensification of the plagues in 9.13–10.29; (5) the last plague, the killing of the firstborn, in 11.1-9 + 12.29-34.

The composition is quite complex. The core is formed by a series of four plagues which occur in accordance with a fixed scheme, as in the Priestly Writing. (1) Moses is sent to the Pharaoh and is to inform him from Yhwh that he must let the people of Yhwh go into the wilderness to serve him there. (2) If Pharaoh refuses permission, a plague is threatened. (3) At the end Pharaoh's heart is hardened (here the root *kbd* is used instead of P's *ḥzq*, except in 8.11). We find this or something similar in 7.14-25 without vv. 19-22 P (I. water into blood), 7.26–8.11 without 8.1-3, 11 P (II. frogs), 8.16-28 corresponding to 8.12-15 P (III. vermin), and 9.1-7 corresponding with 9.8-12 P (IV. pestilence). However, the scheme is not carried through as strictly as in P; there are deviations in the formulations and in the ordering of the individual elements which distinguish II-III from I and IV from I-III. Plague IV deviates most strongly, showing itself to be an addition by the irregular resumption of 8.28 in 9.7b, while II and III differ above all in the intercessory element, and only here does Aaron appear alongside Moses (8.4, 8, 21). If we absolutely have to find an original plague scheme, we can separate out the intercession in 8.4-10 and 8.21-27 as an addition – post-Priestly. But even without petitions, the differences remain, like the position of the prophetic messenger formula 'Thus says Yhwh' (7.17 in I, 7.26 in II and 8.16 in III) or the recognition saying (7.17 in I, 8.6 in II, 8.18 in III). It is also remarkable that the act of inflicting the plague in I (7.20aβb, 21a) is fused with the text of P, and only here, as in P, does Aaron's staff in Moses' or Yhwh's hand play a role (7.15b, 17, 20). In II it is not reported at all, or is dependent on the account of its being inflicted in P, and in plagues III and IV, which are independent in literary terms, it is merely narrated separately (8.20, 28; 9.6f.) and introduced in the same way, namely, in connection with the regulation of the exception for the people and the precise point in time (8.18; 9.4f.), introduced with 'And Yhwh did thus/this' and ending with the hardening of Pharaoh's heart.

The common features and the differences can be explained in two ways. On the presupposition of the source hypothesis they are best explained by a successive origin of the plagues (first I, then II and III, lastly IV), which taken together provided the model for the unitary plague cycle of the Priestly Writing. However, I have not found a convincing argument for the usual assumption that the non-Priestly plagues are also pre-Priestly. Without that presupposition, I and II appear more as a supplement to P, which with the exposition in 7.14-16 is reacting not only to 5.1f. (here too Moses and Aaron!), but in 7.16b also to the failure to listen in 7.8-13; they add to the plagues which are performed without warning by Moses and

Aaron in P (7.19-21; 8.1-3) the announcement to Pharaoh and some details, above all that Yhwh himself inflicts the plagues (7.17, 20; 7.27). By contrast, the independent passages III and IV are duplications of 8.12-15 and 9.8-12 in the scheme of I-II, and precisely for that reason have their own account of the inflicting of the plagues. The supplementary hypothesis does not exclude the successive origin, but cannot explain how the non-Priestly scheme becomes independent in III and IV; the fusion of the non-Priestly and Priestly scheme continues in 9.17–10.29. It is hard to decide which of the two explanations is right, especially as the plagues are an addition to both versions, the pre-Priestly exodus narrative and the Priestly Writing, and have been abundantly glossed. At present I cannot say where the starting point is.

The introduction and conclusion of the series of plagues show a similar picture: 3.9–4.17 in the theophany of Exod. 3–4; 4.20b–6.1 and 9.13–11.8; 12.29-34. Instead of playing the fruitless 'JE game' today, here too a distinction is made between the basic text (non-Priestly and more nearly Yahwistic or post-Yahwistic) and expansions (pre- or post-Priestly, final redaction). With the exception of 3.16-20, the fillings-out of the revelation scene in Exod. 3.9–4.17 – the events on Moses' journey back from Midian in 4.20b, 21-23, 24-26, 27-31; the second address to the Pharaoh after 5.1 in 5.3–6.1, when the forced labour has been made harder; and the three plagues in 9.17–10.27 (hail, locusts, darkness) before the conclusion in 10.28f. – are largely regarded as late expansions which are not independent. At least the instructions in 3.16-20, the approach to Pharaoh in 5.1-2, the ultimate heightening of the plagues in 9.13-16 (with or without 10.28f.), and the announcement and execution of the last plague, the killing of the firstborn, in 11.1-9 and 12.29-34 are reckoned to be the (pre-Priestly) original stratum of the plagues.

But even this state of the text, reduced by all the superfluous incidentals, does not produce a coherent narrative thread. Consistency is lacking right at the beginning. The command to Moses and the elders in 3.16-18, on which the announcement of the plagues in vv. 19-20 depends, goes nowhere, and has evidently been formulated as it is with a view to 4.29-31[64] and the anonymous plural in 5.3ff., in accordance with the different leaders of the negotiations in 5.15ff. In 5.1-2 it is not Moses and the elders but Moses and Aaron who appear before Pharaoh.[65] That presupposes the Priestly Writing. If we want to maintain a pre-Priestly plague cycle, 7.14 must have been directly attached to 4.20a. At the end there are two rival conclusions, each of which results in an ultimate heightening of the plagues: the first is 9.13-16 with the departure of Moses in 10.28f.; the second is 11.1-8 with the departure in v. 8b. Both conclusions pose puzzles. No one knows what is meant by the expression 'all my plagues' in 9.14. Exodus 9.13-16 refer back in vv. 13f. to 8.16, 28 and to 7.17, and in vv. 15f. to 9.1-7; they can equally well be understood as the conclusion to the series of plagues or as an introduction to their continuation (particularly 12.29-33).[66] Exodus 10.28f. can hardly have followed 9.13-16 or 9.13-14, but presupposes a conversation with the Pharaoh of the kind that takes place in the additions in 9.17–10.27, and lastly in 10.24ff. Exodus 11.1-8 picks up the old connection in 3.21f. and anticipates 12.35ff. in order to announce yet again a final plague, one that is not further defined in vv. 1-3, the killing of the firstborn, in the speech of vv. 4-8, which begins suddenly and abruptly. It is impossible for 11.8 to be the continuation of 9.13f.; in a way which corresponds to 10.28f. it concludes the direct speech about and to Pharaoh in 11.4-7. Exodus 11.9 leads over to the Priestly text in 11.10 + 12.1ff. The killing of the firstborn is also announced yet again within the Priestly Passover regulations in 12.1-28 (here vv. 12-13, 23, 27). It is reported only once, in 12.29-33. The command to carry it out can be attached directly to 11.1-3, to 11.1-8 or to 11.1–12.28. As in 5.1f., Moses and Aaron are involved, and 12.1-28 are also addressed to them. In 12.34, 39 as in 12.15ff.; 13.3-10, the regulations about the feast of unleavened bread and in 13.1-2, 11-16 the regulations about the firstborn have attached themselves to the Passover and the plague of the firstborn. If in addition we omit the two quite problematical conclusions in 9.13-16/10.28f and 11.1-8, 12.35 could also once have been attached directly to 8.28 = 9.7b (cf. in P 11.10/12.30ff. or 12.1-28, 40f.).

In short, both the beginning in 3.16-20 and 5.1-2 and the conclusions in 9.13-16/10.28f. and 11.1-8 are associated with the Priestly Writing and the secondary strata in the plague cycle in many ways. Only one of the two conclusions can be original, if either of them are; the other takes account of the insertion of 9.17–10.27 and 11.10 + 12.1ff. As in the case of the plagues, there are two possible ways of interpreting this complicated state of the text. Either 3.16-20; 5.1-2 and 9.13-14 + 12.29-33[67] or 11.1-3 + 12.29-33[68] (with a continuation in 12.35ff.; 13.20ff.) form a pre-Priestly framework around the plague cycle in 7.14–8.28 (+ 9.1-7). But in that case we must reckon with the loss of a considerable amount of text and later interventions in the text. Or, like everything else, the framework passages are post-Priestly expansions which take account of the combination of the exodus narrative (E) and the Priestly Writing (P) and add theological emphases. That perhaps also explains the motif which dominates the non-Priestly plagues, namely the pretext, which is not immediately obvious, of wanting to go in to the wilderness to celebrate a sacrificial feast for Yhwh and 'serve him on this mountain' (3.12, 18; 5.1; 7.16, etc.). This strange motive has prompted a number of speculations on the history of the tradition;[69] however, it is not earlier but later than the basic narrative. The notion, which for the first time is expressed in connection with the theophany 'on the mountain of God' in Exod. 3–4 (3.1, 12), clashes with the earlier motive of the flight in the original exodus narrative (Exod. 2.15; 14.5), and at least envisages the sacrifice of Exod. 18.12 and 24.4-11, if not the foundation of the sacrificial cult on Mount Sinai in the Priestly Writing.

The basic framework of the old exodus narrative was finally filled out not only with the plagues but also in the wilderness itinerary with midrash-like material which is later than the early expansions in Exod. 15 and Num. 20–24. The narratives of Exod. 16–18 have been inserted between Elim and Sinai in 16.1aα and 19.2 (from 'and they came into the wilderness of Sinai'); they are dependent on the doubtless secondary (post-)Priestly itinerary in 16.1 ('to the wilderness of Sin between Elim and Sinai'); 17.1 (from the wilderness of Sin to Rephidim) and 19.1-2a (arrival in the wilderness of Sinai, 'after they had set out from Rephidim'). Exodus 16 (the manna) adds to the provision of water in 15.22-27 the 'bread from heaven' and the discovery of the sabbath. Exodus 17.1-7 (Massah and Meribah) again takes up the murmuring about the lack of water and links it with the question of tempting Yhwh. Exodus 17.8-16 (Joshua's victory over Amalek) was perhaps sparked off by the name of the camping place $r^e p \bar{\imath} d \bar{\imath} m$ (cf. $r^e p e h$ $y \bar{a} d a y i m$, 'slack hands'; $r p d$, 'support') and given a foretaste of the settlement – which has been separated from its prehistory, the exodus from Egypt, by the intervention of the law on Sinai. Like Exod. 17 (v. 6), Exod. 18 is already located on the mountain of God (18.5); the scene resembles the Sinai pericope in Exod. 2–4 and subsequently attributes to the Midianite priest, Moses' father-in-law, a significant role as a worshipper of Yhwh and in the establishment of local jurisdiction (cf. Num. 11; Deut. 1.9ff.). This recalls the role of the priest-king Melchizedek in Gen. 14 and is occasioned here by the fact that Moses' Midianite family is to be declared Yhwh worshippers and, as in Exod. 15.25b-26, even before the revelation of the Torah on Sinai – to some degree on the basis of natural revelation – Moses is to be shown to be a teacher of the law, expert in the Torah.

The itinerary has also undergone midrash-like expansions in being attached to the Sinai pericope – between Exod. 24.18b = 34.28a and Num. 20.1aβb. Here the departure from Sinai in Num. 10.29-36, the narratives in Num. 11–12, parts of the story of the spies in Num. 13–14 and the rebellion of Dathan and Abiram in Num. 16 are usually assigned to the non-Priestly (Yahwistic or Jehovistic) material. In fact, as we saw above (under B.I.2) all these narratives prove to be additions, simply in the light of the itinerary. They incorporate further detours into the itinerary in Num. 10–20 (R^P), which is itself secondary and post-Priestly: Num. 10–12 (here 10.29-36; 11.3, 35; 12.1, 16) have been inserted between Num. 10.11f. and Num. 13; the non-Priestly parts of the text in Num. 13f. do not provide an independent narrative, but supplement the (post-)Priestly basic material: the basic text of the collection of further pieces of writing in Num. 16–18, the rebellion of Dathan and Abiram against the authority of Moses in 16.12-15, 25-34, is dependent on Num. 13f. and heightens the sins of the people. The narratives often refer back to Exod. 15–18 and restore the old connection between Exod. 15 and Num. 20 under the heightened stipulations of the law which has appeared in the meanwhile (Exod. 19–Num. 10).

In Num. 20–21 the departure from Mount Hor in 21.4-9 continues the (post-)Priestly Meribah narrative in 20.1aα, 2-13, 22-29; the passage 21.1-3, which interrupts the connection between 20.22-29 and 21.4, and the confused list of stages in 21.10-20, which bridges the detour round the land of Edom (20.21; 21.4) to the land of Sihon the king of the Amorites (21.21ff.), are even later. After Deuteronomy the conglomerate of post-Priestly expansions in Num. 25.1b–36.13 has accumulated between Num. 25.1a and Deut. 34.5f./Josh 2.1; 3.1. At more or less the same time as the filling out of the exodus narrative in Exodus–Numbers, Joshua was also revised and expanded in many ways in Deuteronomistic and Priestly style.

5.5   Summary. The earliest elements of the Exodus narrative in Exod. 2–Josh. 12 are the miraculous deliverance of Israelites by a victory of Yhwh over the Egyptians at Etam at the edge of the wilderness in Exod. 12–14 (12.37; 13.20; 14.10b, 19b, 20, 24, 25b, 30a), the Song of Miriam in Exod. 15.20f. (vv. 21b), and the Joshua tradition in Josh. 6 (vv. 1-3, 5, 12a, 14, 20b) and 8 (vv. 1-2a, 10a, 11a, 14, 19). These are independent traditions from the time of the pre-exilic monarchy in Israel which stand in no recognizable connection, except that they speak of striking successes of the national god Yhwh in war and in one case (Exod. 14, perhaps also Josh. 6.1) explicitly speak of 'Israelites'. There must also have been some – scant – tradition about Moses and his Midianite origin, presumably from the milieus of wandering semi-nomads and Hapiru people, but no independent tradition can be made out.

Within the framework of the basic document of the exodus narrative (E^G), the individual narratives and traditions which were handed down independently of one another were brought into a narrative and literary complex. Connecting and thus redactional elements are the figure of Moses (Exod. 2.1-22; 3.1-6, 7f., 21f.; 4.18, 20a; 12.35f.; 14.5f., 13f.; 15.22a; Deut. 34.5f.), Miriam and the sea (Exod. 14.21, 27, 30b; 15.20f.; Num. 20.1) and the wilderness itinerary, which takes Israel from Etam on the edge of the wilderness to Shittim in the fields of Moab opposite Jericho (Exod. 15.22a + Num. 20.1aβb + 22.1 + 25.1a), and from there under the leadership of Joshua over the Jordan (Josh. 2.1-7, 15f., 22f.; 3.1, 14a, 16; 4.19b + Josh. 6–8; and 12.1a, 9-24). On this occasion the miracle of the pillars of cloud and fire from Exod. 14 are brought together with the miracle at the sea in the song of Miriam to form one event (Exod. 13.20f.; 14.5f., 10b, 13-14, 19b, 20, 21, 24, 25a, 27, 30; 15.20f.) and gradually the wilderness itinerary is expanded somewhat (Exod. 15.22a + 15.22b-25a, 27; 16.1aα; 19.2, 3; 24.18b

+ Num. 20.1aβb + 20.14-21; 21.21-24a + 22.1 + 22-24 + 25.1a). The leading notion is the remarkable idea that the origins of Israel lie with Moses and the Hebrews in Egypt. The national god Yhwh regards them as his people; he frees them from the misery of Egypt and leads them into a beautiful and broad land (Exod. 3.7f.). Thus Moses is made the fabled figure depicted in the colours of Sargon and the patriarchs, and the leader on the flight of the people of Israel from Egypt initiated by Yhwh. The military superiority of the national God to the enemies of Israel becomes the decisive, sole act of deliverance with which Yhwh makes his announcement in 3.7f., 21f. come true and frees the people from the misery of Egypt. A local tradition of the capture of Jericho and Ai under Joshua becomes the goal of the exodus depicted in Exod. 2–14, the settlement of Israel. The announcement in Exod. 3.7f. which sets everything off and determines the composition is thus fulfilled.

Subsequently the exodus narrative was revised and expanded several times, above all in Exod. 3–4 and 5–13 with the non-Priestly plague cycle, the basic material of which is to be found in 7.14–8.28 (9.1-7); it is prepared for in different ways in Exod. 3–5, and surpassed in different ways in Exod. 9–13 (9.13ff.; 11.1ff.). Furthermore the wilderness itinerary in Exod. 16–18 and Num. 10–16; 21; 25.1ff. is filled out with narrative material which takes account of the law that has meanwhile been inserted. The supplements initially move within the framework of the independent exodus narrative (E^S); however, at many points, for example, Exod. 3.6, 13-15, 16; 4.5 etc., they presuppose the link of the exodus narrative (E) with the Yahwistic primal history and patriarchal history (J) through Gen. 45–50 and Exod. 1 (JE), perhaps in the plagues, and quite certainly in most of the wilderness narratives they also presuppose the incorporation of the Priestly Writing (R^{PJE}).

6.   Result

The basis of the non-Priestly Hexateuch is independent individual traditions, in the case of Abraham and Moses traditions which are very difficult to grasp and which originally had nothing to do with one another: an anthropogony in Gen. 2–4; the Noachite table of nations in Gen. 10; the Lot narrative in Gen. 19; the Isaac–Jacob narrative cycle in Gen. 26–35, which in turn is made up of the Isaac–Esau narrative cycle and the Jacob–Laban narrative; a tradition about the victory of Yhwh over the Egyptians in Exod. 12.37 + 13.20 + 14; the Song of Miriam in Exod. 15.20f.; the Joshua narratives in Josh. 6 and 8. They were brought together redactionally and edited, and thus found their way into two legends about the origin of Israel: the Yahwistic primal history and patriarchal history in

Table C.II.3

Sources	Basic writing (E)	Additions (before and after P)
Exodus		
		1
Moses	2.1-22	2.4, 7-9
	3.1-8, 21-22	3.2a, 4b, 6a, 7b, 8aβ-20
	4.18, 20a	4.1-17, 19, 20b-31
		5.1-11.9; 12.29-34
War narrative	12.35-36	
12.37	12.38	12.39; 13.1-19
13.20	13.21a(b, 22)	
14.10bα, 19b, 20aαβ, 24,	14.5a, 6, 10bβ, 13–14,	
25b, 30a	20aβγ, 21aα²β, 27aα²βb,	
	30b	14.31
		15.1-19
Song of Miriam		
15.20-21	15.22a	
	15.22b-25a, 27	15.25b-26
	16.1aα	16–18
	19.2aα²b, 3a	19–24
	24.18b	32–34
Numbers		
	(10.12a or 33a?)	11–14; 16
	20.1aββ	
	20.14-21	20.14b-16, 19-20, 22; 21.1-13
	21.21-24a	21.24b-35
Balaam	22.1	
22–24	22–24	22–24
	25.1a	25.1b-5; 32
Deuteronomy		
		1.1–34.4
	34.5-6	34.5f. (additions), 7–12
Joshua		
		1
	2.1-7, 15-16, 22-23	2–5
	3.1,14a, 16	
Joshua	4.19b	
6.1-3aα, 5, 12a, 14aα¹, 20b		6–8
8.1-2a, 10a, 11a, 14, 19		
	10–11	9–11
	12.1a, 9-24	12.1b-8
		13–24

Gen. 2–35 with the later appendix of the Joseph story in Gen. 37–45 (J^G and J^S), and the exodus narrative in Exod. 2–Josh. 12 (E^G and E^S). Through the second narrative arch of the Joseph story in Gen. 45–50 and the link in Exod. 1, J and E were brought together, before the origin and insertion of the Priestly Writing, but after the 'Hexateuch' extending from Exodus–Joshua was expanded to form the 'Enneateuch' (Exodus–Kings), in order to form JE (Genesis–Kings); they were abundantly expanded in all phases.

Notes

1   Cf. Wellhausen, *Comp.*, 314f. For the whole cf. the investigations by Blum, Levin and van Seters (above under C.I.1); for partial areas M. Witte, *Die biblische Urgeschichte*, BZAW 265, 1998; D.M. Carr, *Reading Fractures of Genesis*, Louisville, Ky 1996; J.C. Gertz, *Tradition und Redaktion in der Exoduserzählung*, FRLANT 186, 2000. K. Schmid, *Erzväter und Exodus*, WMANT 81, 1999, discusses trends in scholarship.

2   Von Rad, *Genesis*, 127.

3   *Comp.*, 8.

4   The hero of the flood also has different names in the ancient Near Eastern tradition, depending on the context in the tradition: Ziusudra in the Sumerian version (*ANET*^{3}, 42ff.), Atra(m)hasis in the ancient Babylonian version and its Assyrian recension (*ANET*^{3}, 104ff. and Suppl., 512-14), Utnapishtim in the eleventh table of the Gilgamesh epic (*ANET*^{3}, 93ff.) and Noah in Gen. 6–9.

5   Without the 'dust'.

6   In terms of tradition and literary history Gen. 3.20 deserves priority over 2.23f.

7   Also perhaps Gen. 2.18, 20b, 23(f.).

8   The motif of hybris is associated with the serpent, which makes the woman knowingly guilty and desirous of knowledge in order to be like God: 3.1-5, 6aα^2, 13b-15, 16 (only the introduction to the speech), 22a, 23 (cf. Levin, *Jahwist*, 90f.). The expulsion from paradise entails the loss of eternal life; 2.9bα; 3.22b, 24. As a result life becomes dust: 2.7a; 3.19b. The additions in 2.6, 10-14 with the resumption of v. 8 in v. 15 are concerned with the geography of the lost paradise. Gen. 2.7b, 19b are further glosses.

9   The designation of God as 'Yhwh Elohim' is usually seen as an indication of the redactional connection, but the assumption of a secondary supplementation in either of the two possible trends does not work. It does not explain why the terminology in the basic stratum and the expansions (with the exception of 3.1b-5) is limited to Gen. 2–3.

10   A further indication that Gen. 3.22-24 were not yet in the text (with a Yahwistic revision).

11   If it is thought necessary, the names from Gen. 9.18 may also be added: 'And there were the sons of Noah … Shem, Ham and Japheth', who then appear in reverse order in 10.2 as ancestors of the peoples.

12   Cf. Levin, *Jahwist*, 124.

13   In Gen. 11.6a only 'And Yhwh said, "Behold, they are one people"', and perhaps also 'and this is only the beginning of their doing'. The motif of the common language and the confusion of languages in vv. 1, 6, 7, 9a competes with the motif of dispersion; it is not independent but depends on the motif of the dispersion and in

vv. 8b-9 is connected with the original stratum. The decision on priority is made in v. 4.

14   The piece can also be recognized as a supplement from the fact that in Gen. 9.24 it declares Ham to be the youngest brother, contrary to the order in ch. 10, and thus contrary to 10.6, and in 9.27 puts Shem over him and also over Japheth (as 10.21 already does).

15   According to Noth, *Pentateuch*, 28: 6.5-8 . . . 7.1, 2, 3b, 4, 5, 10, *7 (sic), 16b, 12 (sic), 17b, 22, 23aαb; 8.6a, 2b, 3a . . . 6b (sic), 8-12, 13b . . . 20-22; 9.18-27.

16   Gen. 5.29b in Gen. 5; 10.8-19, 21, 24-30 in Gen. 10.

17   Cf. J.L. Ska, 'El Relato del Diluvio: Un Relato sacerdotal y algunos fragmentos redaccionales posteriors', *EstB* 52, 1994, 37-62.

18   Cf. T. Krüger, 'Das menschliche Herz und die Weisung Gottes', in R.G. Kratz and T. Krüger (eds), *Rezeption und Auslegung im Alten Testament und in seinem Umfeld*, OBO 153, 1997, 65-92, esp. 73ff.

19   Cf. *ANET* [3], 95.

20   Gen. 13.14-17; 15; 16.10; 18.18f.; 21.12f.,17f.; 22.15-18; 24.7; 26.3-5, 24; 46.2-4; 50.24. The basic works on this are J. Hoftijzer, *Die Verheissungen an die Erzväter*, Leiden 1956; M. Köckert, *Vätergott und Väterverheissungen*, FRLANT 142, 1988, esp. 162ff.

21   Cf. Isa. 29.22; 41.8f.; 51.2; 63.16; Jer. 33.26; Ezek. 33.24; Micah 7.20; Pss. 47.10; 105.6, 9, 42; Josh. 24.2f.; 1 Chron. 1; 16(= Ps. 105); 29.18; 2 Chron. 20.7; 30.6; Neh. 9; Jub.; Rom. 4, etc. The trio of patriarchs dominates in the Deuteronomistic passages Exod. 3–4 (3.6, 15, 16; 4.5); Exod. 32–34 (32.13; 33.1); and Deut. 1.8; 6.10; 9.5, 27; 29.12; 30.20; 34.4.

22   Cf. H.W. Wolff, 'Das Kerygma des Jahwisten' (1964), in id., *Gesammelte Studien*, TB 22, 1962, 345-73 (for ET see above B.II, n. 4). See also O.H. Steck, 'Gen 12, 1-3 und die Urgeschichte des Jahwisten' (1971), in Steck, *Wahrnehmungen Gottes im Alten Testament*, Gesammelte Studien, TB 70, 1982, 117-48.

23   In 11.27 (P) Haran is the brother, according to 11.29 the father-in-law of Nahor; according to 27.43; 28.10; 29.4 ḥārān is only the place where Laban lives and has nothing to do with the person Haran; the non-Priestly text in Gen. 12–13 does not presuppose that Lot is a son of Haran and the nephew of Abraham (thus 11.27, 31; 12.5).

24   Without Gen. 29.24, 29.

25   Roughly Gen. 29.32-34 and 30.14, 23-24a without the secondary etymologies in 29.32, 33a; 30.24b. The etymologies of Levi in 29.34 and Joseph in 30.23 are crucial for the narrative. Levi has as much or as little to do with the levitical descent of Moses as the choice of the name Joseph does with the Joseph story, which in turn is dependent on Gen. 29f.

26   Roughly Gen. 30.25-26 (+ 28, 31-42); 31.2 (+ 4-5a, 14, 17, 19a, 20), 21-23, 26(-28), 31.

27   The making of the covenant with the aetiology of Gilead in Gen. 31.43f., 46, 48 and the harmonious separation in 32.1-2a are original.

28   Gen. 26.6 is presumably a resumption of v. 1 after the addition of vv. 2-5; vv. 28-29a originally read: 'And they said, Let there be an oath between us ...'

29   Gen. 32.4-9, 14a are basically original. The prayers in vv. 10-12, 13 interrupt the flow of the narrative and are clearly later, vv. 14b-22 (with the additions in vv. 15-16, 20-21a) can be recognized as an addition by the resumption of v. 14a in v. 22.

30   Gen. 33.1a, 4, 12-15 are basically original. Verses 8-11 presuppose the gift in 32.14b-22, vv. 1b-3, 5-7 the secondary births in chs 29–30.

31   This interpretation of the name competes with the interpretations in 25.26 ('āqeb, hold by the 'heel') and 27.36 ('āqab, 'deceive').

32   Cf. Gen. 25.25, 30, 34; 27.11-13, 16, 21-23; 32.4; 33.14, 16 and the sayings about the nations in 25.23; 27.29, 39f.
33   The mention of Abraham in Gen. 26.1, 15, 18 (after 12.10ff., 20); the secondary promises in 26.2-5 (with the resumption in v. 6) and 26.24 (after 12.1-3, etc.); the reminiscences in 27.35-36 (after Gen. 25) and 27.37-38 (after 27.28f.); the oath in 28.20-22 and 35.2-5; the prayers in 32.10-12, 13; the filling out of the gift scene in 32.14-22 and 33.8-11; and perhaps also the offer in 33.12-14; the commandment about food in 32.33; the wives and children of Jacob in 32.23-24 and 33.1b-3, 5-7 (, 12-14); the supplementation of the Priestly text which has been woven into 33.18-20; the reproach of Reuben in 35.22a with a view to the genealogy in 35.22b-26.
34   Gen. 25.1-4, 6 are additions to v. 5, cf. Noth, *Pentateuch*, 29, 149. Levin, *Jahwist*, 193, also connects vv. 18a with v. 6. Gen. 25.11b, 18(a)b are fed by 16.12, 14; 24.62 and are additions to the Priestly text in 25.7-11a, 12-17.
35   The beginning in Gen. 19.1 seems to have been damaged. Originally 'three men' may have stood here, of whom after the departure of Yhwh in 18.33 only 'two angels' remained (cf. also 19.15). Further additions are: v. 9a (from the second 'and they said ...'), 13b, 14aβ, 15aβb, 16aβ.
36   In Gen. 19.17, either 'and they said' should be read, or there is an addition which assumes Yhwh to be the speaker. In what follows the singular is each time secondary: vv. 18-19, 20b-22a. The speech of Lot 'to them', the men of v. 17, introduced in v. 18, is focused directly on the city of Zoar in vv. 20a, 22b, where Lot arrives at sunrise (v. 23).
37   Taken up again in Gen. 13.3f. after the insertion of 12.10–13.1.
38   Presumably without 18.3b. Verses 16b-22a, 33b are an addition, as can be seen from the way in which v. 16a is taken up again in v. 22a and in the inclusion of vv. 16b and 33b. It brings into the picture Abraham as the bearer of the promise through the plans of Yhwh. Wellhausen, *Comp.*, 25f., recognized the conversation between Abraham and Yhwh in vv. 22b-33a as an insertion.
39   *Pentateuch*, 213; for the discussion cf. K. Schmid, 'Die Josephsgeschichte im Pentateuch', in J.C. Gertz et al. (eds), *Abschied vom Jahwisten*, BZAW 315, 2002, 83-118.
40   The number twelve for the brothers in Gen. 37.9-11, 42.3, 13, 32 and of course in the tribal sayings of Gen. 49 is secondary and, like the sons of the maids in 37.2 and the enumeration of the family of Jacob in 46.8-27, presupposes the combination with the Priestly Writing.
41   Genesis 37.9-11 are a duplication which takes into account the twelve sons of Gen. 29–30, but contradicts 35.18-20, the death of Rachel.
42   Still without the Midianites in 37.28, 36.
43   For the differentiation of the material cf. H. Gressmann, 'Ursprung und Entwicklung der Joseph-Sage', in H. Schmidt (ed.), *Eucharisterion* (FS H. Gunkel I), FRLANT 36/1, 1923, 1-55.
44   Cf. the report in Blum, *Komposition*, 234ff.
45   Cf. *ANET*³, 119; the normative representative texts come from the neo-Assyrian period. Moreover the original stratum sufficiently explains the levitical descent of Moses. This has nothing to do with Levi in Gen. 29.34 or the fact that Levi is absent from the Joseph story.
46   If I understand him rightly, now E. Blum, too, following Schmid and Gertz (see C.II, n. 1) regards the transition in Exod. 1.1-9, on which everything further in 1.10-22 depends, as being (post-)Priestly; cf. Blum, 'Die literarische Verbindung von Erzvätern und Exodus: Ein Gespräch mit neueren Endredaktionshypothesen', in S.C. Gertz, *Abschied vom Yahwisten*, BZAW 315, 2002, 119-56: 145-51.

47 Without Exod. 2.4, 7-10aα. Verses 5aβ, 6aβba ('the child ... and she had compassion on him') are individual glosses, as perhaps are also vv. 2b, 3a (up to 'hide him').

48 Originally only Exod. 2.11-12, to which v. 15 joins seamlessly. Verses 13-14 add a second motive for the flight.

49 No one knows why he is called Reuel in Exod. 2.18 and Jethro in 3.1; 4.18; and 18.1, regardless of whether one assumes two independent traditions (sources) or expansions at one or other place or both. The efforts to compensate in Num. 10.29-33; Judg. 1.16; 4.11 and the historical speculations attached to them take us no further.

50 Originally Exod. 3.1 (without the mountain of God), vv. 2b, 3, 4a. Verse 3 adds the angel of Yahweh, vv. 4b-6 pronounce the place of the appearance holy.

51 Without Exod. 3.7b, 8aββ. The rest elaborates the scene: 3.9f. sends Moses alone, 3.16-20 Moses and the elders, ahead to Pharaoh and prepares for the plagues which have been inserted (originally 7.14ff.?); 3.11-12, 13-15 and 4.1-9, 10-12 dismiss various objections; 4.13-17 introduces Aaron, and this prepares for 4.27-31 and 5.1f.; 5.3–6.1.

52 Exodus 4.19 interrupts the context and derives the intention of Moses expressed in v. 18 at a secondary stage explicitly from the command of Yhwh. The assurance that he has nothing more to fear, which goes back to 2.15, distracts from the purpose and again gives more weight to Moses' destiny.

53 Together with Exod. 12.34, 12.39 prepares for the regulations for the feast of unleavened bread in the insertion 13.1-16 and gives it a basis in the salvation history. Exod. 13.17-19 explain the detour via the wilderness and – after the start in 12.37-41 – add the observance of the oath of Gen. 50.25 (cf. Josh. 24.32).

54 Exod. 14.5-6, 10b, 13-14, 19b-20, 21aα^{2}β, 24-25, 27aα^{2}βb, 30. Verses 5b, 7, 19a, 20aβγ can be bracketed off as glosses; vv. 10a, 11f., 15aβ, 31 are post-Priestly.

55 Perhaps without the addition 'the sister of Aaron', if this is not the original place of Aaron before his career as priest and mouthpiece of Moses. The extended version in Exod. 15.1-18 presumably goes back to a core in vv. 6-12 and has attached itself to the hymn quoted in v. 1 in the mouth of Moses (and the Israelites). The thanksgiving genre fits the topic in 3.7f.; 14.13f., 30.

56 The 'from the Reed Sea' is presumably an addition connected with Exod. 13.17-18 (cf. 15.4). There is no mention of this scene either in 13.20 or in Exod. 14.

57 Exod. 15.25b-26 is generally recognized as an addition which, like Exod. 18 and Josh. 24.25, foresees a law alongside the law of Sinai in order to be able to put the people to the test beforehand and measure them by the law.

58 On the basis of the insertions in Num. 10–20, Kadesh in Num. 20.1aα becomes a secondary detour into the wilderness of 'Zin', just as in Exod. 16.1 'Sin' becomes a detour into the wilderness of Sinai, in Num. 13.26 finally even into the wilderness of Paran. For the original geography (Exod. 15.22a + Num. 20.1) cf. Gen. 20.1.

59 The discovery was made by Ulrich Nötzel, whose analysis of Exod. 14 will be presented in his dissertation.

60 Thus in the original stratum only Josh. 6.1, if that has not also been expanded by 'before the Israelites'.

61 Cf. Wellhausen, *Comp.*, 31.

62 Noth, *Pentateuch*, 49; id., *History of Israel*, 111f.

63 For the situation around 840 BC cf. the Mesha inscription (*ANET*^{3}, 320f.). The origin of Balaam has become known through the discovery of the inscription of Deir 'Alla (*TUAT* II, 138-48) and suggests that the complex in Num. 22–24 can be connected with the conditions of the eighth century. In that case the Exodus creed in

Num. 22.5 could be claimed for the ancient tradition only if the perspective was from Transjordan westwards. However, if we are to conjecture that the scene is the borderland between Israel and Moab, north-east of the Dead Sea (Noth, *Numbers*, 172), then the reference to the origin of Israel in Egypt, which does not fit with the permanent state of neighbourliness presupposed, of course depends on the literary context of the exodus narrative. The twofold 'Behold' in Num. 22.5 – the second is the resumption of the first, 'Behold, a people . . . has covered the surface of the land, and it dwells over against me' – is an indication that this is a subsequent insertion (the addition 22.11 is different); the 'in that time' in 22.4b also presupposes the prehistory.

64 The 'elders' also appear elsewhere only in late passages and often together with Aaron, cf. Exod. 12.21; 17.5f.; 18.12; 19.7; 24.1, 9, 14.

65 There is no basis for the correction of the text in Exod. 5.1 apart from the presupposition of the documentary hypothesis. The plural in 5.1, 3 cannot refer over and beyond 4.18, 20a to Moses and the elders in 3.16-20.

66 Noth, *Exodus*, 80f., regarded Exod. 9.14-16 as an addition. More recent scholars find in 9.13f. either the 'summary of the plagues' of 7.14–8.28, though the report and occurrence of them is never reported in this way, but is presupposed in 11.8; 12.30-33 (without the killing of the firstborn) (Levin), or the announcement of the plague of the firstborn which – in connection with 9.13f. + 10.28f. – is announced once again in 11.4-8 and reported in 12.29-33 (Gertz). However, with or without the plague of the firstborn, it is easiest to connect 12.19-33 directly with 9.13-14. Of course the series of plagues in 9.17ff. is also a candidate for a continuation; these are either directly or indirectly aimed at the Pharaoh himself, his servants and his people (cf. 10.6, and 9.19-21, 30; 10.22f.).

67 Possibly expanded by Exod. 9.15-10.28 + 11.1-3 and 11.4-8, 9 + 11.10; 12.1-28 (and 13.1ff.).

68 Possibly expanded by Exod. 9.13–10.28 and 11.4-8, 9 + 11.10; 12.1-28 (and 13.1ff.).

69 Cf. Noth, *Exodus*, 55f.

III.   The Hexateuch

1.   Source division and the composition of the Hexateuch

Wellhausen could start by assuming that the literary-critical differentiation of Yahwist (J), Elohist (E), Jehovist (JE) and Priestly Writing (P) and the 'composition of the Hexateuch' were one and the same. Although he recognized very clearly, and indeed indicated here and there, that the division of sources would not be as successful everywhere as in Gen. 1–3 and the rest of the primal history and the patriarchal history, he regarded it as 'settled' that P and JE 'continue through Genesis as far as the book of Joshua'.[1] However, in the process, for him the two narrative threads J and E became the 'composition JE', which can hardly be disentangled any longer; with this finding was associated the expectation that 'it will not suddenly change from Exod. 1 onwards, especially as in any case Gen. 50 cannot form the conclusion of either J or E'.[2] Moreover Wellhausen has to concede that he has not succeeded in tracing 'the thread of J and E through the whole', because the (Jehovistic) editor in Exod. 1–Num. 10 'dealt far more freely with what he had before him'[3] and 'in the second half of the book of Numbers and in the book of Joshua an element enters which fluctuates undecided between JE and Q, and cannot rightly be defined',[4] the element of a revision which in Joshua 'emerges more strongly and has a far more explicit colouring than in the Pentateuch'.[5] Here, as in Exodus and Numbers,[6] it is difficult to separate it from the Deuteronomistic redaction. In fact, according to Wellhausen we do not have three source documents but two, P and JE, and in JE even Jehovistic material, isolated subsidiary traditions and different revisions, where the revision in Genesis is clearly different from that in Exodus to Joshua.

The differentiation made by Wellhausen was thoroughly misunderstood for a long time, in that each new revision was made a new source document or a new edition. Noth's tradition-historical analysis was directed against this: first of all he limited the source writings again to three versions (J, E and P), and – with Wellhausen's dictum about the end of J in Num. 24[7] – restricted these to the books of Genesis, Exodus and Numbers, that is, to the Tetrateuch; secondly, he separated source division and composition and transferred the further differentiation, Wellhausen's 'composition of the Hexateuch' (now Pentateuch or Tetrateuch), into the prehistory of the 'main themes of the tradition' – oral or written. The 'filling out of the framework given by the themes with narrative material' and the 'growing together of themes and individual traditions' was put here. In this way the composition of the Pentateuch became something fundamentally different from the origin of 'the great literary histories found in the Old Testament', the Deuteronomistic and Chronistic works,[8] though Noth did recognize throughout the significance of the literary shaping of the material by individual authors in giving it form; in this way they put their theological stamp on the tradition that had come down, as in the great literary historical works.[9] Moreover, as the footnotes in the *History of Pentateuchal Tradition*, and even more the commentaries on Exodus and Numbers in OTL show, Noth reckoned with extensive literary supplements to the source documents, not least with the 'Deuteronomistic' revision of the Pentateuch in the sphere of Exodus–Numbers which had already been noted by Wellhausen.

In more recent research the separation of source division and tradition-historical analysis of the composition introduced by Noth has led some scholars only to investigate the written sources on which Genesis–Numbers are based, their basic writing and their supplements, and other scholars to investigate only the composition in Genesis and Exodus–Numbers as it is now. In the one case the written sources generously demarcated by Noth, his predecessors and his successors are reduced over and beyond Wellhausen and Noth to a minimum, in which either the originals or the written sources or the redaction itself – Yahwistic, Jehovistic, Deuteronomistic and Priestly – are discovered. This procedure simply presupposes the 'main themes of the tradition' and largely also the 'growing together of themes and individual traditions', and points to the 'filling out of the framework given by the themes' with narrative material in the subsequent history.[10] In the other case the 'main themes of the tradition' and the 'filling out of the framework given by the themes with narrative material' is presupposed; the composition, the 'growing together of themes and individual traditions', located by Noth in the prehistory, is transferred to the later history and rediscovered in the later and latest (Deuteronomistic) supplementary strata of JE. At any rate for the sphere of Exodus–Numbers, Wellhausen and Noth already thought that these worked over early material but could hardly be separated from it any longer, and finally even the Priestly Writing is counted as a last, formative redactional stratum of a Priestly composition which goes beyond the patriarchal history and exodus narrative, but in substance is also dependent on the continuation in Joshua–Kings.[11] Both approaches drop the question which Noth posed precisely and answered in his own way, as to where the 'main themes of the tradition' come from and above all how the themes came to be brought together. This at any rate presupposes the 'filling out of the framework given by the themes', regardless of whether one puts the 'growing together of the themes and individual traditions' before the (Yahwistic) source writing or redaction and the subsequent 'filling out of the framework given by the themes with narrative material' or simply has the 'filling out' and the growing together in the late (Deuteronomistic and Priestly) composition pass over into one another. Neither the literary-critical reduction of the written sources, which Noth reduced to Genesis–Numbers, to an absolute minimum of originals (sources) and redaction, nor the transfer of the composition, which Noth explained in terms of tradition history, into the late Deuteronomistic and Priestly strata, explains the planned redactional scheme of the Pentateuch which lies behind it, and which moreover does not end in the Tetrateuch but in the Hexateuch or Enneateuch.

In going through the texts, a combination of dividing the sources and analysing the composition has proved to be the way forward. It is and remains right to distinguish the Priestly and non-Priestly texts and to separate out the Priestly Writing (P) as an independent 'source'. Its relationship to the non-Priestly text (JE) corresponds to some degree to that of Chronicles to the books of Samuel–Kings or Genesis–Kings, with the difference that P and JE were subsequently combined into one work (R^{PJE}). As for the non-Priestly text (JE), we must leave further division of sources completely aside and here, as in the other literary historical works of the Old Testament, differentiate between original stratum, basic writing and expansions, and also explain the composition in terms of the distinction between tradition and redaction, that is, correlate the 'growing together' of the 'main themes of the tradition' and the 'filling out of the framework given by the themes' with the development of the text. The 'main themes of the tradition' provide the originally independent narrative units, the originals of the basic document which, if we are not to find ourselves in a fairytale world, can be regarded as originals only to the degree that they have not been worked over and are capable of independent life. Putting them together into a continuous narrative, the 'growing together of themes and individual traditions' is the work of a redactor in the framework of a first composition, in which the reduction to the literary core, the basic writing, reinforces the impression gained from Wellhausen and Noth in the course of the division of sources that the composition of the primal history and patriarchal history in Genesis and that of the Exodus narrative in Exodus, Numbers and Joshua are very different and took place independently of each other. The 'filling out of the framework given by the themes with narrative material' in the basic writing of Genesis and Exodus–Joshua took place before and after its attachment; these are extensive pre- and post-Deuteronomistic and pre- and post-Priestly supplements which, in so far as they are post-Deuteronomistic and post-Priestly, have to do with the piling up of the Hexateuch to form the

Enneateuch and with the incorporation of the Priestly Writing into the Enneateuch or the developing Pentateuch.

2.   J and E in the Hexateuch

Both the patriarchal history in Genesis and the exodus narrative in Exodus, Numbers and Joshua are based on self-contained individual traditions. They are listed above (under C.II.6) and come from the time of the pre-exilic monarchy, some from the north of Israel (Jacob and Laban, Israelites and Egyptians), others from the region around Jericho and Ai in central Palestine (Joshua), and yet others from the Judahite south (Abraham, Lot, Isaac and Esau, Moses and Midian); the Cainite anthropogony and the Noachite table of nations, which put the Cainites and Semites in the East, and Miriam, cannot be localized more precisely. It is striking that the original material does not report either about Yhwh and Israel or, as in the case of Exod. 12–14 (12.37 + 13.20 + 14), Miriam's song of victory in Exod. 15.20f. and Joshua in Josh. 6 and 8, about the history of the people of Israel, but only about individual, spectacular yet quite unspecific victories of Yhwh, the god of the nation and of war. This has been seen as a sign of a pre- or early Israelite tradition, or at least a tradition from before the time of the state. But with this dating one is merely following the suggestion of the later theological overpainting and division into epochs. Taken by themselves, the northern and central Palestinian narratives about Yhwh's war in Exod. 12–14 and Josh. 6; 8 and the song of victory in Exod. 15.20f. presuppose the monarchy of Israel and its chief god Yhwh; the original material of the primal history and patriarchal history also fit the Israelite and Judahite monarchy admirably, provided that we are clear that alongside the central monarchy and its apparatus of officials (administration, army and cult) there were always also other structures: different family and clan alliances, regional and tribal units, which led a life of their own. The original material of the primal and patriarchal history and the narratives about the 'judges' before they were Israelitized and inserted into the salvation history bear witness to this. In both cases the differences are not chronological but geographical and sociological. And the differences by no means indicate that the narratives about the patriarchs and judges were originally anti-monarchical. On the contrary, the more the central kingship and its apparatus of officials was consolidated both internally and externally, the more the other structures could develop, in so far as any notice was taken of the central monarchy at all. However, the degree to which the monarchy and the chief god Yhwh furthered the sense of community is evident from the examples in Exod. 12–14; 15.20f.; and Josh. 6; 8, where regional events or the formation of legends deal with Yhwh the god of the nation and of war, and in one case or another (Exod. 12–14, perhaps also Josh. 6.1) are also specifically about the Israelites. We cannot recognize in them a communal sense of Israel before the state or even the existence of an institution encompassing all of Israel, Israel and Judah, like the 'ancient Israelite amphictyony'. Before the origin of the monarchy Israelites were rather like Ephraimites, Benjaminites, Judahites, Ishmaelites and other Canaanite clans and tribes which called themselves after this or that. As soon as and as long as the two kingdoms existed, there was no need for them and the people of Lot, Isaac, Jacob or Joshua to reflect on who or what Israel was in relation to Judah. Only when the kingdoms perished did the question of what was to become of them arise. The name 'Israel' first became free around 720 BC and therefore was only then filled with new content.

Of the various pieces of original material, the anthropogony in Gen. 2–4, the Noachite table of nations in Gen. 10, the Lot narrative in Gen. 19, the Isaac–Jacob narrative cycle in Gen. 26–35 which first grew up independently, and an Abraham tradition that we can hardly grasp any longer form the basis of the – Yahwistic – primal history and patriarchal history (J). In it the individual traditions are put in a narrative and literary context and brought under the theological sign of Yhwh's curse and blessing. Both Yhwh's curse and blessing and also the conditions of life described in the primal history and patriarchal history largely correspond to the pre-exilic social structures which also prevail in the time of the monarchy and the popular piety at a family and local level, except that there is the special feature that the families and clans represent the small states of the land-bridge of Syria–Palestine associated by kinship. And over all is the one God Yhwh, the national God who stands over the monarchies of Israel and Judah; their relationship is said to be that of father and son. The special sanctioning of the pre-exilic conditions and the depiction of the national religion in the garb of family and local religion are not a matter of course, but needed a special occasion. If we do not want immediately to go to the time after 587 BC for the first redactional version of the primal history and the patriarchal history, a period which is not supported by anything but the current fashion for late dating, the only possible period is the downfall of the Israelite monarchy around 720 BC and the fluctuating situation between 720 and 587 BC, in which the question must have been one of giving 'Israel', which had become stateless and homeless, a new home and its own, non-state identity alongside and in the state of Judah, which still existed. Instead of lamenting the loss of statehood and hoping for the renewal of the monarchy; instead of giving itself up completely and being taken up entirely in the state of Judah, 'Israel' sought a distinctive identity beyond the statehood which had been lost in the northern kingdom of Israel and continued to exist in Judah, albeit exposed to danger, at the level of local and family membership. At this level the small states of Syria and Palestine, often bound together politically in anti-Assyrian coalitions, come closer together, and the submerged 'Israel' becomes the father of 'Judah'. We can regard the combination of the north-Palestinian pair Jacob and Laban with the south-Palestinian pair Isaac and Esau in Gen. 26–35 as a preliminary stage to this; the idea seems to have been fully developed and theologically reflected on in the Yahwistic composition and the basic writing of the primal history and patriarchal history in Gen. 2–35 (J^G).

Someone else has (re)constructed the history of the exodus of Israel from Egypt, the wandering in the wilderness, and the settlement in Exod. 2–Josh. 12 out of the victory over the Egyptians in Exod. 12–14, Miriam's hymn of victory in Exod. 15.20f., the Joshua narratives in Josh. 6 and 8, and a Moses tradition that we can hardly grasp any longer. Here Israel and Yhwh are not redactional but dominate the material from the beginning. Quite manifestly these are formerly independent north-Israelite traditions, which fit best into the thought of the pre-exilic national religion of the time of the Israelite monarchy (before 720 BC), even if they come from different regions and originally represented different interests. The linking of the individual events to the sequence of events of the exodus, in which the national God Yhwh frees 'his people' under the leadership of Moses, Miriam and Joshua from the 'misery of Egypt' and brings them – by-passing Judah – into a 'beautiful and broad land' (Exod. 3.7f.) is the work of the redaction. Of course the notion that 'Israel' is not the monarchy in the north of Palestine but the people of Yhwh which has its origin outside the land in a unique historical act of its God is also redactional. With the exodus narrative in Exod. 2–Josh. 12 the exodus creed comes into being; this is central to the self-understanding of 'Israel' in the Old Testament which separates Israel from all the other peoples inside and outside Canaan and puts it in an exclusive relationship to its God Yhwh – in this it is quite different from the patriarchal history. We can only speculate on why Israel comes from Egypt in particular. Some Israelites must in fact have immigrated from there – with or without Yhwh. The fate of the semi-nomads and Hapiru/Hebrew existences that was behind this was hardly limited chronologically to the period between 1200 and 1000 BC and geographically to the no-man's land between Palestine and Egypt. And finally, the political role of Egypt in the clashes between Israel and Judah and Assyria and Babylon must also have been influential. Liberation from the 'misery of Egypt' at the beginning of the history of Israel is to some degree a counterpart to the misery under Assyria at the end of Israelite history; this did not promise a future beyond the state to the monarchy in Israel, but it did promise such a future to Israel as the people of Yhwh. The *terminus post quem* of the Exodus narrative, for which I use the siglum E, is likewise the downfall of the monarchy of Israel around 720, and its origin falls in the fluctuating situation between

720 and 587 BC in which Israel was without a state and the state of Judah lived on as before. If we may trust the geography at all, according to E, in distinction from the Yahwistic patriarchal history, the future of Israel does not lie in Israel and Judah but solely in the realm of ancient Israel, and especially in the always disputed territory of Benjamin around Jericho and Ai. Evidently Judah is left out of the wandering deliberately.

J and E, the Yahwistic primal history and patriarchal history in Gen. 2–35, and the Exodus narrative in Exod. 2–Josh 12, are two independent legends about the origin of Israel which compensate for the loss of the monarchy by giving a new identity to the people of the state, who have become stateless and homeless. In the one case this is an identity as father of Judah in the alliance of the Syrian-Palestinian family of states. In the other, it is that of the people of Yhwh alongside Judah and the other Canaanite peoples in Palestine. The legends may have been known to each other, and perhaps may even have been assimilated quite deliberately; however, initially they did not constitute a continuous narrative thread but were in competition. Both derive 'Israel' and its stateless existence in the land from the will of Yhwh: for this the one refers to Abraham, Isaac and Jacob, and the other to Moses, Miriam and Joshua.

3.   J, E, JE and P in the Enneateuch

Subsequently the two legends about origins (J^G and E^G) were handed on independently, supplemented and expanded by larger parts (J^S and E^S). The primal history and the patriarchal history in Gen. 2–35 were expanded by the Joseph story in Gen. 37–45. The appendix takes into account the Egyptian Judaism which we know about from reports about the beginnings of the Babylonian period (2 Kgs 25.26; the Jeremiah narratives) and from the Elephantine papyri in Persian times. Without any evidence, I conjecture that the writing was developed further after 587 BC. The fate of the fugitives in Egypt was closer to the heart of the author than the fate of the parts of the people deported to Babylon, perhaps because the Egyptian Diaspora was older and also already had some contact with Judah before 587 BC, and because the Babylonian Golah, like the Assyrian deportations at the end of the eighth century, was thought to be lost. Initially no one envisaged the return of either.

Not long before and soon after 587 BC, the law was implanted in the exodus narrative, which was still independent in the framework of the Hexateuch (Exodus–Joshua): first the Book of the Covenant, then Deuteronomy, and lastly the Decalogue. The law complements the indicative of the exodus creed with the imperative, the obligation to ongoing obedience to the one and only God, which at the latest after the centralization of the cult and the 'Hear, Israel', in Deuteronomy applies to the one 'Israel' made up of Israel and Judah (Jerusalem). The law was the point of contact for the piling up of the 'Hexateuch' (Exodus–Joshua) into the 'Enneateuch' (Exodus–Kings); in E for the combination of the exodus narrative in Exodus–Joshua (E) with the Deuteronomistic narrative work in Samuel–Kings (Dtr^G) through the connecting link of the time of the judges in Judges (Dtr^R), which is the explanation of the (post-) Deuteronomistic additions in Exodus–Numbers and the literary cross-references to the exodus in Deuteronomy–Kings (Dtr^S) which have been observed time and again since Wellhausen.

The Priestly Writing came into being more or less contemporaneously with the building up of the exodus narrative into the 'Enneateuch', Exodus–Kings, in the period of the Second Temple. In it the exodus narrative is integrated into the patriarchal history, and the covenant of Sinai/Horeb and in Moab is replaced by the covenant with Noah and Abraham. The extent is limited to the complex from the creation of the world to the foundation of the sanctuary on Sinai in Gen. 1–Exod. 40 (P^G) or to the revelation of the law on Sinai in Gen. 1–Lev. 27 (P^S). The Priestly Writing for the first time offers a kind of 'Tetrateuch' and preliminary stage to the later Pentateuch.

Presumably the Priestly Writing preceded the prefacing of the primal history and the patriarchal history in Genesis (J) to the Deuteronomistic exodus narrative in Exodus–Kings (E + Dtr), though the combination of J and E into JE was initially quite loose. The expansion of the Joseph narrative in Gen. 45–50 and the hinge in Exod. 1.8-10a, 15-22 produce a literary connection. With this combination (JE) and the incorporation of the Priestly Writing into the Tetrateuch (R^{PJE}), the Enneateuch received its final form before the separation of the two parts of the canon, the Law and the Prophets. This is the explanation for a series of late- or post-Deuteronomistic expansions in Genesis–Numbers and also the corresponding literary references to the patriarchs and Priestly expansions through Genesis–Numbers into Deuteronomy–Kings. Putting Genesis before Exodus–Kings set the law and the history of the people of Israel which came to grief on it and the monarchy under the abiding promise to Abraham and his seed. The separation of the Pentateuch (Genesis–Deuteronomy) as Torah also allowed the history and the law of Moses, the greatest of all the prophets (Deut. 34.10-12), to become an eternally valid promise.

Notes

1 Wellhausen, *Comp.*, 61.
2 Ibid.

3   Ibid., 72, similarly ibid., 94f.
4   Ibid., 207f., Q = P.
5   Ibid., 116f.
6   Ibid., 94 n. 1: 'unless another Deuteronomist is to be assumed apart from him' (viz the Jehovist in Exod. 1–Num. 10 who is like-minded with Deuteronomy).
7   *Comp.*, 116.
8   Noth, *Pentateuch*, 2.
9   Ibid., 228ff.
10 Thus Levin, *Jahwist*.
11 Thus Blum, *Komposition der Vätergeschichte*; id., *Studien zur Komposition des Pentateuch*.

Conclusion

1.   The Israel of the literary tradition is not the Israel of history. As in
the New Testament a distinction is made between the historical and the
kerygmatic Christ, so in the Old Testament the historical and the biblical
Israel must be kept separate. De Wette already taught us to see the
difference;[1] Wellhausen focused it in his distinction between ancient Israel
and Judaism,[2] and Noth again blurred it somewhat by projecting the views
which post-exilic Judaism had of ancient Israel, Israel 'in the language of
confession of faith',[3] as articulated in the Old Testament, into the early pre-
Israelite period. But since the people of Israel did not yet exist in the early
period, we must say good-bye to the notion that everything that makes
Israel what it is or should be in the Old Testament according to the will of
God was already present from the beginning, at least in substance, and to
some degree had been revealed. Archaeology and tradition history point in
precisely the opposite direction. What constitutes the Israel and the Yhwh
of the Old Testament and defines the relationship of the God Yhwh to his
people Israel is the result of a long, painful process of maturing in which the
normality of the two states of Israel and Judah in profane and religious
history gradually became the theological interpretation of the Old
Testament, the 'language of confession and faith', and in which the
peculiarities of God's people Israel, which stand out in analogies with the
ancient Near East, developed.[4]

So the history of Israel told in the Old Testament must not be confused
with the historical Israel. Moreover, as this book has made clear, the
composition and composition history of the narrative works are not simply
identical with the history of Israel. That certainly does not mean that they
are all mere literary fiction and as such can be treated according to the
categories of modern literary criticism. Of course historical insights and the
remnants of authentic tradition have found their way into the Old
Testament, from the earliest strata to the latest. But in no way do we have
direct access to them. Everything is mediated by the tradition. This reflected
on and interpreted the historical circumstances, experiences and traditions
after the event, indeed after the decisive historical breaks of 722–720 BC and
597–587 BC, so as not to lose the link between the history of Israel and
Judah which had been broken off and their own God, but to remember it as
a new foundation which was significant for the future. And even in those

traditions which still know nothing of the sudden ends to the history of Israel and Judah and reflect the conditions of the pre-exilic monarchy, we do not have historical protocols documenting the past or the status quo, but interpretations defining the status quo of a group, a region or a political system by means of its prehistory – shaped by its own ideal. Therefore the Old Testament is not the primary source for the history of Israel and Judah and their religion, but the source of the history of spiritual life and theology in Israel and Judah, in some fragments in the period before, but for the most part for the period after, the historical breaks of 720 BC and 587 BC. At this point the tradition changed into the 'language of confession and faith', Yhwh became the one and only God of Israel, and Israel the one and only people of Yhwh.

2.   A whole series of individual narratives and narrative cycles can be claimed for the period before 720 BC and 587 BC, when Israel and Judah were two independent monarchies in the midst of the world of the states of Syria–Palestine during the first half of the first millennium BC. These once circulated independently and found their way into the composition of Genesis–Kings. From the Israelite north or central Palestine come Jacob and Laban in Gen. 29–31,[5] the Yhwh war in Exod. 12–14,[6] Balaam in Num. 22–24, Joshua and the wars of Yhwh in Josh. 6 and 8,[7] the local heroes in Judg. 3–16,[8] Samuel and Saul in 1 Sam. 1–14,[9] extracts from the 'books of days' of the kings of Israel, and individual traditions (like for example, 1 Kgs 18.41ff.; 2 Kgs 4; 9–10) in Kings. From the south come Lot in Gen. 19,[10] Isaac and Esau in Gen. 26–27,[11] David and Solomon in 2 Sam. 11–12 + 1 Kgs 1–2, Absalom in 2 Sam. 14–20, David–Absalom–Solomon in 2 Sam. 11–1 Kgs 2,[12] extracts from the 'books of days' of the kings of Judah and individual traditions (like 2 Kgs 11) in Kings. The Cainite anthopogony in Gen. 2–4,[13] the Noachic table of nations in Gen. 10[14] and the song of Miriam in Exod. 15.20f. cannot be given a specific location, and the traditions of Abraham and Sarah (Gen. 12–13), Joseph in Egypt (Gen. 39–41), Moses in Midian (Exod. 2) and some splinters of tradition (for example, Josh. 10.12f.), which keep recurring at all literary levels, cannot be demarcated with certainty.

The different types of narrative – patriarchal narratives, narratives of Yhwh wars, legends about heroes, narratives about kings and prophets and official notices – do not represent various historical periods to which one need only assign individual episodes, as the later redactors did, and as modern historians do after them, in order to reconstruct from them the course of the history of Israel. Rather, they are to be regarded as roughly contemporaneous. They all reflect the social and religious conditions of the early, middle or late monarchy and derive these paradigmatically from specific events, often events of the 'beginning' or a critical transition. The difference is that the narratives move on different sociological levels and therefore reflect the same circumstances from different perspectives, with quite different interests. The beginnings of humankind and the patriarchal narratives in Genesis move on the level of the clan, the family and family alliances; the narratives about heroes in Judges which are closely related to them in the environment of tribes, localities and regions; the Yhwh war narratives, the legends about the origin of the kingdom in Israel and in Judah and the extracts from the annals in the environment of the monarchy. The various sociological fields which can be seen from the structure of the action and the living conditions presupposed in it correspond to the three spheres of family, local and state religion typical of the pre-exilic monarchy. The living conditions presupposed in the narratives and the religious phenomena depicted are very modest and small-scale; the mode of narrative is brief and concentrates on essentials. The scantiness of the means of description coincides with the evidence from inscriptions and the historical analogies in Syria–Palestine. It has its foundation in the sparse political and cultural conditions of the small states of Syria–Palestine in the first half of the first millennium; these did not in the remotest approach the order of magnitude of the cultured nations of Egypt and Mesopotamia in the ancient Near East, but became involved in them more and more as time went on.

The sources of the pre-exilic monarchical period contain not only narrative but also a hymn (Exod. 15.21b) and a collection of legal principles, the *mišpāṭîm* in the earliest Book of the Covenant (Exod. 21.12–22.19). This reminds us that the pre-exilic tradition of Israel and Judah was quite varied; indeed, we must even say that the narratives were hardly among the most prominent and earliest traditions. The utilitarian literature which had its place in the court and temple was far more prominent and was earlier. We must understand this to include primarily details of the political, military and above all administrative administration of the court, that is, of its daily business, but we no longer possess all this. The notes from annals in the books of Kings are a miserable fragment. The material also includes festal calendars and sacrificial rituals which found their way into the law,[15] temple songs like the 'Canaanite' hymns[16] or the scheme of the lament and thanksgiving of the individual[17] which have been preserved in the Psalter, the old proverbial wisdom which still awaits a precise literary demarcation from later additions,[18] and Israelite or Judahite prophecy,[19] which is hidden in the prophetic books of the Old Testament, but by nature corresponded more to the picture given by the prophetic narratives in Samuel–Kings and especially the type of what are called 'false prophets' in the Old Testament. Like priests and prophets, the judges too held office both locally, here in the framework of judgment at the gate, and also at the court and temple in the capital. The codification of the law, of which only a modest selection is offered in Exod. 20–21, must have taken place in the same way as the codification of proverbial wisdom for the purpose of education at the court. Sacrificial rituals, hymns and prayers have their natural place in the temple. The old narratives occupy a modest place alongside this stock of old tradition. This can hardly be wondered at, given that only a few elites were able to read and write. In so far as they, too, do not belong in the environment of court and temple, the narratives probably came into being in the groups of which they tell, and through oral tradition fell into the hands of those who made them into literature.

The pre-exilic traditions are marked by the way in which with a certain naivety they simply presume the existing political, social, economic and religious conditions and do not (yet) make these a theme. Theories about the exodus in terms of theology or social revolution, and ideas of the one and only God which brought together the people of Israel and demarcate it from others, are quite remote from them. Life goes on in limited geographical, ethnic and social relationships. A sense of national community is expressed where necessary, but not explicitly unless this is in the face of enemies from outside. As the onomasticon here and in the inscriptions confirms, Yhwh is a national god and at the same time a personal god; he wages war and, as we know from other sources, with 'his Asherah' is concerned for the well-being of those who worship him. In the hymns and prayers he has the features of the west-Semitic chief gods El and Baal; he is king of the gods and lord of the earth; he conquers the sea, gives the rain and is responsible for rescue from the sphere of death. Human intrigues and divine miracles dominate in the narratives. Legal principles, wisdom sayings and even prophetic oracles do not refer to external authorities like the king or the deity, but legitimate themselves. The old tradition may perhaps seem profane to us today, but through and through it has a religious stamp, except that religion and piety are not really reflected. As long as a king ensured peace at home and abroad; as long as wisdom teachers trained the elites and priests and prophets and judges did their duty; as long as the harvest yield was good and life could develop in the families, tribes and localities under the unifying roof of the monarchy and according to its own rules and customs, there was no occasion to think about who or what Israel, Judah or Yhwh was or should be. Israel and Judah were like Moab. And Yhwh was the god of Israel and the god of Judah as Chemosh was the god of Moab.

3.   That changed when towards the end of the eighth century BC Tiglath-pileser III made an appearance and began to incorporate the Aramaean city states and the territorial state of Israel into the Assyrian empire bit by bit from the north. One of his successors, Sennacherib, marched up to the gates of Jerusalem, where around 700 BC for unexplained reasons the Assyrian campaign of conquest ground to a halt.

After the final subjugation of the capital of Samaria around 720 BC and its integration into the Assyrian provincial system, Israel, the kingdom in northern Palestine, no longer existed. Up to 701 BC people in Judah and Jerusalem also had to fear the same fate, but once again they were let off with no more than terror and a reduction of their sphere of rule to the capital Jerusalem and the land round about, in so far as they were not deported. From now on the Israelites lived either in their old territories in the Assyrian province of Samerina or as immigrants in the territory of the kingdom of Judah, on the former border with Benjamin which had formerly been fought over, or in the capital Jerusalem, which was extending westwards. A not inconsiderable number must also have fled to Egypt, where over the years they formed a Jewish Diaspora, but we only hear of this much later.

Unfortunately we do not know precisely what became of the Aramaeans in Syria after the Assyrian invasion. However, as the invasion here began very much earlier and only individual (city) states were ever affected by it, whereas others profited from the presence of the Assyrians and still behaved for a while as loyal vassals, we can at any rate say that life did not cease all at once with the end of state autonomy. Under alien Assyrian rule it followed its accustomed course, with or without a king. The national god Baal or Hadad, who here and there had to suffer a military defeat, survived the Assyrian invasion, whether in the Aramaean capitals which were still ruled by him alone, or in a coalition with the gods of the Assyrian empire regulated by treaty. Things must not have been very much different in Israel and Judah towards the end of the eighth century BC. The prophets of Yhwh in Israel probably saw disaster coming and raised a lament; the prophets of Judah wanted disaster in the name of Yhwh to befall Aram and Israel, who had conspired against Assyria and against Judah. After disaster had struck and danger loomed over Judah, people came to an agreement with the alien Assyrian power as soon as possible; this lasted until the downfall of Assyria at the end of the seventh century and afterwards was overtaken by the next invasion, this time coming from Babylon.

But there were other reactions to the fall of the kingdom of Israel. If one did not want to be taken up completely into the Assyrian province or into conditions in Judah, the question arose where one belonged after the supportive state institutions had fallen away. This question affected above all the relation of Israel to Judah, both of whom had the same god, Yhwh, as their national god. Certainly in the pre-exilic period Yhwh, like other gods, appeared under different names, such as Yhwh of Samaria, Yhwh of Teman and probably also Yhwh of Jerusalem, and it was not unusual for Israelites and Judahites to wage war against each other or enter into coalitions in his name. But now the same god had been defeated by the same opponents in Israel and remained undefeated in Judah. While this was not impossible, at least it was incomprehensible for some. In the prophetic tradition that was growing up, the expedient resorted to was to declare Yhwh himself responsible for the liquidation of his state and his people, and to look for the reasons for this in Israel. The prophetic intimation of the catastrophe became the announcement of a total judgment brought by Yhwh, and the complaint about the chaotic conditions became an accusation and the reason for the judgment which had already taken place in Israel and was still imminent in Judah. Under the impact of the downfall of Israel, and in the face of the Assyrian expansion southwards, in this way there emerged among the prophets for the first time, or at any rate for the first time explicitly, a notion of the unity of Yhwh and his people transcending the oppositions between Israel and Judah.

The prophetic 'no' spoken in the name of Yhwh delivered the people of Israel over to destruction so that the God of Judah might survive. The situation looked rather different for the surviving Israelites, whether they were in the Israelite territories of the Assyrian province of Samerina or in Judah and continued to worship Yhwh in both places. For them a future for Yhwh and the people of Israel had to be found beyond the state. It was found by projecting the unity of Yhwh and the people discovered by the prophets on to the prehistory of the two states in order to gain from there a perspective on the present. Three works of literature which arose in the course of the seventh century BC, each of which offers a legend of the origin of Israel and also explains the relationship to Judah, bear witness to this: the legend of the beginnings of the monarchy and the great Davidic empire in 1 Sam. 1–1 Kgs 2,[20] the Yahwistic primal history and patriarchal history in Gen. 2–35 (J),[21] and the exodus narrative in Exod. 2–Josh 12 (E).[22]

The composition in 1 Sam. 1–1 Kgs 2, which is composed of the legend of the origin of the house of Saul in 1 Sam. 1–14 and the history of the succession to the throne of the house of David in 2 Sam. 11–1 Kgs 2, goes back to the beginnings of the kingdom. David and Saul are brought together through the hinge verse 1 Sam. 14.52 and the connecting passage 1 Sam. 16– 2 Sam. 5(; 8–10), and the house of David, the southern kingdom of Judah, is declared the legitimate successor of the house of Saul, the northern kingdom. The narrative presents a Judahite standpoint, but is painfully concerned to disperse some doubts about the legitimacy and durability of the house of David for Israel. Israel and Judah form a unity under the uniting roof of the Davidic dynasty in Jerusalem, both at the level of the state and as a people.

The Yahwistic primal history and patriarchal history in Gen. 2–35 (J) also refer back to the beginnings of the people, declaring Jacob to be the ancestor of Israel and father of Judah, and describing the genesis of the small states of Syria–Palestine, all vassals of Assyria, in the garb of family history. Recourse is had quite deliberately to traditions from a sub-national milieu which are linked together genealogically and geographically, nationalized and connected with Yhwh, the national god of Israel and Judah. The composition in Gen. 26–35, which is made up of the southern Palestinian Isaac–Esau tradition in Gen. 26–27 and the northern Jacob–Laban tradition in Gen. 29–31 (29.16–32.2a), and deprives Esau of the blessing as firstborn in order to transfer this to Jacob, is a preliminary stage to this. This and the pre-Yahwistic theophanies in Gen. 28 and Gen. 32 were the model for the redactional hinge in Gen. 12.1-3, which spans an arch from the primal history to the Jacob narrative and formulates the perspective in which the people of Jacob and Israel that has emerged from Abraham sees itself in relation to Judah and in the vicinity of the other small states of Syria–Palestine after 720 BC. The Yahwistic primal history and patriarchal history represent a restorative concept which replaces the kingship with the traditional world and life-style of the family and its religious customs from which the material comes and the many personal gods and other national deities (of Aram, Moab, Ammon, Edom and the Philistines) with the one national god of Judah, worshipped in many sanctuaries of Israel and Judah.

Unlike the narrative about the beginnings of the monarchy in 1 Sam. 1–1 Kgs 2 and the Yahwistic primal history and patriarchal history, the exodus narrative in Exod. 2–Josh. 12 (E) presents a markedly Israelite standpoint. The nucleus is formed by the Israelite or Benjaminite narratives in Exod. 14 and Josh. 6 and 8, which like the song of Miriam in Exod. 15.20f. glorify Yhwh as a god of war. By prefacing the narrative with the call of Moses in Exod. 2–4 and the interim links of the itinerary through the wilderness, this became the narrative of the exodus from Egypt and the settlement under Moses, Miriam and Joshua. The redactional plan is governed by the thought that Israel, the people of Yhwh, which has become stateless and homeless, entered the land from outside and in this respect is quite special; it has little in common with its neighbours. In this narrative the old antagonism of Israel and Judah from the time before 720 BC lives on under the conditions of the seventh century. The Israelites do not feel 'related' to Judah and their other neighbours, but claim their independence – cultivated in or near Judah. The exodus credo is given to the brother people, which has meanwhile likewise become stateless, only after 587 BC.

The revision and incorporation of the old collection of *mišpāṭīm* in Exod. 21–22 into the context of the exodus narrative Exod. 2–Josh. 12 represented a step in this direction.[23] The revision added social and cultic laws and gave the material a new framework. At the head stands the law of the altar in Exod. 20.24-26 and at the end the festival calendar in Exod. 23.14-17. The stylizing of the book of the law as a speech of Yhwh and the way in which the people or each individual in the people are addressed in the second person singular is a special characteristic of this revision. In material terms these are not novelties; the only new element is the paraenetic style, which marks out what was taken for granted earlier, namely, the solidarity between members of the people and the usual cultic obligations towards Yhwh, in a special way as God's law. The embedding in the narrative of the Hexateuch makes its contribution to this: the divine law revealed on the mountain of God in the wilderness of Sinai, on Israel's way from Egypt to the promised land, impresses the stamp of the law on the beginnings of Israel which lie outside the land; the Book of the Covenant has to some degree become the foundation document of the elect people of God.

All the works of literature which react to the downfall of the Israelite kingship are still completely based on the pre-exilic convictions. What distinguishes them from the old traditions and the utilitarian literature of this time is not so much the content or any particular theology as the fact that the ancestral conditions of life and ideas have lost their institutional framework and thus are no longer taken for granted. What previously was quite natural all at once needs special foundation and legitimation. And what is grounded and legitimated does not just apply in Israel, but binds Israel and Judah in the framework of the state of Judah into a unity which extends beyond statehood. The exodus narrative has moved furthest away from pre-exilic thought. With a high degree of theological reflection, in it the experiences of vagabond semi-nomads and Hapiru are concentrated in the origin of the people of Israel. Whereas the foundation legend of the monarchy in 1–2 Samuel and the Yahwistic primal history and patriarchal stories in Genesis sanction the status quo of their time, the exodus narrative sees an alternative to this in the people of Yhwh from the no-man's land of the wilderness. Moreover in the seventh century BC the horses and riders of Egypt must have been topical (cf. 2 Kgs 23.29f.).

4.   After the rise of the neo-Babylonian empire under Nebuchadnezzar, in the years 597 and 587 BC Judah also lost its centre, the monarchy and the temple in Jerusalem. Again the prophets, particularly Jeremiah, saw disaster coming and raised the lament. And again the survival of the national god Yhwh and his worshippers, some of whom had been deported to Babylon while others remained in the land, was at risk. Judah and the Judahites would presumably have gradually sunk into insignificance like their neighbours east of the Jordan, or have been completely forgotten, had not the prophets and the three literary works from the time between 720 and 597/587 BC mentioned above done their preliminary work and opened up the perspective of an existence of Yhwh and his people made up of Israel and Judah which went beyond statehood. But in this way it was also natural after 587 BC for the authors of the prophetic books once again to blame the people and acquit Yhwh: the judgment which once came upon

Israel had now also affected Judah. And it was just as natural to compensate for the loss of the centre of the state and the cult after the model of J (Gen. 2–35), E (Exod. 2–Josh. 12) and 1 Samuel–1 Kgs 2 by taking up Judah into the unity of Israel the people of God, which was not a state.

It proved possible to relate the Yahwistic primal history and patriarchal history (J) to the new situation with a bit of retouching. Like the Israelites previously, from 587 BC the Judahites too were in the midst of Aramaeans, Ammonites, Moabites, Edomites and Philistines, or what was left of them; they were left entirely to themselves, their family bonds and the national god Yhwh, who had become their one personal god, and so without further ado they could again find a place in the Yahwistic family of states. Presumably the career of Abraham, the patriarch with his home in Judah, began with this. Whereas the many cultic places that he had founded lost significance in the land, he increasingly turned into the bearer of the promise and the model of faith. At some point people began to perceive that there were also descendants of Israelites and Judahites outside the land of Judah. In the cycles of tradition in Gen. 2–35 people here were not thinking initially of the Babylonian Diaspora but of the Egyptian Diaspora, and they developed the patriarchal history in Gen. 37–45[24] accordingly: Jacob-Israel does not just live on in Judah but also in Joseph, who was sold into Egypt.

As the long later history shows, the Israelite exodus creed was also received and transferred to Judah. The Judaizing began with the incorporation of Ur-Deuteronomy, a novella of the Book of the Covenant, into the exodus narrative of Exod. 2–Josh. 12 (E).[25] Ur-Deuteronomy in Deut. 12–21 is dominated by the idea of the centralization of the cult and wants to do away with the plurality of places of worship sanctioned by J and the law of the altar in Exod. 20.24, which was usual in the pre-exilic period both in Israel and in Judah. The lost centre of Judah, the monarchy and temple in Jerusalem, is replaced by the one place which Yhwh will choose in order to ward off the threat of decentralization. To the unity of the place of worship in Judah the framework in Deut. 6.4-5 ('Hear, Israel!') and in 26.16 adds the unity of Yhwh and the address 'Israel', and thus the unity made up of Israel and Judah at the one place of worship of the one God. The historicizing of Ur-Deuteronomy which is already indicated for 'the place which Yhwh will choose', which assumes Moses as the speaker (Deut. 5.1aα[1] + 'Hear Israel' in 6.4-5, 6 + 12.13ff.) and envisages the situation shortly before the settlement (Deut. 26.1f., 11), serves to aid the literary incorporation into the Hexateuch between the arrival in Shittim (Num. 25.1a) and the death of Moses with the departure from Shittim under the leadership of Joshua which follows (Deut. 34.1a, 5f.; Josh. 2.1; 3.1). Thus in Deuteronomy Moses proclaims in the land of Moab before the people the law which has been revealed to him on the mountain of God, the

Book of the Covenant, and in so doing introduces the necessary changes, the centralization of the cult practised by 'Israel' at the chosen place, prudently never mentioned by name, the one place of worship in Judah.

On the basis of the criterion of the centralization of the cult established in Ur-Deuteronomy, around 560 BC the first Deuteronomist developed the foundation legend of the one Israelite-Judahite monarchy in 1 Sam. 1–1 Kgs 2. In the form of a 'synchronistic chronicle', in 1–2 Kgs he added the history of the kings of Israel and Judah (Dtr^G).[26] Against the background of the initial unity of the kingdom in 1–2 Samuel, here the existence of two states, which lasts until 720 BC, is interpreted as an offence against the demand for centralization of the cult. The breach of the unity of kingdom and cult, the 'sin of Jeroboam', which makes Israel per se guilty and to which the 'high places' bear witness in Judah, leads to the downfall first of Israel and then of Judah. It is not quite clear whether the first Deuteronomist hoped for a renewal of the Davidic monarchy according to the criteria of Ur-Deuteronomy, but that is probable. According to him Israel and Judah, which Yhwh himself gives over to judgment because of the 'sin of Jeroboam', survive in the last Davidic king, who lives in the Babylonian exile and is pardoned. For the first time the Babylonian Golah comes into the field of view of theological reflection.

In time it proves that neither under late-Babylonian nor under Persian alien rule was it possible to reckon with a renewal of the Davidic kingdom. The tradition drew the consequences of this and grounded the existence of 'Israel' wholly in the relationship with God: Yhwh, the king of the gods and Lord of the earth, became king over Israel and the world, the one God became the only God, who in place of the Davidic king chooses the people of Israel and has obligated them to unconditional obedience, not only in the elect place, but throughout the world, wherever Jews are. In the framework of the 'Hexateuch', which extends from Exodus to Judges, this development was recorded by the insertion of the Decalogue in Exod. 20 and afterwards in Deut. 5.[27] From now on no longer the centralization of the cult but the First Commandment is the criterion by which the people of God, 'Israel', made up of Israel and Judah, has to allow itself to be measured. Under this sign the exodus narrative in Exod. 2–Josh. 12 (E), dominated by the law, the history of Yhwh's chosen people of Israel, was combined with the basic writing of the Deuteronomistic work in Samuel–Kings (Dtr^G), the history of the kingship of Israel and Judah rejected by Yhwh, by means of the bridge period of the judges, This was specially constructed for the purpose from a collection of old narratives about heroes from the Deuteronomistic redaction in Joshua and Judges (Dtr^R).[28] The 'Hexateuch' (Exodus–Joshua) grew into an 'Enneateuch' (Exodus–Kings) in which the secondary late Deuteronomistic or post-Deuteronomistic revision, active over a long period, ran its course (Dtr^S).

A similar development took place in other parts of the Old Testament at more or less the same time: in the psalms, for example, the so-called enthronement psalms (Pss. 93–99), and in the prophecy of salvation which was gradually coming into being, above all in Second Isaiah (from Isa. 40). Here the significant difference is that apart from a few late efforts at assimilation, Jacob-Israel, the royally chosen people of God, is not obligated to the law but directly to Yhwh as king of the world and judge of the peoples. Yhwh is the only God, and alongside him there is no other; not Moses, but Israel is his prophet. The development is closer to the Yawhistic primal history and patriarchal history than to the exodus narrative. But it, too, is taken into Deutero-Isaiah and many psalms. In it the exodus creed, which has the history of the people and the law as its content, assumes mythical and eschatological features (cf. also Exod. 15). Creation, patriarchs and exodus are to some degree examples of the presence of eternal salvation, guaranteed by Yhwh since primaeval times and once celebrated in the cult. The pre-Priestly assimilation or combination of J (Genesis 2–45) and E (Exod. 2–2 Kgs 25, which can be grasped in literary form in the second part of the Joseph story in Gen. 45–50 and at the transition to the Exodus narrative in Exod. 1 (vv. 8-10a, 15-16, developed further in vv. 17-22), follow the same line. The Deuteronomistic history of failure is preceded by the creation of humankind and the promise to the fathers, which is combined with the exodus from Egypt up to and including Exod. 15 to form stages of the original salvation, before the law put a stumbling block in the way of Israel. In the scheme of salvation history, the making present of salvation and the demonstration of guilt by means of the law follow each other. Originally these were two opposed positions. The duality also continued to determine the post-exilic history of theology.

5.   The accession of Cyrus in Babylon in 539 BC did not bring the hoped-for change in the direction of salvation. The far more important historical breaks were the rebuilding of the temple in Jerusalem between 520 and 515 BC under Darius I and the building of the wall under Artaxerxes I in the second half of the fifth century, by which Judah became a separate province. Traditions which, while not authentic, still stand very close to the events, have been preserved: the chronicle of the building of the temple in Ezra (4.24;) 5.1–6.15 and the Nehemiah memorial in Neh. 1.1a + 2-6 + 12.[29] According to these the initiative towards building the temple came from the population living in the land; Nehemiah, a member of the Babylonian Golah who had managed to become the king's cupbearer, was responsible for this. Both things were possible only with the assent of the Persian kings, who strongly encouraged the building up of the province of Judah for strategic reasons in accordance with the ideology of rule which

they practised, and which can be read in the Achaemenid royal inscriptions from Darius onwards. People were divided over the signs of favour from the Persian kings. Some were content with them and saw them as the fulfilment of salvation. Others did not want Yhwh to be taken up into the workings of Persian policy and saw the building of the temple and the wall only as the pledge of the promised salvation. Yet others ignored both, confessed their sins and waited constantly for the saving intervention of their God. This and the social splits forming as a consequence of alien rule in the Persian and Hellenistic period in the long run led to splits in the people, expressed theologically in a division into righteous and wicked.

Something of this can be found in the narrative literature of the Old Testament. Those who warmly welcomed the Second Temple but gave it a more far-reaching theological programme included the author of the Priestly Writing (P).[30] What had already been indicated in Deutero-Isaiah, some historical psalms and the combination of J and E appears here in a mature form. Creation, the patriarchs and exodus form a myth which makes salvation present. To some degree, in it the saving beginning of the Deuteronomistic Enneateuch (Genesis/Exodus–Kings) has become independent. The creation of the world focuses on the covenant with Noah, which guarantees the survival of the world. The patriarchs and exodus, subsumed under the toledot of Jacob-Israel, fuse in the covenant with Abraham, which guarantees that God will be God for Israel. The law, by which the people comes to grief, is replaced by the foundation of the sanctuary on Sinai, where the divinity of God is experienced and communicated in the cult (P^G in Gen. 1–Exod. 40 + Leviticus).

The Priestly Writing was conceived as an independent writing alongside the Hexateuch, which had grown into an Enneateuch in Genesis–Kings and was evidently intended as a kind of instruction for reading the first part of the Enneateuch. It presupposes the knowledge of the non-Priestly text in Genesis–Exodus (Numbers) and projects the new beginning in the era of the Second Temple, which historically follows the history of failure depicted in Genesis–Kings, on to the time of the beginnings and foundation of Israel before the settlement and the downfall of the kingdom. In it, 'Israel' and the relationship of the people of God to Yhwh have wholly entered into the language of 'faith and confessing' which in parallel to this – in the late-Deuteronomistic expansions – increasingly also takes over the description given by the Enneateuch in Genesis/Exodus–Kings. Thus more or less because of the difference in theological stamp, it seemed natural to work the Priestly Writing into the literary complex of the Enneateuch (R^{PJE}). On the basis of the tendency of the Achaemenids – discussed by scholars under the key word 'imperial authorization' – to have culture-specific institutions and laws, especially relating to the temple and cult, sanctioned by representatives of the central power, the theologically motivated procedure may also to some degree have been politically in the air. However, as far as we know it was not decreed officially by the king himself or by his governor. This step brought with it a wealth of expansions which in language and theology hover between P and Dtr; these are sometimes more Priestly, sometimes more Deuteronomistic, and sometimes a mixture of the two. It is obvious that it is difficult to keep them apart.[31] It will be the task of future research to find appropriate criteria which allow a distinction to be made in this sphere between pre- and post-Deuteronomistic and pre- and post-Priestly additions. Not everything that is not clearly Deuteronomistic is pre-Deuteronomistic, and not everything that is late- or post-Deuteronomistic and not Priestly is automatically pre-Priestly.

If we put the independent Priestly writing (P^G and P^S) around 500 BC or later, a date in the fifth/fourth century BC follows for the combination of P and JE (R^{PJE}) and the (late- or post-Deuteronomistic and post-Priestly) expansions in the framework of the Enneateuch. The process comes to an end with the separation of the Pentateuch as the Torah of Moses and its translation into Greek. In the course of the third century the books of Joshua–Kings, the Former Prophets, are combined with the prophetic writings which are once again growing strongly, the Latter Prophets, into the part of the canon called Nebiim, 'Prophets'.

Alongside that, the third part of the canon, Kethubim, 'Writings', is already beginning to develop. Its core is the Psalter, which, apart from a few psalms, was finished around 200 BC and was diligently copied in Qumran. The wisdom writings (Job, Proverbs, Koheleth) also gradually take form in the third and second centuries. In them we can hear most loudly the bitter experience that things often go well with the wicked and badly with the righteous; however, these works believe in a just retribution. Since God is often experienced as hidden and is moving increasingly into the distance, intermediaries like the fear of God, personalized Wisdom and the Torah become increasingly important. And what wisdom seeks in this world, Daniel and apocalyptic find in the world to come.

The Chronistic history, which begins to come into being in the middle of the fourth century, also moves in this literary and theological situation. Its beginning is formed by the excerpt from the history of the kingdom of Judah from Samuel–Kings in the basic stratum of 1–2 Chronicles, a document on the prehistory of Judah, the former province of the Persian empire, which was composed not without pride.[32] The excerpt, which here and there also already passes over into special Chronistic material, attaches the utmost importance to the fact that the history of the kings of Judah has run its course in accordance with the principle of retribution advocated by the prophets. Each gets his due in accordance with the law and the model of David and Solomon: the pious honour and power, the sinner just punishment. The consistent Judahite standpoint suggested a link with the foundation legend of the Persian province of Judah, the Nehemiah memoir – in the meantime augmented with the passages about Sanballat and the governorship of Nehemiah. The connecting link is the chronicle of the building of the temple in Ezra 5–6, which has been attached to Chronicles by the redactional hinge in Ezra 1–4[33]and assimilated to the end of the Nehemiah memoir in Neh. 12 by the conclusion in Ezra 6.16-18. In this way the temple and the wall in the Persian empire became the 'post-exilic' equivalent of the kingdom and the temple under David and Solomon and the other kings of Judah in the pre-exilic period. Furthermore the literary link provided the matrix for extensive expansions which in Chronicles and also in Ezra–Nehemiah introduced the genealogies of the tribes of Israel, the law and the whole cultic apparatus, and led the Chronistic history to cover the period from Adam to Nehemiah, in literary terms Genesis–Malachi. Prominent among these introductions in Chronicles are the genealogies in 1 Chron. 1–9 and the foundations by David in 1 Chron. 22–29, and in Ezra–Nehemiah the insertion of Ezra into Ezra 7–8,[34] which continues in Ezra 9–10[35] and Neh. 8–10[36] and stylizes Ezra as the embodiment of Torah piety. In this way Ezra, the priest and scribe, becomes the identifying figure of a scribal Judaism which is faithful to the law. With good reason the tradition, Josephus and *4 Ezra* see him as the last prophet after Moses, the one who is said to have completed the canonical writings or to have written them in accordance with God's dictation. Others did not emphasize Ezra but counted from Moses to Elijah, whose return was expected (Mal. 3.22-24; Sir. 48.1-11; Lk. 1.17). Mark 9.2-8 par. then goes so far as to introduce Jesus Christ alongside Moses and Elijah as the third in the covenant.

Notes

1   Especially in the *Beiträge zur Einleitung in das Alte Testament* I–II of 1806–1807 (reprinted 1971).
2   Stated programmatically by Wellhausen, *Proleg.*,1, and 361ff., etc.
3   Noth, *History of Israel*, 137f., see the programme, ibid., 1-7.
4   Cf. R.G. Kratz, 'Israel als Staat und als Volk', *ZThK* 97, 2000, 1-17.
5   Gen. 29.16-23, 25-28, 30, 32a, 33aα^1b, 34; 30.14, 23-24a, 25-26(, 28, 31-42); 31.2, (4-5a, 14, 17, 19a, 20,) 21-23, 26(-28), 31, 43-44, 46, 48; 32.1-2a.
6   Exod. 12.37; 13.20; 14.10bα, 19b, 20aαb, 24, 25b, 30a.
7   Josh. 6.1-3aα, 5, 12a, 14aα^1, 20b; 8.1-2a, 10a, 11a, 14, 19.
8   Judg. 3.15, 16-26 (Ehud); 4.4a, 5a, 6a, 7 (without 'Jabin's general'), 10a, 12, 13, 14b, 15b, 17a$\beta\gamma$, 18-22 (Deborah and Barak); 6.11a, 19, 21, 24 + 7.1b = 8b, 13-14, 15a, 16-21, 22b + 8.4, 10-12, 18-21bα (Gideon); 9.1-3, 6, 26-41, 50-54 (Abimelech); 11.1a, 3, 5b, 6-8, 11a (Jephthah); 13.2, 6-7, 24a + 14.1–15.8 + 15.9-19 + 16.1-30 (Samson).
9   1 Sam. 1.1-3a, 4-19, 13-20; 9.1, 2aα, 3-8, 10, (11-14,) 16-19, 24b-27; 10.(1,) 2-4, 7, 9, 10aα, 14-16; (10.27b LXX;) 11.1-4, 9-11, 15; 13.2, 3a(bα, 4a), 5abα, (6, 15b-16, 17-

18,) 23; 14.1, 2, 4-5, 8-10aα, 11a, 12a, 13, 14a, 17, 20, (22,) 23a, 46(, 47-51).

10   Gen. 19.1-9 aα[1]b, 10-13a, 14aαb, 15aα, 16aαb, (17-18a, 20a, 22b, 23,) 26(, 30-38).

11   Gen. 26.1aαb, 7-9, 11, 17, 19-22bα, (23,) 26-27, 28 ('And they said, Let it be an oath …'), 29a, 30-31; 27.1-4, 5b, 18a, 24-27bα, 28.

12   2 Sam. 11.1-27a; 12.24bα[2]; 13.1-22; 13.23–14.1, 23, (24, 28-32,) 33; 15.1-6, 13; 18.1–19.9a; 20.1-2, 6-7, 14-22; 1 Kgs 1.(1,) 5-19, 20a, 21-34a, 38-45, 49-53; 2.13-23, 25, 26a, 34-35, 46b.

13   Gen. 2.5, 7a, 8, 19a, 20a, 21-22; 3.20-21; 4.1 abα, 17-22.

14   Gen 9.(18a without 'who went out of the ark'), 19; 10.2-7, 20, 22-23, 31.

15   E.g. Exod. 23.14-19; or Lev. 1–3 (removing the Priestly interpretations).

16   E.g. Pss. 29; 93; or the basic stratum of Ps. 104 (v. 1aα, 2b-4, 10a, 13a, 14b-15, 32, 33).

17   E.g. Ps. 13 and the basic stratum of Ps. 118 (vv. 5, 14-19, 21, 28).

18   There is old sayings material above all in the collections Prov. 10.1–22.16; 22.17–24.22 (on an Egyptian model); 25–29, but it is often interspersed with sayings about the righteous and the wicked, the divine retribution and the maxim about the fear of God.

19   E.g. the prophecy of salvation in Isa. 7.3-9; 8.1-4, the laments over the threat of a catastrophe in Amos 3.12; 5.2, 3, 19; Jer. 4.7, 11-12a, 13, 15f., 19-21; 6.1, 22f., and also desperate laments about the chaos within in Hos. 6.7ff. The charismatic and miracle-worker like Samuel in 1 Sam. 9–10 or Elisha in 2 Kgs 4 is also typical of the early period.

20   1 Sam. 1–14 (see n. 9 above) + 14.52; 16.14-23; 18.17a, 18-19, 20(, 22-27); 19.9-10 (, 11-21); 21–27; 28.1-2; 29; 31; 2 Sam. 2.1aα[1], 3-4a, 8-9, 12-32; 3.(2-5,) 12-13, 21, 22-27; 4.1-3, 6-8aα, 12; 5.3, 6aα, 9(, 13-16; 8–10) + 2 Sam. 11–1 Kings 2 (see n. 12 above).

21   Original stratum, proto-Yahwistic composition Gen. 26–35 and *Yahwistic basic document (with expansions)*: Gen 2.5, 7a, 8, *9abβ*, 16-17, (18), 19a, 20a, *(20b,)* 21-22, *(23, 24,)* 25; 3.*6-13α*, 16-19α, 20-21; 4.1abα, *1bα*, 2-5, 8-12, 16, 17-22, 25-26; **6.1**, *4aββ*; 9.18a (without the ark), 19; 10.2-7, *8-9*, 20, 21, 22-23, *24-25*, 31; 11.2-5, *6a (without 'and they all have one language')*, *8a*; **12.1-4, *6a*, 7-9**; **13**.2, 5, 7a, *8-11a*, *12bβ*, 13, 18; **18.**1-3a, 4-16α; **19.**1-9aα[1], *9aα[2]β*, 10-13a, *13b*, 14aα, *14αβ*, 14b, 15aα, 16aαb, 17-18a, *18b-19*, 20a, *20b-22a*, 22b, 23, *24-25*, 26, 30-38; **21.**1a, 6-8; **26.**1aαb, 7-9, *10a*, 11, *12-14, 16*, 17, 19-22bd, *22bβ*, (23,) 25, 26-27, *28aα*, 29a, 29b, 30-31, *32-33*; 27.1-4, 5a, 5b, 6-10(11-13), 14(-16), *17*, 18a, 18b, 19, 20, (21-23,) 24-27bα, *27bβ*, 28, 29, 30-33, *34*, 39-40, 41-45; **28.**10, [11-12,] *13-16(*, 17-19); **29**.[*1*,] 2-15, 16-23, 25-28, 30, *31*, 32a, *32b*, 33aα[1], *33aα[2]b*, 33b, 34, 35; 30.14, 23-24a, *24b*, 25-26, 27, 28, 29-30, 31-42, *43*; 31.2, 3, 4-5a, 14, 17, 19a, 20, 21-23, 26-28, 31, 43-44, 46, 48, *49*; 32.1-2a, 2b-3, 4-9, 14a, (b-22,) [25-27,] *28-30a*[, 30b, 31-32]; 33.1a, 34.(8-11,) *12-17*; 35.[1, 6-8, 16-20], *21*.

22   Original stratum and *basic writing (with expansions)*: Ex 2.1-2a *(b, 3aα[1])* 3 ('and she took for him … '), 5aα *(β)b*, 6aα(βbα) β, *10aβb*, 11-12 (13-14,) 15-22; **3.**1, *2b*, 3, 4a, *(5, 6b,)*, 7a, *8aα*, 21-22; **4.**18, 20a; **12.**35-36, 37, 38; 13.20, 21a*(b, 22)*; **14.**5a, 6, 10bα, *10bβ*, 13-14, 19b, 20aα(βγ)b, *21aα[2] b*, 24, 25b, *27aα[2]βb*, 30a, *30b*; 15.20-21, 22a; *(15.22b-25a, 27;* **16.**1aα; **19.**2aα[2], 3a; 24.18b; **Num.** 10.*12a or 33a*?); 20.1aββ; *(20.14-21);* 21.21-24a;) 22.1; (22–24;) 25.1a; **Deut.** 34.5 *(only 'And Moses died there'),* 6; **Josh.** 2.1-7, 15-16, 22-23; **3.**1, 14a, 16; 4.19b; **6.**1-3aα, 5, 12a. 14aα[1], 20b; 8.1-2a, 10a, 11a, 14, 19; **(10–11;)** 12.1a, 9-24.

23   *Mišpatim* and *second-person-singular revision*: Exod. 2.1–19.3a (see n. 22 above) + 20.1 *or 20.22a*; 20.24-26; 21.1, 2-11, 12, 13-14, 15-22, 23-25, 26-37; 22.1-16, 17, 18-19, 20a, 22, 24a, 25-29; 23.1-9a, 10-12, 14-17(, 18, 19, 20-33) + **Exod. 24.18b–Josh. 12**

(see n. 22 above). The theophany already presupposes the law in the context: 19.3a + 19.10-20 + 20.1, 24ff. or 19.10-19; 20.18, 21, 22a, 24ff.(–23.17) + 24.18b.

24 Gen. 37.3a(b), 4a,(5-8,) 12-18, (19-20, 23-24,) 25-27, 28a(α^2)βb(, 31-35; 39.1a); 39.1b-41, 54; 42–44; 45.1-4, 14-15, 25-26aα (or -27aαb).

25 **Exod. 2–Num. 25.1a** (see n. 22 above) + **Deut. 5.1aα^1**; 6.4-5; **12.13**, 14a (up to 'Yhwh'), 15-18(, 19-28); **14.22**, (23a, 24a,) 25-26(, 27, 28-29); **15.19-23; 16.16-17, 18** (, 19-20); **17.8-9aαb, 10a; 19.2a**, 3b-7, 11-12, 15-17a, 18bα, 21b; **21.1-4, 6-7, 8b; 26.1-2**, (3-4,) 11, 16; **34.1 a** + **Deut. 34.5-6; Josh. 2-12** (see n. 22 above).

26 **1 Sam. 1–1 Kgs 2** (including 1 Sam. 10.8; 13.1, 4b, 7b-12, 15a; 2 Sam. 2.10-11; 5.4-5; 1 Kgs 2.10-12) + **1 Kgs 3.1-3**; (4.1-19; 5.7-8;) 6.1, 7, 37-38; 7.1; (9.15-23;) 9.24-25; (9.26-28; 10.14-29;) **11.26**, (27-28,) 40-43; **12.2, 20a, 25, 26a, 27aα, 28a, 30a; 14.19-20**, 21 (without 'the city, which …'), 22a, 25-26a, 29-31; **15.1-3, 7-11, 14, 16-28, 31-34; 16.5-6, 8-10, 13abα, 14-26a, 27-31bα; 22.39-46, 48-53; 2 Kgs 1.1, 18; 3.1-2a, 3; 8.16-18, 20-27**; (8.28-29;) **9.14-21bα, 22abα, 23-24, 27, 30-35; 10.1-9, 12-14bα, 17aα, 34-36; 11; 12.1-3a, 4, 18-22; 13.1-2, 7, 8-13; 14.1-5, 7, 18-25a, 28-29; 15.1-11, 13-36; 16.1-3a**, 5-9, 19-20; **17.1-6, 21-23; 18.1-3**, (4aα^1,) 7b, 8, 13-16; **19.36-37; 20.12-13, 20-21; 21.1-2a**, (3a,) 17-20, 23-26; **22.1-2**, 3-7, 9; **23.4a, 11, 12aα^1, 28-36; 24.1, 5-12, 15-19, 20b; 25.1-10, 18-21a, 22, 25, 27-30.

27 Exod. 20.2-17 with 20.22a(b-23) between 19.10-20; 20.1; and 20.24ff.; or with 20.1 between 19.10-19; and 20.18, 21, 22a, 24ff.; Deut. 5.1–6.3 between 5.1.aα^1 and 6.4-5. The First Commandment attracted the making of the covenant: Exod. 24.3, 4-8; Deut. 26.17-18 the piling up of the Hexateuch into the Enneateuch; the reformulation of the covenant under the condition of its transgression: Exod. 32–34; Deut. 27–30 (cf. Josh. 23–24; 2 Kgs 22–23). Exodus 19.3b-9; and Deut. 26.19 along with the paraeneses in Deut. 4.6-11 also belong in the subsequent history.

28 Basic material and *redaction of the book of Judges*: Exod. 2–Deut. 26; (31.*1f.*, *7f.*;) 34.1a, 5-6; Josh. (1.*1f.*, *5f.*;) 2–11 (see nn. 22, 23, 25 above) + 11.16aα^1, (16aα^2-23a,) 23b; 12.1a, 9-24; (23.1b-3; 24.14a, 15-16, 18b, 22.28; Judg. 2.7, *10*;) 2.8-9, *11a* = 3.7aα, 8-14, 15, 16-26, 27-30; 4.*1-3*, 4-22, 23-24; 5.*31b*; 6.1-6, 11-24; (6.25-32; 7.*1a*);7.1b-22; 8.4-21, 28 (29-32); 9; 10.*1-5, 6aα^1*, 7, 8abα, 10a, *17a, 18*; 11.1-11 a(*b,*) 29, (30-33a,) 33b(, 34-40); 12.7, 8-15; 13.*1*, 2-24, 25; 14.1–15.8; 15.9-19, 20; 16.1-30, *31* + **1 Sam. 1–2 Kgs 25** (see n. 26 above).

29 Neh. 1.1a; 2.1-6, 11-18; (3.1-32;) 3.38; 4.4, 6a, 9b; 6.15; 12.(27aα^1,) 31-32, 37-40, 43 and various expansions.

30 Basic document (and expansions): Gen. 1.1–2.4a (1.29f. counting of the days and 2.2b-3); 5.1a, 3-23, (24,) 25-29a, 30-31(, 32); 6.9-22; 7.6-7, 14-16a, 18, (19, 20,) 21; 8.1, 4aα^1b, 15-19; 9.(1-3, 4-6, 7,) 8-11, (12-15, 16-17,) 28, 29; 11.10a(b), 11-26, 27, 31-32; 12.(4b-)5; 13.6a(b), 11b, 12a(bα); 16.1a, 3aα(β)b, 16 or 16.1a, 3aα(β)b, 15-16; 17.1-8, (9-14,) 15-22(, 23-27); 21.1b, (4,) 5 or 21.1b, 2-3, (4,) 5; (23;) 25.7-8, (9-10, 11a,) 12-17; 25.19, 20 … 26b or 25.19, 20, 24, 25aα^1b, 26aα^1βb; 26.34-35; 27.46–28.5(, 6-7, 8-9); (31.18; 33.18; 35.6?;) 35.9-13, 22b-26, 27-29; 36.1-8(, 9-43); 37.1, 2aαb; 46.6-7(, 8-27); 47.27-28; 49.(1a, 29-33a,) 33b; 50.(12-13,) 22; **Exod. 1.13-14**; 2.23aβ-25; 6.2-8; (6.9-12, 13-30; 7.1-7, 8-13, 19-22; 8.1-3, 11,12-15; 9.8-12; 11.10;) 12.(1-28,) 40-41(, 42-51); 14.1-2, (3-4, 8,) 9, 15-16, (17-18,) 21aα^1b, 22(, 23, 26-29); **19.1; 24.16-18a; 25–29; (30–31; 35–39;)** 40.(1-15,) 16-17, (18-33a,) 33b, 34(, 35 + Lev.).

31 I am not even certain whether the expansions indicated within brackets in n. 30 made their way into the text before or after P and JE were brought together, for example, in Exod. 12.1-28, 42-51. At all events, the passages in Exod. 16 (17.1); and Num. 1–20; 25–36, more usually assigned to P, seem to me to be supplements in the framework of R[PJE] which presuppose the non-Priestly itinerary.

32 Excerpt and *special material*: **1 Chron. 2.**1-2, *3a, 4-5, 9-15*; **11.**1-9(, 10ff.); (**13–**) **14**; (**15.***1, 3*, 25-29; **16.**1-3, *43*;) **17.**1–**22.**1; **23.**1; (**28.***1, 2-10*; **29.***20-25*,) 26-30; **2 Chron. 1–** 9; **10.**1–**11.**4, *5-12*; **12**; **13.**1-2, *3, 13-18, 19-21, 22-23*; **14.**1–3, *4, 5, 6, 7, 8-14*; **15.**16– **16.**6, *7, 8-9, 10*, 11-14; **17.**1a*b-5, 10-11, 12-13, 14-19*; **18**; **19.***1-4a*; **20.**31–**21.**1, *5-11, 12-13a, 14-19*, 20; **22.**1–**24.**14, *15-22*, 23-27; **25.**1-4, 11-12, *14-16*, 17-23; **26.**1-4, *5, 6-8, 9-10, 11-15, 16-20*, 21-23; **27.**1-2, *3-6*, 7-9; **28.**1-4, *5*, 6-8, 16-27; **29.**1-2, *3, 4-5, 16-17, 36*; **31.**1, 20-21; 32 (with vv. *24-26, 31* and vv. *2-8, 22-23, 27-29*); **33.**1-10, *11-14*, 18-25; **34**; **35.**1, *2, 7, 16-17, 18-27*); **36.**1-21.

33 Ezra **1.**1-11; (*2*;); **3.**8abα, 10a, 12-13; **4.**1-5 + (*4.24*); **5.**1–**6.**15 + 6.16-18.

34 Ezra **7.**1a(b-5), 6aαb, 11a, 12-13, 21-22, 27-28; **8.**15a, 21-22a(b-23), 24-25 (26-27,) 28- 36.

35 Ezra **9.**1-3, 5-15; **10.**1, 2, 4-5, (9-17,) 18-44.

36 Neh. **7.**4-5a + 5b-72a; **7.**72b-**8.**12/**8.**13-18/**9.**1-11.2 + 11.3ff.

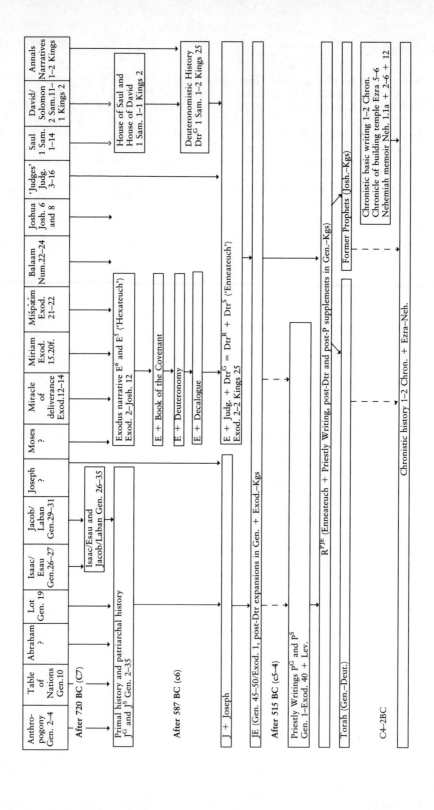

Index of References

219, 324
8.29 187
8.32 193
8.33-55 204
8.33-35 203, 208
9–16 194, 195, 203
9–12 205
9 187, 188, 194, 199, 203,
 205, 207, 324
9.1–16.31 204, 207, 219
9.1-54 208
9.1-3 204, 322
9.1 203
9.4-5 204, 208
9.4 204
9.6 204, 322
9.7-25 208
9.7 204
9.8-15 204
9.16-21 204
9.16 214
9.22-25 204
9.22 193, 195, 205
9.23 215
9.26-41 204, 322
9.42-49 204, 208
9.46 204
9.50-54 204, 322
9.55-57 208
9.55-56 204
9.57 204
10–16 194, 196, 203
10–12 188
10.1-5 187, 193–95, 203, 205,
 208, 324
10.1 193
10.3 193
10.6-18 187
10.6-10 204, 208
10.6 195, 196, 208, 324
10.7 193, 196, 324
10.8 208, 324
10.9 208
10.10-18 204
10.10-16 208
10.10 209, 324
10.11-16 204
10.17-18 208
10.17 204, 208, 324
10.18 324
10.27 214

11.1-11 204, 208, 324
11.1-2 208
11.1 204, 322
11.3 204, 214, 322
11.4 208
11.5 204, 208, 322
11.6-8 204, 322
11.9-10 208
11.11 204, 208, 322
11.12-28 204, 208, 209, 220
11.29 193, 204, 208, 215, 324
11.30-40 208
11.30-33 204, 324
11.30 204
11.33 204, 208, 214, 324
11.34-40 204, 324
12.1-6 204, 208
12.5 204
12.7 187, 193–95, 203–205,
 208, 324
12.8-15 187, 193–95, 203,
 205, 324
13–16 181, 188, 207
13 215
13.1 187, 193, 195, 205, 208,
 324
13.2-24 205, 208, 324
13.2 196, 215, 322
13.3-5 208, 215
13.5 193, 205
13.6-7 215, 322
13.8-23 208, 215
13.24-25 208, 215
13.24 215, 322
13.25 193, 205, 208, 324
14.1–15.8 205, 322, 324
14.1-15 208
14.4 208, 214
14.6 193, 205, 208, 214
14.8 208
14.9-19 208
14.19 205, 208, 214
14.23 214
14.39 214
15.3 208, 214
15.9-19 205, 322, 324
15.9 214
15.10-13 214
15.14 193, 205, 208, 214
15.15-17 214
15.18 214, 215

15.20 187, 193, 205, 208, 324
15.30 205
16.1-30 205, 208, 322, 324
16.13 207
16.17 208, 215
16.20 208, 215
16.23-24 208, 215
16.28 208, 215
16.30 193
16.31 187, 193, 205, 208, 324
17–21 188, 191, 196, 198,
 208, 209, 221
17–18 196
17 196
17.1 196
17.6 188, 196
18.1 188, 196
19–21 196, 220
19.1 188, 196
21.25 188, 196

Ruth
1.1 20
4.12 20
4.17 17
4.18-22 17

1 Samuel
1–31 36, 159, 175, 177,
 180–82
1–15 156, 181
1–14 173, 175, 177, 180, 182,
 183, 209, 210, 310, 314,
 323
1–7 174
1–3 182
1 170, 215, 218, 221
1.1-20 172–74, 183, 184
1.1-3 322
1.1 172, 174, 196, 207
1.3 173, 174, 184, 212
1.4-19 322
1.10-12 173, 184, 212
1.13-20 322
1.19 172
1.21–7.2 184
1.21–3.21 173, 212
1.21–2.11 174
2–3 221
2.12-36 174
2.22 152